Research on Alcoholics Anonymous

Research on Alcoholics Anonymous

OPPORTUNITIES AND ALTERNATIVES

EDITED BY

Barbara S. McCrady
and
William R. Miller

Publications Division
Rutgers Center of Alcohol Studies
New Brunswick, New Jersey USA

This book was supported by National Institute on Alcohol Abuse and Alcoholism grant R13-AA09051. The opinions expressed herein are the views of the authors and do not necessarily reflect the official position of NIAAA or any other part of the U.S. Department of Health and Human Services.

ISBN 911290-24-9
Library of Congress Catalog Card Number: 92-63233
Printed in the United States of America

In memory and honor of Don Cahalan, who encouraged and shaped alcoholism research and researchers for five decades

Contents

Foreword

ALCOHOLICS ANONYMOUS (AA) is many things—a fellowship, a social movement, and a treatment modality. However, its role as a treatment to help people achieve and maintain recovery is its most important function. Because it was developed and implemented before the scientific methods to test treatments were developed, AA has not been evaluated by experimental methods until recently. Because of its importance to alcoholism treatment, as attested to by the experience of hundreds of thousands of people around the world, the National Institute on Alcohol Abuse and Alcoholism (NIAAA) is keenly interested in supporting rigorous methodological studies of AA. The conference that served as the basis of this monograph, with its diverse and rich agenda and expert participants, provides a framework for this important research.

Two overarching questions were addressed by conference participants: Should and can research on AA be done? The answer to the first question is yes—research on AA should be done. It is important to know why AA works, how it works, and for whom. For one thing, it is likely that AA does not work for everyone. Just as we have testimonials from those whose lives were profoundly changed by AA, we also have reports from those for whom AA attendance proved unsatisfactory. Some of these individuals achieved sobriety by other means, and others continued to have their lives destroyed by alcoholism. Knowing why, how, and for whom AA works would help providers to more accurately develop treatment plans for their patients—directing to AA those who are likely to benefit from AA meetings and seeking other therapies for those who are not likely to benefit from AA participation.

The question of whether Alcoholics Anonymous can be studied is more problematic. NIAAA has tried to stimulate research on the questions stated above. Some research has been done, but much proposed research has been hampered by methodological issues that could not be resolved. Some of the methodological problems are listed below. Others are identified by the authors of the chapters presented herein.

1. How do you obtain representative samples of AA participants for survey purposes? If one is restricted to only those who volunteer to participate, and this group is either not a substantial majority of the group nor randomly selected, will this cohort of those who participate and are likely to be atypical of the group as a whole result in flawed conclusions? How do you identify groups that are representative of a city or region of the United States? If you can identify suitable groups, how many have to be studied to yield representative results?

2. How do you define who is in AA? The AA membership is a dynamic population. I have known people who would be very active in the fellowship at one time and not attend meetings at another time, and they would continue to oscillate between involvement and nonattendance.
3. How do you preserve the anonymity of those AA members who choose to participate in surveys? A more general question is how do you study AA without disturbing in a damaging way the unique character of AA?
4. How does one conceptualize what occurs at AA meetings?
5. Can we identify how motivation is related to successful affiliation and outcome? If we can, then that knowledge should be usable to improve affiliation with Alcoholics Anonymous.
6. How does one determine the factors influencing the pathway from attendance to affiliation to sobriety?
7. Can we measure the other benefits, in addition to sobriety, that can occur with affiliation with AA?

Despite these problems, I believe research about AA is possible. The chapters in this book are the result of such work.

I want to end this foreword with a word about a responsibility that investigators have. I have known AA members who did participate in studies but were disappointed at the end of the research because the investigators lost interest in the group and the members at that point. These members felt that the investigators did the research more for self-aggrandizement than as a real quest for knowledge. As researchers plan their studies, they should be sensitive to the feelings of the participants when the study is finished.

Richard K. Fuller, M.D.
Rockville, Maryland
1992

Should and Can Alcoholics Anonymous Be Studied?

CHAPTER 1

The Importance of Research on Alcoholics Anonymous

WILLIAM R. MILLER AND BARBARA S. MCCRADY

Since its inception in 1935, Alcoholics Anonymous (AA) in particular and the 12-step fellowships in general have undergone remarkable growth and change. With an estimated 87,000 groups in 150 countries (Alcoholics Anonymous, 1990a) and over 1.7 million members worldwide, AA is far and away the most frequently consulted source of help for drinking problems. In the United States, nearly one in every 10 adults has attended an AA meeting, and more than one in eight has been to a 12-step meeting of some kind. It is difficult to find an American alcohol/drug abuse treatment program that does not embrace a 12-step approach and recommend AA attendance, or a professional with no opinion about AA. Local court systems in the U.S. now require AA attendance for alcohol-related driving and other offenses, to such an extent that substantial proportions of participants in some AA groups are mandated.

AA has been widely lauded. It has been called "the only continuing and successful group dealing with alcoholism" (Madsen, 1974, p. 156), "medicine's crowning glory" (Father Joseph Martin, 1980), and "the most effective means of treating alcoholism" (Vaillant, in O'Reilly, 1983). The "Big Book" of Alcoholics Anonymous (1976) itself states that "of alcoholics who came to A.A. and really tried, 50% got sober at once and remained that way; 35% sobered up after some relapses, and among the remainder, those who stayed on with A.A. showed improvement. Other thousands came to a few A.A. meetings and at first decided they didn't want the program. But great numbers of these—about two out of three— began to return as time passed" (p. xx). More recently, AA (1990b), in light of current survey data, has clarified that this statement "applied to observations made at an earlier time, and there is no reason to doubt that changes in society and in AA since that time could create a different circumstance today" (p. 13).

For five decades, professionals have called for more scientific research on AA. Wallerstein and his colleagues (1957) observed that "self-help activities of alcoholics as most typically exemplified by Alcoholics Anonymous have not, as yet, been adequately evaluated" (p. 5). Two decades later, Bebbington (1976) commented that "it appears that the state of our knowledge has not improved beyond what we know from clinical experience: that many go to A.A. and that some do very well and attribute their success to their attendance" (p. 579). The Institute of Medicine of the National Academy of Sciences (1990) opined:

> Although it has been in existence since 1935 and has been an important shaping force in alcohol treatment in the United States, Alcoholics Anonymous (AA) has been subjected to surprisingly little scientific study.... The enduring success of this organization in attracting alcoholics to recovery is itself worthy of study. There is, therefore, a pressing need for high-quality research on the impact and mechanisms of AA. (pp. 520–521)

The General Service Office of AA, located in New York City, is itself a remarkable operation. Its budget of over $12 million per year is constituted solely from contributions by members of AA, none of whom are permitted to donate more than $1,000 per year. A staff of 130 provides centralized coordination and advisement. Official publications of AA include six books, the *Grapevine* periodical, 54 booklets, pamphlets and fact sheets, and 7 films, filmstrips, and audiotapes. A random membership survey is conducted every three years to provide current information for the public and professional community. Beyond this, however, AA conducts no research, and maintains no library or clearinghouse of research on AA conducted by others. Its unitary focus is on service to alcoholics and AA groups.

In February of 1992, a unique group of 35 professionals convened in Albuquerque, New Mexico, to discuss "Research on Alcoholics Anonymous: Opportunities and Alternatives." The U.S. Public Health Service participated in support of this meeting through a grant from the National Institute on Alcohol Abuse and Alcoholism. Structured as a "think tank" gathering, the participants came from as far away as Finland and Australia, representing diverse disciplines including anthropology, counseling, history, medicine, nursing, philosophy, psychiatry, psychology, sociology, speech communication, statistics and methodology, and theology. All participants remained for the full proceedings, which lasted for three days. Many had never met each other. Individually, they had attended between zero and thousands of AA meetings. They shared one common interest: to find better ways to conduct meaningful research on AA.

Obstacles to Research

Are there substantial obstacles to research on AA? One clear finding to emerge from the Albuquerque meeting is that empirical research regarding AA has not, in fact, been sparse. Dr. Emrick's review of research on AA (chapter 4 in this volume) covered 115 studies, without including more than 50 unpublished doctoral dissertations. If all published and unpublished studies with at least some data regarding AA were compiled, they would number in the hundreds. At the very least, this indicates that research *can* be done on and within AA.

There are no official barriers to research arising from AA itself. To the contrary, AA publishes a "Memo on Participation of A.A. Members in Research and Other Non-A.A. Surveys" (no date), which states, "In general, within A.A. there is a favorable attitude toward research," and goes on to recommend how investigators and AA members can cooperate to accomplish successful studies. The text of this memo is reproduced, with permission, at the conclusion of this chapter.

Relatively few studies of AA, however, have arisen through the usual channels of federal funding and scientific peer review. Most have been conducted as less formal and unfunded research, often as graduate theses and dissertations. This may be due, in part, to negative attitudes toward and misunderstandings of AA among established researchers. It is also the case that the fluid self-help nature of AA does not lend itself readily to familiar and traditionally valued research designs. For example, a substantial amount of time was devoted, in the Albuquerque meeting, to a discussion of the applicability to AA of the randomized clinical trial. While it was agreed that such trials provide valuable information and represent an important tool for understanding recovery processes, there are particular difficulties in applying this design to such a ubiquitous and variable phenomenon, and many other qualitative and quantitative approaches are available for gaining new knowledge about AA. Furthermore, conducting studies on AA requires certain sensitivity and precautions to ensure that the research does not interfere with or alter the process of AA meetings.

Why Study AA?

Why bother? Some argue that it is best simply to accept AA, without trying to analyze or understand it, or that AA needs no proof or blessing from research. Others argue that the essential processes of AA are not amenable to research and cannot be defined by scientific approaches. We propose six broad reasons why we believe it is important to study AA:

The prevalence of AA. If nothing else, AA is widely recommended and used as a tool for recovery from alcohol-related problems. As the most commonly sought form of help, AA deserves serious attention from those who wish to understand recovery.

Effectiveness. Although traditional controlled trials have not yet yielded evidence for the efficacy of AA, there are reasons to believe that something important is happening within AA, which needs to be better understood. There is the phenomenal growth and popularity of the 12-step fellowships, and the passionate testimony of countless members that AA has helped them. The triennial survey of AA (1990a) reported that 65% of those responding reported sobriety of one year or more. Follow-up studies of alcoholics after treatment commonly find a significant though variable relationship between AA attendance and abstinence.

Cost effectiveness. In a climate of unacceptably accelerating health-care costs, it is important to identify low-cost approaches that can effectively address major health problems (Holder, Longabaugh, Miller, & Rubonis, 1991). Clearly, alcohol problems contribute substantially to health-care costs related to acute and chronic illnesses, injuries, personal and relationship problems, and violence. The treatment of alcohol-related problems is itself a significant cost to public and private health care systems. Help through AA is free, and available almost anywhere at any time.

Matching. The treatment outcome literature to date indicates that there is no single superior approach for treating alcohol-related problems, but rather an encouraging array of alternative approaches (Hester & Miller, 1989). Recently, research has focused on identifying strategies for matching individuals to optimal treatment approaches (Institute of Medicine, 1990). It is reasonable to expect that AA works better for some people than for others, and it would be beneficial to know how to determine, in advance, which approach offers the best initial hope for a given individual.

Persistence. Relatedly, it is clear that a majority of those who attend AA do not continue. The AA (1990b) trienniel surveys reflect a steady decline in the percentage of people remaining in AA over the first year of contact. By three months, 50% have dropped out, and by 12 months the attrition rate appears to be closer to 90%. Further, these survey data indicate that of those who have been sober in AA for less than 12 months, 40% stay sober and in AA for another year. With admirable openness, the observation is added: "It is little comfort to suggest that many who leave return later, because those who have done that are already counted in the numbers shown here" (AA, 1990b, p. 11). Clearly long-term sobriety occurs within in a select minority of those who initially attend AA. AA refers to this as "undoubtedly one of the most significant observations of the survey" (p. 2), and concern is expressed that it is impossible to determine the causes of such attribution through AA's survey research methods, in which dropouts cannot be followed. It seems a worthwhile goal to seek, through research, the causes of this attrition, and methods whereby individuals who could benefit from AA can be encouraged to remain in the fellowship long enough to establish stable sobriety.

Processes of recovery. Finally, AA seems an ideal place to study the processes by which recovery occurs (or does not occur) in a broad population. The literature of AA suggests a rich array of hypotheses about why and how recovery happens. In particular, AA provides unique possibilities to study the influence of a class of variables too often ignored in addiction research: *spiritual* aspects of recovery (Miller, 1990). Much needs to be done in comprehending the processes by which change occurs, particularly outside treatment settings, and research within AA affords many opportunities to advance such understanding.

Toward New Research on AA

The possibilities are many. Discussions at the Albuquerque meeting generated more than 150 important questions that could be addressed in future studies (see Appendix). Our hope is that this volume, which emerged from that meeting, will encourage and assist researchers in designing studies to generate new knowledge about AA.

The remaining three chapters of Part I provide a context for future research. Ernest Kurtz (chapter 2) offers some lessons of history to be pondered and remembered as we look to future studies. Joseph Nowinski (chapter 3) discusses how research interacts with the 12 traditions of AA, and points to special issues that must be considered by researchers in this area. Chad D. Emrick and his colleagues (chapter 4) provide a masterful summary of studies to date on affiliation processes and treatment outcomes within AA.

In Part II, we turn to a broader consideration of how change occurs. Carlo C. DiClemente (chapter 5) sets the stage by presenting a transtheoretical model of change in addictions, through which AA processes might be understood. Margaret Bean-Bayog (chapter 6) discusses the subjective experience of developing alcoholism and becoming involved with AA, emphasizing the heterogeneity of these experiences. In chapter 7, James W. Fowler considers how his model of faith development may parallel transitions that occur over time in AA members. In chapter 8, Stephanie D. Brown compares AA processes with change that occurs in psychotherapy. Finally, Jon Morgenstern and Barbara S. McCrady (chapter 9) discuss unique cognitive processes of change in AA and disease model treatment.

Alcoholics Anonymous does not exist in a vacuum, but is influenced by social context. Four authors in Part III consider the impact on Alcoholics Anonymous and AA research of sociologic (Robin Room, chapter 10), cross-cultural (Klaus Mäkelä, chapter 11), ethnic (Raul Caetano, chapter 12), and gender issues (Linda J. Beckman, chapter 13).

Possibilities for measuring change within AA are the focus in Part IV. Rudolf H. Moos and his colleagues bring their expertise on how to characterize group climate (chapter 14), and Don Cahalan offers his reflections from a long career in longitudinal research (chapter 15). The assessment of relevant individual differences within AA are the subject of chapter 16, by G. Alan Marlatt and his colleagues. Finally, in chapter 17, Richard L. Gorsuch provides a very helpful summary of the vast but often unknown literature on how to measure spiritual variables—a vital dimension for consideration in studying AA.

Part V draws together these pieces in the question, "How could studies of AA be designed?" Ideas are offered for studies in both treatment (J. Clark Laundergan, chapter 18) and community contexts (Alan C. Ogborne, chapter 19). Larry E. Beutler and his colleagues bring their expertise as seasoned psychotherapy researchers to offer perspectives on how one might assess change processes within AA (chapter 20). Finally, Frederick B. Glaser, long a lone voice calling for client-treatment matching, discusses how this important concept of individualized change strategies can be applied in studies of AA (chapter 21).

Part of the work of the Albuquerque meeting involved brainstorming sessions, in which all participants provided their individual written responses to each of 10 questions, then engaged in open discussion to stimulate further ideas. The results of these sessions are reflected, in relatively unedited form, in the Appendix to this volume, and contain a wealth of ideas and issues for those who are considering new research on AA.

The door is open. Studies of AA are not only possible, but much needed. The perspectives offered in this volume are meant to stimulate new studies, to interest new investigators in this important area, and to improve the quality of future research. Though AA itself can never endorse or officially participate in outside studies, there is a long tradition dating to Bill W. of open cooperation between AA members and researchers. This is reflected in the large body of research already accumulating. New studies of AA offer a terrain that will challenge and stretch us, and no doubt cause us to reconsider some of our cherished beliefs. But that is good science, for important new knowledge and breakthroughs often arise precisely when studies *fail* to confirm what we believed to be true at the outset. It is in self-examination and openness to something new that researchers and Alcoholics Anonymous have much in common.

* * *

Memo on Participation of A.A. Members in Research and Other Non-A.A. Surveys

Since the early days of our Fellowship, the participation of A.A. members in research and surveys has been sought—and has occurred. In recent years there has been an escalation of concerns about alcoholism in all parts of our society. As a result, A.A. can expect that requests for participation in research may increase. In general, within A.A. there is a favorable attitude toward research. As Bill W. wrote, "Today the vast majority of us welcome any new light that can be thrown on the alcoholic's mysterious and baffling malady. We welcome new and valuable knowledge, whether it issues from a test tube, from a psychiatrist's couch or from revealing social studies." Historically, participation has been worked out on a case by case basis. Some of the attempts to cooperate have led to strained relationships while more have been successful, mutually satisfying, and produced new insights.

How A.A. members might cooperate with research has been discussed by the trustees' Committee on Cooperation with the Professional Community. At the suggestion of that committee, we offer this memo both to those who would solicit the participation of A.A. members in research and to those A.A. members who will be approached about such requests.

1. The best research relationships between A.A. members and researchers have been those in which the researcher has become thoroughly familiar with the Fellowship before making an inquiry about participation. At the same time, the A.A. members who would be involved have gotten to know the researcher so that they trusted him or her, and have been convinced of the researcher's commitment, competence, integrity, and respect for the Traditions of A.A. The investigator has been forthright in giving the A.A. members all the information about his or her research which they needed in order to make an informed decision about it.

2. For A.A. members, cooperating with a researcher and being part of a research program raises most of the same problems as cooperating with any other non-A.A. professional or engaging in any other non-A.A. undertaking. The problems are amenable to the same kinds of solutions. See: "How A.A. Members Cooperate With Other Community Efforts to Help Alcoholics" and the C.P.C. Workbook. As long as there is frank communication and attitudes of open-mindedness and flexibility, it has proved possible to work out ways of participating in research which do not require A.A. members to compromise A.A.'s Traditions and which permit the researcher to arrive at valid findings.

3. The researcher should be aware that central offices in A.A. cannot offer the kinds of assistance he or she may be used to from the headquarters of other organizations, e.g. access to records, endorsement, etc. However, the researcher may receive some help from the General Service Office, intergroup offices, and local offices of other kinds.

   (a) Individuals in these offices may be willing to give the researcher their opinions about the projects and about their feasibility.

   (b) Literature can be provided which will prove helpful to the researcher in understanding A.A., what it is, what it can and cannot do, as well as on how A.A. members cooperate with non-A.A. undertakings.

   (c) A copy of this memo can be provided.

4. Decisions about whether or not to cooperate in research are always made at the local level where the research will occur. Almost always the request for

participation has been made to individual A.A. members who have then sought the cooperation of other members. In rare instances the request has been made to a group. When A.A. members have decided to cooperate, it has been in their capacity as private citizens.

5. Those individuals approached about cooperation will want to make an informed judgment about whether to participate and about whether to seek the participation of others. Indeed, with the increased requests for research cooperation, it is necessary that selection take place. Some of the kinds of questions the individual might have are: what is being studied, by whom, why and how; who will carry out the research at the local level; what will cooperation involve, e.g. interviews, questionnaires, amount of time; who will evaluate the findings; who will use the findings for what purpose; in the light of A.A. Traditions, is cooperation possible; what arrangements are made to ensure anonymity, etc.

6. A.A. is concerned solely with the personal recovery and continued sobriety of alcoholics who turn to the Fellowship for help. Meetings are devoted exclusively to the A.A. program. No research which could interfere with this goal could be tolerated. Some groups have permitted questionnaires or interviews to occur after meetings provided that participation is on a personal, voluntary basis. Some members look upon research participation as one way of pursuing the above mentioned goal, as using their experience to contribute to long-term solutions for alcoholism. Many more will define it as a distraction from Twelfth Step work which they define in immediate personal terms.

7. A.A. and its members are particularly concerned with anonymity. While most researchers are skilled at ensuring anonymity to subjects, A.A.'s concerns may raise unique issues. For example, as no A.A. can break the anonymity of another, there may be ticklish issues in soliciting cooperation from others. Some research procedures may also require extra precautions be taken, e.g. when data are stored in computers, when granting agencies require consent to participate forms, etc.

And, a final quote from Bill W. about cooperation with non-A.A.'s working to resolve the problems of alcoholism, "So let us work alongside all these projects of promise to hasten the recovery of those millions who have not yet found their way out. These varied labors do not need our special endorsement; they need only a helping hand when, as individuals, we can possibly give it."

We welcome additional information from researchers and from members of A.A. who have experience to share or comments to make.

Acknowledgments

The conference and the preparation of this monograph were supported by National Institute on Alcohol Abuse and Alcoholism grant 1-R13-AA09051. The "Memo on Participation of A.A. Members in Research and Other Non-A.A. Surveys" is reprinted with permission.

References

Alcoholics Anonymous. (1976). *Alcoholics Anonymous: The story of how many thousands of men and women have recovered from alcoholism* (3rd ed.). New York: Alcoholics Anonymous World Services.

Alcoholics Anonymous. (1990a). *Alcoholics Anonymous 1989 membership survey.* New York: Alcoholics Anonymous World Services.

Alcoholics Anonymous. (1990b). *Comments on A.A.'s Triennial Surveys.* New York: Alcoholics Anonymous World Services.

Alcoholics Anonymous. (no date). *Memo on participation of A.A. members in research and other non-A.A. surveys.* New York: Alcoholics Anonymous World Services.

Bebbington, P.E. (1976). The efficacy of Alcoholics Anonymous: The elusiveness of hard data. *British Journal of Psychiatry, 128,* 572–580.

Father Joseph Martin. (1980). Too few counselors effective. *U.S. Journal of Drug and Alcohol Dependence, 3*(12), 9.

Hester, R.K., & Miller W.R. (Eds.). (1989). *Handbook of alcoholism treatment approaches: Effective alternatives.* Elmsford, NY: Pergamon Press.

Holder, H., Longabaugh, R., Miller, W.R., & Rubonis, A.V. (1991). The cost effectiveness of treatment for alcoholism: A first approximation. *Journal of Studies on Alcohol, 52,* 517–540.

Institute of Medicine, National Academy of Sciences (1990). *Broadening the base of treatment for alcohol problems.* Washington, DC: National Academy Press.

Madsen, W. (1974). *The American alcoholic: The nature-nurture controversy in alcoholic research and therapy.* Springfield, IL: C.C. Thomas, 1974.

Miller, W. R. (1990). Spirituality: The silent dimension in addiction research. *Drug & Alcohol Review, 9,* 259–266.

O'Reilly, J. (1983). New insights into alcoholism. *Time,* April 25, 88–89.

Wallerstein, R.S., Chotlos, J.W., Friend, M.B., Hammersley, D.W., Perlswig, E.A., & Winship, G.M. (1957). *Hospital treatment of alcoholism: A comparative experimental study.* New York: Basic Books.

CHAPTER 2

Research on Alcoholics Anonymous: The Historical Context

ERNEST KURTZ

A lcoholics Anonymous has been around for almost 60 years; research on Alcoholics Anonymous has been going on for over 50 years. Yet we still hear mainly about how "inconclusive" are the results of what now number many hundreds of articles. Projects such as this volume seem to verify the law that Mark Keller (1972) formulated two decades ago: "The investigation of any trait in alcoholics will show that they have either more or less of it." That seems even truer of those alcoholics who are members of Alcoholics Anonymous.[1]

As both Dickens and Goethe suggest, "Those who have no memory have no hope." And so if it is important to see Alcoholics Anonymous over time, it is also important to see *research into Alcoholics Anonymous* over time. For research on AA has its own history, and the story of *what* we have learned about Alcoholics Anonymous, and of *how* it was learned, reveals patterns that it would be irresponsible to ignore.

One such pattern is the incomplete parallel, over the past half-century, between research on alcoholism and research on Alcoholics Anonymous. The former has emphasized, in turn, the psychological, the sociological, and the biological. The pattern of research into AA runs differently: first came the sociological, then the psychological, and now more and more interest is shown in the spiritual. Throughout that pattern, uneven though it may be, we find two recurrent motifs; and it is under those headings of, for want of better terms, *accuracy* and *objectivity,* that this chapter is organized.

The First Motif: Accuracy

Most of the earliest research on Alcoholics Anonymous was conducted by sociologists. Their primary method was careful, attentive listening to AA members, both within and outside of AA meetings, followed by analyses of what they had heard and seen. The names of Robert Freed Bales

(1942, 1944), Selden Bacon (1944), and others (e.g., Anderson, 1944; Voegtlin & Lemere, 1942) are surely familiar.

The scope of this earliest research was limited, but the questions asked did derive from accurate, exact data. Later researchers, who ask more sophisticated questions, have not always continued that criterion. One example from the conference that engendered these papers: In conversation, a participant mentioned three studies, observing almost parenthetically that they "demonstrated that Alcoholics Anonymous doesn't work." But as Chad Emrick promptly pointed out, the articles in question all studied individuals mandated to AA by the courts. "What those articles demonstrate," Emrick observed, "is that *coercing* people into Alcoholics Anonymous does not work."

Another, more common, example: whatever the terms used, failure to advert to the AA distinction between mere *dryness* and true *sobriety,* between "putting the cork in the bottle" and attaining a degree of "serenity," signals a very poor understanding of Alcoholics Anonymous. And so claims that "Alcoholics Anonymous emphasizes that drinking is the principal cause of its members' life problems" (Ogborne, 1989) awaken in the aware reader wonder that an apparently serious student of AA seems unfamiliar with the chapter of its book titled "How It Works," wherein may be found the obvious key sentence: "Self-centeredness! That, we think, is the root of our troubles" (Alcoholics Anonymous, 1976, p. 62).

Why this confusion and such decline of accuracy? Are more recent researchers less careful students? Likely not. Much of the problem can, in fact, be laid at the door of Alcoholics Anonymous itself. For especially in recent years, there is a very real sense in which, increasingly, there is no such thing as Alcoholics Anonymous—rather there have developed Varieties of the AA Experience.

Under the impact of alcoholism treatment (through which an increasing number of new AA members arrive at the fellowship [Alcoholics Anonymous, 1990]), shaped also by cultural pressures to widen the concept of addiction, Alcoholics Anonymous, decentralized as it is, now presents itself in a vast variety of groups, of formats, of understandings even of such basic-to-AA realities as *serenity,* not to mention spirituality. This can be a difficult point for people like us to accept, people who want to study Alcoholics Anonymous. Even when we study process, we like our phenomenon to hold still. At the very least, we want it to *be* phenomenon rather than a multiplicity of phenomena.

But AA doesn't hold still, and increasingly it mutates. Current research suggests that most AA members agree that one can no longer assume that every meeting listed in an AA meeting-list is an AA meeting. To take an example recently offered: "I went to this place where a meeting was listed, in Akron itself, for God's sake, and they began by suggesting we go around the table and tell 'how we had nurtured our inner child today.' Hell! I'm a drunk, so I left: that wasn't the kind of meeting I need to keep me sober" (private correspondence).

Note the *kind of* variety addressed here. The concern is not about the different kinds of *subjects* investigated: young or middle-aged or old; also using or not using drugs other than alcohol, legal or illegal; and other such obviously important differences. The point here concerns the varieties of *experiences* available within Alcoholics Anonymous—and the consequent reality that *all* generalizations about Alcoholics Anonymous need careful qualification.

But there is a consolation connected with this caution: Although the *breadth* of AA's varieties is a new phenomenon, the reality of diversity within Alcoholics Anonymous is not merely recent. AA's differences were one reason why it developed in so decentralized a fashion. Early researchers were aware of that, but they fell into the easy (and enduring) trap of researching what was available—studying those AAs who welcomed their research. Influenced also by the secularization hypothesis shared by most sociologists of the era (Tschannen, 1991), they tended to overlook the Akron birthplace of AA and its more Oxford Group-oriented offspring, concentrating their attention on New York AA and its derivatives. The affiliations (and so the locations) of those early students also suggest that they found East Coast AA more convenient to research. Then, too, the strong personality and central role of Bill Wilson had much to do with this focus. Although Bill himself to a perhaps surprising extent welcomed diversity and even disagreement, seeing in them a useful spur to the spiritual virtue of *tolerance,* not all members agreed with him, even about that.

Because most of the differences within AA, then and now, concern "the spiritual," this point will be picked up below when we examine that aspect of research's history. A final example, however, may helpfully conclude this introduction to the importance—and the difficulty—of *accuracy.* Many recent researchers (e.g., Trice & Staudenmeier, 1989), refer to Alcoholics Anonymous as a "self-help" program. As validly as that term may reflect sociological precision, as useful as it may be to distinguish from help-by-professionals, when the phrase spills over to questionnaires or interview schedules, it implicitly sorts the sample: only relatively recent AA adherents accept that term. A majority of those with over 10 years sobriety, my research indicates, object to that label, saying: "No, we tried that, self-help, and it didn't work—that's why we're a God-help program."

And so we are brought back to that ungainly topic, *the spiritual.* Because "the spiritual" is a delicate if not difficult topic for most academicians, let's approach it from a more familiar and congenial direction: our commitment, as researchers, to objectivity.

The Second Motif: Objectivity

By *objectivity* I mean, first, care that the kind of questions asked are true to the phenomenon being studied. Recently, ornithologist Robert Mc-Farlane (1992) reminded that "Science is the art of phrasing questions and identifying their attendant assumptions." And so in the name of science, let me as a practitioner in the humanities raise some questions about the assumptions that have attended the history of research into Alcoholics Anonymous—questions raised by my research into the way later researchers have used earlier research on AA.

Why is it that the most richly accurate as well as most objectively balanced recent studies of Alcoholics Anonymous come in dissertation form, from new rather than established scholars—Taylor (1977), Johnson (1987), Vourakis (1989), Smith (1991)? Why is it that there are so few references to this literature by the major figures currently publishing in the field? Should not research scholars keep abreast of and make available more widely the newest contributions to knowledge? And why are certain other articles so frequently cited—at times in ways that raise questions about the assumptions attending their citation?

Let me be specific. Many (e.g., Ogborne & Glaser, 1984) continue to cite Seiden (1955, 1960), whose 1955 master's thesis was based on a sample of 50 subjects, to the effect that "the use of A.A. members in research as representative of the total alcoholic population is unwarranted." Given the date, that discovery was a real contribution, meriting mention even if only for historical reasons. But in all the references to it over the most recent 15 years, I have yet to see any mention of one finding that led Seiden to his conclusion: "Whether in terms of amount of ego strength, comparability to psychiatric populations or recovery from alcoholism, the A.A. [members] appear to be psychologically 'healthier,' i.e. deviate less from the theoretically normal (nonalcoholic) personality." Is that totally irrelevant or merely unwelcome at a time when the ruling assumption seems to be that only those inclined to "infantilism," "authoritarianism," and "religiosity" (Ogborne, 1989) will do well in Alcoholics Anonymous?

Another example: Studies of AA and spirituality seem bound to cite Robert Kenneth Jones' 1970 examination of the "Sectarian Characteristics of Alcoholics Anonymous" (again with a sample of 50). One wonders how carefully those who cite Jones have read his article, which blends keen sociological analysis with the kind of errors inevitable in an analysis based on observations of AA in just one locality (Merseyside). Jones informs, for example, that "one of the A.A. symbols... is an empty pint beer glass which is placed on the speaker's table." But the habitual citation of Jones troubles for a deeper reason: the context for his description was the English religious situation, which—with its established church and categories of "dissenters"—differs from most other cultures in its understanding of *sectarian;* yet Jones is almost always cited without any advertence to that British context. Why? Because the implications of his terminology are congenial?

A final example: the continued citation (e.g., Ogborne 1989) of Aharan's (1970) criticism that AA members "can't express feelings of depression, disillusionment, fear." Aharan worked out of London, Ontario, and so until I moved to the Detroit area, with its convenient bridge and tunnel, I wondered whether a peculiar reticence might characterize Canadian alcoholics. Not so. But in any case, we are examining citation. And so it is justified to wonder: At how many meetings—and at what kinds of meetings—have those who cite Aharan carefully listened? How many sponsors have they interviewed? Even more importantly, have they attended any after-the-meeting gatherings, the importance of which for understanding AA has been detailed by Rudy (1986), Denzin (1987b,c), Smith (1991), and others? Given our awareness of the impact of treatment therapies on AA practice, Aharan's complaint would seem to invite a follow-up study rather than uncritical citation of a two-decade-old generalization that was questionable even when first formulated.

Question: Do we not have some responsibility to evaluate previous research or at least to place it in some kind of context, or is our obligation solely to pile up the names of those who seem to support some point we are making? This is a pragmatically important as well as a methodologically valid question, for the biases that can creep in are not merely benign. We are all familiar, at least in theory, with the impact of the observer on the observed. What, then, are the effects of the condescension some investigators show toward Alcoholics Anonymous? How self-fulfilling, for example, become prophecies about who will do well, and who poorly, in AA? Not only can such judgments influence who gets sent to AA, but do you think for a moment that the newly sober drunk does not have antennae attuned to the referrer's attitudes?

Let's examine another example. After finding that "affiliates who are younger, male, and lower in SES [socioeconomic status] have more slips, are in AA a shorter time [and] tend to be less stable," Joseph Boscarino (1980) made it the main point of his article that such individuals should still be referred to AA, with "additional efforts... made to maximize the effectiveness" of such referrals. Most citations of Boscarino refer to his "findings" and ignore his recommendations (e.g., Emrick, 1989). Which would seem unfortunate, because a decade after Boscarino, research by Keith Humphreys et al. (1991) indicated that "it would be unwise... to assume that there is a requisite level of education or social stability that must be attained before a client will affiliate with NA or AA." Examining another common assumption, Humphreys' co-authors observed that while it was possible to assume that clients in residential settings were more likely to attend AA because such clients had more severe problems, it was also possible to assume that higher attendance was due to the staff members in such settings more vigorously encouraging clients to such involvement because they themselves were more likely to be "in recovery from substance abuse and to endorse the philosophy of AA/NA" (Mavis & Stofflemayr, 1989). As always, the choice of assumptions lies with the one doing the citing.

A final example of how failure of respect can shape assumptions that may flaw the interpretation if not the results of research. In 1964, Mindlin reported that those "who had attended A.A. meetings were less likely to describe themselves as isolated, lonely, or socially ill at ease." Two decades later, Ogborne and Glaser (1984) offered this as evidence that Alcoholics Anonymous served best those who had a "capacity to function in group settings." That is one possible reading, but is there not the barest possibility that AA attendance helps some to overcome loneliness and isolation? Bacon's 1957 comment on AA's "re-socialization" of the alcoholic supports this view, as does Tremper's almost model sensitivity to the which-comes-first question in his 1972 study of "Dependency in Alcoholics."

By this time, I am sure, you sense my own bias on these questions— and so let me speak directly to it, lest my very real animus be misunderstood. I carry no brief for Alcoholics Anonymous. There are many things about AA that merit questioning, and my sole act of faith here is in the ultimate value of all real research. But the tradition of historical research within which I work holds it to be a fundamental ethic of scholarship that one seeks *first* to understand any phenomenon in and on its own terms; only then can interpretation and criticism worthy of the names result. The ideal is perhaps the clearest in the physical sciences... to be open-minded in the sense of *respecting* what one studies, whether it be the human genome or Jupiter's moons or the AIDS virus. Such respect is not bias: it is rather the prerequisite for accurate study.

When AA's co-founder queried his physician about his spiritual experience in Towns Hospital in December 1934, what if Dr. Silkworth had conveyed the attitude to spirituality that seems to characterize some recent researchers? Why is it that some who choose to research Alcoholics Anonymous seem to bring to that task attitudes toward "the spiritual" that if held toward homosexuality would be termed homophobic? Why, to be more concrete, are pejorative terms such as *religiosity* and *authoritarianism* preferred to the as-descriptive-words *spirituality* and *commitment*? We carefully eschew ethnic epithets and gender slurs: Why can researchers not show a similar sensitivity to the sensibilities of the alcoholics we study? Is it fair to ask their respect if we are unwilling to offer them ours?

Why do I raise so sensitive a point? Because research is that sensitive. An enduring issue in studying Alcoholics Anonymous has been "cooperation" (Aharan, 1970; L. F. Kurtz, 1984, 1985). Given the decentralized nature of the AA fellowship, the autonomy of its groups, the thrust of its traditions, researchers are frequently frustrated in their attempts to get cooperation from AA members. I empathize: historical research, which relies on access to documents, also requires cooperation; and I have discovered that just as we generalize about "members of Alcoholics Anonymous," AA members generalize about "researchers." And so if you gain respect, my research may be easier. And if I violate and lose respect, your research may suffer. As researchers into Alcoholics Anonymous, we are all in this together, whether we like that or not! AA members, after all, are human beings: one thing they do not like—any more than we do—is being scorned, having those realities that hold precious meaning for them demeaned and disrespected.

Let us review but one manifestation of this concern. Respect touches on *ethics,* and our research may require a special sensitivity in this area. Recall the questions raised by Fred Davis (1970) in his discussion of a research project reported by John F. Lofland and Robert A. Lejeune (1970). Wishing to investigate "what features of the social structures of A.A. groups may facilitate or deter affiliation," Lofland and Lejeune undertook field observation of about 70 AA groups (all in Manhattan) to which they sent "agents" who "posed as" AA newcomers. Davis questioned whether there might not be an ethical problem in such "premeditated deception," objecting that in the name of scholarship, it "constitutes a travesty upon A.A.'s identity." Davis went on: "This is not to say . . . that the sociologist is compelled to accept as truth the ideology by which the organization represents itself to outsiders. But, it is a far cry from intellectually detaching oneself from an organization's values to engaging in acts which effectively make a mockery of them."

Note that the point here—the impartiality that can be guaranteed only by respect—concerns not criticism of Alcoholics Anonymous, which has been available for four decades (e.g., Chambers, 1953; Cain, 1960, 1963, 1964), but the specific history of critical research on the fellowship and its program. That history reveals a consistently recurring motif: the problems inherent in attempts to research "the spiritual" in the broadest sense of that much abused term. The story of those research efforts suggest that, for our purposes, it may be helpful to approach that theme from a sensitivity to the distinction between quantitative and qualitative research— or, from another perspective, to the differences between the research approaches of distancing and of immersion.

The earliest research into Alcoholics Anonymous was primarily qualitative, and that remained the norm until fairly recently when, paralleling alcoholism research's turn to the biologically concrete in preference to the psychologically and sociologically amorphous, research on AA also took a strong turn toward quantification. Unlike alcoholism research's yoking of this emphasis with the concretely physiological, however, researchers on AA set off on the quantitative trajectory at just the point where the most interesting research questions seemed to deal in some way with "the spiritual."

Why the turn to quantification took place, although an intriguing question, lies beyond our research concern here; but it does seem worthy of note that the explosion of quantitative studies and the burst of insistence on operationalizing directly correlate in time with the availability of funding disbursed by bureaucratically administered institutions.

At first glance, the turn to quantification would seem a real boon. How better guarantee accuracy and objectivity than by the quantitative approach? Numbers are so precise, so verifiable—apparently, at least, so objectively accurate. Yet quantitative research also has assumptions: not only do we look for what we expect to find, but we see what we look for, as was several times demonstrated at the conference that gave rise to this book. Early in the proceedings, for one vivid example, Robin Room noted that "nine percent of the American population have at some time attended a meeting of Alcoholics Anonymous—that is a number greater than practically any other institution, save the public school and the Catholic Church." A bit later, Don Cahalan, citing the same research study, observed that "*only* nine percent of the U.S. population has even attended an AA meeting" (italics in his voice). Research practitioners, in other words, continue to rediscover the problems inherent in what Nietzsche termed "the doctrine of the immaculate perception" (Jones, 1988). All data are theory-laden: "Perceivers without concepts, as Kant almost said, are blind" (MacIntyre, 1981).

For the deeper difficulty arises from the assumption-turned-demand that "the spiritual" can and should be operationalized. The language is new, but the point at issue is ancient. And although the story of this effort does not necessarily suggest that it cannot be done, that history does suggest wariness of claims to achieve measurement of spiritual entities. Some campuses are still afflicted with the lecturer who each year convinces some freshmen that love can be equated with genital tumescence—a not inappropriate parallel to some studies of AA, if we recall psychiatrist Leslie Farber's (1976) analysis of how the demand to prove love is but one example of the futility of demands to impose *will* on the spiritual, demands for which addiction affords such a fascinating metaphor.

From our perspective, here, perhaps the best evidence that the spiritual cannot be directly measured may be found in our ready (and appropriate) acceptance that there exists no proof of the efficacy of Alcoholics Anonymous—this despite descriptions by hundreds of thousands of members of Alcoholics Anonymous who attest that AA has saved their lives and made it possible for them to live lives worth living. If we have no such proof, despite all the efforts expended over the years by talented and sophisticated researchers, that very lack (1) supports AA members' claims that their program and the spiritual cannot be separated and (2) challenges us to think out research strategies that respect that reality.

A review of research suggests that past endeavors to operationalize the spiritual have produced the same results as attempts to trisect the angle or to prove that four colors suffice the map-maker. Yet recognizing that need not provoke despair. If we can lay aside demands that would require the spiritual to be somehow material, we discover that the spiritual can still be investigated. Historically, in fact, two lines of research into Alcoholics Anonymous have shown particular promise in this area: studies of the affiliation process, and the methodology of content-analysis.

Mindful of the danger of falling into thinly veiled re-pursuits of the alcoholic personality, researchers on affiliation have recently returned to exploring its *process* (Rudy, 1986 and Denzin, 1987c, harking back to Trice, 1957), in this recapturing a research suggestion implicit in a little-known aspect of AA history. AA co-founder Bill Wilson, together with medical researchers Abram Hoffer and Humphrey Osmond, discovered early on that some kind of capacity for the spiritual seemed to be required if an alcoholic was to get the AA program. They understood that capacity not as related to church-going or creedal affirmation or upbringing, but as some kind of process potentially present in every human being, a process that could be prodded. Their efforts to learn its nature in fact underlay Wilson's experimentation with the psychoactive chemical LSD (Alcoholics Anonymous, 1984; Kurtz, 1991 [1979]). I do not recommend that readers continue that exploration, but awareness of it may help researchers deepen sensitivity to the complexity of the pursuit of spirituality, for which "sober intoxication" is a more than two-millennia-old image (McGinn, 1991; Dodds, 1951).

"Capacity for the spiritual" is not a new research category: John Clancy (1962) broached the topic three decades ago. Others (Rudy, 1986; Denzin, 1987c) have touched on it more recently, albeit less directly. To the best of my knowledge, only one person, a hobbyist rather than a scholar, is currently researching how early AA's bibliotherapy worked—the practice of assigning certain books to be read, which was seen as an effective way of "opening to the spiritual" (Dick B., 1992). But studies of the AA practice of sponsorship do follow up on another early hunch about how to achieve that opening (Fichter, 1978, 1982). If those who investigate the relationship that is AA sponsorship can approach that phenomenon not as a manifestation of "authoritarianism" or "infantilism" (Lindt, 1959), but as evidence of the capacity to learn by listening and of a potential for the classic virtue of *humility* (Ripley & Jackson, 1959), then perhaps we are on the road to researching the spiritual (Leech, 1977; Sellner, 1990).

The second promising line of research, although so far more hinted at than carried out, is content analysis—examining the words and concepts used by speakers or in discussions. Used sensitively, content analysis can happily marry quantitative methodology with qualitative sensibility. I can point to no major formal study, but limited examples are sufficiently plentiful both to offer hope and to point out pitfalls. Murphy's (1953) study of the values expressed at AA meetings is one landmark here, and the method has been carried forward informally not only in the dissertations of Taylor (1977), Johnson (1987), O'Reilly (1988), and Smith (1991), but in the studies of Denzin (1987a,b,c) and Rudy (1986) and Rodin (1985)—not to mention the too often overlooked work of George Vaillant (1983).

Conclusion

Accuracy ... Objectivity ... Respect: these must guide not only how we approach the topic of our research, but how we approach each other as fellow researchers into a subject that transcends not only any one of us but, more importantly, any one discipline. The most recent history of research on Alcoholics Anonymous reveals a fault-line not between religion and science—whatever those terms may signify—but between the differing approaches of quantitative and qualitative methodologies, between those who believe that truth is best found by maintaining *distance from* the object of study, and those who think truth is best approached by *immersion in* the subject of interest.

On one side, quantifiers and those who fund research reasonably and responsibly request that the realities we claim to study be in some way operationalizable: let us be able to demonstrate that what we study is real, that we are giving, and getting, our money's worth. Those on the other side insist that to study only those aspects of some realities that are operationalizable is like undertaking to study nonhuman lifeforms and then restricting the scope of investigation to four-footed fur-bearers: convenient as such a research design may be, the sample will not be representative of the population.

How might we bridge this gap, so that we can—truly—learn from each other? Any solution must begin, I suspect, with acceptance that quantitative and qualitative research, the preferences for distancing and for immersion, are in a very real way two different cultures. As in most such cases, although real efforts may be made (as well as lip service given) to tolerance and mutual respect, there always seems to lurk the not-too-well-

hidden conviction that one's own culture is best, that one's own methodology is "number one." The pattern, then, will almost certainly continue
of operationalizing quantitative researchers decrying the fuzzy and unrep-
licable nature of qualitative studies, while qualitative researchers challenge whether what is being so precisely measured has any importance, as
they gleefully point out the assumptions implicit in the supposedly objective quantitative studies.

Two cultures, then; and on the assumption that this reality will resur-
face so long as differently inclined researchers investigate Alcoholics
Anonymous, I think the most apt conclusion to our examination of the
historical context of research on AA is to frame this theme in historical
experience made contemporary by recent film. Reviewing the motion
picture *Black Robe*, one critic praised its avoidance of "easy romanticism"
in portraying the clash of cultures. "Usually today," he noted, pointing implicitly at Costner's *Dances With Wolves*, "one culture does get romanti-
cized and the other trashed." But in *Black Robe:*

> There is a massive, unvarnished dignity, flawed and vulnerable, in both the
> Native American leader and the French priest. The tragedy is that, for all their
> nobility and integrity, they inhabit utterly divergent worlds. What is home for
> one man is chaos for the other. What is beautiful for one is ugly for the other.
> What is heaven for one is devastation for the other. (Kavanaugh, 1992)

The story of past research on such topics does not conclusively demonstrate that such is also our fate, but that possibility remains real. Can we
hope for more than that future historians will be as generous in viewing
the equivalent of these two groups among us? I think we can, if the research inspired by, as well as the research reported in, this volume can
become itself a contribution to healing and to the making whole of the
very diverse efforts of very diverse researchers, by encouraging the commitment of all of us to accuracy, objectivity, and—especially—respect.

Note

1. For the sake of consistency within this volume, the author has revised this article from the Chicago style favored by historians to the American Psychological Association (APA) style beloved by social scientists. This is done
   reluctantly, for I believe that the APA style is itself one source of some of the
   difficulties explored within this chapter. Three points may clarify. First, APA
   style works best when each work cited is a "least publishable unit," having one,
   unambiguous point. Some writing in some disciplines fits that criterion, but not
   all research in all fields. APA style makes it difficult to deal adequately with
   nuanced presentations, often leaving the reader unsure to just which of some
   author's complex findings reference is being made. In the second place, APA-
   style citation, with its initials-only format and foreclosure of parenthetical com-

ment, seems to invite citation of works known only *via* abstract, or at times even only by title. More often than with full-note style, a reader familiar with a cited piece wonders whether the citing author has missed the point or is totally unaware of it. And, finally, APA style privileges distancing over immersion. Other scholars are mentioned rather than engaged with, as full notes invite. But objectivity need not require distancing, from topic or from other researchers. In fact, an objectivity that *respects* even suggests that at least some research be carried on by immersion in rather than by distancing from. At the time of this essay's oral presentation, these thoughts sparked spirited discussion. The editors and the author hope that this expression of them has the same result.

References

Aharan, C. (1970). AA and other treatment programs: Problems in cooperation. *Addictions (Toronto), 17*(4), 25–32.

Alcoholics Anonymous. (1976). *Alcoholics Anonymous: The story of how many thousands of men and women have recovered from alcoholism* (3rd ed.). New York: Alcoholics Anonymous World Services.

Alcoholics Anonymous. (1984). *Pass it on: The story of Bill Wilson and how the A.A. message reached the world.* New York: Alcoholics Anonymous World Services.

Alcoholics Anonymous. (1990). Comments on A.A.'s triennial surveys. New York: Alcoholics Anonymous World Services.

Anderson, D. (1944). The process of recovery from alcoholism. *Federal Probation, 8*(4), 14–19.

B., Dick. (1992). *Dr. Bob's Library.* Wheeling, WV: The Bishop of Books.

Bacon, S.D. (1944). Sociology and the problems of alcohol: Foundations for a sociologic study of drinking behavior. *Quarterly Journal of Studies on Alcohol, 5,* 402–445.

Bacon, S.D. (1957). A sociologist looks at A.A. *Minnesota Welfare, 10*(10), 35–44.

Bales, R.F. (1942). Types of social structure as factors in "cures" for alcohol addiction. *Applied Anthropology, 1,* 1–13.

Bales, R.F. (1944). The therapeutic role of "Alcoholics Anonymous" as seen by a sociologist. *Quarterly Journal of Studies on Alcohol, 5,* 267–278.

Boscarino, J. (1980). Factors related to "stable" and "unstable" affiliation with Alcoholics Anonymous. *International Journal of Addictions, 15*(6), 839–848.

Cain, A.H. (1960). *Philosophical psychology of the socially estranged alcoholic.* Unpublished dissertation, Columbia University.

Cain, A.H. (1963). Alcoholics Anonymous: Cult or cure? *Harper's Magazine, 226*(1353), 48–52.

Cain, A.H. (1964). *The cured alcoholic: New concepts in alcoholism treatment and research.* New York: John Day.

Chambers, F.T. (1953). Analysis and comparison of three treatment measures for alcoholism: Antabuse, the Alcoholics Anonymous approach, & psychotherapy. *British Journal of Addiction, 50,* 29–41.

Clancy, J. (1962). The use of intellectual processes in group psychotherapy with alcoholics. *Quarterly Journal of Studies on Alcohol, 23,* 432–441.

Davis, F. (1970). Comment on "Initial interaction of newcomers in Alcoholics Anonymous." In W.J. Filstead (Ed.), *Qualitative methodology: Firsthand involvement with the social world* (pp. 271–274). Chicago: Markham.

Denzin, N.K. (1987a). *The alcoholic self.* Newbury Park, CA: Sage.
Denzin, N.K. (1987b). *The recovering alcoholic.* Newbury Park, CA: Sage.
Denzin, N.K. (1987c). *Treating alcoholism: An Alcoholics Anonymous approach.* Newbury Park, CA: Sage.
Dodds, E.R. (1951). *The Greeks and the irrational.* Berkeley, CA: University of California Press.
Emrick, C.D. (1989). Alcoholics Anonymous: Membership characteristics and effectiveness as treatment. In M. Galanter (Ed.), *Recent developments in alcoholism: Vol. 7. Treatment research* (pp. 37–53). New York: Plenum Press.
Farber, L.H. (1976). *Lying, despair, jealousy, envy, sex, suicide, drugs, and the good life.* New York: Basic Books.
Fichter, J.H. (1978). Survey of NCCA membership. *NCCA Blue Book, 30,* 11–16.
Fichter, J.H. (1982). *The rehabilitation of clergy alcoholics.* New York: Human Sciences Press.
Humphreys, K., Mavis, B., & Stofflemayr, B. (1991). Factors predicting attendance at self-help groups after substance abuse treatment: Preliminary findings. *Journal of Consulting and Clinical Psychology, 59*(4), 591–593.
Johnson, H.C. (1987). *Alcoholics Anonymous in the 1980s: Variations of a theme.* Unpublished doctoral dissertation, University of California, Los Angeles.
Jones, R.K. (1970). Sectarian characteristics of Alcoholics Anonymous. *Sociology (Oxford), 4,* 181–195.
Jones, S.L. (1988). A religious critique of behavior therapy. In W.R. Miller and J.E. Martin (Eds.), *Behavior therapy and religion: Integrating spiritual and behavioral approaches to Change* (pp. 139–170). Newbury Park, CA: Sage.
Kavanaugh, J., as quoted by Marty Marty (1 February 1992). *Context, 24*(3), 5.
Keller, M. (1972). The oddities of alcoholics. *Quarterly Journal of Studies on Alcohol, 33,* 1147–1148.
Kurtz, E. (rev. ed. 1991; orig. 1979). *Not-God: A history of Alcoholics Anonymous.* Center City, MN: Hazelden.
Kurtz, L.F. (1984). Ideological differences between professionals and A.A. members. *Alcoholism Treatment Quarterly, 1,* 73–86.
Kurtz, L.F. (1985). Cooperation and rivalry between helping professionals and members of A.A. *Health and Social Work, 10,* 104–112.
Leech, K. (1977). *Soul friend: The practice of Christian spirituality.* San Francisco, CA: Harper & Row.
Lindt, H. (1959). The "rescue fantasy" in group treatment of alcoholics. *International Journal of Group Psychotherapy, 9,* 43–52.
Lofland, J.F., & Lejeune, R.A. (1970). Initial interaction of newcomers in Alcoholics Anonymous: A field experiment in class symbols and socialization. In W.J. Filstead (Ed.), *Qualitative methodology: Firsthand involvement with the social world* (pp. 107–118). Chicago: Markham.
MacIntyre, A. (1981). *After virtue.* Notre Dame, IN: University of Notre Dame.
Mavis, B.E., & Stofflemayr, B.E. (1989). Paraprofessionals, staff recovery status, and client satisfaction in alcohol treatment. Paper presented at the 97th annual convention of the American Psychological Association, New Orleans.
McFarlane, R. (1992, January 5). A stillness in the pines: The ecology of the red-cockaded woodpecker. As quoted and cited in "Noted with pleasure," *New York Times Book Review.*
McGinn, B. (1991). *The foundations of mysticism.* New York: Crossroad.
Mindlin, D.F. (1964). Attitudes toward alcoholism and toward self: Differences between three alcoholic groups. *Quarterly Journal of Studies on Alcohol, 25,* 136–141.

Murphy, M.M. (1953). Values stressed by two social class levels at meetings of Alcoholics Anonymous. *Quarterly Journal of Studies on Alcohol, 14,* 576–585.

O'Reilly, E.B. (1988). *Toward rhetorical immunity: Narratives of alcoholism and recovery.* Unpublished doctoral dissertation, University of Pennsylvania.

Ogborne, A.C. (1989). Some limitations of Alcoholics Anonymous. In M. Galanter (Ed.), *Recent developments in alcoholism: Vol. 7. Treatment research* (pp. 55–65). New York: Plenum Press.

Ogborne, A.C., & Glaser, F.B. (1984). Characteristics of affiliates of Alcoholics Anonymous. *Journal of Studies on Alcohol, 42*(7), 661–675.

Ripley, H.S., & Jackson, J.F. (1959). Therapeutic factors in Alcoholics Anonymous. *American Journal of Psychiatry, 116,* 44–50.

Rodin, M.B. (1985). Getting on the program: A biocultural analysis of Alcoholics Anonymous. In L.A. Bennett & G.M. Ames (Eds.), *American experience with alcohol* (pp. 41–58). New York: Plenum Press.

Rudy, D.R. (1986). *Becoming alcoholic: Alcoholics Anonymous and the reality of alcoholism.* Carbondale, IL: Southern Illinois University Press.

Seiden, R.H. (1955). *An experimental test of the assumption that members of Alcoholics Anonymous are representative alcoholics.* Unpublished dissertation, Denver University.

Seiden, R.H. (1960). The use of Alcoholics Anonymous members in research on alcoholism. *Quarterly Journal of Studies on Alcohol, 21,* 506–509.

Sellner, E.C. (1990). *Mentoring: The ministry of spiritual kinship.* Notre Dame, IN: Ave Maria Press.

Smith, A.R. (1991). *Alcoholics Anonymous: A social world perspective.* Unpublished doctoral dissertation, University of California, San Diego.

Taylor, M.C. (1977). *Alcoholics Anonymous: How it works—recovery processes in a self-help group.* Unpublished doctoral dissertation, University of California, San Francisco.

Tremper, M. (1972). Dependency in alcoholics: A sociological view. *Quarterly Journal of Studies on Alcohol, 33,* 186–190.

Trice, H.M. (1957). A study of the process of affiliation with Alcoholics Anonymous. *Quarterly Journal of Studies on Alcohol, 18,* 39–54.

Trice, H.M., & Staudenmeier, Jr., W.J. (1989). A sociocultural history of Alcoholics Anonymous. In M. Galanter (Ed.), *Recent developments in alcoholism: Vol. 7. Treatment research* (pp. 11–35). New York: Plenum Press.

Tschannen, O. (1991). The secularization paradigm: A systematization. *Journal for the Scientific Study of Religion, 30*(4), 395–415.

Vaillant, G.E. (1983). *The natural history of alcoholism.* Cambridge: Harvard University Press.

Voegtlin, W.L., & Lemere, F. (1942). The treatment of alcohol addiction: A review of the literature. *Quarterly Journal of Studies on Alcohol, 2,* 717–803.

Vourakis, C.H. (1989). The process of recovery for women in Alcoholics Anonymous: Seeking groups "like me." Unpublished doctoral dissertation, University of California, San Francisco.

CHAPTER 3

Questioning the Answers: Research and the AA Traditions

JOSEPH NOWINSKI

Imagine that you woke up one morning, picked up the newspaper, and read a front-page story about the discovery of a heretofore secret society for sufferers of chronic depression. This society, whose numbers ran into the millions, supported itself solely by contributions and had a minimal formal organization; on the other hand, it had a rich oral tradition by which it conveyed its program and its philosophy to newcomers. Imagine that this article included testimonials from many of the society's members attesting to how it had helped them find relief from the depression that had clouded their lives. Imagine that some members of the society went so far as to claim that it had literally saved their lives.

The question that presents itself, of course, to the behavioral scientist who reads this astounding article is simply this: Should we attempt to find out more about this society and its program, and to evaluate the claims of its members objectively? Or, should we proceed to develop and improve upon our own cherished technologies for the relief of depression? The question, obviously, is a moral one as much as a scientific one. And to a degree it is even a matter of social policy, for we need to decide if we should invest public money in evaluating what amounts to free treatment for a major and societally costly mental health problem.

The question of whether we *should* study AA, for this writer at least, is unequivocally affirmative. The vectors of scientific curiosity, moral concern, and social policy all converge to indicate that we would be wise to invest some of our resources in efforts to evaluate objectively exactly how effective AA is at helping people to achieve its objectives, how it does this, and who it helps the most. The more difficult questions have to do with deciding *what* about AA we should study and *how* we can do this. In this regard it is probably useful to point out that there is no uniform consensus concerning exactly what the objectives of AA are. To be sure it is a fellowship that exists to help its members stay sober. At the same time, it is portrayed as a program of character growth and spiritual awakening (Alcoholics Anonymous, 1976, chapter 5). It is also important to note that AA, while organized, exists not as a treatment program but as a collection of men and women who are connected by common desires: to not drink again and to be in fellowship with one another. The 12 steps and traditions provide guidelines on how to organize a group whose aim is to help its members achieve the single objective of not taking a drink, 1 day (or 1 hour) at a time, and on how to grow spiritually. The AA group provides a haven for its members who wish to avoid *slippery* people, places, and things (Alcoholics Anonymous, 1975, chapters 6 and 8), as well as a vehicle for pursuing *spiritual progress* (Alcoholics Anonymous, 1976, p. 60). The fellowship is open to anyone who either identifies with the loss of control that it regards as the essence of alcoholism (Alcoholics Anonymous, 1976, p. 24) and/or who simply wishes to stop drinking (Alcoholics Anonymous, 1952, p. 139). It is not necessary to admit alcoholism, or even to stop drinking, in order to avail oneself of AA.

Though rich in concepts, AA lacks a formal theory of change or indeed of causation. It will remain the task of the researcher to translate key AA concepts into operational constructs (without losing their meaning) and to posit hypotheses regarding AA involvement and its relation to sobriety and spirituality. To do this one needs to begin with an understanding of *the answers,* namely the 12 steps and traditions.

Regarding the nature of alcoholism itself, Bill Wilson wrote the following:

> We know that while the alcoholic keeps away from drink, as he may do for months or years, he reacts much like other men. We are equally positive that once he takes *any alcohol whatever* into his system, something happens, both in the bodily and mental sense, which makes it virtually impossible for him to stop. The experience of any alcoholic will abundantly confirm this. (Alcoholics Anonymous, 1976, pp. 22–23)

This is about as specific a theoretical statement as one can find in official AA publications regarding the nature of alcoholism. Basically, *something happens,* physically and mentally, when the alcoholic ingests any alcohol at all, which leads him or her to continue drinking. In the realm of spirituality, we are told the following: "Selfishness—self-centeredness! That, we think, is the root of our troubles" (Alcoholics Anonymous, 1976, p. 62).

All of AA's official statements about alcoholism are, like the above, descriptive. It is remarkably indifferent to etiological formulations. On the other hand, it is remarkably rich in methods for not drinking and for achieving spiritual growth.

Based on its 12 traditions, and using the 12 steps (Alcoholics Anonymous, 1976, p. 59) as a focus, an international and cross-cultural fellowship of millions has evolved (Alcoholics Anonymous, 1990). It is supported by what could be described as a culture, complete with a spiritual philosophy and a body of common wisdom, rites and rituals, and traditions and ethics. This culture exists for the pragmatic purpose of helping its members avoid taking "the first" drink (Alcoholics Anonymous, 1975, p. 5) and for the spiritual purposes of helping its members identify and remove defects of character such as egocentrism (Alcoholics Anonymous, 1976, p. 62) and of experiencing a spiritual "awakening" (Alcoholics Anonymous, 1952, p. 106).

The researcher who wishes to study AA needs to understand, then, that as a fellowship it is founded not on theory or operational constructs but on ideas, ethics, rituals, and traditions. It has strong traditions that run along two parallel lines: pragmatism and spirituality. It has surprisingly little to say about the psychological or biological bases of alcoholism; on the other hand, it has a great deal to say about how to organize an AA group and about the internal processes that lead to personal renewal.

The heart of AA is, of course, its meetings, and to understand these the researcher must understand the traditions, both written and unwritten, that guide AA groups. One could argue that understanding AA boils down to understanding what happens at AA meetings. In fact, the message I would give to patients, based on several years of facilitating alcohol-abusing patients' early involvement in AA as a means of staying sober (Nowinski & Baker, 1992), could be succintly stated as follows: Go to AA meetings and participate; everything else will follow.

This chapter will now focus on some of the important traditions and ethics that guide AA meetings, and which the researcher needs to consider when contemplating research on the fellowship. In a very real sense it is these traditions and ethics that we are speaking of when we speak of research on AA, for it is the traditions that shape the meetings and its meetings are AA. For me the most important traditions, ethics, and beliefs that help to define AA include faith, tolerance, decentralization, anonymity, identification, pragmatism, and sponsorship. Let's look briefly at each one in turn.

Faith

Here is the first tradition:

> For our group purpose there is but one ultimate authority—a loving God as He may express Himself in our group conscience. (Alcoholics Anonymous, 1952, p. 132)

Consider these scenes from the AA way of life:

In January 1992, Alcoholics Anonymous held a regional conference in Connecticut. At the start of the opening session—in other words, the first meeting—all 2,000+ participants stood together and recited the Lord's Prayer.

Every Monday at noon, a men's AA meeting in rural Eastern Connecticut, whose attendance seldom tops six or seven, begins with this same prayer.

Each morning, the men on the Shoemaker unit at Hazelden, a 12-step-oriented treatment facility in Minnesota, begin their day by reading a passage such as the following:

> There is almost no work in life so hard as waiting. And yet God wants me to wait. All motion is more easy than calm waiting, and yet I must wait until God shows me His will. So many people have marred their work and hindered the growth of their spiritual lives by too much activity. If I wait patiently, preparing myself always, I will some day be at the place where I would be. And much toil and activity could not have accomplished the journey so soon. (*Twenty-four hours a day,* 1975)

AA and its sister 12-step programs like Narcotics Anonymous are steeped in spirituality such as this. As researchers we may elect to reframe the first tradition, as well as steps two and three of the twelve steps, in terms of expectancies for change, hope, or interpersonal trust. However we choose to regard AA, ultimately we must respect the fact that it is founded on a belief in and a willingness to rely on some power greater than the individual will. It is faith in this power, more than in science, that sustains the individual AA member. It is prayer, more than therapy, that comforts him or her in times of trouble. It is God, not will, that is seen as the locus of control:

> When a man or a woman has a spiritual awakening, the most important meaning of it is that he has now become able to do, feel, and believe that *which he could not do before on his unaided strength and resources alone.* He has been granted a gift which amounts to a new state of consciousness and being. (Alcoholics Anonymous, 1952, p. 107, italics added)

> The central fact of our lives today is the absolute certainty that our Creator has entered into our hearts and lives in a way that is indeed miraculous. *He has commenced to accomplish those things for us which we could never do by ourselves.* (Alcoholics Anonymous, 1976, p. 25, italics added)

AA is replete with slogans. To the uninitiated these may appear to be little more than bumper sticker psychology, one step down even from pop psychology. In reality, many of these aphorisms stem from, and in turn support, one or more of the fellowship's traditions. With respect to the tradition of believing in a higher power, sayings like "Let Go and Let God," "Came to Believe," and "Turn It Over" embody the wisdom gained from shared experience. They serve as reminders of the pathway that leads to recovery.

It goes without saying that spiritual awakening does not necessarily come easily. Many stories in the "Big Book" (Alcoholics Anonymous, 1952) attest to individuals' struggles with spirituality and a belief in a higher power. The way that AA defines this higher power, moreover, renders it an ultimately personal matter, an existential choice if you will. At the same time that we acknowledge the difficulties in translating spirituality into terms that make it accessible to research, however, we who would study AA must come to terms with the fact that this fellowship admonishes its members to look beyond mere sobriety, to nothing less than a slow, steady, but ultimately profound, personal transformation of a spiritual nature.

Tolerance

The first tradition continues:

> We believe there isn't a fellowship on earth which lavished more devoted care upon its individual members; surely there is none which more jealously guards the individual's right to think, talk, and act as he wishes. (Alcoholics Anonymous, 1952, p. 129)

Another AA saying captures this tradition even more succinctly: "Live and Let Live."

These affirmations of tolerance are an integral part of the AA way of life. The first tradition further reassures us: "No AA can compel another to do anything; nobody can be punished or expelled. Our Twelve Steps to recovery are suggestions; the Twelve Traditions which guarantee A.A.'s unity contain not a single 'Don't' " (Alcoholics Anonymous, 1952, p. 129). Finally, "the only requirement for A.A. membership," the third tradition asserts, "is a desire to stop drinking" (Alcoholics Anonymous, 1952, p. 139).

Collectively, these traditions form the basis for a fellowship whose character is marked by pluralism and adaptability just as surely as it is marked by spirituality. The researcher must be aware of this simple fact: There is no *standard* AA program, no *standard* AA meeting or group, no truly *typical* AA member and, last, no *standard* measure of successful outcome aside from not drinking today. In fact, weeks, months, or years of sobriety are likely to be much more the object of preoccupation for the researcher than for the AA member or group. As one member put it: "Today I had two anniversaries: six years of sobriety, and 24 hours of sobriety." This woman was not being flippant. Rather, she was merely expressing the AA philosophy about alcoholism: A disease whose arrest requires eternal vigilance and active participation in the fellowship of AA.

Decentralization

AA's pluralism is assured in part by its tradition of tolerance and further by its tradition of almost militant decentralization. Everything about AA seems intended to prevent excessive uniformity and minimize central control. Many of its traditions can be interpreted as primarily aimed at protecting the integrity of the individual AA group and the individual AA member. Consider these statements of policy (Alcoholics Anonymous, 1952):

> Each group should be autonomous except in matters affecting other groups or A.A. as a whole. (p. 146)

> Autonomy is a ten-dollar word. But in relation to us, it means very simply that every A.A. group can manage its affairs exactly as it pleases, except when A.A. as a whole is threatened. (p. 146)

> Every A.A. group ought to be fully self-supporting, declining outside contributions. (p. 160)

> A.A., as such, ought never be organized; but we may create service boards or committees directly responsible to those they serve. (p. 172)

> ... our Society has no president having authority to govern it, no treasurer who can compel the payment of any dues, no board of directors who can cast an erring member into outer darkness.... (p. 132)

These words leave little room for interpretation regarding their intent. The result of this commitment to decentralization and local democracy, tempered most modestly with an unenforceable caveat against harming the fellowship as a whole, has been a steady proliferation in different types of AA meetings, as well as a wide range of regional and cultural diversity in the particulars of how AA meetings are conducted. In some areas of the country meetings last an hour and a half, are small, and devote themselves a great deal to a discussion of spirituality. Meetings in Connecticut seldom run longer than an hour, tend to be large, and many are topic-related or speaker-discussion meetings. A patient, recently relocated from Louisiana, complained to me at length about the "superficial" treatment that, in his opinion, the steps got in the North! New Englanders, of course, would never think to require verbal participation in a meeting; on the West Coast some meetings have an explicit rule that "everyone must share." The latest Connecticut AA meeting schedule lists men's, women's, and latinos' meetings. I also know of meetings organized by and for therapists, clergy, lawyers, gays and lesbians.

To a degree the specialization that has crept into AA in recent years could be said to serve the purpose of *identification,* another AA tradition that will be discussed shortly. On the other hand, it also runs counter on some level to Bill Wilson's notion that alcoholism was the great unifier, connecting people who "normally would not mix" (Alcoholics Anonymous, 1976, p. 17). Historically, AA sought to foster identification on the basis of shared spirituality, a common desire to stop drinking, and a belief that this could not be accomplished through willpower alone. Today it has developed a measure of specialization and separation along sexual, cultural, and even socioeconomic lines (e.g., AA meetings for therapists).

One implication of the above for research is this: exactly *which* AA and *which* AA members will one study? Which AA, in other words, is representative? How well can results based on a study of AA in one geographic region (or even one subculture within that region) be generalized to AA as a whole? One logical hypothesis that arises from a consideration of the pluralism of AA is that there may be no single process of change, since there is no single "program" for change. On the other hand it is intriguing to consider how much is achieved by having an organization that can adapt so readily to so many different expectations and proclivities. Does AA adapt, in effect, so as to match individual (or at least subcultural group) needs? And what role does that adaptability play in AA's ability to help its members stay sober through fellowship?

Since the idea of defining a standard AA meeting seems absurd in the context of a fellowship that prizes tolerance and decentralization and that appears to be getting more pluralistic over time, research on AA may necessarily be limited to comparing it on a molar level with alternative approaches to helping men and women stay sober.

Anonymity

The 12th tradition says: "Anonymity is the spiritual foundation of all our traditions, ever reminding us to place principles before personalities" (Alcoholics Anonymous, 1952, p. 184).

One effect of this tradition has been to provide a safe haven from the stigma that has historically plagued alcoholics and addicts. This particular rationale for anonymity is bolstered by another tradition, which is to have both open and closed AA meetings, the latter being reserved for individuals who identify themselves as "alcoholics and those with a desire to stop drinking" (*Connecticut AA Meetings,* 1991). From a researcher's perspective, one might wonder what role AA's tradition of anonymity plays in attracting alcoholics to the fellowship and in facilitating their bonding with the group.

In principle clinical researchers should have no difficulty with the 12th tradition, since they too ascribe to a code of anonymity—in their case a code that requires them to protect the confidentiality of their research subjects. But the problem arises of how one studies closed AA meetings. By definition they are not accessible to outsiders. One might reasonably expect, however, that their dynamics would differ significantly from those of open meetings, and for that reason alone they would be of interest. We know that sponsors routinely encourage those they sponsor to attend at least as many closed as open meetings, as well as a variety of types of meetings, including step meetings, speaker-discussion meetings, and Big Book study meetings.

The researcher who wants to study AA on the level of group dynamics must also deal with the problem of recruitment and the necessity of ensuring truly informed consent. Because of the AA tradition of decentralization there is no central authority or process within the fellowship that could (or would) review research proposals or solicit participation. On the other hand, neither does the General Services Office resist research or advise AA members against participation in it. AA ethics do dictate, however, that even listings of AA meetings are off-limits to researchers and any others who would use them as a means of communicating with groups for reasons other than staying personally sober. Meeting schedules clearly state that they "must not be used as a mailing list, or for any purpose outside A.A." (*Connecticut AA Meetings,* 1991, p. 1). Obviously, the would-be researcher who violated this proscription would be unlikely to succeed in recruiting subjects, no matter what sort of explanation she or he offered. The situation is no better for the recovering researcher, who would be just as clearly in violation of tradition if she or he were to attempt to solicit subjects via AA meeting lists. Recruitment of AA members (or entire groups) for research participation must be very sensitive to the 5th tradition: "Each group has but one primary purpose—to carry its message to the alcoholic who still suffers" (Alcoholics Anonymous, 1952, p. 150). This tradition is universally interpreted to mean that the business of an AA meeting is staying sober. Researchers who respect the priorities of AA, and who manifest sufficient patience, may be more successful in gaining cooperation for empirical studies.

Identification

The tradition of anonymity serves many purposes, one of which, described above, is protection from stigma. Another effect of this tradition, however, and an equally important one in my view, has been to place the welfare of the group over that of the individual. From its inception AA has eschewed the cult of personality that in many ways has characterized this century. Bill Wilson wrote about it this way: "In the world about us we saw personalities destroying whole peoples. The struggle for wealth, power, and prestige was tearing apart humanity as never before" (Alcoholics Anonymous, 1952, p. 130).

Wilson's and AA's response to this perception was to build a fellowship on the principles of decentralization and anonymity. For Bill Wilson and his AA companions, the key to recovery lay in commitment to a group— but one that that would protect their most intimate and shameful confidences, while respecting their individuality. They expressed it this way:

> Most individuals cannot recover unless there is a group. Realization dawns that he is but a small part of a great whole; that no personal sacrifice is too great for the preservation of the Fellowship. He learns that the clamor of desires and ambitions within him must be silenced whenever these could damage the group. It becomes plain that the group must survive or the individual will not. (Alcoholics Anonymous, 1952, p. 130)

AA's organizational structure and certain key policies regarding affiliations with other organizations and promotional activities, embodied in Traditions 9, 10, and 11, ensure that the leader never becomes the focus, but that the group remains the heart of the fellowship.

The AA tradition of emphasizing identification as a cornerstone of recovery is neatly captured by another slogan: "Identify, don't compare." An AA pamphlet titled *Do You Think You're Different?* (Alcoholics Anonymous, 1980) further supports this same idea: That in AA it is not what is different between us that matters most, but what we have in common. This tradition itself suggests an important area for research, namely the process through which identification occurs, and its role in recovery. To be sure, my clinical experience suggests that resistance to identifying with other alcoholics is one of the primary sources of resistance to "getting active" in AA, which in turn impresses me as playing a determining role in staying sober.

Pragmatism

Ernest Kurtz (1988, p. 104), in his history of AA, points out that "it is doubtful that the world has ever seen a more consistent living-out of the pragmatism that so many have thought characterizes American culture." Aside from its spirituality and its admonition to forgo ego for identification, the fellowship of AA is nothing if not pragmatic. This pragmatism is tempered, however, by a reluctance to become overly dogmatic. Therefore, ethics dictate that AA groups always speak of suggestions rather than rules. The official AA publication, *Living Sober,* is subtitled "Some Methods A.A. Members Have Used For Not Drinking," and it opens by telling the reader: "Here, we tell only *some* methods we have used for living without drinking. You are welcome to all of them, whether you are interested in Alcoholics Anonymous or not" (Alcoholics Anonymous, 1975, p. 1). And, as already mentioned, the first tradition makes a point that the "twelve steps to recovery are *suggestions*" (Alcoholics Anonymous, 1952, p. 129, italics added). Within AA there are surprisingly few *shoulds,* and many more *coulds,* than outsiders often expect.

What are the implications of the pragmatic tradition for research? Simply, that there is no one *correct* way to follow the AA program, any more than there is any one *correct* way to conceive of a higher power. Aside from the common advice to go to meetings and not pick up the first drink, AA can be the ultimate in individualized treatment planning, based on its traditions of pragmatism and no-strings-attached sharing. The AA approach to sobriety can be summarized this way: This worked for us—if it works for you, you're welcome to it; if it doesn't, try something else! This approach may represent a significant limitation for researchers who typically prefer more control than this over independent variables such as treatment protocols.

With regard to the pragmatic question, "what works?"—we would offer these suggestions as areas for evaluation. All seem to play important roles in early recovery:

Meetings. Going to meetings and getting active in them (active listening, talking, taking on a responsibility) represents concrete acceptance of the need to seek recovery through fellowship.

Telephone. Getting and using telephone numbers of fellow AA members establishes a support system and builds new relationships.

Sponsorship. Getting an appropriate sponsor is cited by many AA newcomers as crucial to early recovery. The best sponsors are described as flexible (nondogmatic), supportive, and knowledgeable about AA lore, custom, and wisdom.

One day at a time. Keeping the focus on the here-and-now, without getting unduly distracted by yesterday or preoccupied with tomorrow, sets the stage for maximum positive reinforcement.

Sponsorship

AA made a decision early on to remain nonprofessional as opposed to becoming a professional organization. In 1937 Wilson turned down an offer to establish an AA "treatment program" in Towns Hospital (Kurtz, 1988, p. 63), and prior to this there had been discussions among the early AA members of how best to spread the message that had saved their own lives (Kurtz, 1988, p. 57). Later on, the 8th tradition explicitly set the parameters within which AA would grow: "Alcoholics Anonymous should remain forever nonprofessional . . ." (Alcoholics Anonymous, 1952, p. 166).

One apparent purpose for this tradition was to keep 12th-step work— spreading the message of the 12 steps and extending the resources of the fellowship from one alcoholic to another—from becoming a means of profiting personally. Addressing the issue of credibility, Wilson asserted that "alcoholics simply will not listen to a paid twelfth-stepper" (Alcoholics Anonymous, 1952, p. 166). Spreading the message, then, became an integral part of the 12 steps themselves, so that service to others became another means of staying sober: "Having had a spiritual awakening as the result of these steps, we tried to carry this message to alcoholics . . ." (Alcoholics Anonymous, 1952, p. 106).

So the fellowship of Alcoholics Anonymous, as well as other 12-step programs that are molded after it, follows a tradition of extending itself to newcomers through the volunteer efforts of those who have gone before them. The members believe that this helps them to sustain their own sobriety. Of course, consistent with other traditions, there is no training program and no certification process for would-be AA sponsors. There is only the principle, stated in the 12th step, and some guidelines. These are outlined in an official pamphlet titled *Questions and Answers on Sponsorship* (Alcoholics Anonymous, 1978).

Suggestions to the newcomer or the oldtimer seeking a sponsor include: choose someone of the same sex and someone who has at least a year of sobriety. In effect, the message here is that one shouldn't attempt to spread the message until there is some reason to believe that one has gotten it! Sponsorship should be based on trust and personal comfort, as well as mutual respect. The role of the sponsor is one of advisor, resource in times of crisis, and simply another sober person to talk to. As an example of this relationship, one patient of mine, a man in his early thirties with 7 years of sobriety, casually mentioned his interest in joining a pool league (similar to a bowling league). "I think it would be good for me to do that," he said. Then he paused and looked reflective. "But I think they might decide to hold it on Monday nights, and that's my step meeting. I think I'll talk to my sponsor about it, and see what he says."

The institution of sponsorship and its role in the recovery process would no doubt be of interest to researchers. Few if any AA members with any significant sobriety, for example, have no sponsor. Newcomers are advised to find even a temporary sponsor as soon as possible. These ethics point to an important relationship. However, since the stated purpose of sponsorship is to spread the message of AA and nothing else, it may turn out that few AAs would agree to open this relationship to direct observation. On the other hand, many may be willing to answer questions about it. (As an aside, we could reasonably expect many AA members to ask their sponsors for their opinions regarding participation in research, much the way my patient decided to talk to his sponsor about joining the pool league.)

Another, perhaps less intentional effect of AA's decision to remain forever nonprofessional is that it has led to a certain resistance on the part of the fellowship to associating with mental health professionals. It might even be fair to say that a state of mutual antipathy has developed over the years between the mental health professions and AA. After all, AA meetings can still be found in the basements of churches much more often than in the conference rooms of hospitals and mental health clinics. In part this lack of relationship may reflect divergent views on the nature of alcoholism, along with an historic tendency on the part of mental health professionals either to minimize alcohol problems or to treat them secondarily, as symptoms of some more primary disorder.

For AA, of course, alcoholism (or rather, sobriety) is always primary. Although many AA members may be personally sympathetic to the goals of research (and not unsophisticated about it), their primary consideration will rightly be their own sobriety and the sobriety of their fellow AA members. How could it be otherwise if they are to honor their traditions and take their own recovery seriously? The fifth tradition admonishes: "Shoemaker, stick to thy last!" (Alcoholics Anonymous, 1952, p. 150). Those AA members who take this tradition most seriously, regardless of their private feelings about research, can be expected to be less interested in research participation if that research is perceived as invasive or compromising in any way. It could be a mistake to interpret such resistance as reflective of either ignorance or antipathy, when it might simply represent respect for the very traditions that many have come to rely upon for their precious sobriety.

In looking back on my experiences, both professionally and personally, with the fellowship of AA, I conclude that one of the major obstacles to collaboration between researchers and the fellowship may lie not in their competing theories of alcoholism, but in the fact that they are based on different traditions. I recall, for instance, very little discussion of spirituality, of higher powers, or of surrender to the "collective conscience" of a group, in my years of graduate study. I do recall being taught concepts like self-efficacy and locus of control, as well as the most sophisticated methods of statistical analysis that my mind could absorb. I saw little connection between my training as a scientist-practitioner and my early religious education or my adult spirituality; nor can I recall, in all honesty, this issue ever being raised. Years later, when I sat in for the first time on a treatment-planning meeting at the Hazelden Foundation, I was surprised to find a clergyman in the room and puzzled when he began to relate the patient's "spiritual history." Hastily I searched the chart for a psychological evaluation and felt my heart sink when I found none. As you might guess, I experienced an urge to say: "Wait a minute, aren't you missing something here?" Maybe that's a question that we who would study AA need to ask ourselves.

Those who would study AA and its relation to recovery from alcoholism will do well to understand the traditions that are in fact the substance of this fellowship. Based on such an understanding, plus a respectful appreciation of the somewhat different traditions that researchers and AA members may hold dear, those who wish to conduct research may be able to do so while being faithful to the first tradition of the helping professional, which is to do no harm.

References

Alcoholics Anonymous. (1952). *Twelve steps and twelve traditions.* New York: Alcoholics Anonymous World Services.

Alcoholics Anonymous. (1975). *Living sober: Some methods A.A. members have used for not drinking.* New York: Alcoholics Anonymous World Services.

Alcoholics Anonymous. (1976). *Alcoholics Anonymous: The story of how many thousands of men and women have recovered from alcoholism* (3rd ed.). New York: Alcoholics Anonymous World Services.

Alcoholics Anonymous. (1978). *Questions and answers on sponsorship.* New York: Alcoholics Anonymous World Services.

Alcoholics Anonymous. (1980). *Do you think you're different?* New York: Alcoholics Anonymous World Services.

Alcoholics Anonymous. (1990). *Comments on A.A.'s triennial surveys.* New York: Alcoholics Anonymous World Services.

Connecticut AA meetings. (1991). Bristol, CT: P.O. Box 2654.

Kurtz, E. (1988). *A.A.: The story.* San Francisco: Harper & Row.

Nowinski, J., & Baker, S. (1992). *The twelve-step facilitation handbook: A systematic approach to early recovery from alcoholism and addiction.* New York: Lexington Books.

Twenty-four hours a day. (1975). Center City, MN: Hazelden.

CHAPTER 4

Alcoholics Anonymous: What Is Currently Known?

CHAD D. EMRICK, J. SCOTT TONIGAN, HENRY MONTGOMERY, AND LAURA LITTLE

Rarely does one meet a person who does not have an opinion about Alcoholics Anonymous (AA). "It's the only thing that works for alcoholics." "It's a religion." "It's a cult." "It saved my life." "My mom went to AA 10 years ago and she has been sober ever since." "I went to AA and I hated it." "AA is not for me. I don't fit in." The list is endless. Similarly, professional observers of AA have offered a variety of interpretations concerning this entity. It is seen as "systemic" therapy (Berenson, 1990), a semi-cult (Bufe, 1991), and "a protective wall of human community" (Leach et al., 1969). It has been hailed as perhaps the most important phenomenon of the 20th century (Wagenheim, 1991; Whitfield, 1985) and has been pronounced as unquestionably the most effective treatment for alcoholism in history (e.g., Fichter, 1982; Hudson, 1985; Small & Johnson, 1982; Snyder, 1980).

In the final analysis, these opinions, impressions, experiences, beliefs, and revelations are simply that. They do not constitute quantitatively based knowledge, yet they have flourished in the near desert of high quality research into AA. Without scientific investigations into the nature and effects of AA, our society is left with unfounded praises for, unsubstantiated indictments of, and unresolvable disputes about this organization that has survived for better than 55 years. Undisputed is the fact that AA is a major social movement that continues to grow in size and significance not only in helping individuals with alcohol problems but also in influencing the professional community, government agencies and programs, and the general public—all of this without taking a formal public stance on any issue (Fry, 1985; Leach et al., 1969; Levy, 1978; Mäkelä, 1991)! AA's publishing activities alone merit attention for the remarkable influence they have had in shaping public policy and opinion (Littlefield, 1988). Yet the mechanisms by which members are helped and the nature and degree of that help remain inadequately understood (see Bradley, 1988; McCrady & Irvine, 1989; Ogborne & Glaser, 1981).

41

The current anemic state of AA research has occasioned a recent committee of experts convened by the prestigious United States National Academy of Science, Institute of Medicine (IOM) to conclude: "Alcoholics Anonymous, one of the most widely used approaches to recovery in the United States, remains one of the least rigorously evaluated" (Institute of Medicine, 1989, p. 197). The report proceeds to call for "well-designed studies to elucidate the impact and mechanisms of change within AA" (p. 197) and for "outcome research that employs a range of contemporary treatment assessment strategies" (p. 197).

In harmony with this IOM charge, the current project was undertaken to review and analyze the quantitative research that has been conducted to date and reported in the English language in both published and unpublished sources. This effort is an update of previous reviews of the AA literature conducted by the senior author (Emrick, 1987, 1989b; Emrick, Lassen, & Edwards, 1977), but extends considerably beyond those earlier reviews by introducing a formal meta-analysis of the literature under the direction of the second author.

The task of accumulating extant sources of data on AA took the reviewers into unforeseen areas. The disciplines encountered included anthropology, sociology, psychology, medicine, theology, and philosophy. Participant-observational studies, epidemiological surveys, public opinion surveys, ethnographic investigations, and psychotherapy outcome studies were among the research strategies used in the sources. Research designs ranged from the pre-experimental through the quasi-experimental to the formal experimental. Peer-reviewed journal articles, books, unpublished papers, master's theses and dissertations were sought and perused, although time constraints necessitated that most of the master's theses and dissertations be excluded from the present analysis. Besides formal library research, including six data base searches, interpersonal networking led to the uncovering of some hard-to-find treasures. As such the reviewers engaged in a process parallel to the interpersonal networking that some AA members report to be so helpful.[1]

Because the major attention of this review is on the quantitative data that could be gleaned from the sources, the project is most likely to satisfy the appetite for hypothetico-deductive reasoning. Disparagement of qualitative research is in no way intended, however. Although the inductive reasoning involved in qualitative research is not productive of generalizable data, hypotheses, models, and theories can be identified and refined through such efforts (see, e.g., Rudy & Greil, 1988). These hypotheses, models, and theories can then, in turn, be exploited in the service of undertaking better conceived, more complete, and useful quantitative research.

Method

Exploratory meta-analytic techniques were used to integrate findings across studies reviewed (Glass, McGaw, & Smith 1981; Hedges & Olkin, 1985; Hunter, Schmidt, & Jackson, 1982). Application of these techniques had two objectives: (1) to provide a description of the nature of samples used in AA research, and (2) to derive mean weighted correlations (r_w) between variables reported in earlier reviews by Emrick (1987, 1989b) and Emrick et al. (1977). A total of 107 published and unpublished sources were coded and entered into the analyses. Some studies were excluded from the analysis because they did not evaluate AA alone but rather combined AA and other peer groups in samples (Alford, Koehler, & Leonard, 1991; Harrison & Hoffmann, 1987; Humphreys, Mavis, & Stofflemayr, 1991) or because they mixed alcohol and other types of substance abuse into one group (Galanter et al., 1990). Imprecise data reporting caused the exclusion of still other studies (e.g., Hoffmann & Harrison, 1986; Trice, 1957). In another publication, positive correlations between severity of alcohol problems and AA affiliation were found, but inadequate reporting precluded entry of these data into the meta-analysis (Seixas, Washburn, & Eisen, 1988).[2]

Coding was performed by three raters who worked closely together on the first 20 sources to develop interrater reliability. The findings presented need to be taken as preliminary inasmuch as formal interrater reliability is yet to be assessed.

A fundamental assumption of exploratory meta-analysis is that correlations reported in different studies can be averaged in a meaningful way because such correlations are estimates of the same population parameter. Because the stability of an obtained correlation and sample size covary positively, a weighted average is calculated, giving greater weight to those correlations based on larger samples (Hunter et al., 1982). Yet to what extent is it valid to average correlations across studies? Differences in correlations may arise because of potential differences in how variables are defined, measurement error, and differences in sample characteristics. Averaging under these circumstances may obscure the effects of moderating variables. It is valid to average correlations, however, when fluctuations in obtained correlations represent only sampling error. Based on classical psychometric theory, Hunter et al. (1982) developed methods to separate out variation due to sampling error, thus yielding a corrected index of variation of r_w, viz., SD_c. SD_c, therefore, reflects the extent of variation remaining in the estimated population parameter, r_w, after removing variance accounted for by sampling error. In cases when SD_c equals zero, differences among observed correlations reflect only sampling error. In such cases, r_w can be regarded as a stable and unbiased estimate. On the other hand, as SD_c becomes larger, sampling error becomes a less valid explanation of differences in correlations across studies and suspicion increases that moderating variables can be accounting for the variations in correlations.

Two examples may clarify the rationale involved. As will be presented in the Results section, an r_w of .20 was found between anxiety associated with drinking and AA affiliation. The SD_c for this statistic is .00. Differences in the correlations among the four studies contributing to r_w (i.e., .16, .26, .14, .22) can thus be interpreted as reflecting chance fluctuation about a single population parameter and, consequently, one can be relatively confident that drinking associated anxiety and AA affiliation are positively correlated. In contrast, r_w and SD_c for frequency of previous alcohol treatment experiences and AA affiliation were found to be .08 and .13, respectively. Here, a substantial amount of variation remains in SD_c (relative to r_w) after sampling error has been removed. Inspection of the six correlations involved ($-.39$, .00, .00, .16, .26, .40) suggests the presence of a moderating variable in the source from which $r = -.39$ was found.

Source data were rarely in a form immediately suitable for calculation of r_w. Conversion of data into Pearson correlations was accomplished as follows. About 70% of the sources gave sufficient data (test statistic) for converting findings into r using formulas developed by Glass et al. (1981). About 10% of the sources provided means and standard deviations for computing an effect size and pooled error estimate (Hedges & Olkin, 1985). These effect sizes were then converted to r using formulas provided by Hunter et al. (1982). About 12% of the authors reported only probability values ($p < .05$). In these cases, tabled critical values were found that matched both the implied test statistic and the statistic's degrees of freedom. The critical value then was converted to r. Finally, about 8% of the authors simply reported that "no significant" difference was found between variables, giving no additional information. In these situations, an r value of .00 was assigned. The latter two procedures yield conservative estimates of variable relationships. In order for the reader to see what effect the assigning of a value of .00 to inadequately described results has on the r_ws obtained, tabular presentations of r_ws include a separate column (headed "zero out") showing the size of r_ws with the r = .00 estimated values removed.

In this meta-analysis, the sample was the unit of analysis. When multiple publications using the same sample were identified, only unique relationships were used in the calculation of r_ws. No duplicate samples were entered into the coding of sample descriptors. Although there was no limit on the number of correlations that a sample could contribute to the meta-analysis, each sample was restricted to only one correlation for a particular data point. When studies reported data for multiple follow-up periods, Pearson r's were calculated for each follow-up period and then a weighted mean average was computed, which was then used in computing r_w.

Results

Sample Characteristics and Research Design

Table 1 shows that the mean sample size of the 107 sources was 279, with smaller numbers qualifying for entry into the study and a substantially smaller mean size being available for actual data analysis ($N = 191$). Such attrition of subjects is not uncommon in treatment outcome research (see Howard, Cox, & Saunder, 1989). The mean age of the subjects, viz. 42, suggests that AA research was drawn largely from middle-aged members and may therefore underrepresent those members who are 30 years of age and under—an age group that accounted for 22% of the sample in the 1989 General Service Office (GSO) triennial survey of North American members (Alcoholics Anonymous, 1990).[3] Men have been included in this body of research far more than have women. Note that the median sample size for male subjects is 116, whereas for female subjects the median is 9! The small number of women studied in the average sample is remarkable inasmuch as women have comprised about 30% of AA's North American membership in the last five GSO triennial surveys (Alcoholics Anonymous, 1990).

This body of work can be faulted for its failure to measure and describe samples adequately. Over 50% of the sources did not report whether their subjects were all employed, all unemployed, or a mixture of employed and unemployed. Socioeconomic status was not reported by nearly three-fourths of the references. Of those that did assess and report on this variable, over two-fifths indicated that their sample was largely middle-class. Thirty percent of the reporting studies found the samples to be largely lower class with only 7% identifying a higher social class sample. About one-fifth of the reporting studies simply stated that their samples spanned the spectrum of socioeconomic levels. The sources that *did* report on the SES variable may not be representative of all the publications, but the proportion of samples that identified their groups as middle class (i.e., over two-fifths) is consistent with observations that AA tends to be a middle-class organization (see Trice & Roman, 1970b). The most recent GSO triennial survey (Alcoholics Anonymous, 1990) supports these observations, finding 42% of the sample to be sales persons, managers, administrators, professionals, or technical workers. About one-fourth of the sample were skilled or unskilled workers, with the remaining members scattered

TABLE 1
AA Source Sample and Research Design Characteristics ($N = 107$)

Sample characteristic	Mean	Median	SD	N sources
Total sample size	279.15	173	408.90	107
Sample entered	252.75	153	289.11	100
in study				
Sample with data	191.11	134	185.24	76
Total sample age	41.92	42	4.42	60
Male age	41.64	43	7.05	31
Female age	40.27	40	.64	3
Gender				
Male	242.65	116	408.19	88
Female	38.36	9	78.22	86

Employment ($n = 115$)		Author description of alcohol-	
Full-time	13 (12.1%)	related problems	
Unemployed	6 (5.6%)	"Alcoholic"	76 (71.0%)
Both	31 (28.9%)	"Severe"	4 (3.7%)
Not reported	57 (53.4%)	Dependent	13 (12.1%)
		Years problem drinking	4 (3.7%)
Socioeconomic status		"Alcohol problems"	7 (6.5%)
Low	9 (8.4%)	Number prior treatments	3 (2.8%)
Medium	13 (12.1%)		
High	2 (1.9%)		
All groups	6 (5.6%)		
Not reported	77 (71.9%)	Reliability reported for	
		instruments ($n = 98$)	
Sample origin ($n = 101$)		All instruments	19 (19.4%)
Inpatient	69 (68.2%)	Some instruments	32 (32.7%)
Outpatient	15 (14.9%)	Not reported	47 (47.9%)
Community	12 (11.9%)		
Other	5 (5.0%)		
Subject selection ($n = 101$)		Use of corroborating data	
Random	13 (12.9%)	1. Collateral ($n = 100$)	
Volunteers	19 (18.8%)	Yes	31 (31.0%)
Intact group	69 (68.3%)	No	69 (69.0%)

among homemakers, students, military, unemployed, disabled, retired, and "other."

With respect to defining the nature of the subjects' alcohol problems, nearly three-fourths of the sources merely identified their subjects as "alcoholic." About one-eighth described their subjects as alcohol "dependent." A small group of sources measured the alcohol problems of their subjects by years of problem drinking or number of prior specialized alcohol treatments. About one-tenth of the studies described their subjects

TABLE 1 (cont.)

RESEARCH DESIGN CHARACTERISTICS

Subject assignment (n = 100)		2. Biological/medical (n = 95)	
Random	20 (20.0%)	Yes	12 (12.6%)
Nonrandom	69 (69.0%)	No	83 (87.4%)
Matched	11 (11.0%)		
Design (n = 102)			
Correlational	86 (84.3%)		
Manipulation	16 (15.7%)		
Assessment points (n = 97)			
Posttest only	63 (64.9%)		
Pre and post	33 (34.0%)		
Solomon block	1 (1.0%)		

as having "severe" problems with alcohol or simply as having "alcohol problems." The scarcity of *specific* assessment of substance use disorders in this body of research is apparent (see Emrick & Aarons, 1991).

The sources reviewed did describe the settings from which the samples were drawn. Most noteworthy about this variable is the large proportion (over two-thirds) of inpatient samples used and the relatively small percentage (11.9%) of subjects that were drawn from AA in the community. It is not possible to know if this distribution overrepresents AAs who have received inpatient treatment, yet this appears to be so. Although the most recent GSO triennial survey (Alcoholics Anonymous, 1990) found that 68% of active members had received some form of professional treatment before entering AA, certainly not all of these individuals had had specialized inpatient treatment. Also suggestive of there being an overrepresentation of inpatients in the data set is the finding that only about 30% of active members identified alcoholism rehabilitation (i.e., some form of specialized treatment) as a factor in their joining AA (Alcoholics Anonymous, 1990).

Over two-thirds of the investigations examined some already existing intact group; 19% studied volunteers, most of whom were found in community surveys; about one-eighth of the time, subjects were selected from a population at random. With respect to subject assignment, nearly 70% of the studies did not randomly assign subjects to treatment conditions nor match them on certain characteristics. It needs to be stressed that in those studies where subjects were randomly assigned to treatment conditions, in all but two cases (Ditman et al., 1967; Walsh et al., 1991) none of the assignments was to AA, but rather to some other form of treatment. The paucity of randomized clinical trials concerning AA continues.[4]

Regarding research design, only 16% of the sources involved some form of experimental manipulation, and, again, they almost never treated AA as an independent variable. The bulk of the projects were correlational in nature, in which relationships among variables were examined retrospectively in what were generally intact groups (defined by race, patient status in a treatment setting, etc.). Only one-third of the projects assessed subjects at two different points in time. Most simply obtained data at a certain point in the course of an individual's recovery career. The absence of pre-post testing renders it impossible to determine clearly if the status of a subject is a function, at least in part, of a treatment experience. Very conceivably, an individual's status may be a result of variables that are extraneous to the treatment experience.

Nearly half of the sources failed to report on the reliability of the measurement instruments used, and of those that were recorded to have used at least some reliable measurements, the majority of the codings were by inference inasmuch as materials with already established reliability were used. Thirty-one percent of the sources obtained data from collateral informants either to corroborate or to serve as a proxy for self-report data. About 13% of the projects used some type of biological marker or medical record to validate self-report data. These findings indicate that there is considerable room for improvement in this body of research pertaining to the collection of reliable and valid data (see Institute of Medicine, 1989).

Overall, the data presented in Table 1 reveal that AA research has been mostly pre-experimental in design, has failed to use instrumentation of established reliability or at least has failed to report data on reliability, has usually not attempted to check for the validity of the self-report data obtained, has inadequately assessed the nature of subjects' alcohol problems, has been deficient in describing demographic characteristics of the samples, and has sampled an unrepresentatively large number of middle-aged people and an unrepresentatively small number of women.

Although these limitations in AA research by no means stand alone in the alcoholism treatment outcome literature, the composite of the AA literature drawn from this review offers substantial support to the aforementioned conclusion of the Institute of Medicine committee (1989), viz., "Alcoholics Anonymous, one of the most widely used approaches to recovery in the United States, remains one of the least rigorously evaluated" (p. 197). Even strong advocates of AA acknowledge this state of affairs. After asserting the effectiveness of AA, John Wallace recently wrote, "It must be acknowledged, however, that rigorous scientific study of AA has not been possible; all available research is flawed to some degree" (Wallace, 1992).

While descriptive of AA research in toto, a "weak" quality rating may not, however, be appropriate for the more recent publications. Inasmuch as reviews of studies of a broad spectrum of alcohol treatment approaches describe a movement toward better methodology and reporting quality over time (see Emrick & Aarons, 1991) and since many of the studies included in this meta-analysis are drawn from the same data pool on which these reviews have been based, speculation about improved quality of the more recent publications regarding AA seems reasonable. A testing of this hypothesis awaits further analysis.

Affiliation with AA

Results of the review pertaining to relationships between subject characteristics and affiliation with AA are presented in Table 2. Before offering an interpretation of the data, note needs to be made of the fact that the definition of affiliation used in the samples was variable. As McCrady and Irvine (1989) commented in their recent review of AA research, "Affiliation may be defined as attending a certain number of AA meetings; joining an AA group; maintaining involvement over a certain length of time; or self-defined AA involvement" (p. 154). What all these definitions have in common, however, is their reference to some degree of greater exposure to AA. Thus, on the whole, the results in Table 2 may be taken as reporting correlations between certain personal characteristics and having a greater "dose" of AA. The data clearly do not inform us about the effects of AA involvement, only that some relatively greater amount of involvement has occurred.

So who are the individuals who partake of more of what AA has to offer? The relationships in which most confidence can be placed as to their being consistently positive and at least of a low degree of magnitude are those between affiliation and having a history of using external supports to stop drinking, loss of control of drinking and of one's behavior when drinking, consuming a higher quantity of alcohol when drinking, anxiety about one's drinking behavior, being obsessively-compulsively involved with drinking, believing that drinking enhances mental functioning, and religious/spiritual activity. All of these relationships are modest at best, with the exception of having had a history of seeking external sources of support to deal with one's drinking problem. All of the other variables appear to be either unrelated to affiliation (i.e., have r_ws <.10) or difficult to interpret without further analysis because of the presence of a substantial amount of "noise" in the correlations involved (i.e., have high SD_cs).

With respect to this latter group of correlations, it is of note that some samples obviously reported at least a modest level of positive relationship between affiliation and being more physically dependent on alcohol as well as having a more severe overall dependence on alcohol. While factors other than sampling error account for a sizable portion of variation in

TABLE 2
Rank Order of Relationships between AA Affiliation and
Characteristics of Alcohol-Dependent Persons

Personal characteristic	r (weight)	r (zero out)	SD (correct)	N Study	N Subj.
Use external support (more)[1]	.43	.43	.06	4	343
Loss control/drinking (more)[2]	.26	.26	.00	2	368
Daily quant. alcohol (more)[3]	.26	.26	.00	3	318
Physical dependence (more)[4]	.23	.23	.16	5	983
Anxiety about drinking (more)[5]	.20	.20	.00	4	416
Severity of dependence (more)[6]	.18	.20	.25	10	1,219
Obsessive-compulsive (more)[7]	.18	.18	.00	2	233
Enhance mental funct. (more)[8]	.14	.18	.00	2	233
Type of treatment[9]	.14	.23	.12	11	1,256
Social contact (more)[10]	.13	.13	.08	4	1,830
Poly substance abuse[11]	.12	.12	.04	3	1,269
Gender (female)[12]	.12	.12	.08	5	1,746
Spiritual activity (more)[13]	.12	.12	.00	2	1,396
Age (older)[14]	.10	.11	.11	9	2,231
Education (more)[15]	.08	.10	.06	9	1,964
Prior alcoholism trt. (more)[16]	.08	.13	.13	6	2,885
Legal status (fewer prob.)[17]	.07	.07	.00	2	176
Intelligence (higher)[18]	.07	.10	.00	3	175
Marital status (married)[19]	.06	.06	.10	5	1,508
Drk. enhance socialization[20]	.06	.06	.00	2	233
Adult mental health (better)[21]	.05	.06	.15	7	1,185
Employment status (better)[22]	.05	.05	.00	3	283
SES (higher)[23]	.04	.04	.10	4	368
Age first drk. (older)[24]	.03	.03	.00	3	402
Social stability (more)[25]	.02	.19	.00	3	535
Pretrt. drk. pattern (binge)[26]	.02	.06	.00	5	1,494
Internal control w/drinking[27]	.01	.01	.23	2	134
Religion (affil. type)[28]	.00	—	.00	2	1,155
Age of onset (older)[29]	−.01	−.01	.19	2	133
Gregarious drinking[30]	−.09	−.09	.00	2	233
Cognitive functioning[31]	−.53	−.53	.33	2	146

[1]Canter, 1966; Harris et al., 1990; Horn et al., 1987; D.E. O'Leary et al., 1980.
[2]Horn et al., 1987; Ogborne & Glaser, 1981.
[3]Horn et al., 1987; D.E. O'Leary et al., 1980; Seixas et al., 1988.
[4]Haertzen et al., 1968; Horn et al., 1987; D.E. O'Leary et al., 1980; M.R. O'Leary et al., 1980; Schuckit et al., 1985.
[5]Horn et al., 1987; McLatchie & Lomp, 1988; D.E. O'Leary et al., 1980; M.R. O'Leary et al., 1980.
[6]Boscarino, 1980; C.B., 1965; Fichter, 1982; Harris et al., 1990; Horn et al., 1987; McLatchie & Lomp, 1988; Mindlin, 1964; D.E. O'Leary et al., 1980; M.R. O'Leary et al., 1980; Vaillant, 1983.
[7]Horn et al., 1987; D.E. O'Leary et al., 1980
[8]Horn et al., 1987; D.E. O'Leary et al., 1980.

TABLE 2 (cont.)

---

[9]Edwards, 1966; Edwards et al., 1977; Fink et al., 1985; Galanter et al., 1987; Keso & Salaspuro, 1990; Koski-Jannes, 1991; McLatchie & Lomp, 1988; Sisson & Mallams, 1981; Smith, 1985; Smith, 1986; Walsh et al., 1991.

[10]Haertzen et al., 1968; Laundergan & Kammeier, 1978; M.R. O'Leary et al., 1980; Trice & Roman, 1970b.

[11]Laundergan & Kammeier, 1978; McLatchie & Lomp, 1988; D.E. O'Leary et al., 1980.

[12]Alford, 1980; Boscarino, 1980; Kammeier & Anderson, 1976; Laundergan & Kammeier, 1978; McLatchie & Lomp, 1988.

[13]Fichter, 1982; Laundergan & Kammeier, 1978.

[14]Boscarino, 1980; Canter, 1966; Kolb et al., 1981; Laundergan & Kammeier, 1978; McLatchie & Lomp, 1988; Mindlin, 1964; D.E. O'Leary et al. 1980; M.R. O'Leary et al., 1980; Thurstin et al., 1986.

[15]Haertzen et al., 1968; Harris et al., 1990; Laundergan & Kammeier, 1978; McLatchie & Lomp, 1988; Mindlin, 1964; D.E. O'Leary et al. 1980; M.R. O'Leary et al., 1980; Thurstin et al. 1986; Vaillant, 1983.

[16]Boscarino, 1980; Laundergan, 1981; Laundergan & Kammeier, 1978; M.R. O'Leary et al., 1980; Smith, 1986; Vaillant, 1983.

[17]M.R. O'Leary et al., 1980; Vaillant, 1983.

[18]Canter, 1966; M.R. O'Leary et al., 1980; Vaillant, 1983.

[19]Gynther & Brilliant, 1967; Laundergan & Kammeier, 1978; McLatchie & Lomp, 1988; M.R. O'Leary et al., 1980; Vaillant, 1983.

[20]Horn et al., 1987; D.E. O'Leary et al., 1980.

[21]Canter, 1966; McLatchie & Lomp, 1988; Mindlin, 1964; M.R. O'Leary et al., 1980; Thurstin et al., 1986; Trice & Roman, 1970b; Vaillant, 1983.

[22]McLatchie & Lomp, 1988; M.R. O'Leary et al., 1980; Vaillant, 1983.

[23]Boscarino, 1980; D.E. O'Leary et al., 1980; M.R. O'Leary et al., 1980; Vaillant, 1983.

[24]Harris et al., 1990; D.E. O'Leary et al., 1980; M.R. O'Leary et al., 1980.

[25]D.E. O'Leary et al., 1980; Trice & Roman, 1970b; Vaillant, 1983.

[26]Horn et al., 1987; Laundergan & Kammeier, 1978; McLatchie & Lomp, 1988; D.E. O'Leary et al., 1980; Vaillant, 1983.

[27]Harris et al., 1990; D.E. O'Leary et al., 1980.

[28]Jones, 1970; Laundergan & Kammeier, 1978.

[29]D.E. O'Leary et al., 1980; M.R. O'Leary et al., 1980.

[30]Horn et al., 1987; D.E. O'Leary et al., 1980.

[31]McLatchie & Lomp, 1988; Thurstin et al., 1986.

---

these two correlations, the magnitude of at least some of the positive relationships contributing to the r_ws involved is of interest because of the concordance between these two categories and the several drinking problem categories in which consistently positive correlations were found.

Because only a single source was found for relationships between some personal characteristics and affiliation, data pertaining to these correlations were not considered suitable for inclusion in the results of the meta-analysis. Instead they have been entered in Table 3 (which presents single source results for other domains of the meta-analysis). These data *suggest*

TABLE 3
Single Source Findings Across Three Relationship Categories

Category	r	N of subjects	Source
Affiliation and personal characteristics			
Race	.00	39	Thurstin et al., 1986
Ethnic background	.48	49	Vaillant, 1983
Parental SES (higher)	.00	49	Vaillant, 1983
Adult social competence	.00	49	Vaillant, 1983
Cognitive style (flexible)	−.24	47	Fontana et al., 1976
Abstinence before trt.	.00	1,105	Laundergan & Kammeier, 1978
Psychosocial adjustment	−.20	100	Vaillant, 1983
Length of stay in trt.	.00	1,105	Laundergan & Kammeier, 1978
Amount couns. interview	.00	1,105	Laundergan & Kammeier, 1978
Amount clergy couns.	.00	1,105	Laundergan & Kammeier, 1978
Early pred. of adult adjust.	.00	49	Vaillant, 1983
Sociopathy (more)	.00	49	Vaillant, 1983
Self-labeling "alcoholic"	.18	223	Skinner et al., 1982
Primary alcoholism	.00	249	O'Sullivan et al., 1988
Authoritarian attitude	.52	50	Canter, 1966
Introversion (more)	.00	49	Vaillant, 1983
Somatic complaints	−.10	107	McLatchie & Lomp, 1988
Duration alc. problem	−.32	107	McLatchie & Lomp, 1988
No. of drinking situations	.76	107	McLatchie & Lomp, 1988
Intrinsic religion	.35	78	Harris et al., 1990
Extrinsic religion	.00	77	Harris et al., 1990
Religious conflict	−.20	77	Harris et al., 1990
God control	.32	76	Harris et al., 1990
Internal control	−.22	77	Harris et al., 1990
Active-person/active God	.40	77	Harris et al., 1990
Active-person/passive God	−.31	78	Harris et al., 1990
Passive-person/active God	.40	76	Harris et al., 1990
Personal religious exper.	.30	79	Harris et al., 1990
Impression drk. causes social problems	.41	75	Harris et al., 1990
Warm childhood envir.	.28	49	Vaillant, 1983
Alc./Drg. in childhood envir.	.39	271	Haertzen et al., 1968
AA attendance and improvement in criteria other than drinking			
"Skid-row" adjust (better)	.08	100	Vaillant, 1983
Rehospitalizations (fewer)	−.06	83	Finney et al., 1981
Trt. expectancy (higher)	.12	130	Giannetti, 1981
Trt. compliance (better)	.21	143	Baekeland et al., 1973
Participation in AA activities and drinking behavior outcome			
Take-retake step 5	−.12	332	Kammeier & Anderson, 1976
Take-retake step 4	−.08	330	Kammeier & Anderson, 1976
Desire to retake 4-5	.04	305	Kammeier & Anderson, 1976
Active in AA before trt.	.01	350	Kammeier & Anderson, 1976
Reaching out for help	.29	47	Sheeren, 1988

TABLE 3 (cont.)

Category	r	N of subjects	Source
Work step 1	.26	188	Gilbert, 1991
Work step 2	.16	188	Gilbert, 1991
Work step 3	.07	188	Gilbert, 1991

the following very tentative hypotheses: AA affiliation is more likely for individuals who have an Irish background (in a Boston sample), have a less flexible thinking style, have poorer psychosocial adjustment, are more likely to label the self as "alcoholic," possess more of an authoritarian attitude, have had a shorter duration of drinking problems, have consumed alcohol in a greater number of situations, experience their religious life more intrinsically, have less conflict regarding their religious life, are more likely to view God as being in control of life's events, have less of a general internal control orientation, are more likely to perceive control as resting with both the self and with God, are less prone to think of God as a passive influence in their lives with themselves being in control, are more given to thinking of God as being in control of life's experiences with themselves being in a passive role, are more likely to have experienced an intense personal religious experience, are more ready to perceive that their drinking-related problems have caused social/interactional problems rather than vice versa, experienced a warm childhood environment, and lived in a childhood environment in which adults engaged in alcohol and drug use. These hypotheses are certainly provocative and call for researchers to investigate them in future endeavors.[5]

The results of this meta-analysis indicate that systematic distinctions between AA affiliates and nonaffiliates can be identified (see Bean, 1975; Leach, 1973; Ogborne & Glaser, 1981); although the literature is not currently developed enough to provide us with a composite profile of the most likely AA affiliates. Nonetheless, the distinctions drawn from this analysis can contribute to treatment-patient matching decision strategies. This team is therefore inclined to echo the recommendation made by McCrady and Irvine (1989) in their review: "Prospective research studies are needed to facilitate prediction of clients most likely to affiliate successfully with AA. With increasing interest in matching patients to treatment, it seems that further research to identify the distinguishing characteristics of AA affiliates is important" (p. 155). Of course, until such time that affiliation characteristics are more thoroughly identified, all alcohol-troubled individuals "might wisely be regarded as *possible* members of AA" (Emrick, 1989b, p. 41) as well as *potential* rejectors of the organization.

Future investigations into the affiliation process might be most productive, it seems to us, if researchers were to concentrate more on measuring both various aspects of the domain of drinking (e.g., age of onset, quantity of consumption, and consequences of drinking) and sociopsychological variables (e.g., locus of control, spiritual/religious life, thinking style, and emotional health) and were to attend less to typical demographic variables (e.g., age, marital status, and employment status). Until good quality prospective and longitudinal studies using complex multivariate analyses are undertaken, however, it would be premature to conclude that any certain variable is of no value in understanding the affiliation process (see Glaser, 1993).

AA Participation and Adjustment

As noted in the previous section, affiliation with AA is not tantamount to commitment. The latter construct refers to the processes involved in an individual's investing time, energy, talent, emotions, and ultimately his/ her very identity in the organization. Of interest is the question: Do those who invest more of themselves in the organization fare better in their drinking behavior and other domains of life than members who are not as involved?

Some data pertaining to this question appear in Table 4. Note that these results deal only with drinking behavior as the correlate. Relationships between AA participation variables and outcome in other life domains have been so little researched that a meta-analysis concerning such relationships is unfeasible.

The participation variables that were modestly and positively related to drinking outcome are: having an AA sponsor, engaging in twelfth-step work, leading a meeting, and increasing one's degree of participation in the organization compared to a previous time (i.e., being more involved in AA after an alcohol rehabilitation program than before professional treatment). Less sizable but remarkable positive relationships between drinking behavior and AA participation are seen for sponsoring other AA members and "working" the last seven of the twelve steps. Although the r_w for frequency of AA attendance is, in and of itself, of the same order of magnitude as some of the other participation variables, the relatively high SD_c for this variable makes interpretation of the r_w difficult. The sizable SD_c suggests several possibilities, among them being the presence of measurement error, differences in how the variable was defined, and potential moderator and matching variables.[6] Finally, the degree to which one tells one's story about one's history with problem drinking seems to be unrelated to drinking status.

TABLE 4
Relationships between Participation in AA Activities and
Drinking Behavior Outcome

Activity	r (weighted)	r (zero out)	SD (corrected)	N of studies	N of subjects
Tells story at meeting[1]	.07	.07	.00	3	1,142
Leads a meeting[2]	.23	.23	.02	2	1,093
Sponsors AA member[3]	.17	.17	.04	2	1,091
Freq. of AA attendance[4]	.19	.21	.10	13	1,939
Has an AA sponsor[5]	.26	.26	.02	4	539
Does 12-step work[6]	.20	.20	.00	3	1,140
Works steps 6–12[7]	.11	.11	.00	2	1,096
Increased AA participation[8]	.29	.29	.09	2	1,086

[1]Kammeier & Anderson, 1976; Patton, 1979; Sheeren, 1988.
[2]Kammeier & Anderson, 1976; Patton, 1979.
[3]Kammeier & Anderson, 1976; Patton, 1979.
[4]Anderson & Ray, 1977; Armor et al., 1978; Belasco, 1971; Edwards et al., 1977; Finney & Moos, 1981; Gilbert, 1991; Jindra & Forslund, 1978; Kammeier & Anderson, 1976; Patton, 1979; Polich et al., 1980; Rohan, 1970; Sheeren, 1988; Thomas, 1971.
[5]Bohince & Orensteen, 1950; Collins et al., 1985; Sheeren, 1988; Thomas, 1971.
[6]Kammeier & Anderson, 1976; Patton, 1979; Sheeren, 1988.
[7]Kammeier & Anderson, 1976; Patton, 1979.
[8]Kammeier & Anderson, 1976; Wattenberg & Moir, 1954.

On the whole these findings tell us that AA members who "work the program" are more likely to have a better status with respect to their drinking behavior. Thus, the data tend to support the often repeated advice given to newcomers to AA: "If you want to stay sober, get a sponsor and work the steps." AA members are also told that they should go to meetings regularly, attending on average one meeting a day for the first 90 days. This part of the organization's advice is not so clearly supported by the data—there is simply too much "noise" in the pertinent statistic (i.e., the SD_c is too sizable) to render a "supported" interpretation. Phasic variation may account for some of the SD_c size, with attendance frequency and drinking outcome covarying more in the initial stage of AA involvement than during later stages. A prospective study using time series analysis might profitably explore this possibility.

There is nothing in the findings of this review that would cause this team to alter the conclusions of Emrick's earlier work: (1) Successful members "become more actively involved in the organization, adopt its beliefs more completely, and follow its behavioral guidelines more carefully" (Emrick et al., 1977, p. 136), and (2) "AA members who are more active in the organization . . . have an outcome status that is as good as those members who attend or participate less actively. If differences in adjustment are observed, they favor the more active members" (Emrick, 1989b, p. 46). As with other forms of alcoholism treatment, the individual's motivation to engage in the change process appears to be contributory to outcome (see Miller & Rollnick, 1991).

Unlike Emrick's earlier reviews, the results of this meta-analysis provide us with information about the magnitude of the relationships between drinking outcome and participation variables. With the possible exception of "has an AA sponsor" and "increased AA participation," the relationships found are actually modest. One could infer from the data that overall commitment to AA is of limited importance as a correlate of drinking status. Such a cautious conclusion may be premature, however. Well designed future research may be able to identify, through complex multivariate analysis, specific variables that when applied to particular individuals in certain social, cultural, and temporal contexts covary substantially with outcome in AA (see Glaser, 1993).

One final comment is in order about the data presented in Table 4. Much of the data come from large samples of patients treated at the Hazelden Foundation (Laundergan, 1981; Laundergan & Kammeier, 1978). These samples may contain mostly "good prognosis" patients and may, therefore, generate figures that are more optimistic than those that would be derived from a more representative sample of the AA membership at large. Thus the conclusions made about the modest positive relationships shown in Table 4 (except for "has an AA sponsor" which is not based largely or solely on the Hazelden samples) should be regarded as particularly tentative, pending a broader sampling of AA members concerning participation variables.

Before leaving this area of correlates to the drinking status of AA members, a few comments about data that could not be included in the meta-analysis are in order. First, only one data source was found for several participation variables. These data, shown in Table 3, are of only heuristic value at this point. With the exception of "reaching out for help" the variables pertain to specific steps of AA. Because of their size (modest though they may be), "reaching out for help" and "working" Step 1 appear to be particularly worthy variables for inclusion in future investigations of the relationship between AA participation and outcome.

In a study not suitable for our meta-analysis, Tuite and Luiten (1986) analyzed the relationship between step activity and outcome and concluded that only Steps 4 and 5 were of any therapeutic benefit. They dismissed the other steps and practices as "irrelevant, superstitious behaviors" (p. 303). Although we think that Tuite and Luiten go too far in dismissing all but two steps as irrelevant, their work certainly does invite the research community to undertake efforts toward identifying the active ingredients in AA. If such ingredients can be designated, the effectiveness of AA (and by extension other forms of intervention) might be substantially improved.[7]

Drinking Outcome When AA and Professional Treatment Are Combined

According to the most recent GSO triennial survey (Alcoholics Anonymous, 1990), the majority of active AA members receive some form of professional treatment or counseling both before and after joining the organization. Of interest is whether alcoholics do better with a combination of AA and formal counseling than with either alone. Most often researchers have approached this issue from the perspective of determining whether alcoholics fare better if AA is added to professional treatment. Researched in this manner, AA involvement is considered as both a predictor and process variable. Data drawn from this body of research are shown in Table 5. The results suggest that participation in AA prior to professional treatment does not correlate with drinking outcome. Positive correlations were found between drinking outcome and going to AA during or after treatment; however, the magnitude of the SD_cs indicates that factors other than sampling error contributed to differences among the correlations averaged in these r_ws. For example, variables such as previous number of alcohol treatments and length of follow-up assessments each may account for variability in the correlations used to compute r_ws. Despite such "noise" in these correlations, the size of two of them (i.e., "during treatment" and "during or after treatment"), when interpreted in the context of their respective SD_cs, suggests that a consistently positive, if fairly modest, relationship exists between drinking outcome and AA involvement during or after treatment. These findings can be interpreted as suggesting that professionally treated patients who attend AA during or after treatment are more likely to improve in drinking behavior than are patients who do not attend AA, although the chances of drinking improvement are not overall a great deal higher.

Although most of the research attention has been given to the addition of AA to professional treatment, the obverse relationship merits as much consideration: What is the association between drinking outcome and the introduction of professional treatment to AA membership? There are simply not enough available data that are pertinent to this question to perform a meta-analysis. Only four reports that offer some relevant results have been identified by this review team. In two studies (Bissell & Haberman, 1985; Sheeren, 1988) no relationship was found between drinking outcome and having professional ("clinical") treatment during AA participation. Although not a study of "pure" AA, Costello and colleagues

58   Research on Alcoholics Anonymous

TABLE 5
Relationships between Treatment Outcome and AA Members'
Involvement in Non-AA Treatment

Time of AA involvement	r (weighted)	r (zero out)	SD (corrected)	N of studies	N of subjects
Pretreatment[1]	.05	.09	.04	12	5,248
Before/during treatment[2]	.03	.35	.06	3	564
During treatment[3]	.20	.24	.07	6	1,492
During or after treatment[4]	.22	.23	.09	11	1,306
After treatment[5]	.21	.25	.16	31	7,555

[1]Armor et al., 1978; Bateman & Peterson, 1971; Brissett et al., 1978; Corrigan, 1980; Elal-Lawrence et al., 1987; Finney & Moos, 1981; Haberman, 1966; Ritson, 1968; Rossi et al., 1963; Selzer & Holoway, 1957; Tomsovic, 1970; Vaillant, 1983.
[2]Baekeland et al., 1971; Kissin et al., 1968; O'Reilly & Funk, 1964.
[3]Davies et al., 1956; Dubourg, 1969; Finney et al., 1981; Gerard & Saenger, 1966; Mayer & Myerson, 1971; Wattenberg & Moir, 1954.
[4]Anderson & Ray, 1977; Armor et al., 1978; Collins et al., 1985; Corrigan, 1980; Edwards et al., 1977; Elal-Lawrence et al., 1986; Polich et al., 1980; Robson et al., 1965; Tomsovic, 1970; Zimberg, 1974, 1978.
[5]Alford, 1980; Beaubrun, 1967; Brissett et al., 1978; Davidson, 1976; Davies et al., 1956; Edwards et al., 1977; Fagan & Mauss, 1986; Farris-Kurtz, 1981; Fichter, 1982; Fink et al., 1985; Hoffmann et al., 1983; Hoffmann & Noem, 1976; Kammeier, 1980; Kammeier & Anderson, 1976; Kish & Hermann, 1971; Kolb et al., 1981; Laundergan & Kammeier, 1978; Ludwig et al., 1970; McCance & McCance, 1969; McMahan, 1942; Oakley & Holden, 1971; Ogborne & Bornet, 1982; Pattison et al., 1968; Pettinati et al., 1982; Rohan, 1970; Rohan, 1972; Rossi, 1970; Selzer & Holloway, 1957; Thurstin et al., 1986; Vaillant, 1983; Wanberg, 1968.

(1976) reported that when what were essentially "A.A. clubs" underwent replacement by a comprehensive alcohol treatment program (including AA), the 1-year follow-up "success" rate jumped from 18% to 33% ($p = <.0001$). Finally, the recent report of a randomized clinical trial by Walsh et al. (1991) indicated that drinking outcome rates for employer-referred subjects were substantially greater when patients first had professional treatment before participating in community AA (versus starting off with community AA alone). Although these data are very few in number, they at least suggest that AA may not always be "enough" for the person with an alcohol-related problem, particularly when AA is introduced before the professional treatment. Clearly, more research is required to determine when a particular intervention (i.e., community AA alone) is beneficial and when it is unhelpful or, worse yet, actually harmful.

The uncertainty of the relationship between AA involvement and outcome brings this review team to question the very widespread practice in
the professional treatment community of insisting indiscriminately that its
clients/patients join AA and make it the core of their "aftercare." If, for
example, no or only weakly positive (see Miller et al., 1992) or actually
negative relationships (see Peele, 1989) exist between long-term drinking
outcome and either the fact of or the extent of AA membership, then
quasi-coercive or coercive AA involvement is simply inappropriate, if not
unethical or even illegal.

Consistent with this note of caution, alcoholic patients themselves do
not always regard AA as necessary to their recovery. In the United States,
Patek and Hermos (1981) inquired of 45 liver clinic patients who had
improved in their drinking behavior for a year or more as to what factors
they thought had contributed to their good outcome. Only 29% reported
ever having tried AA, and of those who did only 31% had found it to be
beneficial to their improvement. Thus, only 9% of these successful patients had tried AA and found it to contribute to their abstinence (64%)
or to their substantially decreased level of alcohol intake (36%). Consistent with this finding, only 7% of a Swedish sample (Nordstrom &
Berglund, 1986) of 42 "recovered" male alcoholics with good social adjustment who were followed for 21 years reported that the Swedish equivalent of AA had been a contributor to improvement in their drinking
behavior. Of note is that 50% of this sample had established a "social
drinking" outcome and would thus have been unlikely to consider favor-
ably any involvement in an abstinence group (see Emrick, 1989b).

Another reason to question the practice of making indiscriminate referrals to AA is the fact that a very high percentage of individuals who explore the organization drop out. The last five GSO triennial surveys found
a consistent pattern of about a 50% dropout rate by the fourth month and
about a 75% dropout rate by the twelfth month (Alcoholics Anonymous,
1990). Obviously, many referrals do not find AA attractive or beneficial
enough, for whatever reasons, to stay with the organization for any extended period of time.

AA Involvement and Outcome Other Than Drinking Behavior

Although AA was formed and exists today to help alcoholics overcome
their abuse of and dependence on alcohol, the correlates of membership
are not likely to be limited to drinking behavior. Of interest is research on
the relationships between AA involvement and adjustment in life domains
beyond that of drinking. Table 6 presents the results of the meta-analysis
of the pertinent data (with Table 3 showing data from single sources).

TABLE 6
Relationships between AA Attendance and Improvement in Criteria
Other Than Drinking

Outcome criteria	r (weighted)	r (zero out)	SD (corrected)	N of studies	N of subjects
Employment situation[1]	.12	.12	.07	5	1,846
Social, family[2]	.13	.13	.06	6	1,772
Religious life (more active)[3]	.12	.12	.00	5	2,211
Perceived locus of control (internal)[4]	.13	.13	.03	2	1,135
Psychological adjustment[5]	.25	.26	.10	13	1,322
Physical symptoms[6]	−.13	−.13	.00	2	258
Legal situation[7]	.10	.12	.00	2	284

[1]Belasco, 1971; Imber et al., 1976; Kiviranta, 1969; Laundergan & Kammeier, 1978; Vaillant, 1983.
[2]Belasco, 1971; Finney et al., 1981; Laundergan & Kammeier, 1978; Machover et al., 1962; Thomas, 1971; Vaillant, 1983.
[3]Bailey & Leach, 1965; Brown & Peterson, 1991; Corrington, 1989; Laundergan & Kammeier, 1978; Machover et al., 1962.
[4]Bailey & Leach, 1965; Giannetti, 1981.
[5]Bell, 1970; Carroll & Fuller, 1969; Cohen, 1962; Corrigan, 1980; Finney et al., 1981; Giannetti, 1981; Hurlbert et al., 1984; Imber et al., 1976; Pettinati et al., 1982; Seiden, 1959; Spicer & Barnett, 1980; Vaillant, 1983; White, 1965.
[6]Finney et al., 1981; Spicer & Barnett, 1980.
[7]Ditman et al., 1967; Seixas et al., 1988.

Weak positive relationships were found between AA involvement and both employment situation (r_w = .12) and social/family/marital adjustment (r_w = .13), yet high variability in the findings of the studies involved (i.e., sizable SD_cs) makes interpretation of these results difficult. Weak, yet consistently positive, relationships were found between AA involvement and having a more active religious life, possessing a more internal locus of control orientation, and having a better legal situation. AA affiliation was found to be inversely related to the number of physical symptoms reported.

A stronger, though still modest, positive relationship was found between AA involvement and improvement in psychological adjustment (r_w = .25). Since the sizable variability in the findings across studies (SD_c = .10) can be traced to one study that reported a very high positive relationship between AA membership and outcome (Cohen, 1962), one can be reasonably confident of the existence of a positive relationship between AA involvement and improvement in psychological health, at least for those alcoholics who participated in the research projects involved. The generally low magnitude of correlations reported in Table 6 leads us to arrive at a "not demonstrated" or Scotch verdict concerning hypotheses about the benefits of AA on nondrinking measures, with the notable exception of psychological health, which we view as being moderately supported by the data. All of the relationships reported in the table point toward favorable effects, however, leaving critics of AA hard pressed to defend any position asserting widespread deleterious effects of the organization on its members. To the contrary, AA appears to be at least not harmful to affiliates, with one area even showing measurable benefits.

A notable qualifier to the results shown in Table 6 is the self-selective nature of the AA samples from which the data were drawn. AA may not be so benign, let alone beneficial, to all who explore it. Those for whom AA has negative effects may well leave the organization and therefore not be available for inclusion in cross-sectional, retrospective studies of the effects of AA. Prospective investigations need to be undertaken to inform us about the impact of iatrogenic effects on attrition from AA and, by extension, the degree to and manner in which AA has negative effects on participants (see Ellis, 1985; Emrick, 1987; Glaser, 1993). Only by this means will a truly comprehensive assessment of AA's effects on nondrinking criteria be accomplished.

As a final note on Table 6, it is especially surprising to us, because of the emphasis placed in the qualitative literature on the spiritual aspects of the AA experience (see e.g., Bateson, 1971; Kurtz, 1982), that the r_w found between AA membership and religious/spiritual life is so low. One reason for this finding, perhaps, is that amount of religious/spiritual activity may have a nonlinear relationship with membership (i.e., being strongly related to membership for relatively new participants yet unrelated for longer term members), as Brown and Peterson (1991) suggest. Another possible determinant of the fairly low correlation may lie in inadequate definition and measurement of those spiritual/religious variables that are most pertinent to the lives of AA members. Were these variables to be identified, operationalized, and reliably measured, stronger correlations might be observed. Whatever the results, more qualitative and quantitative research into the spiritual/religious/philosophical components of AA involvement is strongly urged along with, of course, investigations of other nondrinking domains.[8]

Discussion

This meta-analysis of the AA literature has given us some foundation points upon which to build our understanding of AA. Yet the overall modest nature of the correlations observed between AA and other variables reminds us that a great deal more research needs to be done before we can know with any precision (1) the factors involved in AA affiliation; (2) the ingredients present in the AA experience that are most helpful, and for whom, and at what time in the course of recovery; and (3) building from these discoveries, the matching strategies that will enhance our ability to use AA effectively.

Statistical Considerations

A problem with the AA research reviewed—and a likely contributor to the overall weakness of the correlations found—was the homogeneity of the samples that were studied. Such homogeneity leads to truncated distributions of variables with the effect of limiting the size of whatever correlations are obtained. Future researchers would be wise to collect data on AA samples of greater heterogeneity than has been typical to date.

In addition to sample composition, investigators need to be attentive to such statistical issues as power considerations and analysis of the practical (not just statistical) significance of results. Otherwise, valuable information about AA's effects might be overlooked when analyzing, interpreting, and reporting findings (see Rosenthal & Rubin, 1979; Rosnow & Rosenthal, 1989).

Investigator Bias

Investigators and funding agencies might wisely give mindful consideration to the impact of "researcher's allegiance" (Robinson et al., 1990) on the planning, conducting, and reporting of AA studies. Given the possible strength of a researcher's opinions about AA as well as the potentially powerful influence of an investigator's theoretical allegiance on research results (see Robinson et al., 1990), research teams might be developed with consideration given to ensuring a diversity of opinions regarding the value of AA, thereby reducing the impact of investigator's allegiance on the design, conduct, analysis, interpretation, and reporting processes.

Theory-Driven Research

Plaguing the reviewed research and thereby limiting its informativeness has been the failure of investigators to identify, understand, and apply theoretical constructs upon which AA is based. We observed, for example, that researchers often approached the variable, attendance at AA meetings, as an indicator of commitment to the organization, yet to our knowledge none of the investigators used commitment theory, a well-developed area of sociological study (see Rudy & Greil, 1987), to guide them in measuring and interpreting attendance data. Mere attendance at meetings may, in fact, be a fairly weak indicator of commitment, with the result that one might not expect to find a consistently strong relationship between a simple frequency count of meeting attendance and the effects of AA on its membership (see Table 4). Theory-based studies of commitment may, on the other hand, reveal strong relationships between certain AA participation variables and outcome.

Because investigators have tended to be weak in theory, their studies have often been inadequately conceived, with the result that important interrelationships among factors within, and contextually associated with, AA have not been explored. Several domains of theory should be taken into consideration when planning further studies: the nature of AA itself, implementation environment (i.e., the contextual environment within which the AA program is offered), outcome, impact (i.e., the causal relationship between AA and its outcome), intervening mechanism, and generalization (see Chen, 1989). If future research is more theory-driven, we anticipate that the results will be even more enlightening than much of what has been reported to date.

Research Gaps and Future Directions

Some noticeable gaps and deficiencies in AA research were identified by the team. For example, female AA members were very underresearched in the sources found. Inasmuch as nearly a third of AA members in North America are female, there is ample opportunity to study the processes involved in AA affiliation, participation, and outcome among women (see Beckman, 1993). Also, the lack of a single study of the youngest segment of the AA community (i.e., those under the age of 21) is of note. Although only 3% of the North American membership of AA is under 21 years of age (Alcoholics Anonymous, 1990), this group should not be overlooked by researchers. In addition, there has been a relative shortage of research on process variables (this being consistent with the lack of theory-driven endeavors); although there has been a trend away from the "black box" approach and toward more investigation of the mechanisms of change. One marker of this trend is the fact that all of the peer-reviewed publications on the effects of "working" individual AA steps have appeared since 1985. One fertile area of process research hypothesis generation is the AA literature which contains many descriptions of change mechanisms.

Perhaps the most serious gap in AA research is the current dearth of prospective and longitudinal studies. These kinds of projects, especially when they include multivariate analyses of data, are considerably more likely to reveal meaningful associations than are the retrospective, cross-sectional studies with univariate analyses that have typified AA research to date (see Glaser, 1993; Mäkelä, 1993). Additionally, the ethnic, cultural, and social contexts of AA data have been inadequately considered (see Caetano, 1993; Mäkelä, 1993; Room, 1993), with the result that important associations between specific groups of alcoholics and the AA organization have gone unidentified. Illumination of meaningful aspects of affiliation, process, and outcome await better quality research endeavors.

On the more positive side, a number of the publications obtained in our literature search did deal directly or indirectly with the issue of matching problem drinkers and AA (e.g., Boscarino, 1977; Chaplin, 1988; Friedman, 1990; Mills, 1989; Ogborne & Glaser, 1981). Yet much remains to be learned about matching strategies. It is hoped that the results of this meta-analysis will serve as a further stimulus for undertakings designed to identify AA-client matching variables.

Finally, although the AA research conducted to date has had its problems, let us not overlook the fact that a tremendous amount of effort has been expended over the years in attempting to understand this most important organization—effort that is to be applauded, particularly given the barriers to research that this organization presents. These endeavors have taken us a bit of the way toward a precise understanding of the organization. May future research lead us along even further.

Acknowledgments

We wish to express our gratitude to William R. Miller, who was instrumental in the formation of the review team and provided valuable encouragement throughout the undertaking. To him, we are truly grateful. We also wish to acknowledge the assistance of Rosemary Kennedy who was helpful in preparing the manuscript.

Notes

1. Although a significant number of sources were unearthed in this search, the reader is cautioned against concluding that the cadre of researchers into the nature and effects of AA is sizable. A considerable portion of the sources reported on AA simply as one variable among many. The target of research was instead on some form of professional treatment or on a particular group of individuals who had problems with alcohol. Consistent with this situation, data on AA were often embedded deep within a report and could not be identified by title or an abstract. Thus, even though a substantial number of resources on AA processes and outcomes were located for this review, the body of research that has dealt with AA as its primary focus is small.

   Also note that in the course of mining for data sources, a large amount of nonquantitative literature was scanned. Some of this material, while not contributing data to the meta-analysis, was perused for observations, ideas, and theories that might aid in the interpretation of the results of the analysis. Some of this nonquantitative literature is cited in the text. These entries are made in order to give the student of AA literature the benefit of having in one place a more comprehensive listing of the material this review team was able to acquire.

2. A comment is in order pertaining to an area of psychotherapy research that was *not* included in this analysis. Time and space constraints caused us to exclude a review of AA's possible iatrogenic effects. As students of psychotherapy research we are all aware that a balanced assessment of any intervention method must always consider the "dark side" of the picture. In reality, very few data have been reported regarding AA's possible negative effects (see Kasl, 1992), with most of the pertinent literature being narrative or descriptive in nature (e.g., Blau, 1991; Bufe, 1991; Emrick, 1989a; Rieff, 1991; Rosen, 1981; Trice & Sonnenstuhl, 1985). Thus, even if we had wished to analyze the literature on AA's harmful effects, such work could not have been performed at the meta-analytic level. Obviously there is a need for qualitative and quantitative research into the potential hazards of AA.

   Another area of the literature excluded from this review is that concerning AA's affiliates—Al-Anon and Alateen. There is a small body of research on the nature and effects of these organizations (Al-Anon Family Groups, 1984; Bailey, 1967; Cutter & Cutter, 1987; Gorman & Rooney, 1979; Hughes, 1977; Wright & Scott, 1978) and the interested reader is encouraged to peruse the references cited.

3. Membership composition with regard to gender, age, socioeconomic class, and drinking and drug histories varies considerably across cultures (Mäkelä, 1993). Restraint must therefore be used in applying the results of the GSO triennial surveys (Alcoholics Anonymous, 1990) to countries outside of North America. This same limitation applies to interpretation of the results of the meta-analysis inasmuch as the vast majority of the data entered into the analysis was obtained from North American samples.

4. One well-known randomized clinical trial of AA (Brandsma, Maultsby, & Welsh, 1980) was not included in the meta-analysis because the data were not suitable for entry in the coding system established for the analysis.

5. If we were to speculate, the results in Table 2 suggest the following composite description of an individual who is likely to consume more of AA: He/she suffers from a relatively strong degree of alcohol problem characterized by losing control of drinking behavior and losing control of one's behavior when drinking, drinking larger amounts of alcohol on the days when drinking occurs, having more worry and anxiety about one's drinking, being more preoccupied with and compulsively involved with drinking, and more often espousing beliefs about how alcohol use improves one's ability to function mentally. Also, the affiliate has more often sought out external sources of help in attempting to deal with drinking problems and has been more active in the spiritual/religious domain of life.

   There is an apparent match between this composite and the nature and function of the nondrinking community experience that AA offers. Individuals who have developed a severe overinvolvement with alcohol, who are anxious about their drinking problems, and who are experienced in looking for support outside themselves by which they can become free of dependence on alcohol are, so it would appear, likely to find AA comparatively attractive. Add to these characteristics a proclivity to engage in spiritual activities and the probability of a drinker affiliating with AA is even greater.

Also of note is the apparent match between the composite picture of the AA affiliate drawn from this review and the description found in the "Big Book" of the drinker who is most likely to join AA.

6. With respect to the possibility of matching variables, for example, there may be an interaction between frequency of AA attendance and sponsorship status such that drinking outcome may relate weakly to attendance for those members who have a sponsor but strongly for those who do not have sponsors and instead rely solely on meetings for support. As another example, an interaction might exist between frequency of attendance and length of abstinence. Frequency may correlate positively with drinking status for members with short-term abstinence yet have no relationship for those with long-term abstinence. Inasmuch as the samples entered into this analysis varied in their length of abstinence (i.e., some samples were of the newly sober while others consisted of individuals who had been abstinent for some period of time), the possibility of such an interaction effect occurring is certainly present. Whatever the case, large SD_cs, such as was found for the frequency of attendance variable, encourage us to search for drinker-AA matching variables that can then guide us toward a more precise and, it is to be hoped, overall more effective utilization of AA.

7. A few sources (Bissell & Haberman, 1985; Dunlap, 1961; Machover et al., 1959; Rather & Sherman, 1989; Thurstin et al., 1986) reported on relationships between drinking status and variables of AA members other than participation. The reader is encouraged to refer to the sources cited for specific information.

8. It is impossible to spend the quantity of time with the AA literature that this review team has and not be enticed into wanting to learn more about definition and measurement of religious, spiritual, and philosophical variables. Even the terms "religious," "spiritual," and "philosophical" are imprecise and require one to call for a consensus process to develop agreed upon definitions in order to pave the way for reliable and valid measurement of these domains. Of course, notable work has already been done in the area of quantifying religious/spiritual variables (see e.g., Gorsuch & McPherson, 1989; Pargament et al., 1988) offering exciting possibilities for the study of these variables in AA (see Harris, Spilka, & Emrick, 1990; Posey, 1988). The reader is referred to a number of publications concerning the religious/spiritual dimensions of life as they pertain to health in general (Bergin, 1991; Woodward, 1992) and to chemical dependency in particular (e.g., Berenson, 1990; Bridgman & McQueen, 1987; Cohen, 1962; Fichter, 1982; Galanter, 1983; Israelstam, 1986; Larson & Wilson, 1980; Miller, 1990; Read, 1989; Rudy & Greil, 1988; Westermeyer & Walzer, 1975; Whitfield, 1985).

References

Al-Anon Family Groups. (1984). *An Al-Anon/Alateen member survey.* New York: Al-Anon Family Groups.

Alcoholics Anonymous. (1990). *Comments on A.A.'s triennial surveys.* New York: Alcoholics Anonymous World Services.

Alford, G.S. (1980). Alcoholics Anonymous: An empirical outcome study. *Addictive Behaviors, 5,* 359–370.

Alford, G.S., Koehler, R.A., & Leonard J. (1991). Alcoholics Anonymous-Narcotics Anonymous model of inpatient treatment of chemically dependent adolescents: A 2-year outcome study. *Journal of Studies on Alcohol, 52,* 118–126.

Anderson W.H., & Ray, O.S. (1977). Abstainers, non-destructive drinkers and re-lapsers: One year after a four-week inpatient group-oriented alcoholism treatment program. In F.A. Seixas (Ed.), *Currents in Alcoholism, Vol. 2* (pp. 511–523). New York: Grune & Stratton.

Armor, D.J., Polich J.M., & Stambul H.B. (1978). *Alcoholism and treatment.* New York: John Wiley and Sons.

Baekeland F., Lundwall L., Kissin B., & Shanahan T. (1971). Correlates of outcome in disulfiram treatment of alcoholism. *Journal of Nervous and Mental Disease, 153,* 1–9.

Baekeland F., Lundwall L., & Shanahan T. (1973). Correlates of patient attrition in outpatient treatment of alcoholism. *Journal of Nervous and Mental Disease, 157,* 99–107.

Bailey, M.B. (1967). Psychophysiological impairment in wives of alcoholics as related to their husbands' drinking and sobriety. In R. Fox (Ed.), *Alcoholism: Behavioral research, therapeutic approaches* (pp. 134–142). New York: Springer.

Bailey M.B., & Leach B. (1965). *Alcoholics Anonymous pathway to recovery: A study of 1,058 members of the AA fellowship in New York City.* New York: National Council on Alcoholism.

Bateman, N.I., & Peterson, D.M. (1971). Variables related to outcome of treatment for hospitalized alcoholics. *International Journal of the Addictions, 6,* 215–224.

Bateson, G. (1971). The cybernetics of "self": A theory of alcoholism. *Psychiatry, 34,* 1–18.

Bean, M. (1975). Alcoholics Anonymous, *Psychiatric Annals, 5*(3), 7–57.

Beaubrun, M.H. (1967). Treatment of alcoholism in Trinidad and Tobago: 1956–65. *British Journal of Psychiatry, 113,* 643–658.

Beckman, L.J. (1993). Alcoholics Anonymous and gender issues. In B.S. McCrady & W.R. Miller (Eds.), *Research on Alcoholics Anonymous: Opportunities and alternatives.* New Brunswick, NJ: Rutgers Center of Alcohol Studies.

Belasco, J.A. (1971). The criterion question revisited. *British Journal of Addictions, 66,* 39–44.

Bell, A.H. (1970). The Bell Alcoholism Scale of Adjustment. *Quarterly Journal of Studies on Alcohol, 31,* 965–967.

Berenson, D. (1990). A systemic view of spirituality: God and Twelve Step programs as resources in family therapy. *Journal of Strategic and Systemic Therapies, 9,* 59–70.

Bergin, A.E. (1991). Values and religious issues in psychotherapy and mental health. *American Psychologist, 46,* 394–403.

Bissell, L., & Haberman, P.W. (1985). Alcoholism in the professions: Follow-up of sobriety and relapses. *Alcoholism Treatment Quarterly, 2,* 69–79.

Blau, M. (1991, September 9). Recovery fever. *New York,* pp. 30–37.

Bohince, E., & Orensteen, A.C. (1950). An evaluation of the services and program of the Minneapolis Chapter of Alcoholics Anonymous. Unpublished master's thesis, University of Minnesota.

Boscarino, J. (1977). Alcohol career patterns in Alcoholics Anonymous: A systemic approach to alcoholic defined behavior. *Dissertation Abstracts International, 38,* 6353A. No. 7803065. University Microfilms International, Ann Arbor, MI.

Boscarino, J. (1980). Factors related to "stable" and "unstable" affiliation with Alcoholics Anonymous. *International Journal of the Addictions, 15,* 839–848.

Bradley, A.M. (1988). Keep coming back: The case for a valuation of Alcoholics Anonymous. *Alcohol Health & Research World, 12,* 192–199.

Brandsma, J.M., Maultsby, M.C. Jr., & Welsh, R.J. (1980). *Outpatient treatment of alcoholism: A review and comparative study.* Baltimore: University Park Press.

Bridgman, L.P., & McQueen, W.M., Jr. (1987). The success of Alcoholics Anonymous: Locus of control and God's general revelation. *Journal of Psychology and Theology, 15,* 124–131.

Brissett, D., Gibson, R., & Kammeier, M.L. (1978). *Relation of pretreatment and posttreatment factors with successful outcome.* Center City, Minnesota: Hazelden Foundation.

Brown, H.P., & Peterson J.H. (1991). Assessing spirituality in addiction treatment and follow-up: Development of the Brown-Peterson recovery progress inventory (B-PRPI). *Alcoholism Treatment Quarterly, 8,* 21–50.

Bufe, C. (1991). *Alcoholics Anonymous: Cult or cure?* San Francisco: See Sharp Press.

C.B. (1965). The growth and effectiveness of Alcoholics Anonymous in a southwestern city, 1945–1962. *Quarterly Journal of Studies on Alcohol, 26,* 279–284.

Caetano, R. (1993). Ethnic minority groups and Alcoholics Anonymous: A review. In B.S. McCrady & W.R. Miller (Eds.), *Research on Alcoholics Anonymous: Opportunities and alternatives.* New Brunswick, NJ: Rutgers Center of Alcohol Studies.

Canter, F.M. (1966). Personality factors related to participation in treatment by hospitalized male alcoholics. *Journal of Clinical Psychology, 22,* 114–116.

Carroll J.L., & Fuller G.B. (1969). The self and ideal-self concept of the alcoholic as influenced by length of sobriety and/or participation in Alcoholics Anonymous. *Journal of Clinical Psychology, 25,* 363–364.

Chaplin, R.T. (1988). *Attitudinal differences between court referred and self referred clients towards the Alcoholics Anonymous program and substance abuse counseling.* Unpublished master's thesis, Western Illinois University, Macomb.

Chen, H.T. (1989). The conceptual framework of the theory-driven perspective. *Evaluation and Program Planning, 12,* 391–396.

Cohen, F. (1962). Personality changes among members of Alcoholics Anonymous. *Mental Hygiene, 46,* 427–437.

Collins, G.B., Janesz, J.W., Byerly-Thrope, J., Forsythe, S.B., & Messina, M.J. (1985). The Cleveland clinic alcohol rehabilitation program: A treatment outcome study. *Cleveland Clinic Quarterly, 52,* 245–251.

Corrigan, E.M. (1980). *Alcoholic women in treatment.* New York: Oxford University Press.

Corrington, J.E. (1989). Spirituality and recovery: Relationships between levels of spirituality, contentment, and stress during recovery from alcoholism in AA. *Alcoholism Treatment Quarterly, 6,* 151–165.

Costello, R.M., Giffen, M.B., Schneider, S.L., Edgington, P.W., & Manders, K.R. (1976). Comprehensive alcohol treatment planning, implementation, and evaluation. *International Journal of the Addictions, 11,* 553–570.

Cutter, C.G., & Cutter H.S.G. (1987). Experience and change in Al-Anon family groups: Adult Children of Alcoholics. *Journal of Studies on Alcohol, 48,* 29–32.

Davidson, A.F. (1976). An evaluation of the treatment and after-care of a hundred alcoholics. *British Journal of Addiction, 71,* 217–224.

Davies, D.L., Shepherd, M., & Myers, E. (1956). The two-years' prognosis of 50 alcohol addicts after treatment in hospital. *Quarterly Journal of Studies on Alcohol, 17,* 485–502.

Ditman, K.S., Crawford, G.G., Forgy, E.W., Moskowitz, H., & MacAndrew, C. (1967). A controlled experiment on the use of court probation for drunk arrests. *American Journal of Psychiatry, 124,* 160–163.

Dubourg, G.O. (1969). After-care for alcoholics—a follow-up study. *British Journal of the Addictions, 64,* 155–163.

Dunlap, N.G. (1961). Alcoholism in women: Some antecedents and correlates of remission in middle-class members of Alcoholics Anonymous. *Dissertation Abstracts, 22,* 1904. No. 61-4688. University Microfilms International, Ann Arbor, MI.

Edwards, G. (1966). Hypnosis in treatment of alcohol addiction: Controlled trial, with analysis of factors affecting outcome. *Quarterly Journal of Studies on Alcohol, 27,* 221–241.

Edwards, G., Orford, J., Egert, S., Guthrie, S., Hawker, A., Hensman, C, Mitcheson, M., Oppenheimer, E., & Taylor, C. (1977). Alcoholism: A controlled trial of "treatment" and "advice." *Journal of Studies on Alcohol, 38,* 1004–1031.

Elal-Lawrence, G., Slade, P.D., & Dewey, M.E. (1986). Predictors of outcome type in treated problem drinkers. *Journal of Studies on Alcohol, 47,* 41–47.

Elal-Lawrence, G., Slade, P.D., & Dewey, M.E. (1987). Treatment and follow-up variables discriminating abstainers, controlled drinkers and relapsers. *Journal of Studies on Alcohol, 48,* 39–46.

Ellis, A. (1985). Why Alcoholics Anonymous is probably doing itself and alcoholics more harm than good by its insistence on a higher power. *Employee Assistance Quarterly, 1,* 95–97.

Emrick, C.D. (1987). Alcoholics Anonymous: Affiliation processes and effectiveness as treatment. *Alcoholism: Clinical and Experimental Research, 11,* 416–423.

Emrick, C.D. (1989a). Alcoholics Anonymous: Emerging concepts: Overview. In M. Galanter (Ed.), *Recent developments in alcoholism. Vol. 7: Treatment research* (pp. 3–10). New York: Plenum Press.

Emrick, C.D. (1989b). Alcoholics Anonymous: Membership characteristics and effectiveness as treatment. In M. Galanter (Ed.), *Recent developments in alcoholism. Vol. 7: Treatment research* (pp. 37–53). New York: Plenum Press.

Emrick, C.D., & Aarons, G.A. (1991). Program evaluation and treatment outcome: Contemporary developments. *Annual Review of Addictions Research and Treatment, 1,* 215–231.

Emrick, C.D., Lassen, C.L., & Edwards, M.T. (1977). Nonprofessional peers as therapeutic agents. In A.S. Gurman & A.M. Razin (Eds.), *Effective psychotherapy: A handbook of research* (pp. 120–161). New York: Pergamon Press.

Fagan, R.W., & Mauss, A.L. (1986). Social margin and social reentry: An evaluation of a rehabilitation program for skid row alcoholics. *Journal of Studies on Alcohol, 47,* 413–425.

Farris-Kurtz, L. (1981). Time in residential care and participation in Alcoholics Anonymous as predictors of continued sobriety. *Psychological Report, 48,* 633–634.

Fichter, J.H. (1982). *The rehabilitation of clergy alcoholics: Ardent spirits subdued.* New York: Human Sciences Press.

Fink, E.B., Longabaugh, R., McCrady, B.M., Stout, R.L., Beattie, M., Ruggieri-Authelet, A., & MacNeil, D. (1985). Effectiveness of alcoholism treatment in partial versus inpatient settings: Twenty-four month outcomes. *Addictive Behaviors, 10,* 235–248.

Finney, J.W., & Moos, R.H. (1981). Characteristics and prognoses of alcoholics who become moderate drinkers and abstainers after treatment. *Journal of Studies on Alcohol, 42,* 94–105.

Finney, J.W., Moos, R.H., & Chan, D.A. (1981). Length of stay and program component effects in the treatment of alcoholism: A Comparison of two techniques for process analyses. *Journal of Consulting and Clinical Psychology, 42,* 120–131.

Fontana, A.F., Dowds, B.N., & Bethel, M.H. (1976). A.A. and group therapy for alcoholics: An application of the World Hypotheses Scale. *Journal of Studies on Alcohol, 37,* 675–682.

Friedman, B. (1990). 12-step is not for everyone. *APA Monitor, 21,* 3.

Fry, L.J. (1985). Social thought, social movements, and alcoholism: Some implications of AA's linkages with other entities. *Journal of Drug Issues, 15,* 135–146.

Galanter, M. (1983). Religious influence and the etiology of substance abuse. In E. Gottheil, K.A. Druley, T.E. Skoloda, & H.M. Waxman (Eds.), *Etiologic aspects of alcohol and drug abuse* (pp. 238–248). Springfield, IL: Charles C Thomas.

Galanter, M., Castaneda, R., & Salamon, I. (1987). Institutional self-help therapy for alcoholism: Clinical outcome. *Alcoholism: Clinical and Experimental Research, 11,* 424–429.

Galanter, M., Talbott, D., Gallegos, K., & Rubenstone, E. (1990). Combined Alcoholics Anonymous and professional care for addicted physicians. *American Journal of Psychiatry, 147,* 64–68.

Gerard, D.L., & Saenger, G. (1966). *Out-patient treatment of alcoholism: A study of outcome and its determinants.* Toronto: University of Toronto Press.

Giannetti, V.J. (1981). Alcoholics Anonymous and the recovering alcoholic: An exploratory study. *American Journal of Drug and Alcohol Abuse, 8,* 363–370.

Gilbert, F.S. (1991). Development of a "Steps Questionnaire." *Journal of Studies on Alcohol, 52,* 353–360.

Glaser, F.B. (1993). Matchless? Alcoholics Anonymous and the matching hypothesis. In B.S. McCrady & W.R. Miller (Eds.), *Research on Alcoholics Anonymous: Opportunities and alternatives.* New Brunswick, NJ: Rutgers Center of Alcohol Studies.

Glass, G.V., McGaw, B., & Smith, M.L. (1981). *Meta-analysis in social research.* Beverly Hills, CA: Sage Publications.

Gorman, J.M., & Rooney, J.F. (1979). The influence of Al-Anon on the coping behavior of wives of alcoholics. *Journal of Studies on Alcohol, 40,* 1030–1038.

Gorsuch, R.L., & McPherson, S.E. (1989). Intrinsic/Extrinsic measurement: I/E revised and single item scales. *Journal for the Scientific Study of Religion, 28,* 348–354.

Gynther, M.D., & Brilliant, P.J. (1967). Marital status, readmission to hospital, and intrapersonal and interpersonal perceptions of alcoholics. *Quarterly Journal of Studies on Alcohol, 28,* 52–58.

Haberman, P.W. (1966). Factors related to increasing sobriety in group psychotherapy with alcoholics. *Journal of Clinical Psychology, 22,* 229–235.

Haertzen, C.A., Hooks, N.T., Monroe, J.J., Fuller, G.B., & Sharp, H. (1968). Nonsignificance of membership in Alcoholics Anonymous in hospitalized alcoholics. *Journal of Clinical Psychology, 24,* 99–103.

Harris, N.A., Spilka, B., & Emrick, C. (1990). *Religion and alcoholism: A multidimensional approach.* Paper presented at the 98th annual meeting of the American Psychological Association, Boston, MA.

Harrison, P.A., & Hoffmann, N.G. (1987). *CATOR 1987 report. Adolescent residential treatment: Intake & follow-up findings.* St. Paul, MN: CATOR.

Hedges, L.V., & Olkin, I. (1985). *Statistical methods for meta-analysis.* New York: Academic Press.

Hoffmann, N.G., & Harrison, P.A. (1986). *CATOR 1986 report: Findings two years after treatment.* St. Paul, MN: CATOR.

Hoffmann, N.G., Harrison, P.A., & Belille, C.A. (1983). Alcoholics Anonymous after treatment: Attendance and abstinence. *International Journal of the Addictions, 18,* 311–318.

Hoffmann, H., & Noem, A.A. (1976). Criteria for the differentiation of success and failure in alcoholism treatment outcome. *Psychological Reports, 39,* 887–893.

Horn, J.L., Wanberg, K.W., & Foster, F.M. (1987). *Guide to the Alcohol Use Inventory* (AUI). Minneapolis, MN: National Computer Systems.

Howard, K.I., Cox, W.M., & Saunders, S.M. (1989, May). *Attrition in substance abuse comparative treatment research: The illusion of randomization.* Paper presented at the NIDA Technical Review Meeting: Psychotherapy and Counseling in the Treatment of Drug Abuse, Rockville, MD.

Hudson, H.L. (1985). How and why Alcoholics Anonymous works for blacks. *Alcoholism Treatment Quarterly, 2,* 11–30.

Hughes, J.M. (1977). Adolescent children of alcoholic parents and the relationship of Alateen to these children. *Journal of Consulting and Clinical Psychology, 45,* 946–947.

Humphreys, K., Mavis, B., & Stofflemayr, B. (1991). Factors predicting attendance at self-help groups after substance abuse treatment: Preliminary findings. *Journal of Consulting and Clinical Psychology, 59,* 591–593.

Hunter, J.E., Schmidt, F.L., & Jackson, G.B. (1982). *Meta-analysis: Cumulating research findings across studies.* Beverly Hills, CA: Sage Publications.

Hurlbert, G., Glade, E., & Fuqua, D. (1984). Personality differences between Alcoholics Anonymous members and nonmembers. *Journal of Studies on Alcohol, 45,* 170–171.

Imber, S., Schultz, E., Funderburk, F., Allen, R., & Flamer, R. (1976). The fate of the untreated alcoholic: Toward a natural history of the disorder. *Journal of Nervous and Mental Disease, 162,* 238–247.

Institute of Medicine (1989). *Prevention and treatment of alcohol problems: Research opportunities.* Washington, D.C.: National Academy Press.

Israelstam, S. (1986). Alcohol and drug problems of gay males and lesbians: Therapy, counselling and prevention issues. *The Journal of Drug Issues, 16,* 443–461.

Jindra, N.J., & Forslund, M.A. (1978). Alcoholics Anonymous in a western U.S. city. *Journal of Studies on Alcohol, 39,* 110–120.

Jones, R.K. (1970). Sectarian characteristics of Alcoholics Anonymous. *Sociology, 4,* 181–195.

Kammeier, M.L. (1980). Chemical dependency: An evaluation of the alcoholism treatment program at St. Joseph's Hospital. *Minnesota Medicine, 63,* 649–652.

Kammeier, M.L., & Anderson, P.O. (1976). *Two years later: Posttreatment participation in AA by 1970 Hazelden patients.* Paper presented at the annual meeting of Alcohol and Drug Problems Association of North America, New Orleans.

Kasl, C.D. (1992). *Many roads, one journey: Moving beyond the Twelve Steps.* New York: Harper Perennial.

Keso, L., & Salaspuro, M. (1990). Inpatient treatment of employed alcoholics: A randomized clinical trial on Hazelden-type and traditional treatment. *Alcoholism: Clinical and Experimental Research, 14,* 584–589.

Kish, G.B., & Hermann, H.T. (1971). The Fort Meade alcoholism treatment program: A follow-up study. *Quarterly Journal of Studies on Alcohol, 32,* 628–635.

Kissin, B., Rosenblatt, S.M., & Machover, S. (1968). Prognostic factors in Alcoholism. *Psychiatric Research Reports, 24,* 22–43.

Kiviranta, P. (1969). Alcoholism syndrome in Finland. *Finnish Foundation for Alcohol Studies, 17,* Helsinki.

Kolb, D., Cohen, P., & Heckman, N.A. (1981). Patterns of drinking and AA attendance following alcohol rehabilitation. *Military Medicine, 146,* 200–204.

Koski-Jannes, A. (1991). *Alcohol addiction and self-regulation: A controlled study on the effectiveness of a relapse prevention program for Finnish inpatient alcoholics.* Unpublished manuscript.

Kurtz, E. (1982). A.A works: The intellectual significance of Alcoholics Anonymous. *Journal of Studies on Alcohol, 43,* 38–80.

Larson, D.B., & Wilson, W.P. (1980). Religious life of alcoholics. *Southern Medical Journal, 73,* 723–727.

Laundergan, J.C. (1981). *The outcomes of treatment: The relationship between previous treatment and client outcome.* Center City, MN: Hazelden Foundation.

Laundergan, J.C., & Kammeier, M.L. (1978). *Posttreatment Alcoholics Anonymous attendance and treatment outcome.* Center City, MN: Hazelden Foundation.

Leach, B. (1973). Does Alcoholics Anonymous really work? In P.G. Bourne & R. Fox (Eds.), *Alcoholism: Progress in research and treatment* (pp. 245–284). New York: Academic Press.

Leach, B., Norris, J.L., Dancey, T., & Bissell, L. (1969). Dimensions of Alcoholics Anonymous: 1935–1965. *International Journal of the Addictions, 4,* 507–541.

Levy, L.H. (1978). Self-help groups viewed by mental health professionals: A survey and comments. *American Journal of Community Psychology, 6,* 305–313.

Littlefield, W.C. (1988). Some key literature of Alcoholics Anonymous. *RQ, 28,* 156–161.

Ludwig, A.M., Levine, J., & Stark, L.H. (1970). *LSD and alcoholism: A clinical study of treatment efficacy.* Springfield, IL: Charles C Thomas.

Machover, S., Puzzo, F.S., Machover, K., & Plumeau, F. (1959). Clinical and objective studies of personality variables in alcoholism: III. An objective study of homosexuality in alcoholism. *Quarterly Journal of Studies on Alcohol, 20,* 528–542.

Machover, S., Puzzo, F.S., & Plumeau, F. (1962). Values in alcoholics. *Quarterly Journal of Studies on Alcohol, 23,* 267–273.

Mäkelä, K. (1991). Social and cultural preconditions of Alcoholics Anonymous (AA) and factors associated with the strength of AA. *British Journal of Addiction, 86,* 1405–1413.

Mäkelä, K. (1993). Implications for research of the cultural variability of Alcoholics Anonymous. In B.S. McCrady & W.R. Miller (Eds.), *Research on Alcoholics Anonymous: Opportunities and alternatives.* New Brunswick, NJ: Rutgers Center of Alcohol Studies.

Mayer, J., & Myerson, D.J. (1971). Outpatient treatment of alcoholics: Effects of status, stability and nature of treatment. *Quarterly Journal of Studies on Alcohol, 32,* 620–627.

McCance, C., & McCance, P.F. (1969). Alcoholism in North-East Scotland: Its treatment and outcome. *British Journal of Psychiatry, 115,* 189–198.

McCrady, B.S., & Irvine, S. (1989). Self-help groups. In R.K. Hester & W.R. Miller (Eds.), *Handbook of alcoholism treatment approaches: Effective alternatives* (pp. 153–169). New York: Pergamon Press.

McLatchie, B.H., & Lomp, K.G.E. (1988). Alcoholics Anonymous affiliation and treatment outcome among a clinical sample of problem drinkers. *American Journal of Drug and Alcohol Abuse, 14,* 309–324.

McMahan, H.G. (1942). The psychotherapeutic approach of chronic alcoholism in conjunction with the Alcoholics Anonymous program. *Illinois Psychiatry Journal, 2,* 15–20.

Miller, W.R. (1990). Spirituality: The silent dimension in addiction research. The 1990 Leonard Ball oration. *Drug and Alcohol Review, 9,* 259–266.

Miller, W.R., Leckman, A.L., Delaney, H.D., & Tinkcom, M. (1992). Long-term follow-up of behavioral self-control training. *Journal of Studies on Alcohol, 53,* 249–261.

Miller, W.R. & Rollnick, S. (1991). *Motivational interviewing: Preparing people to change addictive behavior.* New York: Guilford.

Mills, K.R. (1989). Readability of Alcoholics Anonymous: How accessible is the "Big Book?" *Perceptual and Motor Skills, 69,* 258.

Mindlin, D.F. (1964). Attitudes toward alcoholism and toward self: Differences between three alcoholic groups. *Quarterly Journal of Studies on Alcohol, 25,* 136–141.

Nordstrom, G., & Berglund, M. (1986). Successful adjustment in alcoholism: Relationships between causes of improvement, personality, and social factors. *Journal of Nervous and Mental Disease, 174,* 664–668.

Oakley, S., & Holden, P.H. (1971). ARC: Follow-up survey 1969. *Inventory Journal, NC, 20,* 2–4, 19.

Ogborne, A.C., & Bornet, A. (1982). Brief report: Abstinence and abusive drinking among affiliates of Alcoholics Anonymous: Are these the only alternatives? *Addictive Behaviors, 7,* 199–202.

Ogborne, A.C., & Glaser, F.B. (1981). Characteristics of affiliates of Alcoholics Anonymous: A review of the literature. *Journal of Studies on Alcohol, 42,* 661–675.

O'Leary, D.E., Haddock, D.L., Donovan, D.M., Walker, R.D., Shea, R.A., & O'Leary, M.R. (1980). Alcohol use patterns and Alcoholics Anonymous affiliation as predictors of alcoholism treatment outcome. *Research Communications in Substance Abuse, 1,* 197–209.

O'Leary, M.R., Calsyn, D.A., Haddock, D.L., & Freeman, C.W. (1980). Differential alcohol use patterns and personality traits among three Alcoholics Anonymous attendance level groups: Further considerations of the affiliation profile. *Journal of Drug and Alcohol Dependence, 5,* 135–144.

O'Reilly, P.O., & Funk, A. (1964). LSD in chronic alcoholism. *Canadian Psychiatric Association, 9,* 258–261.

O'Sullivan, K., Clare, A., Rynne, C., Miller, J., O'Sullivan, S., Fitzpatrick, V., Hux, M., & Cooney, J. (1988). A follow-up study on alcoholics with and without coexisting affective disorders. *British Journal of Psychiatry, 152,* 813–819.

Pargamet, K.I., Kennell, J., Hathaway, W., Grevengoed, N., Newman, J., & Jones, W. (1988). Religion and the problem-solving process: Three styles of coping. *Journal for the Scientific Study of Religion, 27,* 90–104.

Patek, A.J., Jr., & Hermos, J.A. (1981). Recovery from alcoholism in cirrhotic patients: A study of 45 cases. *American Journal of Medicine, 70,* 782–785.

Pattison, E.M., Headley, E.B., Gleser, G.C., & Gottschalk, L.A. (1968). Abstinence and normal drinking: An assessment of changes in drinking patterns in alcoholics after treatment. *Quarterly Journal of Studies on Alcohol, 29,* 610–633.

Patton, M.Q. (1979). *The outcomes of treatment: A study of patients admitted to Hazelden in 1976.* Center City, MN: Hazelden Foundation.

Peele, S. (1989). *Diseasing of America: Addiction treatment out of control.* Lexington, MA: Lexington Books.

Pettinati, H.M., Sugerman, A.A., DiDonato, N., & Maurer, H.S. (1982). The natural history of alcoholism over four years after treatment. *Journal of Studies on Alcohol, 43,* 201–215.

Polich, J.M., Armor, D.J., & Braiker, H.B. (1980). *The course of alcoholism: Four years after treatment.* Rand: Santa Monica, CA.

Posey, C.R. (1988). *A study of the correlation between the God-image of the alcoholics and the degree of difficulty in accepting the AA third step.* Unpublished doctoral dissertation. Garrett-Evangelical Theological Seminary, Evanston, Il.

Rather, B.C., & Sherman, M.F. (1989). Relationship between alcohol expectancies and length of abstinence among Alcoholics Anonymous members. *Addictive Behaviors, 14,* 531–536.

Read, E.M. (1989). AA comes alive. *Federal Probation, 53,* 98–100.

Rieff, D. (1991, October). Victims, all? Recovery, Co-dependency, and the art of blaming somebody else. *Harper's,* pp. 49–56.

Ritson, B. (1968). The prognosis of alcohol addicts treated by a specialized unit. *British Journal of Psychiatry, 114,* 1019–1029.

Robinson, L.A., Berman, J.S., & Niemeyer, R.A. (1990). Psychotherapy for the treatment of depression: A comprehensive review of controlled outcome research. *Psychological Bulletin, 108,* 30–49.

Robson, R.A.H., Paulus,I., & Clarke, G.G. (1965). An evaluation of the effect of a clinic treatment program on the rehabilitation of alcoholic patients. *Quarterly Journal of Studies on Alcohol, 26,* 264–278.

Rohan, W.P. (1970). A follow-up study of hospitalized problem drinkers. *Diseases of the Nervous System, 31,* 259–265.

Rohan, W.P. (1972). Follow-up study of problem drinkers. *Diseases of the Nervous System, 33,* 196–199.

Room, R. (1993). Alcoholics Anonymous as a social movement. In B.S. McCrady & W.R. Miller (Eds.), *Research on Alcoholics Anonymous: Opportunities and alternatives.* New Brunswick, NJ: Rutgers Center of Alcohol Studies.

Rosen, A. (1981). Psychotherapy and Alcoholics Anonymous: Can they be coordinated? *Bulletin of the Menninger Clinic, 45,* 229–246.

Rosenthal, R., & Rubin, D.B. (1979). A note on percent variance explained as a measure of the importance of effects. *Journal of Applied Social Psychology, 9,* 395–396.

Rosnow, R.L., & Rosenthal, R. (1989). Statistical procedures and the justification of knowledge in psychological science. *American Psychologist, 44,* 1276–1284.

Rossi, J.J. (1970). A holistic treatment program for alcoholism rehabilitation. *Medical Ecology and Clinical Research, 3,* 6–16.

Rossi, J.J., Stach A., & Bradley, N.J. (1963). Effects of treatment of male alcoholics in a mental hospital: A follow-up study. *Quarterly Journal of Studies on Alcohol, 24,* 91–108.

Rudy, D.R., & Greil, A.L. (1987). Taking the pledge: The commitment process in Alcoholics Anonymous. *Sociological Focus, 20,* 45–59.

Rudy, D.R., & Greil, A.L. (1988). Is Alcoholics Anonymous a religious organization: Meditations on marginality. *Sociological Analysis, 50,* 41–51.

Schuckit, M.A., Zisook, S., & Mortola, J. (1985). Clinical implications of DSM-III diagnoses of alcohol abuse and alcohol dependence. *American Journal of Psychiatry, 142,* 1403–1408.

Seiden, R.H. (1959). The use of Alcoholics Anonymous members in research on alcoholism. *Quarterly Journal of Studies on Alcohol, 20,* 506–509.

Seixas, F.A., Washburn, S., & Eisen, S.V. (1988). Alcoholism, Alcoholics Anonymous attendance, and outcome in a prison system. *American Journal of Drug and Alcohol Abuse, 14,* 515–524.

Selzer, M.L., & Holloway, W.H. (1957). A follow-up of alcoholics committed to a state hospital. *Quarterly Journal of Studies on Alcohol, 18,* 98–120.

Sheeren, M. (1988). The relationship between relapse and involvement in Alcoholics Anonymous. *Journal of Studies on Alcohol, 49,* 104–106.

Sisson, R.W., & Mallams, J.H. (1981). The use of systematic encouragement and community access procedures to increase attendance at Alcoholics Anonymous and Alanon meetings. *American Journal of Drug and Alcohol Abuse, 8,* 371–376.

Skinner, H.A., Glaser, F.B., & Annis, H.M. (1982). Crossing the threshold: Factors in self-identification as an alcoholic. *British Journal of Addiction, 77,* 51–64.

Small, J., & Johnson, N. (1982). Perspectives: An AH & RW interview feature. *Alcohol Health and Research World, 6,* 3–5, 24–25.

Smith, D.I. (1985). Evaluation of a residential AA programme for women. *Alcohol and Alcoholism, 20,* 315–327.

Smith, D.I. (1986). Evaluation of a residential A.A. program. *International Journal of the Addictions, 21,* 33–49.

Snyder, S.H. (1980). *Biological aspects of mental disorders.* New York: Oxford University Press.

Spicer, J., & Barnett, P. (1980). *Hospital-based chemical dependency treatment: A model for outcome evaluation.* Center City, MN: Hazelden Foundation.

Thomas, D.A. (1971). A study of selected factors on successfully and unsuccessfully treated alcoholic women. *Dissertation Abstracts International,* 1863-B. No. 71-23,252. University Microfilms International, Ann Arbor, MI.

Thurstin, A.H., Alfano, A.M., & Sherer, M. (1986). Pretreatment MMPI profiles of A.A. members and nonmembers. *Journal of Studies on Alcohol, 47,* 468–471.

Tomsovic, M. (1970). A follow-up study of discharged alcoholics. *Hospital and Community Psychiatry, 21,* 94–97.

Trice, H.M. (1957). A study of the process of affiliation with Alcoholics Anonymous. *Quarterly Journal of Studies on Alcohol, 18,* 39–54.

Trice, H.M., & Roman, P.M. (1970a). Delabeling, relabeling, and Alcoholics Anonymous. *Social Problems, 17,* 538–546.

Trice, H.M., & Roman, P.M. (1970b). Sociopsychological predictors of affiliation with Alcoholics Anonymous: A longitudinal study of "treatment success." *Social Psychiatry, 5,* 51–59.

Trice, H.M., & Sonnenstuhl, W.J. (1985). Contributions of AA to employee assistance programs. *Employee Assistance Quarterly, 1,* 7–31.

Tuite, D.R., & Luiten, J.W. (1986). 16PF Research into addiction: Meta-analysis and extension. *International Journal of the Addictions, 21,* 287–323.

Vaillant, G.E. (1983). *The natural history of alcoholism: Causes, patterns, and paths to recovery.* Cambridge, MA: Harvard University Press.

Wagenheim, J. (1991). M. Scott Peck's new road. *New Age Journal, 8,* 54–56, 101–105.

Wallace, J. (1992). The value of alcoholism treatment. *Harvard Mental Health Letter, 8,* 4–5.

Walsh, D.C., Hingson, R.W., Merrigan, D.M., Levenson, S.M., Cupples, L.A., Heeren, T., Coffman, G.A., Becker, C.A., Barker, T.A., Hamilton, S.K., McGuire, T.G., & Kelly, C.A. (1991). A randomized trial of treatment options for alcohol-abusing workers. *New England Journal of Medicine, 325,* 775–782.

Wanberg, K.W. (1968). A pilot follow-up study of alcoholism patients. *Journal of the Fort Logan Mental Health Center,* 5, 101–106.

Wattenberg, W.W., & Moir, J.B. (1954). Factors linked to success in counseling homeless alcoholics. *Quarterly Journal of Studies on Alcohol,* 15, 587–594.

Westermeyer, J., & Walzer, V. (1975). Drug usage: An alternative to religion? *Diseases of the Nervous System,* 36, 492–495.

White, W.F. (1965). Personality and cognitive learning among alcoholics with different intervals of sobriety. *Psychological Reports,* 16, 1125–1140.

Whitfield, C.L. (1985). *Alcoholism, attachments & spirituality: A transpersonal approach.* East Rutherford, NJ: Thomas W. Perrin, Inc.

Woodward, K.L. (1992, January 6). Talking to God. *Newsweek,* pp. 39–44.

Wright, K.D., & Scott, T.B. (1978). The relationship of wives' treatment to the drinking status of alcoholics. *Journal of Studies on Alcohol,* 39, 1577–1581.

Zimberg, S. (1974). Evaluation of alcoholism treatment in Harlem. *Quarterly Journal of Studies on Alcohol,* 35, 550–557.

Zimberg, S. (1978). Psychiatric office treatment of alcoholism. In S. Zimberg, J. Wallace, & S.B. Blume (Eds.), *Practical approaches to alcoholism psychotherapy* (pp. 47–62). New York: Plenum Press.

Zimberg, S. (1980). Psychotherapy with alcoholics. In T.B. Karasu & L. Bellak (Eds.), *Specialized techniques in individual psychotherapy.* New York: Brunner/Mazel.

SECTION II

How Does Change Occur?

CHAPTER 5

Alcoholics Anonymous and the Structure of Change

CARLO C. DiCLEMENTE

Since 1935 Alcoholics Anonymous and its 12 steps toward a sober life-style have provided assistance to hundreds of thousands of individuals. Many of its members have experienced significant changes in their lives and attribute these changes to the presence of AA in their lives. This chapter will examine the principles and practices of AA as the author understands them from readings and his experience with hundreds of clients who have used or refused the AA way. The examination will focus on the common process of change across addictive behaviors and explore how AA interacts with this process. The hope is that this examination will provide a detailed description of the active ingredients and potential change mechanisms in AA so that researchers, clinicians, and AA members will understand better when, how, and with whom AA can be most effective.

There has been quite a controversy over whether AA is appropriate for everyone; whether there are deleterious or iatrogenic effects; whether AA is a religion or philosophy as opposed to a support group. This chapter will address and at the same time avoid these controversies by concentrating the level of discourse on the process of change. The questions then change to how does AA promote change, with which aspects of the process does AA do best, at what point in the process of change would AA be most helpful, are there any aspects of AA that could interfere with the process of change, are there certain types of people who would change more efficiently and effectively with AA as the promoter of the change process, and are the principles and practices of AA sufficient by themselves to promote change. These questions will be addressed in this chapter. However, lest the reader be misled or given inflated expectations, this analysis is meant only to initiate a discussion and not to provide definitive answers.

The Transtheoretical Model of Change

Along with my colleague at the University of Rhode Island, Dr. James Prochaska, I have been examining for the past 15 years how individuals change addictive behaviors (DiClemente & Prochaska, 1982, 1985; Prochaska & DiClemente, 1983, 1986, 1992). We and other colleagues have developed and researched a model that we believe captures significant dimensions of this process of change. In fact, we believe we have isolated the central structure of intentional change. The model has been called a transtheoretical approach to the process of change since it utilizes change principles from many theories of psychotherapy and behavior change. Thus, the model attempts to provide an integrative perspective on the process of change that applies to individuals who make changes with or without professional or other types of assistance.

The three basic dimensions of the model are the stages, processes, and levels of change. After a brief introduction of each of these dimensions of change, I will examine how the philosophy and practices of AA relate to each dimension and to the overall process. Our model focuses on intentional change and deals with behavior change that needs the cooperation and collaboration of the individual undergoing the change. This is not a model of coerced or imposed change. The difference is essential. Individuals with alcohol-related problems can be made to stop drinking by being imprisoned and denied access to alcohol. However, stopping drinking is not necessarily changing drinking behavior. Without some intentional, volitional cooperation, lasting behavior change is not possible according to our model.

Let me note a possible, early objection to the application of a model of intentional change to the principles of Alcoholics Anonymous. "Let go and let God" and the belief that "a Power greater than ourselves could restore us to sanity" may appear diametrically opposed to the concept of "intentional change." Some may argue that change in AA is a conversion experience and does not require intention. Others may complain that AA requires more than alcohol behavior change. Still others may resent the attempt to isolate the psychological principles of what seems to be a spiritual process. From my perspective, I would ask these critics to note the following. The 12 steps require the active participation and intentional engagement of each individual who desires to change their drinking and become sober. Second, a conversion experience is not inimical to intentional change and, in fact, requires some individual initiative to achieve lasting behavior change. Finally, I ask readers who are critical to suspend judgment until they have heard the entire argument.

Individuals who successfully modify addictive behaviors appear to move through a series of stages of change (Prochaska & DiClemente, 1992). The stages represent the motivational and temporal aspects of change (Table 1). What is unique about our model is that we have tried to identify both the start and the finish of this process of change. Any change, particularly of alcohol behavior, often begins with a stage of un-

TABLE 1
Basic Elements of the Transtheoretical Approach

Stages of Change:
Precontemplation→Contemplation→Preparation→Action→Maintenance

Processes of Change:

1. Consciousness raising	6. Counterconditioning
2. Self-reevaluation	7. Stimulus control
3. Social reevaluation	8. Contingency management
4. Self-liberation	9. Dramatic relief
5. Social liberation	10. Helping relationship

Levels of Change:
1. Symptom/situational
2. Maladaptive cognitions
3. Current/interpersonal conflict
4. Family/systems conflicts
5. Intrapersonal conflicts

---

willingness to recognize the problem and resistance to seriously consider the need for change. *Precontemplation* stage individuals are not interested in changing. The second step requires serious consideration of change and is labeled *contemplation.* Decision making and a plan of action characterize the *preparation* stage of change. Successfully moving through these first three stages leads to the *action* stage where efforts to cease or modify the target behavior are most prominent. This action phase can be short lived, resulting in relapse or be sustained over 3 to 6 months when the individual enters the *maintenance* stage, whose primary task is to sustain the behavior change over the long haul. These stages have been identified in a variety of studies examining the process of change in smoking cessation (DiClemente et al., 1991), alcohol treatment (DiClemente & Hughes, 1990), weight control (O'Connell & Velicer, 1988; Suris-Rangel et al., 1988), and a wide variety of other health risk behaviors (Prochaska & DiClemente, 1985, 1992).

The "processes of change" are principles or strategies of change that individuals use to negotiate their way through the stages of change and represent the second dimension of the model. We have identified a series of five experiential processes and five behavioral processes that seem to summarize the change principles identified by the major theories of psychotherapy and behavior change. These processes have been examined in several studies of addictive behaviors (DiClemente et al., 1991; Norcross, Prochaska, & DiClemente, 1986; Prochaska & DiClemente, 1985; Prochaska et al., 1988). The list of processes appears in Table 1 and demonstrates a variety of cognitive, affective, and behavioral activities which represent a range of coping functions that promote change. Each process will be discussed in detail when examined within the context of AA practice.

TABLE 2
Levels of Change Addressed by AA Approaches

Symptomatic/Situational Problems:
 • Alcohol Consumption is symptom of disease
 • Consequences of disrupted lives (hitting bottom)
Maladaptive Cognitions:
 • Pride
 • Control
 • Negative and positive thinking
Interpersonal Conflicts:
 • Harm inflicted on others
 • Steps 8-9-10
 • 12 traditions
Family/System Conflicts:
 • Persons harmed/making amends
 • Common welfare comes first (tradition)
Intrapersonal Conflicts:
 • Defects of character
 • Self-centeredness

The final dimension of the model represents the reality that the problem or problems to be changed can occur at various levels of change (Prochaska & DiClemente, 1984, 1986). Each level represents a unique area of functioning that can be problematic (Table 2). The most obvious level is that of symptomatic or situational problems. The level least observable and most difficult to intervene with is that of intrapersonal conflicts. Anyone who has worked clinically with alcohol troubled individuals will recognize that often individuals can have multiple problems at any one level as well as problems at multiple levels. The levels are important because there can be issues at different levels which promote or interfere with change of any one problem behavior and individuals can be at very different stages of change with regard to problems at different levels. Moreover, different theories attribute problems to specific levels which presupposes that changes would need to be made at these levels to obtain successful change of a particular behavior. Keep in mind that although we have identified these five levels, they are all interactive for the individual who is in the process of change. Thus, it is possible for an individual with a drinking problem at the symptom/situational level to ask for help to solve a marital problem at the interpersonal level and, at times, to expect to make changes with the one without modifying the other. The levels help us to understand the range of problems facing an individual and where the focus of change is, should be, or could be.

The model is called transtheoretical and integrative because the three dimensions outlined above all interact to make a complex, but hopefully accurate, picture of the process of change. If an individual has severe drinking problems and comes for help, it would be important to identify which levels are involved, at what stage the individual is with respect to drinking, as well as problems at other levels and what processes, if any, he/she has used or is currently using. This perspective has been quite helpful in conceptualizing and treating client problems (DiClemente, 1985, 1991; Miller & Rollnick, 1991; Prochaska & DiClemente, 1984); understanding other approaches to change (Prochaska & DiClemente, 1986) and developing interventions and research (Abrams et al., 1991; Baranowski, 1990; DiClemente et al., 1992; Prochaska & DiClemente, 1992).

This model was used to guide the development of an outpatient alcoholism treatment program (DiClemente & Gordon, 1983). While designing this program I often thought about how AA involvement would facilitate or hinder the process of change that we were working to achieve. AA was always considered as a potential supplementary intervention for all the clients. It was often recommended but never demanded as a requirement for program participation. My initial assessment was that AA could both facilitate and hinder the process of change. Every advantage could have a corresponding disadvantage. Precontemplators could be helped by attending an open meeting or turned off by the labeling process or by the focus on abstinence as the only acceptable goal. Contemplators could use the 12 steps to promote decision making or resist the spiritual emphasis. Action and maintenance individuals could lose confidence and heart if every slip were seen as a complete relapse or could use the meetings and fellowship to sustain action. So from my perspective there was great potential for undermining the process of change in addition to the potential for significant help or assistance in successfully negotiating the process. Although I believe many of my initial impressions are still accurate, the occasion of the conference on which this monograph is based has allowed me to examine in greater depth the AA philosophy and practice in order to understand better how AA can promote successful change.

AA and Levels of Change

The analysis begins by examining how various levels of change are addressed by AA (Table 2). The 12 steps and 12 traditions of Alcoholics Anonymous understand alcohol consumption as a symptomatic expression of the disease of alcoholism, a disease of the mind. The disrupted life of the alcoholic represents the consequences of drinking that can be viewed as other situational or symptomatic problems. In this sense "hitting bottom" is the confluence of these situational consequences, which become so overwhelming in terms of problems at this level that they motivate or pressure the individual toward acknowledging problems and

TABLE 3
Processes of Change Comparisons with AA Principles and Practices

Processes	AA Practices
Experiential	
Consciousness raising	• Big Book study and other bibliotherapy • Meetings • 12 steps • Sponsor
Dramatic relief	• Personal stories at meetings • Focus on losses attributable to alcohol
Self-reevaluation	• Step 1: unmanageable lives • Defects in character • Moral inventory
Social liberation	• Meeting support alternative lifestyle • Nonalcohol celebrations
Environmental reevaluation	• Bring message to other suffers (Step 12) • Realization of harm inflicted on others
Behavioral	
Self-liberation	• Commitment to attendance and working 12 steps
Stimulus control	• Avoid alcohol and alcoholic network • Affiliate with AA
Counterconditioning	• Meetings cope with urges • Build alternative lifestyle • Prayer and meditation
Reinforcement management	• Desire and sobriety chips • Group support • Step 12: help others
Helping relationships	• Fellowship of acceptance and support • Sponsorship

hopefully taking action, and make it difficult if not impossible for the alcoholic to remain in precontemplation or contemplation stages.

Reviewing the 12 steps, I was struck by the fact that only the first step focuses on alcohol and hitting bottom. The other steps focus either on situational problems or specific conflicts and issues at the other levels of change. It is surprising that there is not more attention paid to alcohol as the problem in these 12 steps. In practice, however, much of the content of many meetings seems to revolve around the presence of alcohol in the lives of the participants, the problems caused by alcohol, and the importance of time away from alcohol. Thus, the symptomatic/situational level of change seems well represented and addressed in the practices but little mentioned in the principles of Alcoholics Anonymous.

Few psychotherapists would consider AA to engage in cognitive therapy or to focus on maladaptive cognitions in the tradition of Albert Ellis, Aaron Beck, David Burns, and others. This level of maladaptive cognitions addresses beliefs, self-statements, and other cognitions or expectancies that are problematic for the individual. Unrealistic expectations or beliefs and negative self-statements are often identified at this level as problems in their own right or problems that contribute to blocking change at the symptomatic or other levels of change. Cognitive and cognitive-behavioral therapies typically focus on this level of change.

A close examination of the 12 steps of Alcoholics Anonymous reveals substantial emphasis on maladaptive cognitions. Step 1 discusses the mental obsession alcoholics have with alcohol. Pride, disillusionment, prejudice, negative and positive thinking, as well as needing some form of belief in God rather than self-sufficiency or self-centeredness are all extensively discussed in the 12 steps as problems with the way alcoholics think. Clearly, AA sees significant problems at this level and has identified changes in these cognitions or beliefs as central to recovery. There are even special phrases like "stinking thinking" which are used to identify thought patterns that can precipitate relapse or rationalizations that interfere with progress toward sobriety. Maladaptive cognitions are a key level of change addressed by AA.

Interpersonal conflicts represent the third level of change. Conflicts experienced at this level are often a precipitating cause for turning to psychotherapy. Relationship problems, marital problems, and specific interpersonal conflicts in work or social friendships are common problems that require change or interfere with change at other levels. In the AA literature and the 12 steps toward recovery interpersonal conflicts appear to be a central part of the process. Steps 8, 9, and 10 directly address interpersonal problems. The AA participant is asked to list persons harmed, make direct amends when feasible, and to continue to anticipate and resolve interpersonal problems. It appears that the alcoholic has created a path of destruction and harm in the wake of his or her drinking. Resolutions of the conflicts and making amends for past transgressions seem to be integral to recovery and, in some way, insurance against the guilt and negative emotions that could trigger relapse. Interestingly, this interpersonal level also has received a lot of attention in the AA traditions. Anonymity, a fellowship of equals, never becoming professionals, and refusing to take money or social stands are all part of the 12 traditions. Most of these positions have been taken to minimize interpersonal conflicts and the petty jealousy, greed, or self-importance that could create havoc among fellowship members (Alcoholics Anonymous, 1952).

In some ways AA minimizes problems at the family/systems level at least in its original principles. There is little mention of how drinking has influenced the entire family system and the children as well as the spouse. Most of the focus is on individual interpersonal relationships described above and not the family system. There is some discussion of how AA members become better partners and family oriented through the 12 steps as described in AA materials (Alcoholics Anonymous, 1952). However, the main concentration of the AA approach is on the individual alcoholic and not the family or employment systems. When it comes to the AA fellowship, on the other hand, the individual welfare or recovery comes behind the common welfare of the AA group (Tradition 1). Here the systemic perspective is more apparent. The AA traditions are designed to minimize organization, bureaucracy, and systemic problems within the AA fellowship.

Finally, we arrive at the level of intrapersonal problems. In many ways this level is a key explanatory level in AA. Restoring sanity, defects of character, self-centeredness, moral inventories, ego puncturing, and the need for vigilance and prayer all point to serious problems that exist at the core of the individual where values and orientation to life are questioned, challenged, and confronted in the process of recovery. The defect in character underlies the drinking behavior and appears to be understood as a primary problem that led to alcohol involvement. Although there has always been significant resistance to seeing alcoholics as having serious emotional disorders, AA principles seem to focus on characterological issues.

This analysis of AA principles and practices from the perspective of levels of change is quite revealing. Although sobriety and resolution of alcohol-related problems is the central reason for the existence of AA, the 12 steps concentrate heavily on the maladaptive cognitions level as well as the inter- and intrapersonal problem levels rather than exclusively or primarily on alcohol consumption or other symptomatic/situational problems. In many ways this is a surprising finding. Researchers who want to examine the mechanisms of change in AA would need to investigate changes and strategies of change at multiple levels. Alcohol involvement is not a major focus of the 12 steps. The levels of change help to identify the multiple problems that the 12-step approach addresses and why this approach can be so readily adapted to other addictive behaviors or symptomatic problems.

The Processes of Change and AA

The processes of change represent coping strategies that are needed to move through the stages of change. They are divided into two distinct subsets representing five experiential and five behavioral processes. We will examine the experiential processes first and then turn to the behavioral processes. Each of the processes is a generic change principle that can be represented by many different specific techniques. For the consciousness raising process, for example, feedback, self-monitoring, confrontation, and education can all be used to help the individual become more aware or engage in this process. In this section the 12 steps and both AA meeting and sponsorship practices are analyzed to see which processes they engender.

Consciousness raising is a prototypic change process that is included in most theories of behavior change. AA provides many avenues for the consciousness raising process. The open and closed meetings have as a primary purpose educating members about alcohol, sobriety, and life problems associated with drinking. The 12 steps are an integral part of this process with "Big Book" (Alcoholics Anonymous, 1976) study and other bibliotherapy encouraged in addition to the meetings. All these activities are in the service of learning more about the ravages of alcohol, the path of recovery, and the pitfalls along the way. Another significant source of education and consciousness raising is the sponsor. The sponsor is an older, wiser counselor in sobriety who offers feedback, confrontation, and information. Both principles and practice contain multiple consciousness raising activities.

Dramatic relief represents the process whereby the individual is moved emotionally by some external presentation about the problem or solution. Psychodrama is a good example of a technique that would encourage dramatic relief or, as some call it, the catharsis process. In AA, the speaker meetings, as well as the closed meetings, offer many emotion generating personal stories about the ravages and losses attributable to alcohol. These dramatic presentations are geared to move listeners to decision making and change of their own behavior. This modeling conveys both information (consciousness raising) and emotionally moving (dramatic relief) messages.

Self-reevaluation is a process whereby the individual revises his or her view of the self with regard to the problem. This seems to be both a cognitive and an affective process. Individuals need to engage in self-reevaluation in order to shift their attitudes and tip the decisional balance toward decision making and action. The process whereby an alcoholic comes to see, feel, and believe that their "lives are unmanageable" would represent best self-reevaluation in the service of change. The need for self-reevaluation is repeatedly addressed in the 12 steps. The search to experience the defects in character and the fearless moral inventory would require or engage the self-reevaluation process.

The final two experiential processes have more to do with the social environment. Environmental reevaluation is a process whereby individuals shift their thinking or views about how their problem affects others, how alcohol is problematic in society, or how the lives of others would be better with this problem eliminated. AA's 12-step perspective on realizing the harm inflicted on others and the emphasis on reaching out to other sufferers in order to experience the larger AA spirit seem to embody the environmental reevaluation process. As individuals become more and more a part of AA, their views of alcohol-related problems and of others shift dramatically as the corresponding activity of self-reevaluation begins to take place. These shifts often include a radical revision of their perspective on the social and interpersonal environment. Social liberation, on the other hand, is an advocacy process whereby individuals engage in expanding options in the community that promote sobriety and resolution of alcohol-related problems. Changing the drinking age or restricting drinking environments are examples of the social liberation process. AA does not take positions on political or social issues in general. However, attempts to provide an alternative lifestyle through involvement in the meetings and organizing as well as sponsoring nonalcohol celebrations and social events seems to represent a social liberation process supported by the organization.

These experiential processes are critical in the earlier stages of change especially in contemplation and preparation stages. AA principles and practice offer numerous activities and opportunities to engage these processes to an individual who begins to "work the program."

The impression often given by individuals who talk about AA from a psychological perspective is that AA is a spiritual program of recovery. That may be. However, AA utilizes many tactics and practices that clearly represent behavioral processes. In fact, AA is a very action-oriented and behavioral program when analyzed in depth using the behavioral processes of change.

In our transtheoretical model the process of self-liberation is a behavioral process that tries to capture commitment or choice. The commitment most encouraged by AA is to attendance at meetings and working the 12 steps. This is expected if the individual is to achieve a stable and productive recovery. The commitment does not appear to be to quit drinking per se but to follow the program that will lead individuals away from alcohol and toward meaningful and productive lives.

The change processes that are most representative of behavior therapy and theory are counterconditioning (changing the response to a particular problem stimulus); stimulus control (changing the stimulus that promotes the problem); or reinforcement/contingency management (rewards and punishments associated with the problem or attempts to solve the problem). Although there have been some heated battles between behavior therapy proponents and the AA community, AA is actually quite behavioral in its approach. Members are urged to avoid alcohol and situations saturated with booze. The AA community and individual meetings help to control cues to drink and offer an alcohol-free environment, all of which represent stimulus control. The emphasis on using meetings to cope with urges, building an alternative lifestyle that substitutes for drinking behavior, prayer and meditation represent counterconditioning techniques. The traditional practice in AA to celebrate the birthdate of sobriety and the use of chips or tokens that represent desire and days in sobriety are obvious reward techniques. The meeting groups offer support and encouragement, which is quite a powerful reward. Finally, Step 12, which encourages helping others, is described as a step that reinforces the sobriety of the helper while offering some help to a fellow drinker. There appear to be many practices of AA that foster the behavioral processes of stimulus control, counterconditioning, and reinforcement management.

A recent study conducted by Snow and colleagues (1992) gathered data on these processes from individuals who currently attended AA compared to those who did so in the past and a group of individuals who had successfully modified alcohol-related problems but never went to AA. Current AA attendees demonstrated greater process use of precisely these behavioral processes and AA meeting attendance was correlated with the behavioral processes.

A process that falls under the behavioral group in our model is the helping relationship. This process is marked by an empathic, open, receptive relationship where the individual is comfortable exploring the problem and one which will support change. This helping relationship process is quite extensively used and represents a major emphasis in AA. The entire organization is called a fellowship where individuals can gain acceptance simply by having the desire to give up alcohol. Sponsorship is another practice that promotes the helping relationship process. Although sponsors can be rather confrontive and not empathic, many individuals in AA talk of their sponsors as offering a supportive and receptive ear.

Behavioral processes abound in the practice and procedures of AA. These behavioral processes are primarily related to attending meetings, using sponsors and the fellowship, avoidance of and abstention from alcohol, and engaging in alternative behaviors. In the transtheoretical model, behavioral processes are important in the action and maintenance stages to achieve successful modification of a problem behavior. In many ways AA seems to be best characterized as an action and maintenance facilitator with much emphasis placed on taking action, reaching out for support, and engaging in protective behaviors like prayer.

AA and the Stages of Change

This analysis of the levels and processes of change can help us examine how AA principles and practices interact with each of the stages of change. This analysis will attempt to point out how the content and procedures of AA can promote or hinder movement from one stage to the next. At the end we will chart what a successful AA member would do to move through the stages of change.

Precontemplation is a much less pejorative term than resistant alcoholic. The 12 steps approach the precontemplator with sensitivity to the difficult task of moving out of precontemplation and "admitting defeat." Exposure to the AA message and a tolerant attitude allowing the individual to experience the continued losses or difficulties brought on by John Barleycorn is considered the best way to get precontemplators to take the first step and admit powerlessness and that their lives had become unmanageable. Presumably this admission would move them through contemplation and into action. In practice, open meetings and "story" telling are geared to reach the precontemplator. If there is discouragement and hopelessness, Step 2 offers hope for the discouraged precontemplator that a "power greater than ourselves" would be there to do the healing.

There are several practices, however, which are often mentioned by precontemplators as reasons why AA is not for them. For them these practices can hinder movement out of precontemplation. The emphasis on the higher power, the labeling process of declaring oneself an alcoholic, and the strong message that abstinence is the only goal have all been pointed to by some precontemplators as impediments to change. The meetings of AA are considered open to all with a desire to stop drinking. However, this can be a mixed message to the precontemplator whose desire is more often than not only a desire to get others to back off. Often a precontemplator will mix meeting attendance with drinking and conceal this from others. There may be openness to precontemplators, but AA appears to assume that movement to contemplation or preparation occurs rather quickly and to condemn precontemplators to drink until the consequences convince them that they have "hit bottom." In summary, most AA principles and practices are not directed to the precontemplation stage drinker.

Before leaving precontemplation, however, it is important to examine ancillary groups spun off the AA tradition. To family, spouses, and children of precontemplators, Alanon, Alateen, and Alatot offer support and work to disengage them from any protective behavior (enabling) that may interfere with the alcoholic "hitting bottom." These groups can provoke the environmental changes or pressure that, at times, can get the precontemplator to move ahead into contemplation, preparation, and action.

The fact that the desire to stop drinking is enough to enter the AA fellowship allows the contemplator to attend AA in order to consider what the problems are and what needs to be done. As described above, there are numerous activities that promote experiential process activity that is needed to tip the decisional balance toward a decision to change. AA activities that educate and move the alcohol troubled person to be convinced of his or her helplessness over alcohol and the need for a higher power are aimed at the contemplator. Throughout the process of recovery AA members are encouraged to engage in contemplation processes to assess problems at various levels. The moral (Step 4) inventory to become aware of current defects in character (Step 6), the assessment of harm to others (Step 8), and the continued personal inventory (Step 10) are all contemplation activities addressing problems at various levels of change.

Contemplators who wish to focus only on drinking behavior, however, may be put off by this emphasis on problems at different levels and could become confused or more ambivalent. Contemplators are asked by the 12 steps to acknowledge issues related to sanity and character defects as well as alcohol consumption. This multi-level emphasis can be quite disconcerting and discouraging. Sponsors can be powerful promoters of contemplation processes but can become quite impatient with too much contemplation and no action. Individuals report being too intimidated to be comfortable calling a sponsor or attending an AA meeting while continuing to drink. In many ways AA seems more comfortable working on contemplation after drinking has ceased.

For individuals who have made the decision to stop drinking and are in the preparation stage of change, AA principles and practices can offer a concrete plan and specific direction. They are encouraged to turn their lives over to a higher power and to attend 90 meetings in 90 days. Choosing a sponsor is also a preparation/action stage endeavor. As discussed above, moral inventories that evaluate needs to change and contain plans to make amends can be considered clear preparation stage activities for various levels of change.

Preparation stage individuals who find it difficult to relate to a higher power or whose focus is on drinking behavior only may find the messages of AA ill suited to their attempts to change. The real challenge is whether the preparation stage individual can accept the AA way as a viable and plausible means to take action and achieve sobriety.

As became obvious in the analysis of the behavioral processes, AA seems to offer action plans for drinking and other levels of change in abundance. Attending meetings, admitting faults, avoiding alcohol, asking Him to remove shortcomings, and making amends all are action activities. The action stage in AA is one that is emphasized and, in practice, action advice appears to be given quite freely in meetings and by sponsors. The whole process of "going public" at meetings is very difficult for individuals not actively engaged in stopping drinking.

Individuals are given the impression that effective action requires active attendance at meetings, and that without this engagement little or no successful change can occur. Thus, alcohol troubled individuals in the action stage who develop their own plan for action can become alienated or undermined by the emphasis that there is really only one way to achieve and maintain sobriety. Another important practice that could undermine as well as promote change is the strict interpretation of relapse. Any contact with alcohol is considered a relapse and sobriety must begin again to be dated from the time of this slip or lapse. This position can be discouraging to slippers and actually promote relapse. However, this strict interpretation can be used by action stage individuals as a support against slipping. AA members will often say, "I thought about drinking but when I realized I would lose all that I gained so far, I decided not to do it." Clearly, for both action and maintenance this strict interpretation of relapse is a two-edged sword.

Once an individual has achieved 3 to 6 months of abstinence, AA offers an unparalleled support system and alternative environment to protect that sobriety. Reinforcement strategies like birthdays and "twelve stepping" can be tremendously helpful for the maintainer. The focus on problems at other levels is probably most helpful for the maintainers. It would be easier to maintain sobriety if interpersonal and intrapersonal problems are effectively solved, minimizing the negative emotions and interpersonal frustration that can trigger relapse.

In practice, the emphasis on perpetual maintenance embodied in the belief that an individual is always an alcoholic and recovering but never recovered can be quite helpful for individuals who experience continued temptations to drink even after years of maintained sobriety. However, continued self-assessment as an alcoholic can undermine maintenance since it does not allow the individual to completely defocus on alcohol and the alcoholic identity. There are indications that continued self-reevaluation long into action and maintenance can contribute to relapse rather than protect against it (DiClemente & Prochaska, 1985). There is also no clear message as to when individuals can disengage from meetings. The implicit and sometimes stated message is attendance should continue forever. However, most individuals who have attended AA and have achieved sobriety have not continued regular meeting attendance although many admit this only with some sense of guilt (McCrady & Irvine, 1989). On the other hand, the 12 steps clearly state that the removal of character flaws (Step 7) and the continued personal inventories, as well as prayer and meditation, are constantly needed to keep the alcoholic on the proper path to maintain sobriety.

Thus far, I have attempted to demonstrate how AA principles and practices address the tasks of each stage of change and can promote or hinder movement from one specific stage. Let me conclude my stage of change analysis by turning to an example of successful movement through the stages using AA. This would be my best estimate of what a successful AA member did to achieve stable, long-term sobriety according to our model.

Table 4 indicates the key elements that the dedicated AA changer would use to move successfully through the stages of change. Ideally the individual would enter at the end of the precontemplation stage having reached his or her own "bottom," identify with the models met in AA, and respond well to the confrontations of twelve steppers. Moving into contemplation the individual would begin not only to see the unmanageability of his or her life with alcohol but also be open to exploring the healing effect of a higher power. This would lead to a rather intensive moral inventory which would demonstrate the need for action at multiple levels. Next there comes a shift to making the commitment to the specific action activities of the 12 steps and the humility to admit to God and another human being (often the sponsor) the wrong and ask for an infusion of proper values. The action plan would include attendance at AA and a single-minded focus on avoiding alcohol as well as making amends to others for past transgressions. Although the 12 steps mention problems or issues at various levels of change, in practice the AA member would concentrate completely on sobriety, leaving marital problems, other therapy, career changes, and education to a time when they have achieved a year or more of sustained sobriety. In AA the maintenance plan is similar to the action plan with the addition of the twelfth step. Any lapse along the way would be considered a relapse that should be followed by a recommitment to AA attendance and a more faithful adherence to the 12 steps.

This brief summary does an injustice to the significant effort and struggle associated with each of the activities mentioned. However, I believe that this is the path through the stages charted by AA principles and practice. Many individuals who have been able to follow this path, accepting the principles and becoming active members in the practice of AA, have been able to achieve significant changes in their drinking behavior and other aspects of their lives including relationships, beliefs, thinking, and the core values by which they live their lives. Although I do not believe that all individuals can or do follow this complete path to achieve change in their drinking and their lives, certainly the ones who have done so are models and advocates of this path to successful sobriety.

TABLE 4

AA Practices and Movement through the Stages of Change

Precontemplation	Contemplation	Preparation	Action	Maintenance	Relapse
Hitting bottom	Unmanageable lives	Commitment to 12 steps	AA attendance	AA attendance	Lapse = Relapse
Modeling	Moral inventory	Turning lives over to higher power	Focus on alcohol only	Focus on alcohol only (1st year)	Attend AA again
Confrontation	Higher power		Making amends	Continued moral inventory	
			Moral inventory	Step 12	

Summary and Recommendation

The preceding analysis demonstrates that there are enough principles of change and a sufficient focus on the various stages of the process to achieve successfully maintained sobriety. At the same time this analysis offers some surprising insights into the AA perspective on the process of change. AA focuses on multiple levels of change and places great emphasis on maladaptive thinking and beliefs, interpersonal conflicts, and intrapersonal issues of values and character. As such it is more concerned with a larger transformation of the individual than drinking behavior modification. The 12 steps are filled with experiential process activity at these multiple levels of change. However, on balance, AA seems to be in practice very action oriented, utilizing all the behavioral processes of the transtheoretical model. As such, the AA approach may be more suited to individuals in the latter stages of change and particularly helpful for individuals in the maintenance stage.

There are principles and practices that appear to address the tasks involved in each stage of change. However, the multiple shifting problem levels, the action orientation, lack of personal skills training, and the focus on the intervention of a vague higher power that needs individual interpretation can make the path to change as defined by AA a difficult one to follow. Lack of engagement in AA certainly can be a sign of a lack of motivation to change but could just as easily reflect mismatches between some AA principles or practices and the individual with the alcohol-related problem. Many individuals achieve change either without using the AA principles or by using only a few to assist them at certain points in the process of change. I would suspect that few individuals used the AA way completely or exclusively in moving through the cycle of change.

What follows are my recommendations that flow from this analysis:

1. More research is needed on the process of change as it relates to AA attendance and 12-step work. This process assessment should include the specific techniques, beliefs, and practices proposed by AA, as well as the generic processes of change described in this chapter.
2. AA involvement needs to be evaluated for relevance and effectiveness among individuals in various stages of change.
3. Researchers evaluating the outcome of AA involvement should assess changes at each level of change and pay particular attention to changes in cognitions and inter- and intrapersonal conflicts.
4. Sponsorship and other practices need to be evaluated in light of stages and processes of change.
5. Although correlational studies offer important information about AA (Emrick et al., 1993), longitudinal studies with comparison or control

groups are needed to understand AA's involvement in the entire process of change from precontemplation through relapse and maintenance.

References

Abrams, D., DiClemente, C., Sorenson, G., Eriksen, M., Emmons, K., & Thompson, B. (1991). Integrating individual and organizations perspectives for workplace cancer prevention. Presented at the annual meeting of the American Public Health Association, Atlanta, GA.

Alcoholics Anonymous. (1952). *Twelve steps and twelve traditions.* New York: Alcoholics Anonymous World Services.

Alcoholics Anonymous. (1976). *Alcoholics Anonymous: The story of how many thousands of men and women have recovered from alcoholism* (3rd ed.). New York: Alcoholics Anonymous World Services.

Baranowski, T. (1990). Reciprocal determinism at the stages of behavioral change: An integration of community, personal and behavioral perspectives. *International Quarterly of Community Health Education, 10,* 297–327.

DiClemente, C.C. (1985). Antonio—more than anxiety: A transtheoretical approach. In J. Norcross (Ed.), *Casebook of eclectic psychotherapy* (pp. 158–185). New York: Brunner/Mazel.

DiClemente, C.C. (1991). Motivational interviewing and the stages of change. In W.R. Miller & S. Rollnick (Eds.), *Motivational interviewing: Preparing people for change* (pp. 191–203). New York: Guilford Press.

DiClemente, C.C., & Gordon, J.R. (1983). Aging, alcoholism and addictive behavior change: Diagnostic treatment models. In *Alcoholism in the elderly: Medical, social and biologic issues* (pp. 263–275). New York: Raven Press.

DiClemente, C.C., & Hughes, S.O. (1990). Stages of change profiles in alcoholism treatment. *Journal of Substance Abuse, 2,* 217–235.

DiClemente, C.C., & Prochaska, J.O. (1982). Self-change and therapy change of smoking behavior: A comparison of processes of change in cessation and maintenance. *Addictive Behaviors, 7,* 133–142.

DiClemente, C.C., & Prochaska, J.O. (1985). Processes and stages of change: Coping and competence in smoking behavior change. In S. Shiffman & T.A. Wills (Eds.), *Coping and substance abuse* (pp. 319–344). New York: Academic Press.

DiClemente, C.C., Carbonari, J.P., & Velasquez, M.M. (1992). Alcoholism treatment mismatching from a stage of change perspective. In R.R. Watson (Ed.), *Alcohol and drug abuse reviews.* Totowa, NJ: Humana Press.

DiClemente, C.C., Prochaska, J.O., Fairhurst, S.K., Velicer, W.F., Velasquez, M.M., & Rossi, J.S. (1991). The process of smoking cessation: An analysis of precontemplation, contemplation and preparation stages of change. *Journal of Consulting and Clinical Psychology, 59,* 295–304.

Emrick, C.D., Tonigan, J.S., Montgomery, H.A., & Little, L. (1993). Alcoholics Anonymous: What is currently known? In B.S. McCrady & W.R. Miller (Eds.), *Research on Alcoholics Anonymous: Opportunities and alternatives.* New Brunswick, NJ: Rutgers Center of Alcohol Studies.

McCrady, B.S., & Irvine (1989). Self-help groups. In R.K. Hester & W.R. Miller (Eds.), *Handbook of alcoholism treatment approaches* (pp. 153–169). New York: Pergamon Press.

Miller, W.R., & Rollnick, S. (Eds.). (1991). *Motivational interviewing: Preparing people for change.* New York: Guilford Press.

Norcross, J.C., Prochaska, J.O., & DiClemente, C.C. (1986). Self-change of psychological distress: Layperson's vs psychologist's coping strategies. *Journal of Clinical Psychology, 42,* 834–840.

O'Connell, D.O., & Velicer, W.F. (1988). A decisional balance measure of the stages of change model for weight loss. *International Journal of the Addictions, 23,* 729–740.

Prochaska, J.O., & DiClemente, C.C. (1983). Stages and processes of self-change of smoking: Toward an integrative model of change. *Journal of Consulting and Clinical Psychology, 51,* 390–395.

Prochaska, J.O., & DiClemente, C.C. (1984). Self-change processes, self-efficacy and decisional balance across five stages of smoking cessation. In P.F. Anderson, P.N. Mortenson, L.E. Epstein (Eds.), *Advance in cancer control* (pp. 131–140). New York: Alan R. Liss, Inc.

Prochaska, J.O., & DiClemente, C.C. (1985). Common processes of change in smoking, weight control and psychological distress. In S. Shiffman & T.A. Wills (Eds.), *Coping and substance abuse* (pp. 345–364). New York: Academic Press.

Prochaska, J.O., & DiClemente, C.C. (1986). The transtheoretical approach: Towards a systematic eclectic framework. In J.C. Norcross (Ed.), *Handbook of eclectic psychotherapy* (pp. 163–200). New York: Brunner/Mazel.

Prochaska, J.O., & DiClemente, C.C. (1992). Stages of change in the modification of problem behaviors. In M. Hersen, R.M. Eisler, & P.M. Miller (Eds.), *Progress in behavior modification 28* (pp. 184–214). Sycamore, IL: Sycamore Publishing.

Prochaska, J.O., Velicer, W.F., DiClemente, C.C., & Fava, J. (1988). Measuring processes of change: Application to the cessation of smoking. *Journal of Consulting and Clinical Psychology, 56,* 520–528.

Snow, M.C., Prochaska, J.O., & Rossi, J.S., (1992). Processes of change in Alcoholics Anonymous: Issues in maintaining long-term sobriety. Manuscript submitted for publication.

Suris-Rangel, A., Cousins, J., DiClemente, C.C., & Dunn, K. (1988). Stages and processes of change in weight control for Mexican American women. Presented at the 22nd annual meeting of the Association for Advancement of Behavior Therapy, New York.

CHAPTER 6

AA Processes and Change:
How Does It Work?

MARGARET BEAN-BAYOG

*If any feel that as psychiatrists directing a hospital for alcoholics
we appear somewhat sentimental, let them stand with us a while
on the firing line, see the tragedies, the despairing wives, the little
children; let the solving of these problems become a part of their
daily work, and even of their sleeping moments, and the most
cynical will not wonder that we have accepted and encouraged
this movement.*

—William D. Silkworth, M.D.
(1976, p. xxvi)

This chapter will use clinical observation to describe how alcoholic
people use or avoid using AA. It is based primarily on clinical work
with alcoholics in and out of AA and distills observations from about
10,000 hours over a twenty year period spent with alcoholic patients seen
individually in treatment, in teaching sessions, and in AA meetings. Most
alcoholic patients sent to me could be called AA avoiders and "rehab re-
fuseniks": they have "failed" at other types of treatment. Making an alliance with them to explore how they deal with their drinking has brought
me to consider paths toward, away from, and around AA.

What makes people willing to attend AA at all? What makes them avoid
it? How do they carry out their first contact? What is it like when they go?
How do they sort themselves into different patterns of use such as refusal
ever to go, refusal to go back, occasional peripheral contact, regular reluctant contact, enthusiastic participation, and embracing AA as a social network and source of new identity as member and even zealous adherent?

And, if someone does go to AA, what effect does it have? How does it
help people think and act differently? How does it facilitate "recovery"
from alcoholism?

The most important single fact about AA use among alcoholics is that
the majority of alcoholic people do not ever go to AA. The numbers vary

according to whose statistics one uses to enumerate alcoholics and AA members (Alcoholics Anonymous, 1989; Secretary of Health and Human Services, 1990). Most people are surprised that the fraction of alcoholics who use AA is small since AA philosophy and ideas have influence disproportionate to their numbers.

This chapter will not attempt to describe AA characteristics, structure, and functions which have been reviewed elsewhere (Bean, 1975a, 1975b, 1991) and discussed throughout this monograph.

Instead, in order to understand how alcoholics decide to use or not use AA, it will be helpful first to review their subjective experiences as they develop alcoholism. What happens to them as their drinking begins to go out of control? How do they react to these experiences? How do they explain their experiences to themselves? What kind of theory and meaning do they develop to make sense of their drinking problems (Bean-Bayog, 1986)?

This is followed by a review of what goes on during recovery from alcoholism: What must the patient change in order to go from being a symptomatic drinking alcoholic to one who has safely stopped?

Finally, a discussion is presented of obstacles in the alcoholic's thinking for the straightforward accomplishment of these tasks. How does AA tackle these obstacles? How does it understand them? How does it engage the alcoholic in changing himself or herself? What resources—human, conceptual, cognitive, psychotherapeutic, and spiritual—does it offer? How does the alcoholic take advantage of these, and in what order? Where are these resources likely to fail? Examples of careers of AA resisters, partial users, and joyous believers will be used for illustration.

Before Contacting AA

Some researchers try to conceptualize affiliation with AA by attending AA meetings themselves and noting their own subjective responses to meetings and members. While helpful, this may also be misleading: Having someone throw a life preserver feels very different to someone standing solidly on dry land than it does to a drowning swimmer.

The alcoholic because of his or her situation and history has a much more intense and ambivalent reaction to AA than does a nonalcoholic. It is important to understand how the alcoholic's experience has changed the meaning of the idea of having alcoholism or making contact with treatment or AA.

How Does It Feel to Develop Alcoholism?

Developing alcoholism is confusing, painful, and complex. The process varies with the patient's age, circumstances, and resources and whether he or she also has mental illness. Generalizations will not always apply, but a sketch of the process will provide a starting point.

Alcoholism usually begins unannounced and gradually. Rarely does the person grasp what is happening at the beginning. What she notices is that she has trouble regulating her alcohol use so that it is safe and within social bounds. She drinks too much. She begins to have symptoms that result from not being able to plan or regulate her drinking. She humiliates herself and disgusts other people or hurts their feelings, causing shame, guilt, decreased self esteem, and trouble in important relationships. She becomes anxious when she drinks because she does not know if she will go out of control or not. This chapter will not discuss etiology. The source of this loss of control, whatever the cause, is not usually conscious.

How the Alcoholic Interprets What is Happening

The alcoholic does not realize what is the matter. In order for her to do this she would have to transform her thinking, accept a stigmatized label, stop using alcohol, and go to treatment (Bean, 1981).

But this is counter-intuitive. The person usually knows she doesn't fit the degraded stereotype of advanced alcoholism, and, besides, the loss of control of drinking is partial and intermittent. *Sometimes* she *can* control her drinking. So she assumes she could always do so if she had more will-power. And she struggles against the loss of control. When she succeeds she feels normal, vindicated, and *not* alcoholic. When she fails, she still does not self-label. She feels helpless, guilty, defective, and demoralized. Self-esteem suffers, but to the extent that her self-esteem is good, she will reject the degraded label. She rejects the idea of help, because to get it she has to stigmatize herself as "alcoholic." This defensive maneuver, denial, seen here marshalled against the earliest mildest problems, is needed more and more if the disorder progresses (Bean, 1981). She may lose health, and the sense of safety, and begin to destroy important relationships.

All this is traumatic, and the alcoholic reacts to it in fascinating ways. Psychological functioning begins to be distorted in order to cope with the threat. As these frightening and painful events occur, the patient does not assume a relaxed, curious, exploratory stance and think, "I wonder if I have alcoholism? Perhaps I should educate myself about that, read, see an addiction specialist, and visit a few AA meetings."

As the threat increases, she rejects the diagnosis and its implications that she should seek treatment with increasing violence. Instead, she fights to regain control of her drinking, and if she fails she rationalizes each episode of trouble to explain her behavior to herself and others: "I must have been more upset about that exam than I realized, I really got drunk"; or "Maybe I am getting my period"; or, "Boy, that was strong punch."

This is interesting. The patient doesn't think she has a respectable medical problem. There is a moral element in drinking problems but the patient takes the idea to an extreme. She develops a moral explanation of what is the matter with her. If she doesn't drink too much she is good. If she does, she is bad and self-indulgent.

This moral free-will model applies to some drinking in alcoholism. At other points, the drinking appears to have a life of its own. But since she clings to the idea that she is good, not bad, and could not be alcoholic, she avoids and even rejects the idea of addiction and the need for abstinence and treatment.

Meanwhile, over time, suppose her pain from her drinking problem is increasing: her losses mount. Her loss of control damages self-respect. Insight and judgment are distorted by denial; they may also be impaired by the neurotoxic impact of the alcohol. If she is drinking often and heavily, she may experience confusion, self-preoccupation, regression, irrationality, and mood swings, because of the effect of the alcohol on her brain.

If she becomes addicted and develops withdrawal when she stops drinking, psychological dependence intensifies massively because if she cannot obtain and drink alcohol she will be physically sick.

She is increasingly out of control. Her experiences are terrifying, but so is the threat of the loss of alcohol and the acceptance of the label. But the worse her symptoms, the greater her helplessness, and the larger the threat, the more she clings to her increasingly farfetched insistence that she *can* control herself. Denial here may be global and frantically held.

Cognitive Positions Alcoholics Hold During Drinking

This is the cognitive content of the thinking of the untreated alcoholic:

1. He denies that he cannot regulate his alcohol use, because that would mean he was defective, diminished, subhuman.
2. He believes he drinks abnormally because of the pain of his circumstances and that drinking relieves this pain. He does not realize that by now much of his pain *results* from drinking.
3. He is hopeless and ignorant about how to go about solving his problem.

Meanwhile, like most people, somewhere along the line he has heard of AA. He may know someone who goes, or someone that he thinks should go. He may have heard of other treatments as well, and he may have seen an article or two about alcoholism or a celebrity talking about treatment. His family may have planted pamphlets for him to find. His reaction to these cultural phenomena is usually intense interest, even fascination, often furtive, as well as with fear, shame, repression, revulsion, and outrage. *"No,* that is not *me.* I don't need *that."* But he may keep the phone number of an advertisement in his wallet for several years.

Impact of Alcoholic Psychological Distortions on Entry into Treatment

A look at the alcoholic's experience and interpretation of her drinking problem may help one to understand how she thinks about contacting a treatment facility or AA.

The most important point is that diagnosis and treatment of an alcohol problem in any context *hurts.* When the patient's husband criticizes, she is angry and humiliated and guilty. When the doctor, worried about her hypertension, takes an alcohol history, she cringes and bristles, feeling punished and ashamed. And when she sees a TV special on alcohol flash a hotline number on the screen she may write it down, or she may just switch channels and go get something to drink.

For every person who actually goes to an AA meeting, there are dozens more who are considering it, resisting it, thinking about it and, almost always, hating the idea. Most people who telephone AA do so with shaking hands, a terrible sense of defeat, a sense of having been caught, accused, and punished and with an intense fear of public exposure. Understanding this psychology makes it much easier to answer the questions about AA affiliation posed in the introduction.

Just as the main reason people avoid AA is pain, the main reason they think of going to AA is also pain. Alcoholic drinking is a horrible way to live. When an alcoholic resists, part of him knows that the drinking is dangerous. Every time he experiences a negative result from drinking he thinks about contacting treatment.

We have here a balance of pain, shame, fear, and hope. Pain comes from consequences of drinking, and also from fear of loss of alcohol and of humiliation in treatment. Fear of consequences of drinking weighs against fear of the pain of treatment. And the hope that he can figure out how to drink safely and socially counterbalances the hope that, if he goes to AA or other treatment, he could get safe, get sober, get stopped.

The way any given alcoholic behaves at the point of seeking treatment is a vector, the strength and direction of which depends on the opposing forces acting on his thinking. How sick is he? How addicted? How bad is his pain? Can he make the causal connection between pain and drinking, or does he equate drinking with relief? Docs he have any knowledge of hopeful outcomes resulting from seeking treatment?

The AA Response to Resistance to Treatment

Suppose she picks up the phone and calls AA. How does AA tailor its responses to its own perception of the psychology of the alcoholic?

The most important intervention AA makes into the pain and despair of the thinking of the alcoholic is the instillation of hope.

It is despair and fear that force the alcoholic to rely on her primitive defensive denial, and it is usually a crack in her defenses, brought about by a crisis in her life, a confrontation with a medical or legal complication of the drinking, or the threat of damage or loss of an important relationship that drives her into the arms of AA. AA wants her to be able to stop denying the severity of her drinking problem, to bear the painful feelings this entails, and to seek an alternative to her habitual reaction of reaching for a drink. Here, AA intercedes by instilling hope. It tells the alcoholic that there is a way out of her current anguish. It offers general promises that she can break the addiction and specific instructions how. Most important, it promises to help her bear the pain she must face. It is only in the presence of such support that she can begin to relinquish her denial and resistance and come to meetings.

What does AA do with her pain? Generally, they acknowledge the pain of drinking and predict more. They talk about the well-being possible from recovery (i.e., they predict an eventual decreasing pain from joining: "Are you sick and tired of feeling sick and tired?"). They tend not to focus initially on the pain and shame of contact, though they empathize, nor do they depict the demands of getting permanently sober. They break the job down into small simple steps: "Just don't drink," "Go to a meeting," "Don't pick up just one drink for just one day," "One day at a time." They help the alcoholic simplify her complex psychological experience by reducing the perceptual and cognitive field to the question of her relation to alcohol and nothing else. Everything else is called, "people, places and things."

Shame is dealt with by a range of devices. The most powerful is that everyone there says they bear the stigmatized label, which the newcomer so fears. "Hi, I'm Mary and I am an alcoholic," can be looked at as masochistic, but to the newcomer it says that maybe human beings, and some respectable ones at that, can call themselves alcoholic. The relief from shame resulting from attending a single meeting can be tremendous.

There are several other brilliant maneuvers to deal with shame about alcoholism. One of the most remarkable is the device of defining membership in such a minimal way. The only requirement for membership is a desire to stop drinking. Notice that it is emphatically *not* necessary to have stopped or to self-label as alcoholic. These are considered to be later, separate, and demanding tasks. The only suggestions for newcomers are "don't drink" and "go to meetings."

Fear is dealt with by another range of devices, including support, reassurance, clarification, explanation, nurturing relationships, and, most powerfully, example. If someone goes to an AA meeting he sees people struggling with alcohol, who are sober and at various stages of recovery. AA also copes with shame by providing a patient who interprets his drinking problem as a moral failing with an alternative conceptualization. AA defines alcoholism as a "disease" or "allergy," and provides the alcoholic with a form of sick role, "recovering alcoholic" and "AA member," to substitute for "drunk," "bum," and other pejoratives. This legitimizing and nonshaming role, while controversial, does make it easier for some alcoholics to attend AA and to describe how they got there, what obstacles they had to overcome, and what it is like. At the meetings there are people who are sober such a short time that they remember vividly what it was like to be a newcomer and there are others who have been sober longer and provide role models of full recovery with which to identify.

Engagement in AA

When someone who contacts AA is able to engage with and use this healing community, the results can be wonderful. But many do not.

Sometimes this is a result of denial of the alcohol problem. Someone goes and says, "I'm not *that* bad," and flees. Sometimes she is right, she isn't *that* bad. Sometimes she is very ill but the pull of the dependence on alcohol leads her to rationalize or minimize her alcohol problem so that she can flee AA. Most people who go to AA are looking both for help, or at least a decrease in pain, and, contrariwise, for a rationalization so they can get out of having to go.

The typical first-meeting attendee is full of fantasy and hearsay about AA, full of shame and defensiveness about his drinking, and is loudly signalling his ambivalence by sitting in the back (dubbed "half measures" row, after an AA quote about not wanting to have to be fully committed). He is usually alone and skeptical, and is searching the experience for data to corroborate a decision never to return. This is easy enough to do, as AA is full of characteristics that are tempting to criticize and reject.

I try to deal with this with my own patients by asking them to visit a half-dozen different meetings and to come back and tell me what they hated the most about each one. Perhaps they can get past their negative reactions. Perhaps not. If they do not, they will have to find other resources and approaches to deal with their drinking. If they *can* go and if they do participate in AA, we are now in a position to describe what AA does to help people recover (Bean, 1975a, 1975b). For the purposes of this discussion we will assume that recovery is based on abstinence from alcohol and on changes in thinking, as well as on actions that stabilize abstinence from a momentary decision to a committed lifestyle.

Recovery from Alcoholism

Whether someone is using AA, other treatment, religion, or individual willpower in recovery from alcoholism, it is helpful to have a concept of what is involved. What is the transformation from an actively drinking, out of control, untreated alcoholic to a safe, solidly recovering one? What must the alcoholic do to change from one to the other?

One way to describe this information is to list a series of actions or tasks that people carry out in the process of moving from active alcoholism to mature abstinence.

Life-threatening conditions must be resolved first, then potentially life-threatening ones such as breaking treatment or continued drinking, then those that block recovery such as denial and neurologic damage, and, last, the luxuries of grieving and psychological growth.

Tasks of Recovery from Alcoholism

These first five tasks require two years.

- Establish a relationship to alcoholism treatment. See a counselor, attend AA, or get admitted to an alcoholism treatment program.
- Secure a safe environment. People do not learn new behavior well when they are in pain or danger.
- Learn how to get sober. AA suggests, "don't drink, go to meetings, join a group, get a sponsor."
- Learn why to get sober. Change the distorted psychology of alcoholism. Resolve denial so person realizes he has alcoholism. Make the causal connection between suffering and drinking, that drinking brings short-term relief but long-term misery. Teach the person how to use treatment so he or she does not have to drink.
- Cope with the effects of stopping: family turmoil, facing stigma and shame, and protracted withdrawal syndrome.

These last three tasks require at least three years more.

- Grieve the losses incurred from alcohol use.
- Remodel psychological and cognitive habits developed during alcoholism such as denial.
- Seek psychotherapeutic treatment for any antecedent or concomitant psychiatric disorder.

The recovery process can roughly be expected to occupy five years of the patient's life, although this varies widely. Most change occurs in the first 18 months, and what follows may be as much maturation and psychological growth as healing from a physical and emotional disorder (Bean-Bayog, 1985).

This list of tasks of recovery is one simple, commonsense way of describing the process of change in recovery from alcoholism. Most clinicians, alcoholism counselors, and others who care for alcoholic people follow some such conceptual sequence in their work, whether implicit or explicit. For example, Brown describes a developmental model of recovery (Brown, 1985). Of course, alcoholics vary and simple cookbook sequences do not serve for patients who present with simultaneous crises (e.g., the paranoid schizophrenic alcoholic who needs both detoxification and inpatient psychiatric treatment as well as medical care and housing).

AA provides its own list of tasks of recovery in the 12 steps, but I find that what AA does for a new alcoholic approaching membership is far more complex and powerful. The 12 steps are component techniques appropriately used mostly in middle and late recovery, after the initial phase of instilling hope, engaging the new member, establishing sobriety and healing from the recent damage of heavy drinking.

Psychological Shifts in Recovery in AA

As we can see from the description of the psychology of the drinking alcoholic, drunkenness is only part of the problem. Recovery entails a set of related maturing sequences in the patient's defenses, self-image, identifications, and object relations.

Defenses. Consider first what happens in AA to the primitive defenses the alcoholic was driven to use during active drinking: denial, minimization, avoidance, projection, and acting out by drinking. In AA there are specific, orderly mechanisms offered to facilitate the development of mature mechanisms and the relinquishment of these crude ones.

The use of hope and support to help the patient abandon denial has been mentioned. The new member is not expected to give up denial immediately, but bit by bit. Initially, it is enough for her to attend meetings. Everyone understands that she will be able to "admit" she is alcoholic long before she can stand to "accept" it. She may be nudged along, but not pushed to give up her denial until she is ready.

Avoidance can be abandoned because as she stops drinking, her pain and shame and sickness abate and she has less she needs to avoid. Projection of blame is the primitive way active alcoholics handle guilt. In AA, guilt is decreased by confession (4th, 5th, and 6th step), expiation, atonement, penance (6th, 7th, and 8th steps), and making amends; there is thus less need for projection.

Magical thinking is let go as the new member begins to implement the sequences of small constructive steps to make real progress in her life.

Impulsive self-destructive action is contained by AA structures, limits, supports, and controls. The prescriptions, "Don't drink," "Go to meetings," provide the framework. Dependence on a "Higher Power" allows narcissistic defenses such as grandiosity and omnipotence to attenuate while rituals such as asking for help not to drink everyday provide controls. Meanwhile, activities in meetings and the larger AA subculture foster the development of maturer defenses.

Repression takes over many of the protective functions denial served during drinking. Reaction formation, the transformation of the unacceptable into its opposite, allows love of drinking to shift toward love of sobriety.

Later, reaction formation may mature even further toward altruism and sublimation in 12th step work, where the person uses his own recovery as the basis for helping others.

AA fosters other mature defenses such as anticipation ("think through a drink before you take it"), humor, altruism, and sublimation. But it also allows people to choose their own pace.

Not all alcoholics use the same defenses or follow the same path in recovery. AA offers a smorgasbord of options from which each new member chooses and tailors his own program.

Limits of AA's Expectations of Change

What AA does *not* undertake to change is as interesting as what it does. It understands that the new alcoholic's experience is chaotic and painful, dominated by impulses to drink, neurologic impairment, high levels of psychic distress, and damaged relationships. Grasping that it is hard to get and keep the new member's attention, it makes few, brief, repeated suggestions adapted to his level of functioning.

New members are told not to change things in their lives (jobs, housing, relationships), just to focus on not drinking. They are taught to take care of themselves and to keep things simple.

Later, more complex ideas, such as using a sponsor, will be conveyed. Working through the 12 steps and defensive maturation are deferred until after the early phases of tenuous control, confusion, withdrawal, and craving. The alcoholic is not expected to scrap his defenses abruptly, but only to discard and replace them by stepwise changes. He does not change his identity initially, only certain aspects of his behavior, (e.g., "don't drink"). Recognizing how human beings resist change, AA focuses initially on a single goal, changing the drinking, putting off character change until later. Alcohol remains a major focus, as it was during drinking, and its loss is expected to require substantial mourning.

Self Image and Identification

I have described how the alcoholic's self-esteem was damaged by drinking. During recovery, self-esteem improves as he defines himself as an alcoholic who can stop, then as a sober alcoholic, and finally as a "recovering" alcoholic. He moves from role of new member, to helping with coffee at meetings, to speaker, to group member, to sponsor.

He is able to do this by following the example of AA members already in these roles. He sees them at meetings, hears them speak, may ask one of them to be his sponsor. It is a kind of apprenticeship learning structure focused on helping the new member learn how to keep sober, make use of what AA offers, and adjust to living without alcohol. This empirically developed body of skills and knowledge with the private language norms, values, and beliefs of the AA subculture is transmitted mainly orally, through informal caring relationships, sponsorship, group membership, going on "commitments" to speak at meetings, as well as more formally in the "Big Book" (Alcoholics Anonymous, 1989) and the "Twelve Steps and Twelve Traditions" and other AA literature (Alcoholics Anonymous, 1952).

The Process of Participation

In order for a person to be able to participate in this subculture, he must have the social skills to use the group and be able to suspend his own values to participate in those of the group. He is told "identify, don't compare," when listening to speakers. "Identify" is used here to mean "find what you have in common with the speaker, don't look for differences."

This is an important way AA has to handle newcomer resistance and objections to the value system in AA. As noted, incoming alcoholics are looking for differences, ways they can justify not returning to AA.

Most new alcoholics identify most easily when the focus is on alcohol. They do share that problem and can "identify." When it comes to accepting the other norms of the group, however, many newcomers balk. Common criticisms are of the religious beliefs and rituals; the party line depiction of alcoholism as progressive, arrested but never cured; the insistence on AA as the only way to recover; and the norm that AA attendance must be permanent. The insistence on abstinence ("It's the first drink that gets you drunk") has been exhaustively reviewed elsewhere in the controlled-drinking controversy. Many alcoholics, both in and out of AA, hope desperately to avoid having to make a commitment to sobriety.

The Crucial Source of Confusion

What makes newcomers' rejection of these norms interesting from the point of view of how AA works is that *the aspects of AA that may repel both alcoholic and nonalcoholic observers often fit exactly into the distorted psychology of alcoholic thinking.* This point is essential to understand both the alcoholic's resistance to AA and the researcher's sympathy with this resistance and failure to identify it as problematic. While everyone has a point that AA may be rigid, dogmatic, or nonscientific, it is also true that many alcoholics who may need help in getting sober and who could use many aspects of AA to do so will reject AA because of these characteristics. That is, there is a congruence between the intellectually honest and understandable rejection of distasteful values of the subculture and the distorted psychology of the drinking alcoholic dominated by denial who rejects AA because entry into it requires painful losses.

Clinical Examples

It is now possible to see how various alcoholics approaching AA might fan out into a range of responses to it.

A substantial majority, either because they find the group's qualities inconsistent with their own or because they are resisting treatment generally, simply never go. Some of these people can be brought in if they enter another form of treatment (see a physician, enter an alcohol rehabilitation center, or are coerced by the courts). Some of these, when they get sober, stop resisting AA and may take to it. Their resistance was to abstinence and treatment in general. Or, they are able to work through and forgive AA its faults, which they no longer find threatening. One reason newcomers are so judgmental of AA is that they are terrified of the power of what is happening to them and fear AA won't be good enough to help them. As it starts to work, they reject and judge it less.

Some, even if they stop drinking and use other supports, still refuse to go to AA. One patient, who spent his life building dreams into businesses by sheer force of will, never could abide it. "Fatuous and self-indulgent," he said, despite never having been to a meeting. "It's not for me." He stopped drinking at my suggestion after his first phone contact with me before we even met. I never did get him to go to AA.

Others find it difficult to use because of psychopathology independent of alcoholism. One phobic and depressed woman was terrified of the meetings. She went to one every three or four weeks until some friendly soul asked her out for coffee. Panicked, she never went back. She got sober with medical monitoring, antidepressants, and disulfiram. She thought about AA a lot and was jealous of people who were "brave enough to go."

Some refuse to go because no one educates them on what to expect or encourages them to use AA even though it is imperfect. Many patients who initially reject AA can use it if they are given some latitude to reject aspects that are culturally or personally alien to them. Others get help by ventilating their anxieties about AA, their experience that all the talk about alcohol made them want to drink, their fear of exposure, their shame, or their dislike of some individual interaction with a particular AA member. New attendees are shaky, self-preoccupied, sensitive, and judgmental. They may get their feelings hurt, and conclude they don't like AA.

Others refuse to use AA, but may be able to make use of some of the groups like Women for Sobriety or Rational Recovery that have spun off from AA in response to some of the common criticisms of it.

Others have difficulty with AA because of painful personal experience of it. One patient's mother had faked sobriety in AA for nearly ten years, celebrating anniversaries while secretly drinking. The patient naturally hated AA as a fraud. He was finally able to go to AA and became an enthusiastic participant, when I was able to convince him there might be many AAs and that all he needed to do was to find an AA that was not his mother's version (or perversion) of it.

AA can vary widely from region to region, from meeting to meeting, and even from night to night. Sometimes people need to be encouraged to sample a variety of meetings.

Some early alcoholics reject AA because they really can return to moderate drinking patterns and they simply cannot fit into the abstinence-based AA belief system. They threaten AA, and AA denies that what they are doing is possible. One patient who liked AA very much and stopped drinking for over a year before he returned to occasional, very abstemious alcohol use, kept going to a couple of meetings a month for four more years, but was troubled that he couldn't talk about his occasional drinking, which ranged around two drinks per month. He eventually stopped going after hearing a sponsor telling someone who had taken a single drink that he was "relapsed," "in denial," and "had to get honest."

On the other hand, when I suggested to one patient, an obsessional man, eager to please, and anxious, that he go to AA, he fervently plunged in. Despite the fact that he was literally a rocket scientist, the anti-intellectual aspect of AA didn't faze him, perhaps because he was so secure in his scientific identity. He was deeply comforted by the spiritual aspect of the program, and soothed and supported by its nurturing relationships. I was surprised. I never would have predicted he would be comfortable in AA.

Conclusion

These examples are intended to show how different people select and focus on different aspects of AA when they contact it. They find different things to love in AA and different things to hate. Sometimes, the fear and contempt and despair that create resistance can be overcome by exploration and encouragement. Sometimes not. People are surprising and intriguing in their needs and choices.

But arching over and embracing its discussion of the diversity of possible interactions that occur when different alcoholics approach AA, this chapter has attempted to show how alcoholics in general share experiences and characteristics that determine their response to AA. It has described the distorted thinking of alcoholism itself as one of the greatest obstacles to AA use or participation in any treatment.

The chapter has also tried to show how AA has tailored a range of responses and problem-solving efforts to addressing the alcoholic's resistances.

The goal of this article is to suggest how these complex subjective phenomena may operate generally so that they can be considered in "treatment matching" efforts, noted in treatment outcome studies, and perhaps evaluated in study designs for future research, especially the questions of why alcoholics are so resistant to treatment and what types of approaches make treatment more accessible to them.

References

Alcoholics Anonymous. (1952). *Twelve steps and twelve traditions.* New York: Alcoholics Anonymous World Services.

Alcoholics Anonymous. (1989). *Alcoholics Anonymous.* New York: Alcoholics Anonymous World Services.

Bean, M.H. (1975a). Alcoholics Anonymous, Part I. *Psychiatric Annals 5,* 7–61.

Bean, M.H. (1975b). Alcoholics Anonymous, Part II. *Psychiatric Annals 5,* 7–57.

Bean, M.H. (1981). Denial and the psychological complications of alcoholism. In M.H. Bean & N.E. Zinberg (Eds.), *Dynamic approaches to the understanding and treatment of alcoholism.* New York: Free Press.

Bean-Bayog, M. (1985). Alcoholism treatment as an alternative to psychiatric hospitalization. *Psychiatric Clinics of North America, 8,* 501–512.

Bean-Bayog, M.H. (1986). Psychopathology produced by alcoholism. In R. Meyer (Ed.), *Psychopathology and addictive disorders.* New York: Guilford Press.

Bean-Bayog, M.H. (1991). Alcoholics Anonymous. In D. Ciraulo & R. Shader (Eds.), *Clinical manual of chemical dependency.* Washington, D.C.: American Psychiatric Press.

Brown, S. (1985). *Treating the alcoholic. A developmental model of recovery.* New York: Wiley.

Secretary of Health and Human Services. (1990). *Seventh special report to the U.S. Congress on alcohol and health.* Rockville, MD: Public Health Service, Alcohol, Drug Abuse and Mental Health Administration, National Institute on Alcohol Abuse and Alcoholism.

Silkworth, W.D. (1976). The doctor's opinion. In *Alcoholics Anonymous* (3rd ed.). New York: General Service Office of Alcoholics Anonymous.

CHAPTER 7

Alcoholics Anonymous and Faith Development

JAMES W. FOWLER

The purpose of this chapter is to explore the usefulness of faith development theory as a vehicle for operationalizing for research the role of spirituality in Alcoholics Anonymous. Here we will assess the congruence of a dynamic, generic conceptualization of faith with the dimensions of spirituality fundamental to AA. We will also explore the potential of structural-developmental stages of faith to characterize phases and quality of recovery.

Since 1971, with research teams at Harvard and at Emory Universities, I have engaged in conducting interview research and building theory in the area of faith development (FD). Faith, as used here, is an inclusive category, not limited to religious belief or practice. It refers to the dynamic human process of finding and creating meaning in one's life. Rooted in the Piagetian (1967, 1970, 1976) psychological and epistemological tradition, also incorporating the neopsychoanalytic perspectives of Erikson (1963, 1964, 1968), our constructive developmental theory has identified seven multidimensional stages by which to give formal characterizations of developmental levels of faith consciousness.

Faith development theory has been widely employed by theorists and practitioners in the fields of religious education and pastoral counselling. We know of two graduate students who presently are writing dissertations using faith development theory to study recovering alcoholics and adult children of alcoholics. This chapter, however, marks the first occasion for me to look into the field of recovery research, and particularly to begin to relate faith development theory and research to understandings of the dynamics of Alcoholics Anonymous.

Faith Development and AA: Meaning-Making and Conversion

The Focus on Faith

In the perspective taken here, faith is understood to be a dynamic factor in the lives of all human beings and communities. Ernest Becker

113

(1968) has called our species *homo poeta*, the human creature who lives by the making and sharing of meaning. In this sense faith is a generic feature of human life.

Faith, in this generic sense, is not reducible to belief or to religion. It is true that religious traditions are intrinsic to most cultures and have evolved so that most of humankind continue to find the most comprehensive contexts for the nurture and shaping of their faith in religious traditions. For several reasons, however, it is useful to distinguish religions— or, as Wilfrid Cantwell Smith (1963) calls them, cumulative traditions— from the dynamics of faith. Faith, here, refers to the personal actions and responses involved in awakening to meanings and values, and in committing the self to centers of value, images and reality of power, and core stories that link persons to others who share them, and to an ultimate frame of reference which gives them coherence. Belief and believing constitute one important dimension of faith. But faith also involves dimensions of both the unconscious and conscious composing of and responding to meanings that are at once more personal and more generic.

Faith, then, involves relations of trust in and loyalty to centers of value, images and realities of power, and shared core stories. Faith is never purely individual. As a part of the forming of selfhood, it arises and develops in the relationships where human lives take form. Faith is a construing and shaping of relationships. In faith persons construe and shape the self's relations to others, to the self, to the world, in light of images of transcendence or an ultimate environment. Faith's construing includes cognitive, affective, and imaginal structuring. It holds together the rational and the passional.

In sum, we describe faith's activity here in the most formal terms we can muster. Faith is a dynamic process of construal and commitment in which persons find and give meaning to their lives through trust in and loyalty to shared centers of value, images and realities of power, and core stories.

Alcoholics Anonymous and Faith: A Reading Both Implicit and Explicit

AA's interpretation of human action and meaning making places an especially significant focus on emotions, attitudes, and construing cognitions and on their roles in shaping and distorting a person's patterns of relating and acting. I want to suggest that AA depicts these affective and interpretative patterns in ways that connect with the foci of FD theory. Let me explain:

Let us begin with AA's delineation of "instincts" or "drives" which have as their object the fulfillment of "natural" human needs. With these terms the author of *Twelve Steps and Twelve Traditions* (Alcoholics Anonymous, 1952, pp. 44–54) refers to the human needs for relationship; for love, sex, and reproduction; for security; for social status; for power or affectance; and for wealth or economic well-being. Due to the distorting power of emotions, attitudes, and construing cognitions, attachments to the objects or activities that fulfill these "instincts" can become excessive and addictive, constituting "sins" in AA nomenclature. These excessive attachments would correspond to distorting centers of value and images of power in FD theory.

Both implicit and explicit in AA philosophy is the assertion that alcohol addiction is linked with a destructive core story, a story that is both consciously and unconsciously operative. This core story, in its various versions, centers in the person's taking on an excessive demand for self-reliance: One is responsible for establishing one's worth, one's significance, one's viability as a person in terms of one's deeds, productivity, power, wealth, status, heroic qualities, self-control, and the like. One learns early to carry the largely unconscious burden of presenting a "false self" to the world. The strain, anxiety, and lack of real intimacy that accompany one's effort to maintain the false self and to live its core story both give rise to and rely upon the use of alcohol as a numbing for pain and as a catalyst for pseudo-spontaneity and intimacy. The use of this kind of formal language in speaking of these matters must not be allowed to mask the crucial role of alcohol in both maintaining the false self, and continually subverting it, as one falls deeper and deeper into addiction. The trapped and increasingly desperate alcoholic uses the chemical in the struggle to keep the false self going as long as possible; at the same time the chemical dependence increasingly results in behavior that is not tolerable to others and, at the deepest level, to the self. Bottoming out, and the degenerative process leading to it, can be a horrible experience.

AA's analysis of alcoholism, we may say, describes a crippling faith of use. Persons in thrall to this faith experience a lack of deep trust in either other persons or a higher power, although those holding such faith may be religious and be part of loving families. For such persons, "God" is likely to have been constructed in childhood along the lines of the primary relations in which they first took on the burden of the false self. Such a deity functions as a taskmaster God, loving conditionally and providing grace only as one continually strives to earn it.

Conversion in Faith Development Theory and Alcoholics Anonymous

Conversion in faith development perspective can be defined in this way: a significant redirection of life defining attachments, as regards one's previous conscious or unconscious centers of value and images of power, and the conscious adoption of a new identity and new core story, as part of the commitment to reshape one's life in a new community of interpretation and action. This characterization implies a process that has decisive moments of turning and redirection, but which extends over a significant period of time and involves a succession of transforming re-integrations of one's way of being a self.

Conversion in AA perspective begins when one reaches and acknowledges a state of helpless desperation in the effort to maintain the false self and the illusion that one can manage one's drinking. Bottoming out comes when some combination of self-disgust and fright at the extent of one's absolute loss of control, the terror of recognizing the devastation of one's own and others' lives, and some dim hope that one can be released and restored, coalesce. Real change begins with the readiness to admit powerlessness, to accept a new identity as an alcoholic, and to embrace the humbling identification with a community of others who have also relinquished the illusion of self-control and have admitted powerlessness *vis.* their drinking. It can mean days and weeks of going to meetings for no more conscious reason than the feeling of safety of being in rooms with accepting others where there are no bottles. Gradually it comes to mean making a commitment to enter into the 12 steps and become part of the 12 traditions of Alcoholics Anonymous. It means developing the willingness to ask for support from and accountability within its fellowship. In ways that will deepen and widen as one works the program, a person commits to a step-by-step process of transformation that combines sobriety with a growing reliance upon sponsor and friends and one's higher power, or "God as you understand Him." This conversion turns one in the direction of a core story that offers the model of a life of noncontrolling serenity, of reconciling and nondistorting relations with others and with God, and of generative investment of the self in carrying the AA message to others. As theorists like Gregory Bateson (1975) frame it, this conversion involves an epistemological shift from seeing and experiencing the self as being in symmetric (competitive, prideful) relations with others and the world, to seeing the self as being in complementary relations with others and the world. This shift means embracing a paradoxical truth: There is a kind of power that issues from acknowledged powerlessness. There is a capacity for choice and the exercise of will that is made possible by giving up the illusion—or the demand upon the self—that one can or should control everything. The admission of powerlessness allows one to move from an all-or-nothing stance to a responsible self stance.

Both in faith development and AA terms, conversion marks the beginning of an ongoing process of transformation involving fundamental change in the contents of one's faith—a change with regard to one's centers of value, one's images of power, and the core story or stories by which one unconsciously or consciously lives. In both perspectives, conversion involves appropriation of and growth in the beliefs, attitudes, skills, and action patterns of a new community. In both frameworks there is a shift from fearful and prideful self-distantiation toward the risking of trust in and the reliance upon the power of the transcendent and/or of the group. In both contexts, there may be a transformation from a "false self" to a more authentic or "true self." In both frameworks there is a shift from an ego-focused self-actualization to the mutual concerns of vocation or calling.

Stages of Faith: Patterns of Cognitive and Emotional Restructuring

A Brief Introduction to Faith Development Theory

Faith development research and theory emerged in the late seventies and early eighties. It was preceded by the work on the development of moral reasoning of Lawrence Kohlberg and his associates (1981, 1984). They, in turn, were dependent upon a tradition in philosophical psychology that began with Immanuel Kant (1969) and included centrally the cognitive developmental structuralism of Jean Piaget (1967, 1970, 1976), the symbolic interactionism of George Herbert Mead (1967), and the genetic epistemology of J. Mark Baldwin (1915). In addition, faith development theory has depended upon the psychosocial theory of ego development offered by Erik H. Erikson (1963, 1964, 1968). In its theological background it has relied upon the work of Paul Tillich (1957), H. Richard Niebuhr (1960), and the comparative religionist, Wilfred Cantwell Smith (1963).

Faith development theory attempts to account for the operations of knowing, valuing, and committing that underlie a person's construal of self/other relations in the context of an explicitly or implicitly coherent image of an ultimate environment. Faith is understood dynamically as involving both the finding of and being found by meaning; both the construction and the reception of beliefs and commitments; and it is meant to include both explicitly religious expressions and enactments of faith, as well as those ways of finding and orienting oneself to coherence and meaning in relation to an ultimate environment which is not explicitly religious. In virtually all the interviews we have conducted with recovering persons involved in AA, the distinction between being "religious" and being "spiritual" has been important to the respondent. Most affirmed that they are spiritual persons; a much smaller number claimed to be spiritual in explicitly religious ways.

In its empirical research and theory building the faith development perspective has identified seven formal, structurally definable stages in the ways persons compose and maintain their life-orienting systems of meaning and valuing. Each stage represents a structural ensemble, a set of operations of knowing and valuing, but which the person composes and maintains commitment to his or her life-grounding meanings.

Development through the stages requires both time and physical maturation, though it is not inexorably tied to either. The sponsorship of traditions, group membership, and the critical relations and experiences arising from interaction in life all affect the rate and extent of a person's ongoing development through the stages. Persons may equilibrate or arrest in a stage or a transition between stages, either for long periods of time or permanently. Certain groups support persons in their development to particular stages, but may also "seal" or "cap" their possible development to further stages. We believe that the stages are sequential and invariant. We do not have sufficient data to indicate the extent of their universality or cross-cultural validity. The following descriptions will serve as a brief overview of the structural developmental stages of faith:

- *Primal faith* (infancy): A pre-language disposition of trust forms in the mutuality of one's relationships with parents and others to offset the anxiety that results from separations which occur during infant development.
- *Intuitive-projective faith* (early childhood): Imagination, stimulated by stories, gestures, and symbols, and not yet controlled by logical thinking, combines with perception and feelings to create long-lasting images that represent both the protective and threatening powers surrounding one's life.
- *Mythic-literal faith* (childhood and beyond): The developing ability to think logically helps one order the world with categories of causality, space, and time; to enter into the perspectives of others; and to capture life meaning in stories.
- *Synthetic-conventional faith* (adolescence and beyond): New cognitive abilities make mutual perspective-taking possible and require one to integrate diverse self-images into a coherent identity. A personal and largely unreflective synthesis of beliefs and values evolves to support identity and to unite one in emotional solidarity with others.
- *Individuative-reflective faith* (young adulthood and beyond): Critical reflection upon one's beliefs and values, utilizing third-person perspective taking; understanding of the self and others as part of a social system; the internalization of authority and the assumption of responsibility for making explicit choices of ideology and lifestyle open the way for critically self-aware commitments in relationships and vocation.
- *Conjunctive faith* (early mid-life and beyond): The embrace of polarities in one's life, an alertness to paradox, and the need for multiple interpretations of reality mark this stage. Symbol and story, metaphor and myth (from one's own traditions and others') are newly appreciated (second, or willed naivete) as vehicles for expressing truth.

• *Universalizing faith* (mid-life and beyond): Beyond paradox and polarities, persons in this stage are grounded in a oneness with the power of being. Their visions and commitments free them for a passionate yet detached spending of the self in love, devoted to overcoming division, oppression and violence, and in effective anticipatory response to an inbreaking commonwealth of love and justice.

The Faith Stages by Operational Aspects

The emergence of these stages depends upon development across several structural aspects. We think of these aspects as "windows" or "apertures" giving us access to a unified ensemble of operations—a Piagetian "structure of the whole"—which underlies and gives form to faith consciousness. These aspects include level of cognitive development, social perspective taking, and moral reasoning, as well as locus of authority, bounds of social awareness, form of world coherence, and symbolic functioning.

Table 1 provides a summary overview of the structural transformations that occur in each of these aspects in the movement from one stage to another. The purpose of providing this table in this context is not to give a fully detailed orientation to this depiction of the structural dynamics of the faith stages. This can be found elsewhere (e.g., Fowler, 1981, 1986; Moseley, Jarvis, & Fowler, 1986). Rather, we introduce this overview here for reference as we turn, in the next part of this chapter, to an examination of the mutually enriching perspectives of developmental stages of faith and developmental phases of recovery through involvement with AA.

Stages of Faith and Phases of Recovery

Stephanie Brown is a pioneer in the study of how psychotherapeutic approaches and AA programs can work jointly with greater effectiveness in the recovery process. As a newcomer to this field, and as one deeply grounded in developmental theories, you can imagine my interest at being steered to the groundbreaking work of Brown and her associates on developmental phases in the recovery process. Her work has correlated developmental patterns in the recovery process with an adaptation of Piagetian structural-developmental psychology. Piaget's work is epistemological in focus, and highlights the patterns of cognitive restructuring that come with normal intellectual development. Brown has sought to integrate affective and behavioral dimensions into a Piagetian model. I have found the results stimulating and helpful.

Due to the invitation to prepare this chapter I agreed to help form and co-lead a research team at Emory to study relations between the

TABLE 1
Faith Stages by Aspects*

Aspect Stage	Form of Logic (Piaget)	Role-Taking (Selman)	Form of Moral Judgment (Kohlberg)	Bounds of Social Awareness	Locus of Authority	Form of World Coherence	Role of Symbols
0	*	*	*	*	*	*	*
I	Preoperational	Rudimentary Empathy (Egocentric)	Punishment— Reward	Family, primal others	Attachment/ dependence relationships. Size, power, visible symbols of authority	Episodic	Magical-Numinous
II	Concrete Operational	Simple Perspective-taking	Instrumental Hedonism (Reciprocal Fairness)	"Those like us" (in familial, ethnic, racial, class and religious terms)	Incumbents of authority roles, salience increased by personal relatedness	Narrative-Dramatic	One-dimensional; literal
III	Early Formal Operations	Mutual Inter-personal	Interpersonal expectations and concordance	Composite of groups in which one has interpersonal relationships	Consensus of valued groups and in personally worthy representatives of belief-value traditions	Tacit system, felt meanings symbolically mediated, globally held	Symbols multi-dimensional; evocative power inheres in symbol
IV	Formal Operation (Dichotomizing)	Mutual, with self-selected group or class— (Societal)	Societal Perspective, Reflective Relativism, or Class-biased Universalism	Ideologically compatible communities with congruence to self chosen norms and insights	One's own judgment as informed by a self-ratified ideological perspective. Authorities and norms must be congruent with this.	Explicit system, conceptually mediated, clarity about boundaries and inner connections of system	Symbols separated from symbolized. Translated (reduced) to ideations. Evocative power inheres in *meaning* conveyed by symbols

V	Formal Operations (Dialectical)	Mutual with groups, classes and traditions "other" than one's own	Prior to Society, Principled Higher Law (Universal and Critical)	Extends beyond class norms and interests. Disciplined ideological vulnerability to "truths" and "claims" of outgroups and other traditions	Dialectical joining of judgment-experience processes with reflective claims of others and of various expressions of cumulative human wisdom.	Multisystemic symbolic and conceptual mediation	Postcritical rejoining of irreducible symbolic power and ideational meaning. Evocative power inherent in the reality in and beyond symbol *and* in the power of unconscious processes in the self
VI	Formal Operations (Synthetic)	Mutual, with the Commonwealth of Being	Loyalty to Being	Identification with the species. Transnarcissistic love of being	In a personal judgment informed by the experiences and truths of previous stages, purified of egoic striving, and linked by disciplined intuition to the principle of being	Unitive actuality felt and participated unity of "One beyond the many"	Evocative power of symbols actualized through unification of reality mediated by symbols and the self

*Undifferentiated combination of basic trust, organismic courage, premonitory hope with admixtures of their opposites—preconceptual, prelinguistic mutuality.

¹Reprinted with permission from *Stages of Faith* (pp. 244–45), by J.W. Fowler (copyright 1981 by Harper & Row).

development of faith and persons in recovery through the programs of AA. We call ourselves the Project on Spirituality and Alcoholics Anonymous. As part of a pilot study to initiate our work together, in consultation with AA central offices and carefully adhering to AA principles and traditions, we designed and administered a 78-item questionnaire to volunteers personally solicited from a wide variety of AA meetings in the Atlanta area. Of the 130 persons completing questionnaires 93 (72%) agreed to be interviewed on AA and spirituality. At this writing 14 interviews with persons we selected from the volunteers have been completed, transcribed, and preliminarily analyzed. The 14 respondents (seven men and seven women) are clustered into four groups based upon the length of their sobriety. Four respondents had 3–6 months; three had 12–24 months; three had 4–6 years; four had 8 years or more. Our interviews lasted from 45 minutes to one and a quarter hours. They were recorded and transcribed.

On the basis of my analyses of this pilot sample I have found significant parallels with the phases of recovery cited by Brown (1985). (See Figure 1.) Drawing on our data and upon the operational aspects of faith development theory, I believe we have begun to be able to identify some additional dimensions of recovery as a developmental process. Table 2, building upon the framework given in Table 3-1 on page 62 of Brown (1985), outlines some of the results of our preliminary work.

As a way of illustrating and giving particular voice to the cognitive, affective, and behavioral structuring described in the enriched descrip-

FIGURE 1
Phases of Recovery[1]

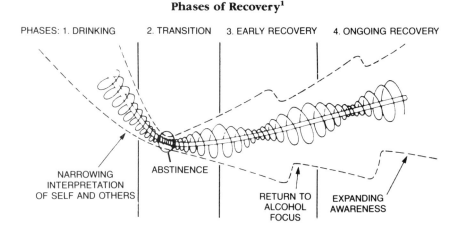

PHASES: 1. DRINKING   2. TRANSITION   3. EARLY RECOVERY   4. ONGOING RECOVERY

NARROWING
INTERPRETATION
OF SELF AND OTHERS

ABSTINENCE

RETURN TO
ALCOHOL
FOCUS

EXPANDING
AWARENESS

[1]Reprinted with permission from *Treating the Alcoholic: A Developmental Model of Recovery,* by Stephanie Brown (copyright 1985 by John Wiley & Sons, Inc.).

tions of phases of recovery offered here, let me introduce three persons we have come to know through our interview research. Since we conducted no interviews with persons in the active drinking phase, I turn first to a voice from the transition phase (pseudonyms have been assigned in all cases).

Misty: A Voice from the Transition Phase

Misty, 31 years old, grew up in a home with an alcoholic mother and stepfather and an overbearing fundamentalist grandmother. She experienced emotional, physical, and sexual abuse in her home. She consumed a lot of mouthwash before age 11. From 11 on she drank, and from 15 on had various cross addictions. Her present sobriety has extended for 13 months.

From as early as Misty can remember she has had a sense of negative identity that carried religious overtones:

> I didn't deserve for God to love me because, you know, I was out there doing all of these bad things. I was born a bad kid anyway, and you know, as I recovered I found that... God is not punishing... my God is not... because I acted... because I... drank for 15 years.... No matter what I do, God is there.

Asked how she knew she was born a bad child, she replied:

> I heard stories, all the stories, when I was growing up... from my family were about how bad I was from the start when I was a baby... they'd take me out and I'd cry all the time. I'd throw fits and later on I'd get angry and throw things.... I believed for years that [it] was true that I was born that way and my poor family had to put up with this little satan child.... I'm just now starting to change those messages around.

Earlier in the interview Misty described as spiritual experiences times when she felt wonder and a sense of safety. She said:

> I guess they help me in just feeling okay and feeling safe, when I feel like... I want a spiritual past, like there's a power greater than me, that can guide me and... that's always going to be there whether I veer off the road or whatever.... It's safety, it's hope... that if things get bad they can get good again.... That I will be okay, that I don't have to be miserable, that I don't have to die, that I have choices... I feel like now that it's not always going to be a desolate road.... There are times when I get depressed or get sad or go through a hard time and I know that there will always be other feelings that will follow good times.... I know that I can stick it out and my belief is that God tells me

TABLE 2
Relations Between Stages of Faith and Phases of Recovery*

Phase	Cognitive & Affective Structures	Stages of Faith	Therapy Strategy
Drinking	Compartmentalization & affective dissociation. Denial and selective screening of input relative to self and behavior. Fetishing on alcohol axis. Perspective taking in service of defense and manipulation. False self and pseudo self-esteem.	While cognitive functioning may be at early or full formal operations, emotional levels and selfhood likely at either the PRIMAL (age 0–2), the INTUITIVE-PROJECTIVE (age 2–6), or MYTHIC-LITERAL stage (age 7–13).	*Cognitive:* Breakdown belief system and denial. *Behavior:* Facilitate epistemological shift. *Object attachment:* Is to alcohol.
	ABSTINENCE: ALCOHOLIC IDENTITY & ADMIT OF LACK OF CONTROL, OR PRO-TEM QUITTING		
Transition	Shift in core personal identity—admits loss of control and being alcoholic. Taking new affiliation, actions and behaviors, and beginnings of new language. Imitation and concrete guidance—"getting the motions right." Follow rules, learn steps, traditions, slogans, etc. Depression or "Pink Cloud."	First efforts at relinquishing "false self." Giving up defenses and compartmentalization. Either overwhelming affect or numbness. Reduced to sensory-motor dependence (PRIMAL); magical-imitative dependence (INTUITIVE-PROJECTIVE); or rule-grounded affiliation (MYTHIC-LITERAL).	*Cognitive:* Emphasis on identification with AA stories, learning new language of recovery. *Behavior:* Emphasis on action, learning, new behaviors. *Object attachment:* To books, phone, AA meetings. *Steps:* Focus 1–3; emotions, reimaging.
Early Recovery	Begins to integrate new attitudes and behaviors: "Letting Go . . .," Asking for help. Experiences emerging "subjectivity"—new reliance upon own feelings. Begins to attend to own interiority, and to that of others. Mutual interpersonal perspective-taking. Begins to face life issues, relational changes, and layered guilt and shame. Relies upon group acceptance and support and upon sponsor.	Relying upon group and sponsor feedback to begin reimaging self. Develops first suspicions that deep core negativity about self could be mistaken. Begins to seek *personal* relation with reimaged higher power. From group meetings absorbs *tacit* understandings of AA. Struggles w/accepting acceptance. Transition to SYNTHETIC-CONVENTIONAL stage.	*Cognitive:* Self-exploration with 12 steps (& therapy): first grasp of paradox of freedom through admitted dependence. *Behavior:* Practice learnings, read literature; facing new aspects of primary relationships. *Object attachment:* Adds sponsor, principles/higher power.

| Ongoing Recovery | Begins to be able to articulate for self and others the sense of the 12 steps as ongoing process. Identifying character defects and distorting life-patterns leads to family of origin work. Learning to use methods of steps as "tools" to discipline subjectivity and to deal with the legacy of toxic emotions and emotional lability. Shapes patterns of meditation and emotional processing to maintain "balance" and serenity. | Using sponsor, group, friends and/or therapy, develops and practices third-person perspective. Reflects critically on beliefs and practices. Turns AA principles and lore into *explicit* knowledge rather than *tacit.* Combines these operations to underwrite "executive ego" and to maintain firm self-boundaries. Transition to INDIVIDUATIVE-REFLECTIVE stage of faith and frequently, to the CONJUNCTIVE stage. | *Cognitive:* Person practices cognitions & language of abstinence. Activates cognitive emphases by attending AA, reading and talking with other alcoholics. Constructs new identity as alcoholic integrates affect with alcoholic identity and behavior, reconstructs past. *Behavior:* Practices behaviors of abstinence. Activates behavioral emphasis if needed. *Object attachment:* AA principles, book, meetings, higher power. |

Note: A most salient addition to this emerging model will come from the work of the *Women's Ways of Knowing* collective (Belenky et al., 1986). With persons in the transition phase I expect we frequently will find (as with Misty in the interview discussed on page 123) that the recovering person has to emerge from the "voice" of "silence" or "received knowing." The "Women's Ways..." group have combined a structural developmental perspective with power analysis arising from feminist theory. Their discussion of the emerging of "subjectivity" is particularly pertinent for understanding more of the dynamics of the movement from the transition to the early recovery phase. Learning to "discipline" subjectivity, to use the steps to develop "procedural knowing," we believe, is a key factor in the process of moving successfully into the ongoing recovery phase.

*The phases of recovery on which this chart are structured are derived from the work of Stephanie Brown (1985). The columns dealing with "Cognitive and Affective Structuring" and "Stages of Faith" were created by James W. Fowler, Ph.D. and are based on the analysis of data from a pilot study of 14 interviews with recovering men and women who identified themselves as members of AA. Four had 3–6 months of sobriety; three had 12–24 months; three had 4–6 years; four had 8 years or more. There were seven men and seven women interviewed. The interviews were conducted by Seth Copeland, M.Div. The column entitled "Therapy Strategy" is adapted from Brown's original chart.

that ... things are going to get better. I'm not put on this earth to be miserable, and things can always get better.

Safety plays a key role in Misty's concept of her higher power:

> I guess the safety thing comes because I feel like a higher power is like a ... almost like a parent you know, within, like you know, some things, maybe when I was a child I didn't get a whole lot of good nurturing parenting, and my higher power almost like fills that need.

In speaking about the ways she is working the steps she said:

> Well, you know, it seems like when I get in the worst trouble is when I forget the fact that I'm an alcoholic ... and, I think that I have control over, and not only alcohol but other people, places and situations ... when I forget that the only control I have is over my own actions. And that's when I get in ... the worst space. And the closest to a drink. Or the closest to death.... The third step is really important for me. Cause it gives me ... that's where I mean the heart of my spirituality lies in that third step ... that's where I'm, you know, admitting there is a God, but also taking some responsibility in there, you know.

After some initial difficulty in finding an appropriate sponsor relation, Misty has found one with an older woman who has 15 years of sobriety. She describes their relationship:

> I would describe it almost like ... a parent-child relationship. And not that I'm a child like, you know, this is what you're gonna do and ... you know, the guidance part is, you know, the specific guidance, you know, like I don't know what to do, and sometimes I don't. Sometimes I need that ... and if I didn't do it that way, I know my sponsor would not ... you know, say, "Oh well," want to write me off and say, "You don't listen to me" or whatever.

Asked what kind of things she would take to her sponsor, Misty replied:

> Things involving work, involving relationships ... roommate stuff, you know, where I had to confront my roommate ... I felt like my boundaries were being violated. A lot of boundary stuff ... family, you know, how to deal with my family situations.

Misty explained that when she feels a compulsion to drink, instead of calling her sponsor she usually goes to a meeting.

Then asked how she is like or different from other people in the program, Misty says:

Well, I'm like in that . . . I'm an alcoholic and I'm powerless over alcohol and everything. I'm like them because I have the same issues as everybody that sits in the room. You know, sexual issues of all types of abuse. . . . I don't, you know, I have trouble setting boundaries, dealing with people . . . and I think all those things, dealing with low self-esteem . . . all the things I had before I came in, like I shared with probably everybody in there.

Reflecting on how she has changed since coming into recovery, Misty said,

I guess the accepting myself. . . . Before I came into recovery I didn't have a clue, as to who I was, what I like, outside of getting drunk and getting high. . . . And this is something I'm starting to discover, and I have a long way to go . . . and accepting those things, too. Accepting the good with the bad, you know, character defects with everything. . . . I used to be a person that felt like I had to be the center of attention. I had to be the entertainer and all that, and now I'm learning to just, like, sit back and be there. And just be able to, you know, to be, and not have to earn my place.

Misty's emotional and cognitive structuring of self, others, and her higher power have a great deal of quality of the intuitive-projective stage of faith. She has tried to rid herself of the accusing God who she felt cursed her with an original badness. She seeks, and sometimes feels, the presence *in her* of a loving, protecting, parent-like, nurturing God. The accepting and protecting community of AA; a sponsor who is like a guiding, but not a blaming parent; and the language that enables her to recognize some of her difficulties maintaining boundaries and claiming self-esteem and their origins; all these factors combine to give her a place to cling on a steep and scary cliff. She has difficulty identifying with many of the stories in the "Big Book." She struggles with depression and tendencies toward isolation. She still has to largely invent each new day. She has serious needs for a context where a deep reworking of her poor parenting can be experienced. Nonetheless, she finds hope and strength and caring persons in AA, and the steps are beginning to become part of her daily way of life. She is beginning to construct and trust a higher power that offers the love and the sense of safety she so deeply needs. With each new week and month of sobriety, she gains strength. Recently she has stood up to her boss and renegotiated her hours so that she doesn't have to work such erratic and dangerous shifts. Still in the transition phase, AA meets Misty supportively in many of the places where she needs to be met. The program provides a scaffolding of relationships, language, concepts, behavioral guides, and spirituality, which help lay foundations for her move into the less fragile structures of the early recovery phase.

Bob: Stable in Early Recovery

Bob is 55 years old. Eight years of sobriety have restored him to a stable job in finance, to being a sponsor for five other persons in recovery, and to an intensely committed reclaiming of his boyhood Catholic faith. He grew up in a rigidly pre-Vatican Catholic family with an alcoholic father and began drinking at 16. A product of parochial education, he considers the discipline, the dogma, and the "black and white" certainty of his boyhood Catholicism as a plus. He had a warm feeling of a loving and supporting God in his early years and "spent a tremendous lot of time meditating, praying, as part of the discipline that I was exposed to." He says that during that period when he was drinking most heavily, "in that part of life that was insane almost to the point where drinking managed my whole life, while I never openly denounced God, I was not practicing my religion as devotedly as I thought I should... there was that lull in my life where I think I lost it." Asked about the "it" he felt he lost, Bob replied:

> The *it* that I lost was what I considered to be a contact with him [God].... As I grew towards maturity and I started to look at life, and when alcohol entered my life, I lost that childish, good feeling that I had in my relationship with God. I knew he was there, I knew he was a friend, but I didn't call on him as regularly as I had prior to my drinking.... It wasn't a dislike for him, it was almost as if I wasn't visiting him anymore.

Bob speaks of his discomfort over the fact that his own four children resisted his efforts to involve them in church and parochial education. With them, and partly under the impact of the liberalization of the Catholic church after Vatican II, Bob said he decided to become a "liberal" father, letting his children make their own choices. He says, "As I look back at it at least, it was a dishonest attempt on my part, trying to rationalize my inability to manage my family the way I thought it should be."

From his present perspective, Bob seems to feel that the post-Vatican changes in the church really let him down.

> Forget all of those disciplines that you were given as a child, start using your own brain, and your own rational thought process—and my rational thought process was contaminated with alcohol, mind-altering substances.... I just saw the church as not having the same old-fashioned solid foundation it had before, when I was a child.

Bob has returned to his church and seems to rely upon its authority structure and dogma in ways that reflect the tacit knowing and reliance upon external authority characteristic of the adult synthetic-conventional stage of faith. In a similar fashion, his reliance upon AA principles and traditions exhibits a tacit (as opposed to explicit) understanding, and an unquestioning reliance upon consensual interpretations of the program. He is not aware of changes in himself, except as reflected by others with whom he interacts. Both his dependence upon interpersonal relations for support and self-knowledge, and the absence of consistent third-person perspective taking in his relations with others, begin to become clear in the following statement: "I see more of myself when I'm surrounded by other people, especially in the program, who have what I would like to have, and that is a higher level of spirituality than I do . . . I feel best about myself when I am surrounded by those kinds of people." Rather than one particular sponsor, Bob has 10 persons whom he regularly calls and who seem to function for him as a variegated group ego.

As seems characteristic of persons who have equilibrated in the structural position of early recovery, Bob's characterization of the steps and how he works them remains tacit and nonreflective:

> Oh, gracious, I never get off of step one. And that's good for me. I have, you know, they say in the program of AA, these are the steps we take, not these are the steps we work. And I have taken, I believe, to the best of my ability every one of the steps. But the one I continue to come back to each and every day, just as a reminder, is the fact that I'm an alcoholic, and my life is unmanageable, and if I can accept that, the rest of the day seems to move along in the way it's going to move along.

Largely missing in Bob's structuring in early recovery is in-depth work on family of origin issues, or addressing the issues of control, shame, and guilt in his life. His "spreading" of sponsors and his relatively surface working of the stages collude with the truce he has made of the early recovery position. He is sober and effective in his work: He has meaningful relationships with a lot of persons in AA and through his church. Though he says little about it, his marriage seems to be stable. It is a truce that seems to work for him.

CK: Emerging into Ongoing Recovery

CK is 34 years old. Like both Misty and Bob, she had some college. She works as a writer. She came from a religiously mixed home and experienced both emotional and physical abuse. She began drinking at 13. Until she joined AA at 26 she was cross-addicted with marijuana and other substances. She said, "I consider myself deeply spiritual, but not in the least religious. Spirituality plays a major positive part of my life." Asked if she has spiritual experiences, CK says:

Definitely. Almost every day now. Some bigger than others, I mean, just being alive is a spiritual experience for me. It comes in little things. I can't say that I've ever had one of those "burning bush type" experiences. . . . But, there are times, it's really when I know that I'm really having that, is when I feel life so much . . . I'm so grateful to be able to contribute in some way and to feel alive. . . . I have cats . . . I love the cats. And there are moments when I sit and, you know, the cat will be laying socked out on the sofa . . . and I'll look over and I won't see my cat anymore, per se, but I see this living thing, you know, that's also alive, and that has a life of his own. And he shares that life with me . . . I know it may sound a little sappy, but that's a whole lot of how that works. . . . Everything to me is one. And it mostly has to do with feeling, feeling a life force as it is.

Reflecting the reclaiming of subjectivity and feeling that can come with the early recovery phase, CK said:

It's important to me that I can feel anything. I spent a number of years not feeling and that's why I drank and why I did drugs, is to not feel. To not feel anything, because I couldn't deal with it. It didn't matter if it was a bad feeling or a good feeling or anything. It was all too strong, or so I thought, for me to take. And so, I anesthetized myself frequently . . . all the time. I mean, I don't pretend to know what the purpose of life is other than to be alive and so, I can't say that by not drinking and not doing drugs I have now accomplished the purpose of life, except I have! Because to me, drinking and doing drugs was a walking deadness, you know, and now it's not . . . Those kind of feelings are things I never had before. It's important to feel them, because I didn't feel anything for a long time.

In a long passage CK speaks about how sobriety has brought a widened aperture for feeling emotions of all sorts. She focuses particularly on recent work in meetings on the emotions of anger and fear. Especially interesting are her reflections on anger:

I used to think that . . . I shouldn't feel anger . . . that anger is a bad thing. And even in the Big Book it talks about, you know, "anger is a luxury that we can ill afford." What it means is that anger is one that we can't hold onto for a long time, you know, cause it's impossible, I think, to totally eradicate ourselves of anger. . . . And what I've learned . . . that there are really good ways to express anger, that anger in and of itself is not a bad emotion, but how you express it is the important thing.

I quote this long passage partly to illustrate CK's capacities for constructively critical interaction with the classic text and teachings of AA. But I also call to your attention the robust use of the pronoun, "I." CK is experiencing through AA and therapy the emergence of the strong "executive ego" that is part of the individuative-reflective stage of faith. Please note that this is not the "inflated" or "grandiose" ego that must be relinquished with Step 1. This is the chastened, hard won sense of self and self-responsibility that emerges in the processes of successful ongoing recovery.

If space permitted we could document from CK's interview how she has appropriated the steps of AA as a finely honed set of tools for working with the childhood and family of origin backgrounds of current relational or situational issues in her life. She says about the steps: "That's the kind of structure that I need, you know. Some very basic guidelines that I can just follow, no matter what it is that's bothering me.... They don't tell me what to do about a situation, they don't give advice, they are tools that if I pick them up and I use them the way that I've heard so many people in the rooms say, then I'm going to get somewhere with it. I'm going to see some change, and to me that's what it's all about, is change." She says the steps are harder now, "because I found out it's not just about not drinking and not taking drugs anymore.... The steps really work to... help me come to terms with myself and how I fit into the world. And it's a harder thing... it's a really humbling experience to really work the steps."

CK describes her relation with sponsors in AA as moving from "mentor-student" relations—"They were the gods, they were my gods through AA and what to do when I got there"—to more friend-like relations, over time. She spoke of the tremendous importance of the welcoming acceptance she felt from the beginning in AA. In recent years she has used sponsors less and has relied more upon a therapist who functions as a sponsor for her. CK is a sponsor for two other persons at present.

Summing up her experiences and how she has changed with AA, CK said:

> When I walked in the door, they said, "You only have to change one thing: everything." And I have done that... I've become a completely different person... everything is different. The way that I look at the world is different. The way that I look at life, the way that I look at me. I don't hate myself so much anymore. Every now and then I have bouts with it, you know, self-doubt mostly. Lack of confidence. I think really I don't hate myself at all anymore. I do have bouts of low self-esteem, or doubting my abilities, sometimes, but as far as the complete hatred that I had for myself before, it's gone. It's completely gone. I like myself a whole lot better now. I think other people do, too.

In some ways CK is a textbook case of successful entry and progress within the ongoing recovery phase. With the mystical turn in her spirituality, she exhibits qualities that likely will move her toward the conjunctive stage of faith. At present, however, cognitively, affectively, and behaviorally, she seems to exhibit a growingly integrated motion structured in the individuative-reflective pattern of faith and selfhood.

Conclusions and Questions for Further Research

Alcoholics Anonymous may be thought of as a richly evolved social practice—lay-led and democratic in spirit—that meets recovering persons at many of their points of need and provides community, behavioral, emotional, and spiritual disciplines that help members sustain sobriety and nurture personal transformation. From the standpoint of this observer, some of the crucial elements of AA include:

1. The practice of total acceptance and nonjudgmental solidarity, coupled with strong group accountability.
2. An insistence upon and modeling of a deep-going honesty.
3. A paradoxical account of liberation through the recognition and admission of bondage.
4. The provision of firm, yet flexible behavioral and attitudinal guidelines aimed at a safe and gradual movement toward self-responsibility.
5. The preservation and use of classic texts that offer orientation, a spiritual philosophy or theology, and narrative accounts (constituting a collective core story) that provide models of and models for recovery.
6. A system of lay and peer sponsorship grounded in the practice of tough-enough love.

In reviewing the dimensions of the AA approach to recovery I find absolutely no grounds for the popular charge that AA induces or perpetuates undue or prolonged dependence, or that it can be dismissed as the mere substitution of one addiction for another. Brown's account of the transitional, early recovery, and ongoing recovery phases, and their correlations with our stages of faith, begin to help model the dynamics of transformation and growth in quality of sobriety that AA, frequently combined with therapy and other treatment approaches, can nurture. The model also helps us understand how persons can become arrested or blocked in what AA members call "dry drunk" or "so-driety" positions.

I find that the spiritual foundations of AA participate in the democratic, pragmatist character of the movement taken as a whole. In the spirit of William James (1936), AA acknowledges and sponsors a full variety of spiritual orientations and functional images of one's higher power. At the same time, AA guards against spiritual tendencies that are divisive or that perpetuate detrimental forms of individualism. Spirituality in AA aims at a recovery of self-worth grounded in a deep-going honesty, an appropriate interdependence, making possible the recovery of feeling and creative imagination. Continuing participation in AA, with the forms and intensity of participation evolving in accordance with the quality of recovery, aims at the maintenance of balance and serenity based on a realistic recognition of one's limits, and on trust in a higher power, coupled with a pattern of generative care for others who need help in recovery.

This chapter, building on an empirical and theoretical joining of faith development theory with the work of Stephanie Brown, has argued and tried to demonstrate that there are qualitative stages or phases in the recovery process. The addition of the faith development perspective, with its seven structural aspects, provides what promises to be a helpful framework for operationalizing the dynamic range of dimensions addressed in the practices and spirituality of AA. Further enrichment and refinement of this developmental model of phases and degrees of quality of sobriety promises to be of help in studying and understanding the spirituality of AA and the role of spirituality in treatment programs of other kinds, as well.

To a new student of AA one of the most impressive factors in its cumulative practical wisdom is the way its culture of slogans, stories, terms, and practices have evolved to provide a unified system of diverse supports that meet and sustain persons in each of these phases of recovery, and in the transitions between phases or stages. Our awareness of the practical wisdom of AA practices becomes focused and vivid through the lenses of empirically observed stages of recovery. Further research refining and extending our understanding of the processes by which AA supports persons in these different phases, and in the transitions between them, could make the following desirable contributions:

First, it would be possible to communicate more adequately to the medical, psychiatric and social scientific communities, as well as to families and the lay public, the transformational dynamism of AA principles and practices. Such communication can be especially important for nonalcoholic mental health personnel, clergy, and educational communities that need to be able to work effectively with recovering persons.

Second, such research could make the AA paradigm of conversion, healing, and transformation more widely available in a culture that is riddled with addictive behaviors, and that is presently increasing the number of family contexts in which abuse, neglect, and spiritual confusion or emptiness are normative. Many persons who are not alcoholics or substance abusers are nonetheless in desperate need of places where their "false self" can be recognized and allowed to deflate. Sadly, religious communities are often not effective in providing such places or help, and, in fact, often exacerbate dynamics of shame and false selfhood. In a shame-based society we are in need of practical spiritualities that can foster personal healing and transformation. Many individuals have difficulty with the appropriate embrace of limits and strengths in spiritualities of self-responsibility. Better empirical and theoretical accounts of spiritual transformation through AA could make significant contributions toward meeting these broader societal and religious needs.

Third, such research might offer AA members perspectives that could help to make sponsorship a more reflective and informed practice. In my beginning research in this area, sponsorship strikes me as a very uneven and chancy link in the recovery support chain offered by AA.

Finally, deepened and refined research on quality and phases of sobriety could illumine such matters as the following: (a) What patterns of AA support and of treatment programs tend to contribute to *capping* persons' faith development or qualitative advances in recovery. (b) The processes by which persons choose groups or sponsors, or make changes in these in relation to the developmental changes in different phases of sobriety. (c) Why and how persons in extended recovery that includes qualitative growth gradually internalize the practice of the steps and adopt more flexible and self-responsible patterns of working their programs and of participating in meetings.

Notes

The author expresses appreciation to the following persons affiliated with Emory University who have made material contributions to the preparation of this chapter and to the perspectives that inform it: Elizabeth Howell, M.D.; Fred Marsteller, Ph.D.; Lani Walsh, M.S.; Seth Copeland, M.S.; Margaret Blevins, M.T.S.; Michael Wyatt, M.Div.; and Karen DeNicola, M.T.S.

References

Alcoholics Anonymous. (1952). *Twelve steps and twelve traditions.* New York: Alcoholics Anonymous World Services.

Bateson, G. (1975) *Steps toward an ecology of mind.* New York: Ballantine.

Baldwin, J.M. (1915). *Genetic theory of reality.* New York: AMS Press.

Becker, E. (1968). *The structure of evil.* New York: Macmillan.

Belenky, M.F., Clinchy, B.M., Goldberger, N.R., & Tarule, J.M. (1986). *Women's ways of knowing.* New York: Basic Books.

Brown, S. (1985). *Treating the alcoholic: A developmental model of recovery.* New York: John Wiley.

Erikson, E.H. (1963). *Childhood and society* (2d ed.) New York: Norton.

Erikson, E.H. (1964). *Insight and responsibility.* New York: Norton.

Erikson, E.H. (1968). *Identity, youth and crisis.* New York: Norton.

Fowler, J.W. (1981). *Stages of faith: The psychology of development and the quest for meaning.* San Francisco: Harper and Row.

Fowler, J.W. (1986). Faith and the structuring of meaning. In C. Dykstra and S. Parks (Eds.), *Faith development and Fowler.* Birmingham, AL: Religious Education Press.

James, W. (1936). *The varieties of religious experience.* New York: Mentor Books.

Kant, I. (1969). *Critique of pure reason* (Norman K. Smith, Ed.). New York: St. Martin.

Kohlberg, L. (1981). *Essays on moral development, Vol. I: The philosophy of moral development.* San Francisco: Harper and Row.

Kohlberg, L. (1984). *Essays on moral development, Vol. II: The psychology of moral development.* San Francisco: Harper and Row.

Mead, G.H. (1967). *Mind, self and society* (Charles W. Morris, Ed.). Chicago: University of Chicago Press.

Moseley, R.S.M., Jarvis, D., & Fowler, J.W. (1986). *Manual for research in faith development.* Atlanta, GA: Center for Research in Faith and Moral Development.

Niebuhr, H.R. (1960). *Radical monotheism and western culture.* New York: Harper and Row.

Niebuhr, H.R. (1989). *Faith on earth.* New Haven: Yale University Press.

Piaget, J. (1967). *Six psychological studies.* New York: Random House/Vintage Books.

Piaget, J. (1970). Piaget's theory. *Carmichael's manual of child psychology* (P. Mussen, Ed., 3d ed., Vol. 1). New York: John Wiley.

Piaget, J. (1976). *The child and reality.* New York: Penguin Books.

Smith, W.C. (1963). *The meaning and end of religion.* New York: Macmillan.

Tillich, P. (1957). *Dynamics of faith.* New York: Harper and Row.

CHAPTER 8

Therapeutic Processes in Alcoholics Anonymous

STEPHANIE D. BROWN

Despite the longevity of Alcoholics Anonymous (AA), now almost 60 years old, there has been little formal study on "how it works." There is some consensus (Kurtz, 1982; Leach, 1973; Ripley & Jackson, 1959) that it does work, in that affiliation with AA helps people stop drinking and stay stopped, although even this assumption is questioned because of a limited research base. With several exceptions (Bean, 1975a, 1975b; Beckman, 1980; Thune, 1977) there continues to be little understanding of what contributes to the achievement and maintenance of abstinence, what constitutes the process of change within AA, and what facilitates both.

The best source of information on the process of change has been AA's "Big Book" (Alcoholics Anonymous, 1955, 1976), which contains descriptions of what it was like during drinking, what happened, and what it is like now during abstinence, compiled by the first 100 members. The book combines practical experience and guidelines for change embodied in the 12 steps, also called the "program" (Alcoholics Anonymous, 1955, 1976).

Two important observers of AA also have provided interpretations of the process of change: Gregory Bateson (1971), from an anthropological-epistemological-cybernetics frame, and Harry Tiebout (1944, 1946, 1949, 1953), from a psychoanalytic perspective.

In recent years, S. Brown (1977, 1985) used all three sources as the theoretical foundation for exploring the process of recovery for self-identified abstinent members of AA. She outlined stages and tasks for the alcoholic patient and the therapist, defining a process of change that includes behavioral, cognitive, and psychodynamic factors.

These four perspectives on AA share a common theme: power and control. In this chapter, I will examine the therapeutic processes within Alcoholics Anonymous around that core issue—the relationship of beliefs about power and control to the maintenance of abstinence and the process of long-term change.

Alcoholism and Power

Alcoholism and other addictions are fundamentally related to power (Bateson, 1971; Brown, 1977, 1985; Mack, 1981; Tiebout, 1944, 1946, 1949, 1953). In its essence, addiction is characterized by a distorted, faulty belief in the power of self—the power to control one's use of a substance (Alcoholics Anonymous, 1955, 1976). The process of recovery is also related to power, but in a paradoxical way. The move from addiction into recovery is grounded in challenging and relinquishing the belief in one's power over self. Recovery does not involve finding the best way or the right way to control one's intake of a substance. Instead, recovery involves relinquishing the core belief in power over self and accepting the reality of loss of control over one's drinking or use of a substance. Drinking alcoholics often believe they are empowered by alcohol when in fact they are victimized by it. Recovering alcoholics acknowledge that they have no power over alcohol and are, in turn, empowered by this truth and their acceptance of it.

Defining Addiction and Recovery

Those who support the disease concept of addiction (Bean, 1975a,b; Jellinek, 1960; Royce, 1981) and the treatment philosophy of Alcoholics Anonymous (1955, 1976) accept the reality of the loss of control over one's use of a substance and the inability to ever regain control. Abstinence is implicit in treatment and recovery. Others (Armor, Polich, & Stambul, 1978) challenge the disease model and AA program, believing instead that addiction is a learned behavior disorder. Loss of control is the problem, but for some it is a problem that can be treated, with the ability to control one's use of a substance reclaimed or relearned. The treatment emphasis is on improved function, with a return to the use of substances considered possible. The differences in definition and emphasis are mutually exclusive and based totally on beliefs about the power of the self.

Development of Addiction

The process of developing alcoholism includes behavioral, cognitive, and affective components (Brown, 1985). In its behavioral manifestation, the individual needs to drink increasing amounts of alcohol while maintaining (the cognitive dimension) that he or she has no problem with drinking. As the addiction develops, the alcoholic is guided in behavior, perception, and explanations of reality by a belief in control. The individual must maintain two core beliefs: (1) I am not alcoholic, and (2) I can control my drinking. Evidence to the contrary must be denied, rationalized, or explained as something else. The faulty belief in the power to control one's drinking serves as an organizer of beliefs about self, others, and the world (Brown, 1985).

As addiction progresses, the individual's view of self, others, and the world becomes increasingly influenced by the need to deny the reality of the drinking behavior and, at the same time, to maintain it. Alcohol, or the need for alcohol, and the denial of that need become the central organizing principle in the individual's life. The core of the faulty logic and denial system rests on the following premise:[1]

> I am not drinking too much. I have not lost control *and* I need to drink this much because....

The reason is, of course, something else that becomes identified as the "real" problem:

> I need alcohol to cope with the kids, to regulate my mood swings, to bind my anger at my husband, to compete with men for power or for prestige, to enhance my self-esteem, to provide insulation for my nerves, to get to sleep, or to treat my depression.

According to Alcoholics Anonymous (1955, 1976) and, more recently, self-psychologists (Khantzian, Halliday, & McAuliffe, 1990), alcohol or other substances provide the substitute for something missing in the structure of the self. The substance provides a false illusion of security, esteem, and power, all of which feel as if they come from within. Thus, they soon become essential to provide a sense of well-being that is not present without the substance. The illusion of power comes from outside the self. This illusion, and the increasing need for more of the substance, create a growing bind:

> My belief in my own power—my ability to control my drinking—kept the whole addictive cycle intact.

Theory Foundation

Tiebout (1944, 1946, 1949, 1953) and Gregory Bateson (1971) have provided conceptual frameworks based on the concept of control to explain the logic of addiction and recovery and the processes of change that occur within AA. These theorists have emphasized the faulty belief in the power of the self as a central dynamic of addiction, and the relinquishment of that belief in self-power as central to recovery.

Central to a "theory" of change within AA are the concepts of surrender and acknowledgment of powerlessness, or loss of control. At the core is paradox: it is precisely the deep acceptance of loss of control—surrender—that forms the foundation for empowerment and deep internal change of individuals in recovery.

In psychiatric theory, the move from drinking into abstinence has been compared to a conversion phenomenon that follows an act of "surrender" (Tiebout, 1949). The process is developmental. The alcoholic requires more and more alcohol to produce the same effect. The individual also begins to experience consequences related directly to drinking or to denial and distorted thinking. The alcoholic begins to be "cornered" by the tension of the double bind: needing more alcohol, but denying that need or explaining it as something else.

According to Tiebout (1944), surrender is the point when the tension breaks and reality wins. Surrender is the acceptance of reality on the unconscious level, the giving up of one's belief in self-power or control. Reality is the loss of control—powerlessness over alcohol.

Several members of AA tell the "story" of their drinking, illustrating the conversion of their beliefs about control.

> I don't know how I went on for so long! It was so obvious to everyone in my family that I *had* to have my drinks. I never allowed myself to know that. I simply explained my drinking as a "choice," to treat myself, to relax, to pamper my hurt feelings, or to drop out emotionally and get some space. And I blamed everyone else for the stress in my life that made me need to treat myself in the first place. What a vicious cycle of denial. Then one day it all broke. While driving, I was stopped for weaving across the center line. I was so humiliated. I just couldn't believe it was me standing beside my car with the light shining in my eyes. I knew, for a brief moment, that it was over—that I had failed the sobriety test—that I was an alcoholic. That moment was a relief. But it only came after I was backed into a wall.

Another individual illustrates:

> I had carried on for years with no sign of any chips in my denial. I insisted, or screamed if necessary, that I could control my drinking, and everyone should mind their own business. Then one day I saw the hurt on my daughter's face as I staunchly upheld my right to drink. Her look bore the truth as I could not see it in myself. I knew I was an alcoholic, and I could not control my drinking. I have not had a drink since that afternoon.

These two examples illustrate the AA concept of "hitting bottom," surrender, and the conversion experience. Together they involve a personal challenge to one's deepest beliefs, in this case related to the belief in the power to control one's drinking. Tiebout suggested that the belief in self-power, which precludes surrender and acceptance of reality, is fueled by defenses of defiance and grandiosity: "Grandiosity claims that there is nothing you cannot master and control, though the facts demonstrate the opposite" (1953, p. 52).

Defiance means that individuals hold tenaciously to their belief in self-control by simply defying the reality of its opposite. "Defiance is a trustworthy shield against the truth and all its pressures. Defiance masquerades as a real and reliable source of inner strength and self-confidence since it says, in essence 'nothing can happen to me because I can and do defy it.' For people who meet reality on this basis, life is always a battle" (Tiebout, 1953, p. 51).

Bateson outlined a theory of alcoholism in cybernetic terms (the relationship of parts to a whole and the process of establishing and maintaining a dynamic equilibrium or balance) emphasizing, like Tiebout, the critical significance of defeat, or what Tiebout and AA call "hitting bottom." Bateson outlined how AA embodies in its form, structure, and language his concept of a system in which the parts are in a complementary rather than a competitive relationship and balance with one another. According to Bateson:

> The first two steps of AA are as follows: (1) We admitted that we were powerless over alcohol and that our lives had become unmanageable. (2) We came to believe that a power greater than ourselves could restore us to sanity (A.A., 1939). Implicit in the combination of these two steps is an extraordinary, and I believe, correct idea: the experience of defeat not only serves to convince the alcoholic a change is necessary; it is the first spiritual experience. The myth of self-power is thereby broken by the demonstration of greater power. (Bateson, 1971, p. 3)

Like Tiebout, Bateson characterized the individual as locked into a paradoxical and vicious cycle of alcoholic drinking and thinking, maintained by pride (that is, the belief in the ability to maintain control of one's drinking). Alcoholic pride places alcoholism—the reality of loss of control—outside the self with the individual engaged in resisting or controlling it. Pride is closely related to power. The individual is engaged in an endless struggle to disprove or defy the reality of loss of control.

Bateson characterized the drinking alcoholic as locked into a symmetrical, competitive relationship with the self and other. Drinking alcoholics must prove repeatedly that the bottle cannot kill them, that they *can* control their drinking.

According to Bateson, the symmetrical, competitive relationship is a dichotomous one, with an implicit winner and loser. The individual is winning, losing, good, bad, powerful, not powerful. The battle or contest is centered on control. The symmetrical position is also grounded implicitly in a concept of "power over," meaning that one person dominates another, or one part of the self willfully conquers or controls another part.

Bateson suggests that the conversion outlined by Tiebout and experienced by AA members reflects a dramatic shift from the dichotomous, symmetrical position to "an almost purely complementary view of his relationship to other and to the universe or God" (1971, p. 11).

Acceptance of loss of control over alcohol—precisely the acceptance of defeat within a symmetrical frame—frees the individual to make this shift to a complementary frame. Central to the complementary framework is a sense of being part of something larger than the self: the philosophy of AA emphasizes the importance of the belief in a power greater than the self. The shift from symmetrical pride to a complementary view of oneself in relation to others describes the core internal change necessary to sustain abstinence and recovery. Bateson underscores the central significance of the systemic, part-to-whole relationship:

> The single purpose of A.A. is directed outward, and is aimed at the noncompetitive relationship to the larger world. The variable to be maximized is a complementary one and is of the nature of "service" rather than dominance. (1971, p. 16)

Bateson emphasized the critical and necessary function of a belief in a higher power to facilitate and maintain the shift in personal view. Central to the shift is relinquishment of a belief in self-control.

Other theorists have examined a more general process of change. Watzlawick, Weakland, and Fisch (1974) include paradox in differentiating first- and second-order changes. First-order change occurs within a consistent and logical framework, with no change in underlying premise; second-order change requires a leap and a shift in underlying premise. Second-order change corresponds to Tiebout's conversion phenomenon and Bateson's shift from symmetrical to complementary.

Higher Power

The concept of personal power "over" is grounded in the symmetrical, dichotomous frame that automatically places the individual in a position of self-evaluation, based on relative standing. A belief in "power over" one's control of a substance is at the heart of the addictive struggle.

A "power from within" model may still be embedded in a symmetrical frame. It is the corresponding dichotomous struggle internalized. The individual experiences extreme ambivalence or becomes pitted against opposing internal wishes, needs, values, or beliefs, while struggling to control one part of the self *against* the other.

The dichotomous frame is self-reinforcing, primitive, and resistant to change because attempts at resolution remain anchored within the symmetrical frame. Only by shifting the frame or the basic premise can the dichotomy be resolved. The shift involves paradox. Still within the symmetrical frame, individuals must come to "know" at the deepest level the deepest truth: they are powerless to control their own drinking or use of a substance. It is the surrender of one's belief in self-power or control. Paradoxically, surrender—still within the symmetrical frame—is the essential first step toward the ultimate acquisition of power from within. In its most simple form, the individual transfers the belief in power from the self to a power greater than the self, a power paradoxically constructed by the individual.

This transfer moves the person to a complementary frame. In essence, the relinquishment of a false belief in the power of the self enables the individual to place the self *in relation to* others on an equal level. Power or control is vested in something greater than the self *and* greater than another.

Only with a shift to a complementary frame can the struggle for power over or against be transformed. The alcoholic acknowledges lack of power over self, turns the source of control "over" to an abstract, external, "higher power" that the individual defines, and then, through the process of recovery, reclaims and internalizes. Individuals in long-term recovery experience deep feelings of safety, trust, well-being, and power coming from within by virtue of having relinquished the very source of that power.

In AA, the repeated relinquishment of self-power and the construction of belief in a power greater than the self form the base for deep change in a long-term process of recovery.

The Process of Recovery

The acceptance of loss of control of one's drinking forms the heart of what is called in AA "hitting bottom" or surrender. With acknowledgment of loss of control, the individual becomes ready to make the shift into abstinence and recovery. While the move into recovery is facilitated by acknowledging loss of control, sustained recovery also requires a corresponding acceptance of one's inability to regain control, which is implicit in accepting the identity of an alcoholic. Loss of control is seen as permanent rather than temporary, with a hope to return to drinking and corresponding "self-control" relinquished.

Recovery is a radical process of second-order change, of transformation in one's deepest beliefs and behavior. Whereas the drinking individual ordered the view of self around a belief in control, the recovering person learns to do just the opposite: the acknowledgment of loss of control and the identity as an alcoholic become the new organizing principles ordering behavior as well as cognitive and affective development in recovery (Brown, 1991a,b).

Acknowledgment of lack of power is a first step in halting the vicious cycle of addiction. But it does not in itself sustain recovery. Acknowledgment of lack of power within a complementary schema does.

In the move from drinking into recovery, and frequently during the process of recovery, acknowledgment of lack of power remains embedded within a symmetrical frame, and therefore must be interpreted as a defeat, failure, or victimization. From a symmetrical view, loss of control is viewed as a pathological surrender, a weakness. The inclination is to look for "solutions" that will help the individual regain control. This first-order (Watzlawick et al., 1974) framework typically focuses on what action to take. The individual remains locked into a view of self as failing or inadequate, with efforts directed toward reversal: how to regain control *over* self or *over* another; how to be the winner, rather than the loser; how to be the one in power, rather than the victim. This symmetrical, dichotomous frame eliminates the possibility of equality, and it may contribute to relapse as well. A patient named Peggy illustrates this well:

> I struggled for months in early recovery. I just couldn't let go of the notion that being alcoholic was bad, and I had failed miserably by losing control. I kept thinking of all the ways to get it back so I could be a "normal" drinker like everyone else. I just couldn't accept it, and get on with my life as a sober alcoholic. My idea of recovery was not to be an alcoholic anymore. I finally started drinking again. Luckily, it was just as awful as before. I was not going to become "normal" at this business of drinking. After a few months I really surrendered, and now understand much better what being powerless really means.

It is only with the acquisition of a complementary framework and the development of a "higher power," to which control is turned over, that acknowledgment of lack of power becomes in itself empowering within a complementary frame. Acknowledgment of lack of control functions as an equalizer—a universal reminder of ultimate human frailty. Individuals in recovery, by acknowledging their loss of control and lack of power, come to recognize that the basic fundamental equality of all human beings rests in helplessness and an inability to control self or other. Peggy continues:

> When I could really feel the depth of my defeat and my complete inability to control by drinking, I could recognize my need for help. Gradually the idea of a higher power made perfect sense, though it's taken me years to really develop

a working relationship with a power greater than myself. Now I see myself as a small part of a much larger universe, running without my control or authority. I have come to trust and feel safe with my own conception of my higher power.

Individuals do not move from dependence on a substance to no dependence. In fact, there is no such thing as "no dependence." Surrender and the process of recovery involve acceptance of one's ultimate dependence instead of denial, with a fundamental shift in the object: the individual moves from a belief in control or reliance on the self or substance to reliance on the AA group, the 12 steps of recovery that AA members call "the program," and, ultimately, to a more abstract higher power, at first constructed and attributed outside the self, and later internalized. The result is paradoxical, as an alcoholic with many years of recovery illustrates:

I am dependent on my higher power, I am dependent on the fellowship of AA, and I am more independent in all areas of my being than I have ever known.

This thinking—that dependency is a natural and normal aspect of ongoing human development—matches current psychoanalytic views. Theorists such as Mahler (1975), Erikson (1963), and Bowlby (1980, 1988) now emphasize the significance of human attachment and lifelong dependence to healthy development.

The road to sustaining and solidifying the transformation or conversion is difficult. The ongoing process of recovery involves active and continuing change in behavior and in the deepest beliefs and values about one's self. This behavioral, cognitive, and affective developmental process is ordered and contained by the 12 steps.

The 12 Steps

Many observers have cataloged their subjective and objective impressions of and hypotheses about Alcoholic Anonymous' success (Alibrandi, 1982; Beckman, 1980; Kurtz, 1980; Maxwell, 1984; Thune, 1977), Brown (1985) suggests that the process of change in AA can be compared with good psychotherapy—success is defined as behavioral abstinence for alcoholics, along with a greater capacity and tolerance for complex self-knowledge and potential for change at behavioral, cognitive, and affective levels. This view also fits with Bateson's and Tiebout's schemas.

Brown (1985, 1991a) suggests that AA, the 12 steps, and the structure of "the program" (AA, 1939, 1955, 1976) embody a complex multidimensional model of long-term treatment and change that surpasses any single-focused psychotherapy intervention or treatment for alcoholism. She offers the radical suggestion (Brown, 1991a) that AA can be viewed as a comprehensive primary treatment itself, rather than an adjunct to traditional forms of psychotherapy. Brown (1991a) further suggests that the form and structure of AA provide a model for integrating different levels of traditional psychotherapy (behavioral, cognitive, psychodynamic) to better fit the changing needs of the alcoholic according to stage in recovery.

As outlined earlier, the 12 steps of AA are organized around acceptance of loss of control (Step 1), with the acceptance of powerlessness over alcohol seen as the base for liberation and change, following surrender and an experience of defeat in one's efforts to control drinking. There is recognition that continuing acceptance of powerlessness cannot be maintained in a void. Step 2 offers a "power greater than self" to hold the individual's dependence. In addition to facilitating the shift from symmetric to complementary, the higher power also offers a continuing challenge to feelings of omnipotence, defiance, and grandiosity, character traits that accompany active alcoholism. It is suggested in AA's *Twelve Steps and Twelve Traditions* (Alcoholics Anonymous, 1952) that ongoing ego reduction is necessary to maintain sobriety.

Step 3 is seen as an action step that also cuts away at self-will. The first three steps are a direct assault on pathological egocentricity or narcissism, a condition that includes an inflated unrealistic belief in self-power.

Step 4, the moral inventory, introduces rigorous uncovering self-examination and introspection, a process of piercing psychological defenses of denial, projection, rationalization, and self-delusion through acknowledging the realities of past behaviors and beliefs.

Steps 6 and 7 reflect a change in attitude, from self-power and egocentricity to deference, with a willingness to learn from others and become "part of." Acceptance of basic dependency and human need is implicit. So, too, is the cultivation of humility, a realistic view of one's self as part of a larger whole. From a symmetrical frame, deference and humility are equated with passivity and negative defeat and therefore must be resisted.

Steps 8 and 9 involve restitution, an acceptance of responsibility for the consequences of one's drinking, which also relieves guilt and thus frees the individual to move forward in the present. These steps also introduce a focus on interpersonal relationships.

Steps 10, 11, and 12 are often called maintenance steps by AA members (Alcoholics Anonymous, 1952). Geared toward the present, these steps emphasize continuing reliance on a higher power that allows the individual to maintain a stable attitude of ego reduction, honesty, humility, deference, gratitude, and responsibility to help others—all attitudinal qualities or character traits that maintain the individual in a complementary frame, part of something larger, rather than the center. With these steps as a structure, which both contains individuals in and provides the guidelines for a reorganization of the self, individuals move through the stages of recovery.

Stages of Recovery

The processes of addiction and recovery are developmental (Brown, 1977, 1985), proceeding in stages, each with defined tasks. The first stage is drinking, based on a belief in self-power. The process of recovery is built on abstinence, grounded in a transformation in belief: the individual acknowledges lack of self-control or self-power and identifies as an alcoholic. The process of recovery then proceeds through the stages of transition, early recovery, and ongoing recovery.

Transition

The transformation of belief heralding the transition from drinking to abstinence is radical and profound. It is a period of high vulnerability and dependence requiring a very active, concrete focus to sustain the new truth and the new behaviors that support it. Initially, individuals involved in recovery programs, particularly the 12-step programs of AA and Al-Anon, will learn to replace their addictive dependence—on a substance or another person—with dependence on new objects, including 12-step meetings, literature about recovery, and an abstinence-oriented support group.

Rather than frustrating or denying dependency needs, newly recovering alcoholics are instructed to ask for help and to gratify their needs through the structure of the recovery program. This is a critically important mechanism: acknowledgment of loss of control and lack of self power is not tantamount to frustration of need and helplessness. Nor is it a prescription for inaction or the solidification of a victim position, as Mike believed.

> When I was first sober, I was determined not to be dependent, helpless, or wishy-washy, but I couldn't get myself out of the bind that said the only way not to be dependent is to be able to drink and control it. I would hear others talking about being dependent on AA and their higher power and it drove me crazy. I seemed to think I could live without any dependency at all. It took a long time to realize that I am a very needy person and that is perfectly fine! I have learned that I have needs and that I can take care of them. The AA program provides the source for meeting my dependency needs in a healthy way.

The critical task of transition is to refrain from acting on impulses, returning to old beliefs based on self-power and the behaviors that accompany those beliefs: use of a substance with the illusion of power and self-control regained.

The process of transition involves active behavior change—learning behaviors that support abstinence rather than drinking, as Mike illustrates:

> In the beginning, all I could think about was alcohol—my beloved drinks! I had to pay strict attention so I would not suddenly, surprisingly find myself taking a drink when I had no conscious intention of doing so. I listened closely to others and asked advice: what did I need to do in order not to drink? For a while, it meant coming to AA meetings every day, talking on the phone, reading about alcoholism, and going for a walk at cocktail hour. I was amazed that I had no idea how to change my behavior when it got right down to it. And changing my behavior certainly came first.

The transitional stage also involves cognitive change. The recovering person begins to challenge denial, uncovering evidence to support the reality of loss of control. This process is the beginning of cognitive reconstruction, a central task of recovery, congruent with behavior change. As recovering alcoholics begin to solidify their new behaviors, they also begin to reconstruct their "stories" of themselves and their drinking. Newly recovering individuals in AA construct a revised narrative of their lives related to drinking: what was it like in the past while drinking, what happened (the elements leading to or comprising surrender), and what it is like now in recovery. Recovering alcoholics in AA order their reconstructed views of self, their identities, around the centrality of their drinking in the past and the reality of loss of control. At the same time, they begin an ongoing process of cognitive construction, building new identities in the present as recovering alcoholics, also based on continuing acknowledgment of loss of control.

The alcoholic in transition is dealing with a radical shift in basic premises about self and is usually focused on concrete behavioral and cognitive changes, as Mike demonstrated. These individuals are more likely to feel frightened (Royce, 1981) than empowered, as they relinquish the false safety of the belief in control. They may, however, feel a sense of freedom, of a tremendous burden lifted, as they are freed from their own denial and distortion. The great danger in this period of transition is the threat of reverting to a symmetrical frame of thinking from which they must view abstinence and loss of control as a defeat. A newly abstinent individual may be faced immediately with acknowledging the reality of behavior and the functions it served. For many, the transition stage is fraught with conflict and fear. What does it mean to be alcoholic? What will it mean to be abstinent?

Problems in recovery may not center on the first step of acceptance of loss of control, but rather on the exploration process, as recovering individuals begin a process of deep self-examination similar to an in-depth uncovering psychotherapy, ordered and contained by the 12 steps.

Early Recovery

Early recovery is distinguished from the transitional phase primarily on the basis of impulse (Brown, 1985). The recovering person is less threatened with impulses to return to old behavior and belief, although the lure of the belief in control and the behaviors that accompany it is always a potential threat. Resistance may continue as a problem.

The shift from the symmetrical power-focused victim position requires development of a sense of self independent of a tie to the substance. For many, the intuitive recognition of this basic developmental task is tremendously threatening. Recovery signifies for many the development of autonomy and the threatened loss that independence or development of self implies. Peggy again illustrates:

Once I really acknowledged my lack of control, recovery was more difficult in a way. Then I had to face the horrible anxiety I felt about every change I made on my own behalf. It took a long time to figure out that I had any needs of my own—I used to answer every question about myself with a statement about my husband or children. Much of recovery has been a struggle, as I repeatedly resist making positive changes which feel aggressive or damaging to my husband and family at the same time. Anything that will result in a stronger sense of myself also feels hostile to them.

Many men and women revert to the illusion of control with the hope of finding a diversion from or alternative to the responsibilities of self-development. It is extremely difficult to relinquish the illusion of finding a good parent or caretaker outside the self in the form of another individual or a substance. The problem reverts again to finding the individual or substance that will provide what is missing or divert the individual from self-development. The latter means "digging," deep introspection and challenge of old beliefs and behaviors, outlined in Steps 4 and 10. This in-depth self-exploration focuses on the past and the present and involves awakening unconscious and unknown aspects of the self. The threat of this focus on self-development often sends the individual back to a symmetrical position, evidenced by the following logic:

There is something wrong with me that I can't find a caring partner. . . . There is something wrong with others because I always end up being hurt. If only I could find the right person, or the right strategy, I could make this person love me. . . . One drink or pill will provide what is missing. The bottle fills the hole.

In early recovery, like transition, individuals are instructed to maintain abstinent behavior and to "fill the hole" with 12-step meetings, literature, and association with abstinent friends. The focus remains on behavioral or cognitive change to support abstinence. The continuing development of self, in concert with the development of a belief in a higher power, is the task of ongoing recovery.

Ongoing Recovery

Alcoholics in ongoing recovery maintain a concrete behavioral and cognitive focus but also incorporate deeper uncovering self-exploration, which occurs through the structure of the 12 steps and frequently the process of psychotherapy as well. The work of ongoing recovery is very similar to and compatible with a psychodynamic, uncovering therapy process. Through Steps 4, 8, 9, and 10, individuals question past and present, conscious and unconscious motivation, challenging behavior and beliefs. The security and stability of sobriety, maintained by a continuing behavioral and cognitive focus, permit the emergence of affect, also related to past and present, without stimulating a return to drinking.

People in 12-step programs also speak of the heart of ongoing recovery as spiritual development (Brown, 1985), encompassed in the belief in a power greater than the self. This higher power may take different forms, from concrete reliance on the greater power of the AA group in early recovery to an abstract personal concept of God developed in ongoing recovery. It is the function rather than the form that is significant (Brown, 1985). Recovering alcoholics acknowledge loss of control over drinking and extend that acceptance to all areas of their lives. They recognize their ultimate helplessness and basic dependency fundamental to all human beings. They experience what Tiebout referred to as ego deflation or reduction, a continual striving for humility. These are challenges to the natural resurgence of grandiosity, defiance, and an inflated belief in the power of the self—all threats to sobriety.

In drinking, transition, and even early recovery, individuals frequently reject the notion of a higher power, particularly referenced to concepts of God. In fact, much resistance to AA rests in the erroneous belief that AA is religious. Individual AA members describe their fellowship as spiritual instead. As Bateson noted, the concept of a higher power is profound in function, as it facilitates relinquishment of a belief in the power of self. Yet, ironically, individuals remain locked in the destructive, painful cycle of addiction, precisely because they must deny dependence. Individuals continue to assert that the bottle or the substance will not win. The power of the self is seen as ultimate, and it locks the individual into pathological dependence. Mike sums it up:

> I'd say the essence, the heart of my recovery, has been the development of my relationship with my higher power. In the beginning, I was a real skeptic. I cringed when people spoke about God or a higher power. Yet all the while I was trusting myself to learn from others in AA meetings. Though I couldn't see it, I could feel it. I knew intuitively that other people in AA had something special, and if I let them show me, I could have it too.
>
> In the beginning it just meant sobriety, and of course it still does. But recovery is so much more. I have a good relationship with myself and others based on getting myself out of the center. All of this came when I could really believe in a higher power and learn to live with that reality guiding my life. It just means there's something bigger than me.

Acceptance and active construction of a higher power sustain individuals in a complementary frame, which then provides a new foundation for relationships with self and others. The individual is dependent on a higher power and equal with others. The work of recovery involves the development of autonomy, grounded in acceptance of one's basic human dependence, and the development of mature interdependent relationships with others. Paradoxically, by relinquishing a belief in self-power, people in recovery experience themselves as autonomous and empowered from within.

Note

1. Material in block quotes represents statements of individuals whose names have been changed or deleted.

References

Alcoholics Anonymous. (1939, 1955, 1976). *Alcoholics Anonymous: The story of how many thousands of men and women have recovered from alcoholism.* New York: Alcoholics Anonymous World Services.

Alcoholics Anonymous. (1952). *Twelve steps and twelve traditions.* New York: Alcoholics Anonymous World Services.

Alibrandi, L. (1982). The fellowship of Alcoholics Anonymous. In E.M. Pattison and E. Kaufman (Eds.), *Encyclopedic handbook of alcoholism.* New York: Gardner Press.

Armor, D.J., Polich, J.M., & Stambul, H.B. (1978). *Alcoholism and treatment.* New York: Wiley.

Bateson, G. (1971). The cybernetics of self: A theory of alcoholism. *Psychiatry, 34* (1), 1–18.

Bean, M. (1975a). Alcoholics Anonymous I. *Psychiatric Annals, 5*(2), 7–61.
Bean, M. (1975b). Alcoholics Anonymous II. *Psychiatric Annals, 5*(3), 7–57.
Beckman, L. (1980). An attributional analysis of A.A. *Journal of Studies on Alcohol, 41*(7), 714–726.
Bowlby, J. (1980). *Attachment and loss: Volume 3.* New York: Basic Books.
Bowlby, J. (1988). *A secure base.* New York: Basic Books.
Brown, S. (1977). *Defining a process of recovery in alcoholism* (Doctoral dissertation, California School of Professional Psychology, Berkeley).
Brown, S. (1985). *Treating the alcoholic: A developmental model of recovery.* New York: Wiley.
Brown, S. (1991a). Adult children of alcoholics: The history of a social movement and its impact on clinical theory and practice. In M. Galanter (Ed.), *Recent developments in alcoholism: Vol. 9. Children of Alcoholics* (pp. 267–285). New York: Plenum Press.
Brown, S. (1991b). Children of chemically dependent parents: A theoretical crossroads. In T.M. Rivinus (Ed.), *Children of chemically dependent parents: Multiperspectives from the cutting edge.* New York: Brunner/Mazel.
Erikson, E. (1963). *Childhood and society.* New York: Norton.
Jellinek, E.M. (1960). *The disease concept of alcoholism.* New Brunswick, NJ: Rutgers Center of Alcohol Studies.
Khantzian, E.J., Halliday, K.S., & McAuliffe, W.P. (1990). *Addiction and the vulnerable self.* New York: Guilford.
Kurtz, E. (1980). Why A.A. works. *Journal of Studies on Alcohol, 43*(1), 38–80.
Leach, B. (1973). Does Alcoholics Anonymous really work? In P.G. Bourne and R. Fox (Eds.), *Alcoholism: Progress in research and treatment.* New York: Academic Press.
Mack, J. (1981). Alcoholism, A.A.., and the governance of the self. In M.H. Bean and N.E. Zinberg (Eds.), *Dynamic approaches to the understanding and treatment of alcoholism.* New York: Free Press.
Mahler, M., Pine, F., & Bergman, H. (1975). *The psychological birth of the human infant.* New York: Basic Books.
Maxwell, M. (1984). *The A.A. experience.* New York: McGraw-Hill.
Ripley, H.S., & Jackson, J.K. (1959). Therapeutic factors in Alcoholics Anonymous. *American Journal of Psychiatry, 116,* 44–50.
Royce, J.E. (1981). *Alcohol problems and alcoholism.* New York: Free Press.
Thune, C. (1977). Alcoholism and the archetypal past: A phenomenological perspective on Alcoholics Anonymous. *Journal of Studies on Alcohol, 38*(1), 75–88.
Tiebout, H.M. (1944). Therapeutic mechanisms of Alcoholics Anonymous. *American Journal of Psychiatry, 100,* 468–473.
Tiebout, H.M. (1946). Psychological factors operating in Alcoholics Anonymous. In B. Glueck (Ed.), *Current therapies of personality disorders* (pp. 145–165). New York: Grune and Stratton.
Tiebout, H.M. (1949). The act of surrender in the psychotherapeutic process with special reference to alcoholism. *Quarterly Journal of Studies on Alcohol, 10,* 48–58.
Tiebout, H.M. (1953). Surrender vs. compliance in therapy with special reference to alcoholism. *Quarterly Journal of Studies on Alcohol, 14,* 58–68.
Watzlawick, P., Weakland, J., & Fisch, R. (1974). *Change.* Palo Alto, Calif.: Science and Behavior Books.

CHAPTER 9

Cognitive Processes and Change in Disease-Model Treatment

JON MORGENSTERN AND BARBARA S. MCCRADY

A lcoholics Anonymous is a significant social movement in the United States. Through its activities and ideology, or used as one aspect of a broader treatment approach, its therapeutic message impacts the overwhelming majority of alcoholics seeking treatment in this country. Moreover, when viewed as the model for other 12-step programs and for the "recovery movement," its influence may rival that of professional treatment for mental health problems (Room, 1993). Both because of its popularity and its unique nonprofessional approach to treatment (e.g., the use of peers as therapeutic agents and its emphasis on spirituality), the therapeutic mechanisms employed by AA have been the focus of professional comment. While theorists have offered a variety of systematic interpretations of change processes occurring in AA (e.g., Brown, 1985; Kurtz, 1982), there have been few empirical studies. The topic of this chapter is cognitive change in AA and disease model treatment. We will describe some aspects of ongoing empirical research we are conducting on treatment processes in alcohol treatment. Our aim is to provide a conceptual framework for understanding how change processes in AA might be studied as well as to suggest how the research methods we used might serve as one paradigm for studying cognitive change in AA.

Unlike the study of psychotherapy, there has been relatively little research on treatment process in alcohol treatment. Until quite recently the majority of clinical research on alcoholism has entailed endpoint evaluations of treatment outcomes. As a result, little is known about change processes that occur during treatment which facilitate positive outcomes. Lack of a well-documented understanding of how change occurs in alcohol treatment has left a vacuum, which has, at times, been filled with rather dramatic and contradictory claims, particularly concerning disease model treatment. For instance, some have claimed (McElrath, 1988) that this approach "is the most successful form of treatment for chemical dependency in recorded history." Others have stated that such an approach is not only not helpful, but actually detrimental to many individuals trying to resolve an alcohol/drug-related problem (Peele & Brodsky, 1991). More study is needed to learn how change occurs in specific alcohol treatment models, whether there are common change processes that occur in alcohol treatment, irregardless of treatment approach, and how such processes differ from those occurring in "natural recovery."

Two approaches have been used to study treatment process in the psychotherapy literature. One approach has centered on examining broad nonspecific factors such as "combating demoralization" (Frank, 1974) or relationship factors, such as having "a helping relationship with a therapist" (Luborsky et al., 1975). Such elements are common to most treatment models. Another approach has studied change processes that are specific to a particular treatment approach. One example of this is the work of DeRubeis, Hollon, and others (e.g., Hollon, DeRubeis, & Evans, 1987) examining the role of cognitive change as a causal mediator in cognitive-behavioral treatment for depression. The broad aim of these studies is to establish that the focus of the therapist's interventions, in this case altering dysfunctional cognitions, is the causal mediator of symptom reduction. This would indicate that the active ingredients of change are related to the specific and unique effects of that treatment model rather than to nonspecific factors.

Examining Treatment Process in Alcohol Treatment

We have been interested in extending the study of specific therapeutic effects to alcohol and drug treatment models. Broadly speaking, the two dominant models in alcohol treatment—the disease model and the behavioral model—propose very different factors as causal mediators of change. For the disease model approach, change is associated with such factors as accepting powerlessness over alcohol, whereas in the behavioral model increasing self-efficacy is one key to positive outcome. On a formal level, a study of theory-specific change processes would involve identifying "core" processes or therapeutic mechanisms for that treatment approach, operationalizing and measuring these processes and then establishing a link between these processes and positive outcomes.

In a first study, we attempted to identify treatment processes or therapeutic mechanisms associated with disease model and behavioral treatment for alcohol-related problems. We culled the alcohol/drug treatment literature for references to treatment processes. For disease model treatment this included the work of Anderson (1981), Cook (1988a,b), Laundergan (1982), and Wallace et al. (1988), and that of Cermak on codependency (1986). We also surveyed the behavioral treatment literature. Thirty-five different treatment processes were identified, although

TABLE 1
Disease Model Treatment Processes

Process	Abbreviated Name
Help client accept disease notion of chemical dependency.	Disease
Reduce denial. This includes helping client become aware of the destructive aspects of alcohol use and helping client to acknowledge a loss of control over drinking.	Denial
Help client understand that recovery is a lifelong process and that s/he will require the help of others in order to remain sober.	Attribute/CD
Facilitate client's identification with people in recovery.	Id/Recovery
Facilitate client's commitment to attend AA meetings, find a sponsor, and work the 12 steps	AA
Reduce codependent denial. This includes codependent's acknowledgment that their partner has a drinking problem and that their behavior contributes to that problem.	Codependent I
Help partner accept codependent label and make a connection to an appropriate self-help group.	Codependent II
Facilitate a spiritual experience in recovery and help client to believe in a Higher Power.	Spiritual
Help client understand that recovery is a lifelong process and that s/he will require the help of others to stay sober	Lifelong

one of these processes, pharmacological treatment, contained several sub-processes. Nine of these processes could be categorized as disease model processes, 17 as behavioral processes, seven as general psychotherapy processes and two as pharmacological treatment mechanisms. A complete description of the methods and results of this study is beyond the scope of this chapter and has been reported on elsewhere (Morgenstern & McCrady, 1992). The following presentation will be limited to a discussion of disease model experts' views on disease model treatment processes. Table 1 presents a list of the disease model processes and a short referent name for each process.

Two processes categorized as general psychotherapy processes, but which were prominently mentioned in the disease model literature, appear in Table 2. The other treatment processes identified were either general or behavioral in nature and not directly relevant to a discussion of change processes in AA. We then surveyed a representative sampling of doctoral-level experts on the treatment of alcohol-related problems. This group was composed of a random sample of members of the American Society of Addictive Medicine, the Society of Psychologists in Addictive Behaviors, and first authors of empirical publications on alcohol treatment. We asked this group to rate how essential or detrimental each of the 35 treatment processes were to resolving an alcohol-related problem.

TABLE 2
General Psychotherapy Processes

Process	Abbreviated Name
Help client accept need to find more gratifying relationships with others.	Relationships
Increase client's acceptance of responsibility for change in drinking behavior and for changes in behavior in general.	Responsibility

Table 3 contains the ranking and ratings for these 11 processes given by those experts who identified themselves as using an exclusively disease model approach to treating alcohol-related problems. Reducing denial was ranked as the most essential treatment process by disease model experts. Its mean rating was 2.92 on a 7-point Likert scale with the anchors of $+3$ labeled *essential* and -3 labeled *detrimental.* The mid-point zero was labeled "no effect." Facilitating identification with people in recovery was ranked second, followed by helping a client understand that recovery is a lifelong process requiring the help of others to stay sober. Accepting the disease notion of chemical dependency was rated fourth and committing to attend AA/NA meetings was rated fifth. Other disease model processes, such as reducing codependent denial and helping the client to understand that most of the problems he or she is experiencing are attributable to the effects of chemical dependency, were ranked lower, but still rated as important to treatment. Surprisingly, facilitating a spiritual experience in recovery was ranked 22nd and received a mean rating of 1.58. This seems to reflect that fact that, at least for doctoral-level professionals, "spirituality" is not considered an essential aspect of their disease model treatment approach.

Overall, these results seem supportive of our attempts to identify disease model treatment processes. With one exception, disease model experts rated the disease model processes as essential to treatment. In addition, we asked respondents to comment on the accuracy and comprehensiveness of our list. Only one respondent suggested that we had missed an important disease model process. This process was dealing constructively with shame and guilt issues during recovery.

Next we attempted to operationalize these treatment processes and develop an instrument to measure them in clinical populations. We chose to focus on the cognitive aspect (i.e., relevant beliefs and attitudes) rather than on either affective or behavioral changes. Our decision was partly a pragmatic one related to one of the immediate goals of the study. This was to measure treatment process or within-treatment change occurring in typical inpatient alcohol treatment programs. In these programs, interventions are geared toward persuading clients to adopt new beliefs and atti-

TABLE 3
Ratings of "Experts" Using a Disease Model Treatment Orientation

Process	Rank	Rating
Denial	1	2.92
Id/Recovery	2	2.67
Lifelong	3	2.57
Disease	4	2.50
AA	5	2.50
Responsibility	6	2.42
Attribute/CD	11	2.22
Codependent II	12	2.21
Codependent I	17	2.00
Relationships	18	1.92
Spiritual	22	1.58

Note: Ratings were made on a 7-point Likert scale with +3 labeled *essential*, −3 *detrimental*, and 0 *no effect*.

tudes. While behavior change is the long-term goal, individual differences in this dimension are difficult to measure during treatment, since all clients participate in a highly structured milieu. Furthermore, measures of cognitive change are easier to construct, administer, score, and interpret than measures whose focus is on affective or behavior change. Finally, both disease model and behavioral approaches place an important emphasis on attitudinal and other cognitive changes that need to occur as part of the treatment process.

As many items as possible were generated to measure each of the treatment processes. Where possible, relevant descriptive statements culled from disease model and behavioral literature were used in constructing items. These items were then reviewed for intelligibility, simplicity, face validity, and conceptual clarity. Items finally selected were given to several judges with expertise in treatment and research on alcohol-related problems, including several with expertise on disease model approaches. Judges were asked to discard items that were not sufficiently face valid or not likely to be understood by a treatment population.

These items were then used to construct a self-report questionnaire using a 5-point Likert scale with *strongly agree* and *strongly disagree* as anchors. This measure, titled the Client Change Questionnaire, was administered to 153 subjects who were in inpatient treatment for alcohol/drug-related problems. Subjects were drawn from four private treatment centers in Wisconsin, New Jersey, New York, and Connecticut. Results from this study were used to analyze the psychometric properties of the questionnaire. Items were examined for minimally acceptable response distributions, and internal consistency for items representing each process was

TABLE 4
Items Loading Highly on Disease Model Factor

Item	Loading
Attending AA meetings is an important part of my recovery.	.77
It feels good to be with other people who are recovering and know what I've been through and am trying to do every day.	.74
Believing in a Higher Power isn't going to help me solve my drinking problem.	−.71
I will continue to need others' help in order to recover.	.69
I believe I should never use alcohol or any mood altering chemicals again.	.69
I can rely on God or a Higher Power to help me through my life.	.68
I plan to have regular contact with my AA sponsor.	.67
I find I have a lot in common with people who are dealing with their own drinking problem.	.67
Once I'm not under so much stress, I'll be able to drink in moderation.	−.67
I plan to attend AA meetings regularly.	.66
I should never have another drink.	.66

calculated. Many of these analyses are only of narrow interest to the scales' construction and further development, and are of little relevance to this chapter. However, some results have implications for measuring cognitive processes in disease model treatment. Items representing two general processes (increasing responsibility and making gratifying relationships) and two disease processes (codependent denial and codependent labeling) either were not sufficiently discriminating or internally consistent. However, items representing the other seven disease model processes were sufficiently discriminating and did have acceptable levels of internal consistency. Items from the five processes rated most highly by disease model experts did have acceptable items distributions. We constructed subscales with these items and then looked at intersubscale correlations to ascertain whether subscales were measuring different processes. When we examined the interscale correlations of these items, they were high in the .5 or .6 range. We then decided to factor analyze the 45 items in these subscales to provide a more empirically derived set of processes.

An exploratory factor analysis with promax rotation was used for these 45 items. The eigenvalue of the matrix suggested one strong factor. At the same time, the scree test suggested extraction of six more specific factors. Thirty-five of the 45 items loaded .5 or better on the first factor, which accounted for 33% of the variance. Table 4 shows a list of the 11 items that had the highest loadings. Only three items loaded poorly, .30 or less, on this factor. The existence of one strong factor suggests that clients in treatment are readily able to identify relevant disease model beliefs as belonging together. The items presented in Table 4 have a high level of face validity and represent diverse aspects of disease model ideology such as a concern with Higher Power, commitment to attend AA, having an abstinence goal, etc. Clients indicating strong agreement with these items could be said to strongly endorse a disease model perspective. Indeed, one goal of disease model treatment is to provide clients with experiences that facilitate adopting these beliefs.

The scree test also suggests that six more specific factors exist. These factors can be interpreted as specific facets of the larger domain of disease model beliefs. Table 5 presents the six specific factors extracted using the scree test and the items that loaded .4 or better for each factor. These six factors accounted for 56% of the variance. Three factors, Commitment to Alcoholics Anonymous (Factor 1), Belief in a Higher Power (Factor 2), and Identifying with Others in Recovery (Factor 3), are almost identical to the earlier, conceptually constructed subscales. All items representing the first two factors loaded highly on their respective process. For Factor 3, many of the original items were retained. Items not retained seemed to share their variance between Factor 1 and Factor 3. For instance, the item, "I find I have a lot in common with people who are dealing with their own drinking problem," loaded at about the .35 level on both factors. Interfactor correlations between these factors were highest at .47. An additional item, "It feels good to be with people who are recovering and know what I've been through and am trying to do every day," also loaded on both factors. Conceptually, it appears that Factor 1 taps a commitment to adhere to the structure of AA, such as attending meetings regularly and maintaining contact with an AA sponsor. Factor 3 measures some processes facilitated by AA, such as sharing a common problem with others and learning better methods to solve problems. While similar and related, these processes are not identical.

Problem Recognition/Commitment to Abstinence (Factor 4), Disease Beliefs (Factor 5), and Loss of Control (Factor 6) differ somewhat from the earlier conceptually derived processes. Items loading on Factor 4 were drawn both from our original "reducing denial" items and from abstinence items we had conceptually grouped under beliefs that alcoholism is a disease. As framed, these beliefs, while consonant with disease model treatment, would also be a focus of change in any treatment model using abstinence as a treatment goal. Items loading on Factor 5 were those that emphasized the incurable aspect of disease. Interestingly, items related to abstinence or simply labeling oneself an alcoholic did not load on this factor. However, the item, "I'll *always* have a drinking problem," did load on this factor.

Items loading on Factor 6 pertain to beliefs that drinking caused a loss of control. It is important to note that here loss of control refers not only

TABLE 5
Disease Model Factors

Factor	Loading
1. Commitment to AA	
I plan to attend AA meetings regularly.	.87
I plan to have regular contact with my AA sponsor.	.77
Attending AA meetings is an important part of my recovery.	.77
Someone who doesn't attend AA meetings isn't serious about stopping drinking.	.71
Trying to stop drinking without AA is like scuba diving without an oxygen tank.	.65
I plan to make 90 AA meetings in 90 days.	.62
I will continue to need others' help in order to recover.	.56
It feels good to be with other people who are recovering and know what I've been through and am trying to do every day.	.47
2. Belief in a Higher Power	
God, as I understand him/her, will bring back sanity to my life.	.78
I believe in a power greater than myself.	.78
I can rely on God or a Higher Power to help me through my life.	.70
A belief in God or a Higher Power is an important part of my recovery.	.65
When I have a problem I can turn it over to my Higher Power.	.55
3. Identifying with Others in Recovery	
I learn a lot from listening to other recovering people who have gotten through difficult situations.	.63
I need to solve my personal problems before I can stop drinking.	−.60
Listening to how other people solve their drinking problem won't be very helpful to me.	−.59
My drinking problems aren't like those of other people.	−.52
I find it easy to identify with the experiences of other recovering alcoholics.	.45
I drank too much because of stress or personal problems, otherwise I don't have a drinking problem.	−.45
It feels good to be with people who are recovering and know what I've been through and am trying to do daily.	.42
4. Problem Recognition/Commitment to Abstinence	
I have a drinking problem and should work on it.	.65
I'm not planning on drinking again because it gives me problems, but I will use other drugs in moderation.	−.53
My efforts to control drinking have failed.	.49
I should never have another drink.	.47
I am an alcoholic.	.42
I believe I should never use alcohol or any mood altering chemicals again.	.42
Once I'm not under so much stress, I'll be able to drink in moderation.	−.41

(continued)

TABLE 5 (*cont.*)

Factor	Loading
5. Accepting Chemical Dependence as a Disease	
I am an alcoholic and can never be cured of my disease, but I can learn to live with it.	.75
Once an alcoholic, always an alcoholic.	.75
Alcoholism is an incurable disease, not just a bad habit.	.65
I have an incurable, potentially fatal disease called alcoholism.	.64
I'll always have a drinking problem.	.43
6. Loss of Control	
My life was out of control because of my drinking.	.72
When I drank I got into trouble.	.68
Once I started drinking, I couldn't be sure I could stop.	.48
Maybe I have some problems, but the main reason my drinking got out of hand was because I'm an alcoholic.	.48
Drinking has caused serious problems in my life.	.47
I have a disease and will always need help coping with it.	.44
My efforts to control my drinking have failed.	.42

to loss of control over alcohol consumption, but to loss of control over one's behavior and life. In this regard, it is similar to the AA notion of life becoming unmanageable. Most of these items were drawn from the original "reducing denial" items. While the primary content of the items is loss of control, some items loading on this factor, such as "I have a disease and will always need help coping with it," connote a sense of helplessness or powerlessness. Taken together, Factors 4, 5, and 6 might be seen as comprising conceptually distinct facets of the disease model notion of reducing denial. Factor 4 (Problem Recognition/Commitment to Abstinence) would seem an appropriate initial focus of cognitive change in many treatment models. However, in disease model treatment a further, more controversial focus is on changing beliefs regarding powerlessness, loss of control, and acceptance of permanent incurability.

One process that is not represented in the factors is "Help client understand that recovery is a lifelong process and that s/he will need the help of others in order to stay sober." This process was rated as highly important by the "experts." An analysis of item loadings for this process suggests that the process itself contains two conceptually distinct ideas. One relates to the need for indefinite, continuing efforts to maintain recovery; the other refers to a dependency on others. In a further iteration of the scale we intend to write separate items for these concepts. In general, we felt that items assessing attitudes related to dependency and powerlessness were not sufficiently represented and will add more items to assess these.

FIGURE 1
Factor Structure of Disease Model Beliefs

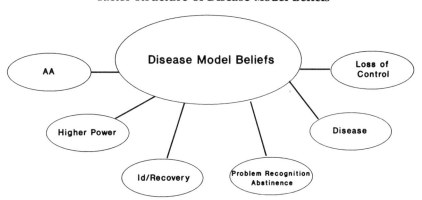

Implications for Understanding How Change Occurs in Disease Model Treatment and AA

Our study suggests that it is possible to identify processes that are hypothesized as causal mediators of change from the perspective of disease model theory. Most if not all of these processes have an important cognitive component. Some processes, such as committing to AA, involve behavioral and cognitive aspects. Others, such as accepting the disease notion or attributing problems to the effects of chemical dependency, are exclusively cognitive in focus. While our study considered formal treatment, AA places important emphasis on similar cognitive changes, at least during the initial phases of AA involvement. Thus, assessing cognitive change is a useful and perhaps necessary aspect of any study of change processes in AA.

The list of disease model processes and beliefs is not presented as a final or authoritative one. Rather, its value is primarily heuristic. Emrick, Tonigan, Montgomery, and Little (1993) note that an important limitation of past research on AA has been a failure to identify, understand, and apply the theoretical constructs upon which AA is founded. Our current works uses a theory-driven perspective to identify causal mediators of change from within the disease model framework.

Figure 1 presents a graphic illustration of the results of the factor analysis. Six sets of beliefs comprise a larger construct of disease model beliefs. The concept that AA focuses on changing several sets of attitudes is not surprising. However, being able to identify them may be useful in tracking change occurring during AA involvement and in matching clients to disease model treatments.

One can ask which of these beliefs might present a barrier to AA involvement, which beliefs AA is capable of changing, and which of these beliefs may be predictive of positive outcome. For instance, one can ask whether individuals who are strongly opposed to spirituality and have controlled drinking goals end up affiliating with AA. Are these barriers absolute or can they be moderated by other factors, such as extreme distress or hitting bottom?

Figure 1 also suggests that clients are able to differentiate from among various aspects of disease model beliefs, endorsing some while rejecting others. This suggests that those affiliating with AA may selectively endorse certain aspects of its ideology while remaining neutral or rejecting other aspects. It is commonly assumed that accepting powerlessness and surrender to a Higher Power is an essential part of every AA member's recovery. However, this remains an empirical question. It is possible that AA members use different processes available within the framework of their involvement with AA in resolving their drinking problems. Some may use the classical AA ideology of surrender and humility, while for others AA involvement may facilitate better coping and more effective use of social supports.

A final comment concerns the search for specific effects. Our model examined change processes from within an AA perspective. However, in order to understand how change works in AA it will be necessary to examine other process models as well. Our study identified three aspects of the process of "reducing denial." One aspect, problem recognition and having an abstinence goal, would be common to many treatment models. The other two, believing that alcoholism is a disease and causes loss of control, are specific to AA. Further study is needed to assess whether AA works through facilitating recognized curative processes, such as creating social supports, increasing hopefulness, or helping to initiate cognitive coping, or by more unique effects, such as inducing humility, surrender, or some process of spiritual conversion, or by some combination of these.

Conclusion

In this chapter, we have attempted to provide a conceptual framework for studying change processes in AA. Specifically, we used a theory-based approach to identify and measure important disease model treatment processes. These can be viewed as change processes which are responsible for mediating positive outcomes. A strength of this approach is that it allows one to assess whether these changes take place as a part of treatment or AA involvement and whether these changes can be linked to outcome. As noted above, AA's focus on curative processes such as surrender and spirituality has been the subject of much controversy. Further empirical research should help clarify which types of change processes are operative in AA and disease model treatments and whether and for whom these processes are uniquely effective.

References

Anderson, D.J. (1981). *Perspectives in treatment.* Minneapolis, MN: Hazelden.

Brown, S. (1985). *Treating the alcoholic: A developmental model for recovery.* New York: Wiley Press.

Cermak, T.G. (1986). *Diagnosing and treating co-dependence: A guide for professionals who work with chemical dependents.* Minneapolis, MN: Johnson Institute Books.

Cook, C.H. (1988a). The Minnesota model in the management of drug and alcohol dependency. Part I. *British Journal of Addictions, 83,* 735–748.

Cook, C.H. (1988b). The Minnesota model in the management of drug and alcohol dependency. Part II. *British Journal of Addictions, 83,* 735–748.

Emrick, C.D., Tonigan, J.S., Montgomery, H., & Little, L. (1993). Alcoholics Anonymous: What is currently known? In B.S. McCrady & W. R. Miller (Eds.), *Research on Alcoholics Anonymous: Opportunities and alternatives.* New Brunswick, NJ: Rutgers Center of Alcohol Studies.

Frank, J.D. (1974). Psychotherapy: The restoration of morale. *American Journal of Psychiatry, 131,* 271–274.

Hollon, S.D., DeRubeis, R.J., & Evans, M.D. (1987). Causal mediation of change in treatment for depression: Discriminating between nonspecificity and noncausality. *Psychological Bulletin, 102,* 139–149.

Kurtz, E. (1982). A.A. works: The intellectual significance of Alcoholics Anonymous. *Journal of Studies on Alcohol, 43,* 38–80.

Laundergan, J.C. (1982). *Easy does it! Alcohol treatment outcomes, Hazelden and the Minnesota Model.* Minneapolis, MN: Hazelden.

Luborsky, L., McLellan, A.T., O'Brien, C.P., & Auerbach, A. (1985). Therapist success and its determinants. *Archives of General Psychiatry, 42,* 602–611.

McElrath, D. (1988, June 16) The Hazelden treatment model. Testimony before the U.S. Senate Committee on Governmental Affairs, Washington, DC.

Morgenstern, J., & McCrady, B.S. (1992). Curative processes in the treatment of alcohol and drug problems: Behavior and disease model perspectives. *British Journal of Addictions, 87,* 615–626.

Peele, S., & Brodsky, A. (1991). *The truth about addiction recovery.* New York: Simon and Schuster.

Room, R. (1993). Alcoholics Anonymous as a social movement. In B.S. McCrady & W.R. Miller (Eds.), *Research on Alcoholics Anonymous: Opportunities and alternatives.* New Brunswick, NJ: Rutgers Center of Alcohol Studies.

Wallace, J., McNeil, D., Gilfillan, D., McLean, K., & Fanella, F. (1988). Six-month treatment outcomes in socially stable alcoholics. *Journal of Substance Abuse Treatment, 5,* 247–252.

SECTION III

Contexts of Change

CHAPTER 10

Alcoholics Anonymous as a Social Movement

ROBIN ROOM

There are many potential ways to approach the topic of Alcoholics Anonymous (AA) as a social movement, and only a few of them will be given attention in this chapter. We will first give brief consideration to the place of Alcoholics Anonymous in the formal sociological literature on social movements. Secondly, we will consider the current extent of membership in Alcoholics Anonymous in the United States: How broadly spread is AA's influence in the society, both directly through attendance at AA meetings and more indirectly through attendance at other groups modeled on AA's approach? Next, in view of AA's unique status as an organization that has to a large extent broken Michels' "iron law of oligarchy" (1958), we will consider in detail its organizational principles and practices. We will also consider how AA's ideology and organizational principles were from the beginning aimed at overcoming not only alcoholism but also egoistic individualism, which might be viewed as the leading disorder of modernism. Lastly, we will consider the relation of AA's ideas and AA as an organization to the generalized 12-step consciousness that has come to the fore in the 1980s, and possible directions of future development of the movement.

AA and the Social Movement Literature

Traditionally, for sociologists the prototype of a social movement was a workers' movement—a class-based movement to change society in the interests of its members' class. It has been pointed out, however, that already in the 19th century, in addition to such "beneficiary" movements, movements such as abolitionism and temperance based largely on "conscience" constituencies were prominent on the American scene (Zald, 1988). In recent years, there has been a mostly European literature on "new social movements," bringing into the analytical frame movements such as the ecology movement or the peace movement, whose members are aiming at social change, but are not acting on behalf of their

167

own class or sectional interest. Considering AA in the light of this literature, Bloomfield (1988) and others have concluded that AA shares some characteristics of these "new social movements."

In other ways, however, AA does not fit the usual sociological meaning of "social movement." A social movement is usually thought of as aiming at change in the society in which it operates, while AA seeks only personal change among its members and specifically renounces any ambition to change the surrounding society. It is clear that the conceptualization of social movements, and the focus of the literature, will have to be rethought if AA is to be fitted in. On the other hand, as we will discuss, there are signs of the emergence alongside AA of a generalized "12-step movement" with a greater resemblance to the traditional model of a social movement.

An alternative framing of AA is as a religious movement. To those approaching AA from a strictly rationalist frame (as many researchers do and as a self-consciously scientific approach usually does), the references to "God as we understood Him" and the requirement to surrender to a higher power are clinching evidence that we are dealing with a religious sect or movement. Further evidence, if it were required, can be drawn from AA's connection with the Oxford Group Movement at its inception and from the parallels between AA's ideology as spelled out in the Twelve Steps and the ideology of the Oxford Group Movement (Bufe, 1991; Peterson, 1992).

On the other hand, when Bufe (1991), who is critical of AA from a rationalist position, compares AA's characteristics with those of a presumptively destructive religious cult, he concludes that AA does not fit many of the characteristics he enumerates for such a cult. In AA's own self-definition, it is a movement of spiritual renewal, but it is not a religion. Comparing AA with religious movements in general, Mäkelä (1990) has noted that it would be an unusual religion indeed which showed as little interest in origins and afterlives as AA does.

As an organization, AA thus does not neatly fit the usual descriptive categories of social science. This is of course more of a problem for social science than for AA. AA began as an organization *sui generis*, but it has become the prototype of a burgeoning category of mutual-help organizations. It is time that the sociology of movements and organizations took note.

The Extent of Membership in AA and Other Twelve-Step Groups

Alcoholics Anonymous was founded in 1935, but grew slowly at first, attaining about 100 members by the time it gained national media attention in 1940. After a period of sharp growth in the 1940s, AA's rate of growth flattened out in the 1950s, and then resumed a steady growth in the late 1960s and up to the present ("A Generation . . . ," 1987; Leach & Norris, 1977). AA's own estimate of its membership in the U.S. and Canada in early 1990 was 978,982 ("Triennial surveys . . . ," 1990)—about 0.48% of the population over age 18 of the two countries.

We recently were able to compare AA's own estimate of membership with estimates derived by other means (Room & Greenfield, 1991). As part of a 1990 nationwide study of drinking practices and problems, interviews were conducted with 2,058 persons aged 18 and over, constituting a national adult probability survey of the conterminous United States (completion rate 71%). As part of this survey, respondents were asked a small series of questions about their attendance at Alcoholics Anonymous, other 12-step groups, and other support or therapy groups. In another section of the questionnaire, respondents were asked about going to any form of treatment for "a problem in any way related to your drinking," and those answering yes were asked about attendance at each of a list of agencies including AA.

Altogether, 3.1% of the adult population reported that they had ever been to an AA meeting about an alcohol problem of their own and 1.5% reported that they had been within the last year. The 1.5% figure for attendance in the current year is three times AA's own statistics for current membership, suggesting that AA's membership counts are quite conservatively derived. On the basis of our respondents' answers on frequency of AA attendance, the top 0.5% of the sample (only a handful of cases, of course) each reported attending AA meetings 100 or more times in the last year.

However, these figures for attendance about one's own alcohol problem by no means exhaust the range of AA's influence in the population. Asked more generally about attendance at AA meetings, implicitly for any reason, 9.0% of U.S. adults reported having done so at some time in their life, and 3.4% reported having done so within the last year. Comparing these results, it is clear that attendance at an AA meeting does not necessarily imply a definition of oneself as having an alcohol problem; the attendance may be prompted by many factors, including curiosity or concern about someone else's drinking. On a lifetime basis, only about one-third of those who have been to an AA meeting acknowledge it to be for help with a drinking problem of their own; for the last year, the proportion is 42%.

Attendance at AA meetings far exceeded the proportion who had attended "another support or therapy group for an alcohol problem of your own" (1.9% lifetime, 0.9% in last year). On the other hand, substantial proportions had gone to meetings of other 12-step groups: 4.6% on a lifetime basis for Al-Anon (1.7% in the last year), 1.7% lifetime for other Adult Children of Alcoholics (ACOA) groups (0.8% in the last year), and

2.8% lifetime for any other 12-step group (0.8% in the last year). Eliminating overlaps in attendance, altogether 13.3% of the population had attended a 12-step meeting at some time in their life and 5.3% had done so within the last year. This compared with 2.6% who had been to a non-12-step support or therapy group for nonalcohol problems and 8.1% who had seen a therapist or counselor in the last year about a personal problem (not about drinking, and not in a support or therapy group). Thus, 12-step meeting attendance plays a dominant role in support or therapy group attendance in the United States, and the reach of 12-step groups into the population is not far short of the reach of therapy or counseling of any kind.

A much larger portion of the general population, then, has some familiarity with AA practice and ideas than would be implied by AA's claimed membership of about 0.5% of the adult population. The results also make clear that AA's influence is not limited to those who have attended its meetings. Apart from the 9% who have ever attended AA meetings, another 4.3% have attended meetings of some other 12-step group, with more attending Al-Anon than any other group. Thus, about half as many people in the general population have attended an Al-Anon meeting as have attended an AA meeting. On the other hand, these figures remind us that, despite the proliferation of other 12-step groups, AA still plays a dominant role in 12-step attendance.

While there is a well-developed research literature on AA, literature on other 12-step groups, other than the groups' own literature, is not well-developed. The new developments of the last 10 years—the burgeoning of new 12-step groups, notably including the ACOA movement and the development of a new consciousness of membership in a general 12-step movement—have received only sketchy attention and little analysis. Yet these developments in organization and consciousness may well be among the more significant aspects of recent social changes in America. It may be argued that the radiation of the 12-step movement outward from AA is part of a process that bids fair to restore alcohol issues to the central position they occupied in American history in the century before 1930.

Organizational Principles of AA

Any continuing organization must make a series of choices about its internal organization and its relation to the outside world. How is membership in the organization to be defined—to what extent inclusively or exclusively? What is the basic unit of organization: the individual, a face-to-face group, or some larger group? What are the forms of relation within the organization, both between individuals and between groups: egalitarian, hierarchical, a client/professional relation, or some mixture of these? Where in the organization are its assets held and who controls them: the face-to-face group, the organization as a whole, an oligarchic trustees committee, etc.? How does the organization approach the outside world: evangelically, seeking alliances, or with a stance of splendid isolation?

AA's organizational principles steer a clear path through these questions. Membership is defined inclusively; on the other hand, the stance to the outside world is isolationist, neither accepting nor seeking outside influence. Power resides at the base, in the "group conscience" of the face-to-face group; all superstructures are defined as responsible to the base-group level. Forms of relation are egalitarian, both within the group and between groups. Thus group officers and delegates are elected by group members, and incumbency is expected to rotate between members. Groups are autonomous, and cannot be subject to control either by other groups or by some superior body. The problem of where assets are held is solved in large part by a prohibition on owning property or holding substantial assets. As we shall note, there are nuances and even exceptions to these general choices, but their general direction is clear. To an unprecedented extent, AA has succeeded in creating an organization that breaks Michels' "iron law of oligarchy" (1958) by building in structures and principles that minimize the professionalization of leadership and keep effective organizational power at the level of egalitarian face-to-face interaction. From another perspective, Bufe (1991) has remarked how well AA has carried into practice the organizational ideals of classical anarchist thought.

The heart of AA is a quintessentially oral occasion: the meeting. The movement certainly has written texts, in the form of conference-approved literature, national and local magazines and newsletters, and a rich diversity of unofficial publications. But much of how AA operates is carried on in an oral rather than a written tradition. Even a feature of AA as important as sponsorship is carried in the oral tradition; it is nowhere discussed in *Twelve Steps and Twelve Traditions* (Alcoholics Anonymous, 1952). For another example, there is no central specification of an order of proceedings at an AA meeting, nor is it handed out in written form to participants; if it is written at all, it is on a dog-eared sheet handed on from one group secretary to another.

Like much else in AA, then, its organizational principles are carried in part in written form and in part orally. The primary written locus of AA's organizational principles is the 12 traditions, first published in *Grapevine,* AA's magazine, in May 1946, and adopted in revised form at the first AA International Convention in Cleveland in 1950. But there are principles of AA's organization that cannot be found anywhere in the 12 traditions, or otherwise spelled out in writing. Our discussion of the organizational principles is therefore not organized around the twelve traditions, although they are cross-referenced as appropriate.

(1) *Openness of membership* (Tradition 3). "The only requirement for membership is a sincere desire to stop drinking." AA has none of the ordinary means of maintaining a boundary between membership and nonmembership: there is no membership roster to sign and there are no membership dues. An important corollary of this is that there are no procedures for excommunicating or excluding from membership; AA defines itself as open to all comers.

This is an unusual organizational characteristic. Most political, religious, or other voluntary organizations have a well-defined boundary between membership and nonmembership. AA's ban on property and on professionalism (see below) help make its open membership structure feasible: there are no tangible assets for the members to share in or quarrel over, and the AA group is not financially burdened with maintaining professionals (a burden that tends to force a definition of membership in most religious congregations, for instance). The lack of any procedure for exclusion from membership has probably helped in avoiding splits within groups and fractionation of AA as a movement, by removing the possibility of permanent victory in any internal faction fights.

On the other hand, openness of membership and attendance at meetings does sometimes create problems in the management of meetings. While AA meetings generally show a substantial tolerance for deviations from decorum, it is not unknown for obnoxious participants, and particularly drunken participants, to be physically ejected from meetings. Thus Johnson (1987, p. 245) reports that in Southern California "on rare occasions someone who is extremely disruptive may be expelled from a group by disallowing him or her to use the club premises where the meeting is held." The standard AA texts offer no guidance on what to do about a recurrently disruptive attender. Al-Anon texts, which spell out some organizational matters in greater detail than AA texts, do contemplate a kind of informal excommunication from an individual group. For instance, where a member persists in spreading information from the meeting outside the group, "for the 'greatest good of the greatest number,' he may have to be warned and asked to leave the group if he continues" (Al-Anon, 1981, p. 73). A major safety valve is the ability of one or another party in a continuing conflict to simply form another group (see (2)(b) below). Thus Al-Anon's advice about dealing with a domineering group chairman, if persuasion fails, is that "stronger measures may have to be taken, perhaps ultimately to ask her to leave the group. . . . In some instances the members of such a group have left it and re-formed it without her" (Al-Anon, 1981, p. 71).

(2) *The group as the autonomous organizational base* (Tradition 4). The fundamental organizational unit of AA is the group. A group is defined in terms of those who meet face-to-face at meetings scheduled for a particular place and time or times of the week. Individual members may consider themselves members of several groups, although there is informal encouragement to pick one as the "home group." Each group is "autonomous, except in matters affecting another group or AA as a whole" (Tradition 4). In principle, then, on most matters the group makes its own decisions. Just as there is no exclusion rule for individuals, there is no exclusion rule for groups.

The primacy and autonomy of the group is reinforced by several specific organizational principles.

(a) *The group as self-governing, subject to no external authority or superstructure* (Tradition 9). The discussion in *Twelve Steps and Twelve Traditions* emphasizes the distinction between "the spirit of vested authority and the spirit of service" (p. 174). AA has an elaborate structure of service boards and committees, elected directly or indirectly by AA groups, but power is firmly defined as lying at the base rather than in the structure: "Our leaders are but trusted servants; they do not govern" (Tradition 2). Accordingly, it is noted in *Twelve Steps and Twelve Traditions* (pp. 173–4), a headquarters communication to a group will be worded in the form of suggestions: "Of course, you are at perfect liberty to handle this matter any way you please. But the majority of experience in A.A. does seem to suggest.... "

In practice, there are some forms of recognition or nonrecognition of AA groups. Johnson (1987, pp. 427–431) reports that in southern California the local central office sends out a delegate to observe procedures in a new group, "to see that the group is not violating the Traditions," before listing it in the area directory of groups and meetings. Listing in the area directory is an important means of recruitment of new members, often by referral by others, so that denial of a directory listing may affect the continuation or growth of the group. But there is nothing to stop an unlisted group from continuing and considering itself to be an AA group. Certainly failure to participate in and support AA's service structure does not hinder recognition; about half the groups listed in the directory for a northern California county fail to participate in and support AA's general service structure.

(b) *No exclusive territories or franchises.* No existing AA group can hinder a new AA group from forming, even if it is appealing to the same population as the existing group. This is a fairly unusual provision for a multicelled organization. In many denominations, the existing congregation has exclusive jurisdiction in a parish or locality; chapters of fraternal organizations usually have an exclusive franchise for some defined population.

The lack of exclusive jurisdictions might be regarded as a corollary of the autonomy of the group, extended to new as well as existing groups. But the wording of the 4th tradition ("each group should be autonomous except in matters affecting other groups") could have lent itself to an alternative interpretation, since the formation of a new group might well adversely affect the status of an existing group.

The lack of exclusive territories or franchises provides both a safety valve for internal conflicts and a mechanism for organizational growth. As an AA proverb puts it, "All that is needed to start an AA meeting are a resentment and a coffee-pot," reflecting that a new group often starts as the resolution of a conflict between members of an existing group. From an organizational perspective, the lack of any inhibition on forming new groups turns resentments and conflicts which might otherwise threaten group continuance into an instrument of organizational growth.

(c) *The group as self-supporting* (Tradition 7). Each group is enjoined to be "fully self-supporting, declining outside contributions." The expenses of the group are met from "passing the hat" during the meeting. Normally, these expenses would include rent, refreshments, literature purchases, and contributions to activities at the intergroup and general service levels. As noted above, not all groups in fact contribute to the AA structure beyond the group level. Refreshment expenses may be paid for by members separately, and the net literature expense may be small. Rental costs vary greatly from group to group; in some places, groups meet in public spaces that would not normally be charged for, though they may arrange to pay some kind of nominal rent to preserve the principle of self-support. Traditionally, many U.S. groups have met in church basements and rooms, rented for a relatively small charge. In hard times and with the growth of 12-step groups, however, rents have tended to rise as churches come to view them as a significant source of income.

In the "long form" of the 12 traditions (Alcoholics Anonymous, 1952, pp. 189–192), the injunction to decline outside contributions is further spelled out: "We think that... any public solicitation of funds using the name of Alcoholics Anonymous is highly dangerous;... that acceptance of large gifts from any source, or of contributions carrying any obligation whatever, is unwise."

(3) *No affiliations or distractions.* The principle that groups should be self-supporting obviously supports the maintenance of a bottom-up organization, where no group is financially dependent on another or on AA superstructures. However, AA texts give at least equal emphasis in the discussions of the self-support principle to the importance of refusing fis-

cal support from outside AA. The principle of self-support is thus also one of several principles designed to ensure that AA maintains a single-ness of purpose (Tradition 5) and a central focus on the egalitarian fellowship of the AA meeting. Likewise, the principle of external anonym-ity, discussed below, among its other functions helps keep AA free of imputed affiliations by breaking the link between the external commit-ments of individual AA members and the fact of their AA membership. Other organizational principles aimed at avoiding affiliations or distrac-tions include:

(a) *Prohibition on external affiliations and endorsements* (Traditions 6 and 10). The prohibition on affiliations goes in both directions: AA groups should not affiliate with any other organization, and neither will AA allow any other groups to affiliate with it. There is de facto a partial exception to the latter for Al-Anon, which is indeed separately organized but has long had a special relationship to AA. However, with other 12-step groups, AA's relationship is fully at arm's length.

While AA has kept true to its prohibition on organizational affiliation with alcohol treatment programs, this may well seem a fine distinction to a client of a "Minnesota model" or "12-step-based" treatment program. In medical and other professional perspectives on treatment for alcohol-related problems, AA is often viewed as an adjunct to treatment, in par-ticular as a cheap "aftercare" program. In the numerous U.S. treatment agencies that are 12-step-based, therapists and counselors will usually be members of AA themselves, and AA-like or AA meetings in the institu-tional setting will form much of the substance of the treatment program. AA has thus been co-opted by the U.S. alcohol treatment system to the extent that the uninitiated will tend to presume an affiliation exists.

(b) *Prohibition on property ownership* (Tradition 6). AA groups, and AA as a whole, are enjoined from owning any real property, "lest problems of money, property and prestige divert us from our primary spiritual aim." This principle is the most radical departure from usual organizational practice in the United States: The greatest aspiration of a new congrega-tion or fraternal club is normally to own its own building, and most vol-untary associations would jump at such a chance. AA's rule recognizes that property issues, on the other hand, are often sources of collective and individual strife in churches and voluntary associations. In the "long form" of the traditions, the potential utility of property to AA is recog-nized, but a clear organizational separation from AA itself is enjoined: "Any considerable property of genuine use to A.A. should be separately incorporated and managed, thus dividing the material from the spiri-tual. . . . Secondary aids to A.A., such as clubs or hospitals . . . ought to be incorporated and so set apart that, if necessary, they can be freely dis-carded by the groups" (Alcoholics Anonymous, 1952, p. 190).

The most extensive exception to the prohibition on property ownership is the copyrights maintained on AA publications and the registered
trademarks on AA symbols. AA's publishing effort is at one and the same
time an intrinsic part of the organizational program and a substantial
source of revenue which has long been used to support the costs of the
AA structure (service worker wages, travel, etc.) above the group level.
Preliminary data from the International Collaborative Study of Alcoholics
Anonymous suggest that in North America as well as in some other indus-
trial countries literature sales account for as much as half of the total revenue of the national level AA.

The issue of whether and how much AA's superstructure should depend
on profits from literature sales has been a source of recurrent discussion
in AA, leading sometimes to downward adjustments in literature prices to
diminish the profits and thus the organizational dependence on them.
Legal action to protect trademarks is a more recent phenomenon, and
those opposing it regard it as a break with the traditions. Thus a letter to
Recovering, a San Francisco-area 12-step newspaper, comments that controversies over AA's trademark lawsuit "demonstrate the unexpected
and uncontrollable problems that often result from property ownership.
Why does AA own a trademark? Doesn't that ownership violate the [Tra-
ditions]? ... Lawsuits and public controversy? That's not How It Works"
(W., S. 1991).

(4) *Internal equality and democracy.* AA texts emphasize the equal
status of AA members, an equality symbolized by the expectation that
each member should take on a common status identification, traditionally
heavily derogated in the world at large: "My name is X, and I'm an alcoholic." In discussing leadership in the context of the 2nd tradition, *Twelve
Steps and Twelve Traditions* does acknowledge that old-timers in the
movement often play a role of moral leadership, but it distinguishes
between "bleeding deacons" and "elder statesmen," with the latter subordinating their personal judgment to the group decisions of the "group
conscience." In line with this discussion, seniority in the movement does
play a considerable part in who ends up in what position in the structure,
and groups often impose a minimum length of sobriety as a prerequisite
for election to office in a group, but the formal equality of AA members
carries much more substantive weight than the formal equality, say, of U.S.
citizens or of Communist Party members. A number of principles and procedures weigh against the build-up of hierarchy or oligarchy within AA.

(a) *No professional relationships* (Tradition 8). "Alcoholics Anonymous will never have a professional class" begins the discussion of the 8th
tradition in *Twelve Steps and Twelve Traditions* (p. 166). Although mutual help between members is at the heart of AA's practice, such help
("12th-step work") within the context of AA must not be paid for, but

must be freely given. This principle, of course, radically distinguishes AA from "12-step based" treatment agencies, in which recovering alcoholics are routinely employed as counselors. Since the 1950s and the rise of "12-step-based" treatment institutions, the complex and often blurred roles of the "two-hatter," the AA member who is also a professional alcoholism therapist, have been a continuing issue for concern and discussion within the AA movement. *Twelve Steps and Twelve Traditions* tends to emphasize the lure and distraction of money in discussing the rationale for the 8th tradition, but perhaps more important is its role in excluding the status relationship of professional versus client from AA's process. Such a status relationship would fundamentally compromise the principle of equality of members.

It is curious that neither in the discussion of the 8th tradition nor elsewhere in *Twelve Steps and Twelve Traditions* is there mention of the role of sponsor, although sponsor/pigeon relationships have long been an important element of AA's practice. Instead, the reference is simply to the "12th-stepper." Perhaps it was felt that any reference to the sponsor role in the canonical texts would tend to undercut the norm of the equal status of members.

(b) *Elected and rotating leadership.* The discussion of the 2nd tradition in *Twelve Steps and Twelve Traditions* clearly favors elections as the method for choosing group leadership, although in line with the principle of group autonomy elections are not mandated. The *AA Service Manual* lays out a suggested method of election to be used by group delegates, involving successive ballots to seek an absolute majority, with a drawing of lots in case of a tie. Rotation of representation and leadership is mandated in the service structure and is recommended to groups concerning their own leadership (Alcoholics Anonymous, 1952, p. 191).

The principle of election, of course, enforces the ideology of a bottom-up structure, and the principle of rotation helps keep the leadership structure open and relatively free of oligarchy. That voting is implicitly open to all members, no matter how new, supports the ideology of equality of status of members.

Rotation and election rules within a group are in the end up to the group, on the principle that groups are self-governing. Groups clearly vary considerably in the extent to which there is in practice a regular rotation of leadership.

(c) *Decisions by consensus.* The only formulation concerning processes for group decision-making offered in *Twelve Steps and Twelve Traditions* is in the 2nd tradition: "For our group purpose there is but one ultimate authority—a loving God as He may express Himself in our group conscience." "Group conscience" in AA terminology has come to mean decision-making by consensus. This does not necessarily mean complete unanimity, but neither does it mean decisions by majority vote. Instead, it entails a frequently lengthy discussion in search of common denominators before the group decision is taken.

Although the Higher Power is almost omnipresent in the steps, this is its only appearance in the traditions. Thus, while other elements of the organizational principles are worded and justified in rational terms, the process of group decision-making is associated with the sacred and the mysterious. This is no accident: as we will further discuss, Bill W. saw "self will run riot" as the central vice of the alcoholic, and thus would have seen the subordination of the individual ego to collective interests as the stress-point in making the organization work.

As noted above, elections of officers and delegates are excluded from the principle of decision-making by consensus, although here, too, the widest possible consent is sought. Otherwise, the consensus principle is almost universally applied. But not quite: In California, at least, decisions about whether a meeting is to be a smoking or a nonsmoking meeting, as consciousness changed on this issue, have sometimes come down to majority voting. Johnson (1987, p. 443) observed two majority votes on this at successive meetings of a group, in a situation complete with meeting-stacking and other manipulations reminiscent of party politics.

(d) *Internal openness—no secrecy of process, partial anonymity.* Although, as discussed below, anonymity with respect to the outside world is firmly maintained, information, including names, is relatively freely available within AA. This is partly a matter of convenience or necessity: AA groups often circulate a list of names and addresses of members to their members, as an aid to twelfth-step work and to organizational maintenance. Worldwide listings of AA groups and meetings facilitate visiting and networking by traveling members. But the transparency of AA as an organization and the availability of information to members is also an important means of limiting oligarchic tendencies and subordinating the service structure to members' governance.

(e) *External anonymity* (Traditions 11 and 12). The principle of external anonymity invoked in the organization's name is justified on several grounds. It facilitates AA's policy of "attraction rather than promotion" in public relations. As noted above, it reinforces the principle of avoiding affiliations and distractions. But it also is a crucial element in maintaining equality and democracy within AA. It is a common experience of social movements with a democratic style and a collective leadership that these principles are inexorably undermined by the results of media attention to the movement. Reporters and authorities want to deal with leaders, preferably as few as possible, and a spokesperson for the movement soon becomes a celebrity. The enhanced status in the outside society tends to be reflected back into the organization's internal processes. An oligarchic leadership for the movement can thus be created not by internal but by external processes. Again, the ideological emphasis on individual egoism as a main problem for alcoholics may have tended to underline the special importance of anonymity in an organization of alcoholics. Certainly, AA as an organization struggled with and over the anonymity principle in its early days, and the principles enunciated in the 11th and 12th traditions were hard won.

AA, Individualism, and Modernity

AA came into being in a culture and a social class fond of quoting the verse, "I am the master of my fate, I am the captain of my soul." Success and happiness were defined, particularly for men, as ideals one created for oneself and as goals that would be attained by hard work and utmost attention to duty. To give this cultural milieu labels, it was characterized by radical individualism and by a belief in the inevitability of progress at the level of the individual as well as of the society. As feminist ideas spread in the early twentieth century and middle-class women began to make careers of their own, the ideas were increasingly applied for women, too.

In the early and middle life of the men of the generation that founded AA, with a mean birth year of 1895 (judging by the stories in the first edition of the Big Book—see Room, 1989), the idea of progress came in for some rude shocks. The First World War put the whole idea of the progress of civilization in doubt, although it probably did not greatly disturb the ideal of individual betterment for those who survived it in one piece. But the Great Depression made a mockery of the idea that hard work would bring individual success. AA was born in the depths of the depression, among middle-class men many of whose lives had also be affected by the war. Its founding generation were by then middle-aged, and often had a tumultuous marital and family history, reflecting that their generation had also been at the leading edge of a half-realized shift from patriarchal to companionate gender relations, and had pioneered the idea of divorce as a thinkable option for the middle class.

To borrow Madsen's term (1979), at its foundation AA was indeed a "crisis cult." It arose at a moment when the boat captained by the self-directed middle class man had run aground on the reefs—on the conflicting realities of a structural economic depression and of an increasing willingness on the part of women to contemplate (at least) kicking out their men.

As Levine (1978) has argued, the particular focus on alcohol as the destroyer of the dream was a well-worn groove in the culture. As an explanation of personal failure in a no-longer-Calvinist culture committed to redemption and to second chances, drinking had the wonderful feature of being externalizable. The bottle could be cast away, and the dream restored. In a generation committed from youth to heavy drinking as a symbol of revolt against "Victorian morality," it is no accident that the crisis cult coalesced around alcoholism.

But AA took on a larger agenda than simply stopping drinking—perhaps it had to, since the changes that came with the repeal of Prohibition made stopping drinking more complicated than avoiding the bootlegger. What AA took on was nothing less than the ideology of radical individualism and the patterns of thinking that sustained it. For, in the new social conditions, the ideology was no longer sustainable—it had become a "soul-sickness."

First, AA took the individualist ideology on at the level of ideology. This is what lies behind Bill W.'s singling out of pride, of egoism, and of "big-shot-ism" above all other vices of the alcoholic and behind his failure to mention self-confidence among potential virtues (Alcoholics Anonymous, 1952). To get anywhere in the new circumstances, one had to deflate the ego, to abandon the notion that "I can do it for myself." But if one could not do it for oneself, where was the responsibility for its happening to lie? One answer was to rely on a professional. But professionals have limited mandates. A doctor may agree to take on responsibility for treating a disease, but cannot take responsibility for one's life. A second answer is to rely on a social group—perhaps on AA itself. Synanon, for instance, adopted this solution, with eventually disastrous results. This answer might solve the problem for the foot-soldier, but it did not solve it for the group's leaders. AA chose a third answer: the responsibility should be given to a "Higher Power." Functionally, the Higher Power solution removed the burden from the individual, without transferring it either to another person or to an institution.

AA's particular form of the Higher Power, however, came from radically individuated Protestant traditions: this was a Higher Power characterized by the individual him/herself and who spoke unmediated to the individual. Like a homeopathic remedy, the cure for the pathology of individualism itself was drawn from individualist thinking. The focus on pride as the besetting vice, on surrender, and on a Higher Power can all be seen as antidotes to the ideology of radical individualism.

Second, AA took the individualist ideology on at the level of ways of thinking, attacking the legitimacy of offering reasons for behavior, particularly when they are offered as justifications. The idea that an individual's actions should be justified by an individual-level set of reasons only makes sense in an individualistic world-view. The modern middle-class adult has spent many years in school learning what are acceptable reasons to offer where one's interests are at stake. With greater education, one becomes more adept at offering the proper reasons for what one is doing, ones which do not, for instance, sound racist or sexist. "Consciousness-raising" to a considerable degree is a matter of efforts to change the acceptability of particular rationales in everyday discourse. AA's identification of reasons as suspicious and of justifications as erroneous thought can be seen as an attack on individualist, self-regarding habits of thought and talk. Thus Bill W.'s discussion (Alcoholics Anonymous, 1952) focuses on pride and its correlates as the underpinning that invalidates justifications.

Third, AA took individualism on at the level of practice and organization. In this arena, its attack took many forms—but again, there was often an individualist cast to the remedies for the pathology of individualism. The 12th step taught the duty of helping others even when it was trouble to oneself, but noted that this was really the best, perhaps the only effective, way of helping oneself. The sponsor system built strong links between individual members, but sponsorship was left as a matter for the two individuals involved, rather than for central direction. Most obviously, the AA structure of nonhierarchical relations and of regular meetings as a central element of the program built a sense of community and sought to subordinate the individual will to the collective conscience ("our common welfare should come first").

It has long been fashionable for sociologists to focus on the individualism in American life (e.g., Bellah et al., 1985), but there is also a strong communalist countertheme in American history. Much of AA practice and organizational structure borrowed from or reinvented older forms in the culture. The Quaker meeting offered a model of a nonhierarchical meeting composed of personal testimonies and of a decision rule of substantial consensus rather than majority voting. Protestant denominations with "congregational polity"—the wing of Protestantism that applied the Reformation to church organizational structure—offered examples of acephalous organization, with anyone allowed to set up a new congregation. Fraternal organizations such as the Masons, the Oddfellows, and the temperance fraternities, all of which flourished greatly in late 19th-century America, offered models of mutual-interest groups with a strong emphasis on regular meetings and on fellowship, and in some cases on secretiveness with respect to the outside world. Since the time of de Tocqueville's observations of the early temperance movement, the United States has been a society of meeting-goers, of voluntary organizations arising spontaneously and autonomously for a myriad of purposes. Whether in student governments in school or college, in New England town meetings, in congregational business meetings, or in professional conventions, middle-class Americans, and many working-class Americans also, have considerable life experience with collegial meetings with regular meeting-times, set rules of order allowing challenges from the floor to any "railroading," and a regular rotation of meeting organizers. AA was able to draw on this unnoticed reservoir of cultural experience as its traditions developed.

What is perhaps most unusual about AA in this cultural context is its decision about collective property—that its meetings would not own any substantial collective property (distinguishing it from church congregations and many fraternal organizations) and would not hold any franchise on a territory or population (distinguishing it, for instance, from Rotary). In this, AA chose to set itself apart from U.S. capitalist traditions, at the collective as well as individual level. Again, Bill's discussion of the rationale and experience behind the 6th tradition is in terms of counteracting the individualistic egoism of alcoholics—"nearly every one of us had wished to do great good, perform great deeds, and embody great ideals. We are all perfectionists who, failing perfection, have gone to the other extreme and settled for the bottle and the blackout" (Alcoholics Anonymous, 1952, p. 156).

The general burden of the argument above is that AA is, in many complex and often ironic ways, a movement entwined with modernity, both in ideology and practice (compare argument in Kurtz, 1979, p. 216 ff.). At the obvious level of its characterization of its opponent as alcoholism, it depends for the logic of its existence on a conception of drinking deviance arising after Foucault's "shift of gaze" in the early 19th century (Levine, 1978). At a deeper level, its attack on pathologies of individualism, and particularly on egoistic pride, makes sense particularly in societies (or sections of societies) with a radically individualist ideology. If we find AA growing successfully in milieux outside these limits, we may hypothesize that AA's ideology there will have shifted considerably from its origins.

AA is also entwined in modernity in its solutions to the problems it takes on. It asks that the newcomer act and think individualistically—in defining for himself/herself a Higher Power, in finding a suitable meeting and sponsor, in speaking up about his or her own experience. It offers organizational forms and traditions that assume a democratic culture and, to some extent, urban rhythms of life. In throwing their weight towards the collectivist side of modern traditions, AA's methods often take for granted aspects of an individualist frame of thought.

In the context of North America, AA can be seen as a corrective to pathological aspects of the culture of individualism. But in a wider world context, its cultural thrust is more equivocal. In contexts such as Central America, AA may be the carrier of modernity and may be on the cutting edge of the introduction of individualist habits of thought and action into the culture.

The Future: AA and the Emergence of a
Generalized 12-Step Consciousness

In the course of the 1980s, many of those who participated in Alcoholics Anonymous and other 12-step groups came to think of themselves as members of a more general phenomenon, a "12-step movement" or a "recovery movement" transcending AA or the other particular groups which they attended (see Room, 1992). This shift in consciousness came in the wake of the growth of the Adult Children of Alcoholics (ACOA) movement, which got under way in the early 1980s. This shift may have been associated with the personal odysseys of many ACOA members. Some, for instance, moved on from the ACOA movement to AA as they became concerned about their own drinking, and then to Women Who Love Too Much groups or Sex and Love Addicts Anonymous groups as they moved to do something about their current pattern of relationships.

A conviction on the part of growing numbers of people that they were multiply addicted was probably a precondition for moving towards a general 12-step consciousness. The conventional recourse has been to attend a different 12-step meeting for each problem, often tackling the problems one at a time so that the individual's group membership is serial or cumulative. But many seem to find this problematic: "If I deal with my codependency at one meeting, my addiction at another, my abuse issues at yet another, where, when and how do I put it all together?" (W., M., 1991). No formal response to this problem has yet emerged, although it is reported that "there are unofficial 'All Anonymous' meetings where sharing on any addiction is allowed. There are unofficial Twelve Step meetings where those from many programs gather for step study and don't discuss individual diseases" (M., 1991).

Undoubtedly some members of AA would welcome a unified organizational form that reflected a generalized 12-step consciousness. This is unlikely to emerge from AA or other condition-specific 12-step groups themselves, however, if only because of their polity. Group-level consensus decision-making, with little in the way of a hierarchical decision-making structure, is about the most conservative possible form of organization: innovation can be effectively blocked by a small minority at multiple levels. Neither a solution in which AA expands its scope to cover other problems, nor one in which there is a substantial merger of associations, seems at all likely. If a unified 12-step fellowship were to emerge, it would probably be as a new organization which gradually drew strength away from existing fellowships.

A more likely scenario for greater unification is in terms of continuation of present trends: the growth of facilities formally outside the 12-step groups but providing services across associations. Clubhouses serving a variety of 12-step groups, newspapers like *Recovering,* sections on "recovery" in bookstores, and 12-step stores, cruises, and conferences serving all in the "recovery community" are already well established. The commercial impulse that often takes over outside the associations themselves dictates appealing to the widest possible market.

The movement toward a generalized 12-step consciousness complicates personal and social responsibilities: instead of having a master status as an "alcoholic" or "overeater," and organizing oneself around recovering from that addiction, increasingly one is expected to examine and feel responsible for a wide variety of addictive behaviors. This shift in part lies behind the decline of smoking in California AA meetings; even the totemic coffee-pot has come under increasing scrutiny. One letter to *Recovering* complains about what the author calls "12-step bashing": the Overeaters Anonymous members, for instance, who tells "the recovering alcoholic that he or she is not really sober if they still drink coffee, eat sugar, or smoke" (G., 1991). At an institutional level, *Recovering* has felt constrained to limit its advertising to events or behaviors that would not feed any of the recognized addictions of its readers (Atkins, 1989/90). The ideology of "codependence," which subjects to scrutiny any behavior that might be seen as enabling another's addiction, conflicts with the traditional AA live-and-let-live ideology.

There is also a deeper conflict between general 12-step movement ideology and some strains of the ACOA movement, as some *Recovering* correspondents have noted (B., 1991). Locating the source of one's life problems not in one's own behavior but in family processes around another's behavior, ACOA ideology encourages self-reliance, self-regard and indeed putting one's own interests first. The emphasis on giving up trying to control another's behavior was there from the beginning of Al-Anon, but before the 1980s it was applied in the context of family dynamics, rather than to life in general. Now the ideology has been generalized, often in the concept of "codependency"—"a general tendency toward being too other-directed." Alongside the various strands of the ACOA movement, Co-Dependents Anonymous, which began at the end of 1986, had grown to 1,600 meetings by mid-1990; an observer wondered: "Is CoDA what we've all been waiting for, an opening to the general population, the 12-step program for everybody?" (W., 1990).

Such an ideology is, of course, quintessentially individualistic, and putting it into practice tends to undermine any altruistic or community-building behavior. The ideology thus potentially subverts important features of 12-step groups—12th-stepping, sponsorship, and the empathy and service ethics—features that are, in fact, the most crucial for institutional survival.

The ideology of the coalcoholism and codependency movements holds further hidden conflicts with AA's original ideology. Where AA members are taught to be suspicious of any rationalizations of their behavior ("your best thinking got you here"), the "co" movements start from a rationalization and interpretation of one's own behavior in terms of external factors—the behavior of others. In emphasizing the effects on one's current life of patterns in the family of upbringing, the ACOA movement chooses a psychodynamic view of life problems, akin to the psychoanalytic views of the 1930s (Roizen, 1977), as opposed to AA's more phenomenological view. Hand in hand with this epistemology, the thinking of the "co" movements is much more heavily dominated by professional therapists. The central texts of the movements are not anonymously compiled, but are written by therapists who have acquired a celebrity status. Some groups, such as Robin Norwood's Women Who Love Too Much groups, are organized explicitly around the writings of a particular therapist. Quite a few "co" groups have deviated from 12-step practice in having a professional-led or hierarchical structure.

We might therefore guess that 12-step groups built around codependency concepts will not find it easy to maintain themselves as self-governing nonhierarchical organizations. But the influx of codependency ideas may also weaken AA itself. This may be part of the explanation of some recent reports of attenuation of AA 12th-stepping traditions (see Room, 1992), and of the finding in a study of AA in Marin County (Kaskutas, 1989) of increasing difficulties in getting people to fill the minimum service positions to keep meetings operating. The attractive power of the movement is likely to lessen if its meeting structures and processes weaken.

All movements, in any case, eventually reach a saturation point, where they have exhausted the population pool from which they draw. Usually, the high-water mark of a movement is still only a small fraction of all those who were eligible. From this point of view, AA may be approaching saturation in the United States. Comparing the 9% of the U.S. adult population who have ever attended an AA meeting with the one-fifth or so who ever drank at all heavily, we might guess that the upward curve of AA membership in the U.S. cannot long continue. As a whole, the broad spectrum of 12-step groups must be seen as further from saturation, but it is worth keeping in mind that already about as many U.S. adults went to a 12-step group in the last year as went to any kind of psychotherapist or counselor (Room & Greenfield, 1991).

Against this, it must be noted that each stage in AA's growth could hardly have been predicted before it occurred. It would have been a brave observer of AA before 1939 who would have predicted its take-off in the early 1940s. A commentator in the 1950s might well have concluded that

AA was associated with a particular age-cohort, and would dwindle like, say, the Women's Christian Temperance Union as its founding generations aged and died. A social analyst in the 1970s might have predicted that AA's organizational vitality would be sapped by the growth of public and private alcoholism treatment institutions. An observer in the 1980s might have expected recruitment to AA to decline with the fall in U.S. per capita consumption after 1981. So far, AA has confounded any such predictions, growing to become a pervasive influence in American life, with an expanding presence also on the world stage. When the history of the twentieth century is written, AA will merit discussion, not only for its influence in the specific field of alcohol problems, but also for its influence as a general organizational model—a model of how mutual help efforts can be workably organized on a nonhierarchical, nonprofessionalized and flexible basis.

Acknowledgments

This chapter draws on drafts written for the International Collaborative Study of Alcoholics Anonymous and thus reflects the shared thinking of participants in that study. Parts of the chapter were drafted at the Alcohol Research Group, Medical Research Institute of San Francisco; preparation of these were supported by a National Alcohol Research Center grant from the National Institute on Alcohol Abuse and Alcoholism. The chapter was completed at the Addiction Research Foundation of Ontario. Opinions expressed are those of the author alone.

References

A generation faces alcoholism. (1987, August 10). *San Francisco Chronicle*, p. 8.
Alcoholics Anonymous. (1952). *Twelve steps and twelve traditions.* New York: Alcoholics Anonymous World Services.
Al-Anon. (1981). *Living with an alcoholic with the help of Al-Anon.* New York: Al-Anon Family Group Headquarters.
Atkins, L. (1989/90, Dec./Jan.). Editor's desk, *Recovering,* p. 4.
B., B. (1991, August). [letter to editor], *Recovery,* pp. 4, 6.
Bellah, R., Madsen, R., Sullivan, W.M., Swidler, A., & Tipton, S.M. (1985). *Habits of the heart: Individualism and commitment in American life.* Berkeley and Los Angeles: University of California Press.
Bloomfield, K. (1988). *Beyond sobriety: The cultural significance of Alcoholics Anonymous as a social movement.* Unpublished working paper, University of California, Berkeley, California.
Bufe, C. (1991). *Alcoholics Anonymous: Cult or cure?* San Francisco: See Sharp Press.
G., P. (1991, September). [letter to editor] *Recovering,* p. 4.
Johnson, H. (1987). *Alcoholics Anonymous in the 1980s: Variations on a theme* (Doctoral dissertation, University of California at Los Angeles).
Kaskutas, L. (1989). *A study of Alcoholics Anonymous in Marin County.* San Rafael, CA: Marin Institute for the Prevention of Alcohol and Other Drug Problems.

Kurtz, E. (1979). *Not-God: A history of Alcoholics Anonymous.* Center City, MN: Hazelden Educational Services.

Leach, B. & Norris, J.L. (1977). Factors in the development of Alcoholics Anonymous. In B. Kissin & H. Begleiter (Eds.), *The biology of alcoholism: Vol. 5. Treatment and rehabilitation of the chronic alcoholic* (pp. 441–543). New York and London: Plenum.

Levine, H.G. (1978). The discovery of addiction: Changing conceptions of habitual drunkenness in American history. *Journal of Studies on Alcohol, 39,* 143–174.

Madsen, W. (1979). Alcoholics Anonymous as a crisis cult. In M. Marshall (Ed.), *Beliefs, behaviors, and alcoholic beverages* (pp. 328–388). Ann Arbor: University of Michigan Press.

M., V.R. (1991, Jan.). The twelve steps: Meeting the challenge of our success. *Recovering,* pp. 1, 9.

Mäkelä, K. (1990, October 10–11). AA as a social movement. Paper presented at a conference on popular mass movements and the society in 2010, Espoo, Finland.

Michels, R. (1958). *Political parties: A sociological study of the oligarchical tendencies of modern democracy.* Glencoe, IL: Free Press.

Peterson, J. (1992). The international origins of Alcoholics Anonymous. *Contemporary Drug Problems, 19,* 53–74.

Roizen, R. (1977). A note on alcoholism treatment goals and paradigms of deviant drinking. *Drinking and Drug Practices Surveyor, 13,* 13–16.

Room, R. (1989). Alcoholism and Alcoholics Anonymous in U.S. films 1945–1962: The party ends for the "wet generations." *Journal of Studies on Alcohol, 50,* 368–383.

Room, R. (1992). "Healing ourselves and our planet": The emergence and nature of a generalized twelve step consciousness. *Contemporary Drug Problems,* forthcoming.

Room, R. & Greenfield, T. (1991). *Alcoholics Anonymous, other 12-Step movements and psychotherapy in the U.S. population, 1990* (Working Paper F281). Berkeley: Alcohol Research Group, Medical Research Institute of San Francisco.

Triennial surveys profile A.A. membership over the years. (1990, Fall). *About AA,* pp. 1–2.

W., C. (1990, May-June). ACA vs. CoDA, *Changes,* p. 9.

W., M. (1991, June). Left-handed non-smoking pagan AA meeting here tonight! *Recovering,* pp. 1, 13.

W., S. (1991, June). [letter to editor], *Recovering,* p. 3.

Zald, M.N. (1988). The trajectory of social movements in America. *Research in Social Movements, Conflicts and Change, 10,* 19–41.

CHAPTER 11

Implications for Research of the Cultural Variability of Alcoholics Anonymous

Klaus Mäkelä

The aim of this chapter is to illustrate some dimensions of cultural variation within Alcoholics Anonymous (AA) and to discuss implications for research of this variability. The international diffusion and structure of AA is described in the first section. This is followed by a discussion of cross-national variation in membership composition. Variations in the structure and dynamics of AA as a social movement are described in the third section, followed by a discussion of the meaning of spirituality as one aspect of the belief system of AA. In the fifth section, the interaction order of AA and the AA meeting as a speech event are analyzed. The last section points to some implications for research of the cultural variability of AA.

Alcoholics Anonymous as an International Fellowship

International Diffusion of AA

By looking at the diffusion of Alcoholics Anonymous we may shed light on what is essential in AA and what features are accidental reflections of its time and place of birth. The cultural specificity of AA has been formulated on many different levels, on the level of American middle-class values (Trice & Roman, 1970), on the level of white male Anglo-Saxon experience (Denzin, 1987, pp. 164–165), or on the level of temperance cultures (Levine, in press). Levine discusses AA as a continuation of temperance traditions characteristic of English-speaking and Nordic countries. In these countries, distilled liquor was historically the dominant alcoholic beverage, and Protestantism was the dominant religion. The combination of disruptive drinking and Protestantism lead to an obsessive concern about alcohol-related problems and to enduring and powerful temperance movements. To Levine, AA is a continuation of the same concern about alcohol in a new historical situation. The distribution of AA groups in the

TABLE 1
AA Groups and Members in the World in 1965 and 1986 by Linguistic
and Cultural Region (percent)

	GROUPS		MEMBERS
	1965	1986	1986
United States and Canada	81.1	57.2	53.8
Other Anglophone countries	8.3	7.2	5.2
Scandinavia	2.0	1.4	1.3
Other European countries	2.3	5.5	4.6
Latin America	5.7	27.8	34.5
Other countries	0.6	0.8	0.6
Total	100.0	99.9	100.0

Source: Annual statistics collected by the General Service Office in New York.

world by linguistic and cultural region (Table 1) provides partial support to Levine's interpretation. Levine's temperance cultures accounted for 60% of the membership of AA in 1986. The trends over time, however, point in a different direction. The share of all active AA groups in English-speaking and Scandinavian Protestant countries diminished from 1965 to 1986 while the share in central and southern European and particularly Latin American countries substantially increased. In 1986, Latin America accounted for more than one-third of the world membership of AA. Consequently, the relationship of AA to temperance traditions has to be reformulated.

By the end of the 1980s, the diffusion of AA had definitely moved beyond the cultural confines of the Anglo-Saxon and Protestant world. Long-lasting AA activities had typically been established in all wealthy non-communist, non-Islamic countries. After the upheavals in Eastern Europe, we can safely predict that AA will be established all over Europe. The fellowship also has established bridgeheads in some industrialized Asian countries (Mäkelä, 1991a).

Mechanisms of Diffusion of AA

American culture has often been actively exported or promoted by centralized organizations. In contrast, there are no military, political, commercial, or even national cultural interests connected to the spread of AA.

A summary of the influences on the early beginnings of AA in seven countries is presented in Table 2. The diffusion of AA has been based mainly on the efforts of individual members, often with a middle-class background, in connection to their regular work and everyday activities (diplomatic or military missions, commercial or professional travel, tourism). It is worth pointing out that direct influence by U.S. residents or visitors has been significant in only three of these countries. Direct contacts with the United States have nevertheless been important since in five countries key roles have been played by local natives who have visited or emigrated to the United States. Once AA has been established within a linguistic region, local members often support AA activities in other countries sharing the same language. Latin America has a system of international sponsorship whereby countries formally sponsor each other. At the First Ibero-American Service Meeting in 1979, Mexico was given the task of sponsoring Spain; Colombia sponsored Panama, Ecuador, and Peru; and Argentina sponsored Chile, Paraguay, and Bolivia. Austria and Switzerland provide examples of similar but less formalized mechanisms of support.

Professional conferences and networks usually play a decisive part in the diffusion of health technologies and techniques. Until recently, this mechanism of diffusion has not been of great significance to AA, although alcohol professionals have played some role in the early stages of AA in many countries. Lately, institutional treatment systems based on the AA program also have been important for the diffusion of AA at least in Iceland and Sweden (Stenius, 1991).

Unlike religious groups, AA does not have paid employees for missionary work, although the General Service Office in New York has from early on provided centralized advice and occasionally assistance in, for example, translating the literature to national languages. Individual members sometimes have carried out energetic campaigns to strengthen AA in some region. In 1958, an AA veteran from the United States, Gordon M., traveled to the Caribbean on what was later known as the "Caribbean crusade" (Rosovsky, 1989a). In the late 1980s, a certain kind of AA diplomacy emerged, particularly with respect to the Soviet Union. Private foundations closely related to AA supported several North American AA delegations visiting the Soviet Union (Alcoholics Anonymous, 1989b; Don P., 1989; Zink, 1990).

In the main, AA continues to spread from drunk to drunk as an authentic grass-roots movement. This is in clear contrast to many other innovations bearing the imprint of American culture, such as the new religious movements of the last decades. The implantation in Europe of the Unification Church, Scientology, Transcendental Meditation, and other related cults has been centrally directed from the United States (Beckford & Levasseur, 1986).

TABLE 2
Influences on Early Beginnings of Alcoholics Anonymous in Seven Countries

	A	SF	IS	MEX	PL	S	CHF	CHI	CHG
Year of first attempt to start AA inspired activities	1959	1946	1948	1941	1969	1939	1948	1974	1962
Year when first autonomous AA group in national language was established	1960	1950	1954	1947	1974	1953	1956	1976	1963
Significant influence of local natives having emigrated to the United States	−	+	+	+	+	−	−	−	−
Significant influence of local natives having visited the United States	−	−	+	+	+	+	−	−	−
Significant influence of American residents									
Members of AA	−	−	−	+	−	−	−	−	−
Treatment professionals	−	−	−	−	−	−	+	−	−
Significant influence of American visitors									
Members of AA	−	−	−	+	+	−	−	−	−
Treatment professionals	−	−	−	−	+	−	−	−	−
Significant influence of visitors from other countries									
Members of AA	+	−	−	−	+	−	+	+	+
Treatment professionals	−	−	−	−	−	−	+	−	+

Direct financial support from GSO in New York	–	–	–	+	–	–	–
Direct financial support from AA in other countries	–	–	–	–	+	–	–
Professionals playing important role as initiators of the first few groups							
Medical doctors	–	+	–	+	–	+	+
Psychiatrists	–	–	–	–	+	–	+
Social workers	+	–	+	–	–	+	+
Professionals playing important supporting role for the first few groups							
Medical doctors	–	+	–	+	–	+	+
Psychiatrists	–	–	–	+	+	+	+
Social workers	–	–	–	–	+	+	+
Institutional 12-step treatment important in growth of AA	–	–	+	–	–	–	–

Note: The column titles designate countries by international identification letters used on license plates on cars: A = Austria, SF = Finland, IS = Iceland, MEX = Mexico, PL = Poland, S = Sweden, CH = Switzerland. Letters attached to CH refer to French, Italian, or German speakers in Switzerland.

Relationships Between the North American
and the International Service Structure

In the beginning, the cofounders acted as leaders and advisers for the fellowship worldwide. In 1955, the responsibility for the leadership of the fellowship was taken over by the General Service Conference. At that time, groups were already meeting in a number of countries and languages, and Bill W.'s vision AA was to spread around the globe—but the conference delegates came from only the United States and Canada (Bill W., 1986, p. 16).

Following Bill W.'s vision, the original version of the North American conference charter foresaw that "other Sections of the Conference may sometimes be created in foreign lands as the need arises out of language or geographical consideration" (Alcoholics Anonymous, 1986, p. 24). In a revision adopted in 1987, the reference to future "other Sections of the Conference" was deleted from the North American conference charter. The present version only refers to the World Service Meeting and speaks of encouraging consultation between national service conferences (Alcoholics Anonymous, 1988a, p. S29).

In October 1967, an inquiry was sent to representatives of 11 countries and two zones (Central America and South America) asking whether they would like to send two delegates to a World Service Meeting ("not a conference, since it would not be fully representative of world A.A."). The First World Service Meeting was held in New York City in 1969. Twelve countries that had developed central headquarters were represented. At the 11th World Service Meeting held in Munich in 1990, 21 countries were represented.

The World Service Meeting represents the international voice of the fellowship but it has no power to make decisions in the name of the world conscience of AA groups. As shown by the following excerpt from an interview with a Finnish oldtimer, there are members who would like to change this situation:

> The present World Service Meeting structure was a failure from the very beginning. The meeting was created when countries like Finland wanted to have their voice heard. At the World Service Meeting their voice is heard alright but it is of no consequence.

Occasionally, delegates may also feel that more account could be taken of the cultural variability of the world in planning World Service Meeting discussions. One of the agenda items of the 1988 World Service Meeting was as follows: "Discuss instances where the original literature does not reflect local conditions, e.g., 'too American.' " Some concern was expressed with respect to the cultural specifity of the content, but the discussion was mainly restricted to purely linguistic matters and to whether other English-speaking countries would need local idiomatic expressions instead of the original American formulations (Alcoholics Anonymous, 1988b). English continues to be the main language of the World Service Meeting, but simultaneous translation in Spanish has been provided since 1982 (Alcoholics Anonymous, 1990b).

Within a few years, it is very likely that less than half of the Alcoholics Anonymous members will be living in the United States or Canada, but the North American General Service Conference continues to represent the ultimate authority of the movement.[1] The somewhat ambiguous international structure of AA has not, however, caused real conflicts.

In matters of international service, the key role is played by the General Service Office (GSO) in New York. If divisions occur within national movements, it still is up to the office in New York to determine which faction is the official one.[2] In Mexico, there are two parallel service structures, known as Central Mexicana and Seccion Mexico. They both have a large following and count approximately 600 groups in Mexico City alone. Both publish translations of American AA literature, but only Central Mexicana has been granted legal copyright by the GSO in New York (Rosovsky, 1989b). The loose and unbureaucratic structure of AA makes it understandable that legal aspects of AA activities are recurrent topics at World Service Meetings where representatives of the GSO encourage national delegates to pay attention to the legal protection of AA logos and literature.

The moral authority of the North American General Service Conference as representing the legacy of the cofounders and of the early experiences of the fellowship probably suffices to explain why this situation has not caused conflicts. Financial factors may also contribute. The majority of groups outside North America function in relatively poor countries. Through the GSO in New York, North American groups continue to support international service activities financially, including a considerable part of the expenses connected with the World Service Meeting.[3]

Due to the structures of AA, issues of international service structure are of little concern. In most organizations, ordinary members show little interest in organizational matters, and in AA this is accentuated by the total autonomy of individual groups. National AA movements also function independently, and the power of the General Service Office in New York is strictly limited. As time goes on, there develops a national elite of oldtimers who work at various levels of the service structure, but there is little growing ground for a diplomatic elite that would feel the vocation to pursue their cultural perspectives on an international level. World service representatives usually are regular members and not paid employees of AA. The principle of rotation also results in few delegates having time to learn the craft of international meetings.

It is unlikely that in near future AA will establish any supranational bodies with power to represent the conscience of the fellowship. It may be of some symbolic significance, however, that, based on floor action, the 11th World Service Meeting (Alcoholics Anonymous, 1990b) decided to establish a fund for promoting AA literature worldwide. This fund is the first to be administered directly by the World Service Meeting and not by the GSO in New York.

Despite the worldwide diffusion of AA, its American origins are still clearly visible in its international service structure. Research on AA has been even more strongly dominated by North American perspectives and by issues that have to do with the specific impact of AA on the American treatment system and on cultural images of alcoholism in the United States.

Membership Composition

The most striking differences in the composition of the membership of AA relate to gender (Rosenqvist, 1992). The proportion of women among members of AA varies from 10% in Mexico to 44% in Austria and up to 50% in Switzerland. The proportion of female members in AA has an immediate impact on the internal character of the movement, but it should also be put in relation to the number of heavily drinking women in each country. Interestingly enough, in all study countries for which data are available, women seem to be overrepresented in AA compared to their share among heavy drinkers or in clinical populations seeking treatment. According to population estimates based on a general population survey in the United States in 1988, 26.5% of those meeting proposed DSM-IV criteria for alcohol abuse and dependence were women (Grant, 1992, Table 2). According to AA's own membership survey of 1989, the proportion of females was 35% (Alcoholics Anonymous, 1990a). In Finland, 10% of all heavy drinkers were women, as estimated by the 1984 drinking survey (Simpura, 1987), but their share among alcohol clients at outpatient treatment facilities was 20% in 1987 (Lehto, 1991). Their share among AA members is even higher, around 25%. In a clinical screening in Mexico, 8% of the patients classified as alcoholics were women (de la Fuente, 1991), whereas women accounted for 10% of the Mexican membership of AA.

Studies of gender relations in AA would be important for an understanding of how AA meetings in many countries attract an overrepresentation of women, as compared to professional treatment systems. The original literature of AA has a rather patriarchal flavor. Many AA groups still seem to be based on very traditional sex roles, but there may well be as much variability in gender roles within AA as there is in the surrounding societies.

The proportion of members less than 30 years old is less than 10% in Finland, Poland, and Sweden but around 30% in Iceland and Mexico (Bloomfield, 1991b). These figures indicate that there is no simple relationship between the age structure of the membership and the maturity of the movement or the nature of the surrounding culture.

In the literature, AA is described as a predominantly middle-class movement (Bean, 1975; Trice & Roman, 1970), but historical contingencies may have a long-lasting influence on the class composition of the membership. In Finland, the first autonomous AA groups grew out of the so-called Home Clubs for alcoholics working under the auspices of the social democratic temperance movement (Mäkelä, 1989). The first Home Club was led by a social worker who recruited members mainly from her working-class clientele. As a consequence, the first AA members in Finland much more frequently had a working-class background than was the case in the United States.[4] In Mexico, urban workers and rural poor are strongly represented among the membership of AA.

The class background of AA members may be related to their channel of recruitment. People coming from institutional 12-step treatment centers are particularly likely to belong to the upper social strata, partly because of better insurance coverage. In Sweden, the early oldtimers often were blue-collar workers whereas the newer members coming from Minnesota treatment centers are predominantly middle class.

Meaningful data on drinking and drug experiences of members of AA are even harder to get than data on their demographic composition. It is very likely that multiple drug use is much more common among AA members in North America than elsewhere; in 1989, 42% of the membership reported that they were addicted to other drugs besides alcohol (Alcoholics Anonymous, no date). It is generally thought that the number of newcomers with less extreme drinking careers has been on the rise in the United States, but corresponding cross-cultural speculations are not available.

Because of the cross-cultural variation in membership composition, great caution is required in any generalizations about which types of drinkers feel at home in AA and which do not. Insofar as the recruitment of new members is based on informal networks and social identification, the composition of membership tends to perpetuate itself. Historical contingencies may therefore have a long-lasting influence on the nature of AA in each country.

Structure and Dynamics of the Movement

Important differences are related to the phase of development and rate of growth of AA in each country. In Austria, AA activities started in 1960. It took 18 years before the number of groups exceeded 20. Internally, the movement has reached a considerable degree of maturity, but it remains relatively small (Eisenbach-Stangl, 1991). In Finland, the first autonomous AA group started in 1948. In five years, more than 20 groups were active. Finland now ranks third in Europe after Iceland and Ireland in terms of the number of groups relative to the population (Mäkelä, 1991a). The annual growth rate of the membership was extremely high in the 1950s, oscillated around 20% in the 1960s and 1970s, went steadily down in the 1980s, but was still above 10% in 1988 (Mäkelä, 1989, Table 2). In Poland, the first autonomous AA group started in 1974. The socialist government was suspicious of the movement, and it took 10 years before the number of groups reached 20. During the last few years of the 1980s, the growth was truly amazing, and in 1989 there were more than 300 AA groups (Woronowicz & Zielinski, 1992).

In some countries, institutional 12-step treatment has had an important impact on membership recruitment. Although the early growth of AA in North America was spectacular, the rate of growth slacked somewhat in the 1950s and 1960s (Mäkelä, 1992). The increase in membership was considerably steeper in the 1970s and 1980s, very likely because of the growing symbiosis between AA and the professional treatment system and the influx of new members through rehabilitation centers. In Sweden, AA for a long time had great difficulties surviving in the shadow of a native self-help movement, the Links (Kurube, 1991a, 1991b). The situation was suddenly changed in the mid-1980s with the advent of institutional 12-step treatment of the Minnesota type (Helmersson, 1991). From 1977 on, Iceland similarly experienced a sudden expansion of institutional 12-step treatment. As a result, an astonishing 10% of all men in their forties had by the end of 1985 been admitted to inpatient alcoholism treatment at least once in their life (Olafsdóttir, 1988).

The rate of growth and maturity of the movement in each country is reflected in the length of sobriety attained by members of AA. According to group surveys carried out in the course of the international AA project, the percentage of members with less than one year of sobriety varied from 26% in German-speaking Switzerland to 67% in Poland. At the other end of the continuum, more than one-tenth of the membership had at least 10 years of sobriety in Finland, German-speaking Switzerland, and the United States, whereas there were fewer experienced members in, for instance, Iceland, Mexico, Poland, and Sweden.

There also are differences in the complexity of service structure and the degree of diversification among AA groups. In Austria, Iceland, Sweden, and Switzerland, service meetings are held at two levels above the group level, whereas the number of levels in the service structure is four in Finland and five in the United States. Another indicator of the complexity of the service structure, the number of subcommittees of the national service board, varies from none in Austria to 11 in the United States and 13 in Mexico.

Numerical strength and maturity tend to lead to a diversification of groups and meetings (Olafsdóttir, 1992). All-women's groups exist in all study countries except Austria and Switzerland, but only Finland and the United States have all-men's groups. Special groups for young people exist in Iceland, Mexico, Sweden, and the United States. Iceland and Poland are the only study countries not having at least one AA group for gays and lesbians. In most countries, however, the number of special-interest groups and meetings is low, and only in the United States have special-interest meetings any quantitative significance.

Interpretations of Spirituality

Members of AA vary widely with respect to the content of their beliefs concerning many aspects of the program. There are significant differences in exactly what sense alcoholism is defined as a disease. Another example is provided by the beliefs concerning the nature of the 12 steps. To some members, each step should be taken only once, with the exception of the maintenance steps; to other members, each step should be worked on continuously. In the following, the focus is on interpretations of spirituality as one key aspect of the belief system.

In a report published in the World Health Forum (Stewart, Didon, & Johnson, 1991), AA in the Seychelles is described as containing "a healthy dose of prayer." This may be true in the Seychelles but not necessarily in other parts of the AA globe. Kurtz (1979) describes how the language of the 12 steps reflects the conflict between those early members who wished the AA program to be Christian in doctrine and other who objected to any references to God. According to Kurtz (1979, p. 71), "neither Wilson nor A.A. did ever solve this problem." Indeed, to Kurtz the unresolved tension between these two perspectives is a central feature of AA.

Although the wording of the steps has remained unaltered, Peterson (1992) points to the important shifts in the discussion of the steps in official AA literature. In comparison to *Alcoholics Anonymous* (Alcoholics Anonymous, 1939, 1955), in *Twelve Steps and Twelve Traditions* (Alcoholics Anonymous, 1952) the second step has been transformed from a preparation for a third step, involving a formal statement of surrender to God, to an acceptance of the AA group or the AA program as providing the help to overcome the powerlessness over alcohol acknowledged in the first step.

As can be expected, there are regional and cross-national differences in interpretations of spirituality. As an outward sign of this variability, we may note that AA meetings are closed with the Christian Lord's Prayer in many parts of the United States and in some Icelandic groups (Olafsdóttir, 1991). This custom is uncommon or nonexistent in, for example, Austria (Eisenbach-Stangl, 1992b), Finland (Mäkelä, 1991b), France (Alcoholics Anonymous, 1989), and Poland (Woronovicz & Zielinski, 1992). Madsen (1980) suggests that within the United States, a traditional religious orientation is more typical in the Midwest and the South, while a nonreligious approach is more prevalent in California and the urban Northeast. In a survey of the membership of AA (Bloomfield, 1991a), 88% of the Mexican sample but only 28% of the Swedish sample endorsed the following statement: "I know God really exists and I have no doubts about it." In Mexico, 35% said that the "power greater than ourselves" mentioned in the 12 steps "refers to the AA fellowship or the power of the group" whereas the corresponding figure was 47% in Iceland and 59% in Sweden. The differences with respect to participation in organized religion were even more marked. In the Swedish sample, 63% attended worship less than once a year, whereas the corresponding figure in Mexico was only 15%.

Spirituality is an extremely complex field of meaning (Eisenbach-Stangl, 1992a). Percentage figures about specific beliefs provide a crude picture of different lines of thought but they certainly illustrate the wide diversity of beliefs held by members of AA.

The AA Meeting as a Speech Event

Part of practicing the AA program is individual action, such as reading the literature, prayer and mediation, or taking the 4th-step inventory, but most of the program is carried out in social interaction. Any contacts between members may be part of the program, but the most important interactive events are AA meetings. Against this background there are surprisingly few studies or detailed descriptions of concrete AA meetings in the literature. What we usually get is a summary description of "a typical meeting" and perhaps a discussion of the emotional and social dynamics of AA meetings. An analysis of AA based on small-group dynamics runs, however, the danger of remaining too general since an AA meeting clearly differs from most other face-to-face encounters. AA is at the same time a *system of beliefs* and a *system of interaction* based on a specific set of rules of talk.

The specificity of AA meetings is related more to ways of speaking than to what is said. The lack of cross-talk and of overt negative feedback to previous turns of talk make AA meetings unique speech events. A Finnish oldtimer put it this way: "Comments and advice must be given privately, otherwise the spell of the meeting may be broken."

Members of AA are well aware of the uniqueness of AA meetings. The following excerpts are from interviews with Finnish members of AA:

> The secret of AA is that you get the feeling that 'those bastards are not even interested in me.' Nobody in AA asks where you come from and where you are going and there is no compulsion to do anything.

> AA is like a long-time analysis with the group as the analyst. It is important that members do not comment on each other but that each member is allowed to draw her own conclusions.

The problem is that the rules of talk remain implicit. AA meetings are robust in the sense that blatant transgressions of the rules of discourse most often are simply ignored and are thus not allowed to disturb the main line of the meeting. The variability of meetings also contributes to make it difficult to pin down the core of the interaction order of AA. The following are examples of some of the most evident differences.

In Austria, most meetings have circular seating arrangements. An audience type seating is common in Mexico.

In Finland and in Iceland, most meetings are closed and speaker's meetings are the exception. In northern California, the majority of meetings are open meetings and speaker's meetings are quite common.

There is a lot of variation in turn-taking rules. In Finland, everybody usually speaks in seating order. In northern California, speaking on request is the most frequent format. In Switzerland, it is up to the chair to select the next speaker. At some meetings, the current speaker selects the next speaker. Differences in turn-taking rules are significant since they obviously have an impact on the topical coherence of the discussion.

Corresponding to differences in surrounding culture, there is much more eye contact, body contact, and positive feedback to previous turns of talk at American than at Finnish meetings.

At 12-step treatment centers, meetings tend to be much more confrontative and interpretative than traditional AA meetings. One could perhaps say that here the belief system takes precedence over the interaction order of AA. More generally, if we focus on the belief system of AA, variations in rules of discourse are marginal. It can be argued, however, that there are significant differences between AA meetings and other types of peer groups or professional group therapy. If this is true, it is important to carry out detailed naturalistic studies of concrete AA meetings as speech events.

Implications for Research

The cultural variability of AA and its nature as a social movement have important implications for the research agenda. AA is not a pill (Glaser & Ogborne, 1982). No attempts should be made to evaluate AA as such since social movements cannot be evaluated in any technical sense. What should be evaluated is not the movement itself but actions taken by the public health and social control system with respect to the movement. If medical doctors recommend that their patients attend AA meetings, it is this advice that should be evaluated and not AA. If courts use mandatory attendance in AA as an alternative to other penalties, this sentencing practice is what should be evaluated and not AA. If inpatient or outpatient treatment systems apply the 12-step program, the efficacy of the treatment can and should be evaluated but not AA. The 12-step program can and should also be used as a source of inspiration for experimental studies of the impact of specific tools and methods commonly used within the AA movement. The treatment evaluation perspective should, however, be complemented with a social movement perspective. The basic issues may remain the same, but the research questions are formulated differently. For example, the social movement perspective formulates its questions in terms of membership turnover rather than in terms of treatment efficacy.

Affiliation and Attrition

We may distinguish between questions of recruitment or affiliation and questions of attrition: Who joins AA? How long do members stay in the fellowship and how do they leave the movement?

The recruitment process can be analyzed in terms of the demographic characteristics, drinking experiences, personality traits, and opinions and values of those who join and those who do not join the fellowship.

Because of selection bias, retrospective studies of clinical populations are particularly ill suited for an analysis of factors affecting the likelihood of affiliation with AA. Clinical populations consist of people with current drinking problems. Clinical patients with previous AA contacts are a selection of members who have failed. It is worth emphasis that four-fifths of the studies included in the meta-analysis by Emrick, Tonigan, Montgomery, and Little (1993) were based on inpatient or outpatient samples, and most of them were retrospective.

Identification with older members is an important aspect of the affiliation process, and it is easier to identify with "people like me" (Vourakis, 1988). If the first members of AA in a country or a community represent the working class, local groups will initially attract people having the same class background. If the founding fathers are college graduates, middle-class people will be particularly likely to join the movement.

Recruitment may also differ depending of the phase of development of the movement in any particular country. The analysis of membership characteristics should therefore be complemented by a discussion of the internal structure and social context of AA and of different pathways to the movement. Early pioneers join a different movement compared to later newcomers who are surrounded by experienced oldtimers. The relationship of the fellowship to institutional treatment also makes an important difference. If a high proportion of members are recruited from inpatient treatment units based on a 12-step program, the movement looks different than if most members come directly from the field.

It may well be that public referral programs could fare better if the variability of AA meetings could somehow be taken into account. If atheists could be assisted to find agnostic meetings and college graduates to find upper middle-class meetings, this might prove even more useful than any attempts to determine which general characteristics have an impact on the likelihood of affiliating with AA.

It is possible that after a careful examination of historical particularities general characteristics may be found that distinguish AA members from those who choose not to affiliate. It is likely, however, that these common features have to be conceptualized at a higher level of abstraction than the statistical associations found in particular studies. This requires emphasis since most studies do not analyze their reported correlations as historically contingent. Empirical studies often report conflicting results with respect to factors associated with AA membership (Emrick, 1987, 1989; Ogborne & Glaser, 1981). The way out of the confusion is to complement statistical meta-analysis with an analysis of the concrete cultural and social context of each statistical relationship.

Attrition processes can be studied in terms of the same characteristics as the affiliation process. In addition, the probability of terminating AA membership should be studied in relation to time spent in the fellowship and participation in its various activities. It is also important to distinguish between different reasons for membership attrition (deaths, dropping out of AA and relapsing to problematic drinking, growing out of AA without problematic drinking, etc.).

Spirituality

Spirituality should be approached as a field of meaning and not only as a set of variables. It is extremely difficult to design measures of individual spirituality that would be independent of specific ontological and cosmological beliefs. This is not a problem in situations where the content of spirituality is the same for most people. If spirituality for most Polish or Mexican members is synonymous with Catholicism, their degree of commitment to the Catholic faith can perhaps be measured. In more heterogeneous situations, problems of measurement may be almost insurmountable. Few Finnish members of AA participate in organized religious activities, and it may be impossible to design a simple measure that would adequately take into account all existing varieties of spirituality (Arminen, 1991). Using Whitfield's Spirituality Self-Assessment Scale, Corrington (1989) found no clear correlation between spirituality and length of AA membership. One possible explanation lies in the many items that refer to the new codification of spirituality taught at professional 12-step treatment institutions ("I live in the here and now"; "I have a sense of being able to differentiate my mind (or ego) from my spirit [or higher self]"). It is conceivable that this particular type of spirituality is more alien to AA oldtimers than to newcomers from rehabilitation centers.

In any case, it is clear that successful attempts to measure spirituality require an analysis of the actual beliefs held by individual members in different cultural settings. Fields of meaning are mutually understandable to people who do not share the same beliefs. We can understand sentences and concepts we do not believe have external referents. Descriptions of inner states are similarly understandable, up to a point, to persons who do not share similar experiences. But understanding spirituality requires dialogue and conceptual analysis before measures can be designed. In a case of analysis, Miller (1988) reports how religious discussions with a patient suffering from severe depression helped him to restructure his belief system. Niemelä (1990) presents a qualitative analysis of interviews with former drunks who had experienced a religious awakening. There seem to be interesting differences between those who reported that their desire to drink had simply vanished and those who still had to struggle against the temptation.

A hermeneutic approach to spirituality does not preclude experimental research. In Probst's (1980) controlled experiment, cognitive therapy was more effective when it incorporated the client's own spiritual perspectives, irrespective of the religious orientation of the therapist. Therapists (two) and treatments were completely crossed. Neither therapist was religious but both were successful in adopting spiritual imagery.

The AA Meeting as a Speech Event

My final plea is for naturalistic studies of AA meetings as speech events. We would need a combination of detailed micro-analytical studies in the tradition of conversation analysis and more global descriptions in the tradition of ethnography of speaking. This is a long road since naturalistic studies of speech are extremely laborious, but the road is worth taking. There are experimental indications that rules of speech do matter. In a controlled study of volunteers screened for their patterns of drinking, verbal strategy used in giving feedback on the test results had a significant impact on the level of drinking in the follow-up (Miller, Benefield, & Tonigan, in press). If one single speech event can be this important, it should make sense to study the rules of talk at AA meetings.

Acknowledgment

This report has been prepared as part of the International Collaborative Study of Alcoholics Anonymous with participation from Austria, Finland, Iceland, Mexico, Poland, Sweden, Switzerland, and the United States. It is very much based on joint efforts in data collection and on a collective exchange of ideas.

Notes

1. It may be symptomatic that Kurtz's (1988) excellent history of AA contains next to nothing on international issues. Interestingly enough, AA diplomacy with respect to the Soviet Union, the second superpower at the time, belongs to the few international topics referred to. The World Service meeting is not even mentioned in the index.
2. Applications for membership in the WSM are made to GSO in New York and sent by GSO to the World Service Meeting Policy/Admissions/Finances Committee for approval by a two-thirds vote of committee members (Alcoholics Anonymous, 1990).
3. The expenses of the Ninth World Service Meeting (1986) totalled US $101,000. Of this, 52% were covered by delegate fees and contributions and 48% by the General Service Board (U.S. and Canada) (Alcoholics Anonymous, 1987b).
4. No recent data for Finland are available, but Kiviranta (1969) presents information from the early 1960s on the occupational structure of the membership of AA compared to the clientele of outpatient A-clinics and municipal or state owned asylums for alcoholics. Of the three groups, asylum inmates quite clearly were recruited from the lowest social strata. In comparison to A-clinic patients, both lower white-collar workers and unskilled workers were overrepresented among members of AA whereas the A-clinics had a larger proportion of skilled workers. There were no differences in the percentage of upper white-collar workers.

References

Alcoholics Anonymous. (1939, 1955). Alcoholics Anonymous. New York: Alcoholics Anonymous Publishing.

Alcoholics Anonymous. (1952) *Twelve steps and twelve traditions.* New York: Alcoholics Anonymous World Services.

Alcoholics Anonymous. (1986). The A.A. service manual, 1986–87 ed. New York: Alcoholics Anonymous World Services.

Alcoholics Anonymous. (1987a). Advisory actions of the General Service Conference of Alcoholics Anonymous, 1951–1986. New York: Alcoholics Anonymous World Services.

Alcoholics Anonymous. (1987b). Ninth World Service Meeting: Final Report. New York: Alcoholics Anonymous World Services.

Alcoholics Anonymous. (1988a). The A.A. service manual, 1988–1989 ed. New York: Alcoholics Anonymous World Services.

Alcoholics Anonymous. (1988b, October). Tenth World Service Meeting: Report of the Literature/Publishing Committee.

Alcoholics Anonymous. (1989a, January). A noisy distraction. *AA Grapevine,* 20–21.

Alcoholics Anonymous. (1989b). Thirty-ninth Annual Meeting of the General Service Conference of Alcoholics Anonymous: Final Report. New York: Alcoholics Anonymous World Services.

Alcoholics Anonymous. (1990a). Alcoholics Anonymous 1989 membership survey. New York: Alcoholics Anonymous World Services.

Alcoholics Anonymous. (1990b). History and recommendations of the World Service Meeting, 1969–1988.

Alcoholics Anonymous. (no date). Comments on A.A.'s triennial surveys. Unpublished report, Alcoholics Anonymous World Services.

Arminen, I. (1991, January-February). Characteristic features of spirituality within A.A. in Finland. Paper presented at the Third Working Meeting of the ICSAA, San Rafael, California.

Bean, M. (1975, February-March). Alcoholics Anonymous. Psychiatric Annals reprint. New York: Insight Communications.

Beckford, J.A. & Levasseur, M. (1986). New religious movements in Western Europe. In J.A. Beckford (Ed.), *New religious movements and rapid social change* (pp. 29–54). Paris & London: Sage/UNESCO.

Bill W. (1986). A.A.'s legacy of service. In *The A.A. service manual, 1986–87 ed.* (pp. 5–19). New York: Alcoholics Anonymous World Services.

Bloomfield, K. (1991a, January-February). Spirituality. Paper presented at the Third Working Meeting of the ICSAA, San Rafael, California.

Bloomfield, K. (1991b, January-February). The membership of AA. Paper presented at the Third Working Meeting of the ICSAA, San Rafael, California.

Corrington, J.E. (1989). Spirituality and recovery: Relationships between levels of spirituality, contentment and stress during recovery from alcoholism in AA. *Alcoholism Treatment Quarterly,6,* 151–165.

Denzin, N.K. (1987). The recovering alcoholic. Newbury Park, CA: Sage.

Don P. (1989, July). Experience, strength, and hope—A visit to the Soviet Union. *AA Grapevine,* 28–35.

Eisenbach-Stangl, I. (1991, January-February). A good-natured anarchy: History and structure of the AA community in Austria. Paper presented at the Third Working Meeting of the ICSAA, San Rafael, California.

Eisenbach-Stangl, I. (1992a, October). AA as a spiritual community. Paper presented at the Fourth Working Meeting of the ICSAA, Mexico City, Mexico.

Eisenbach-Stangl, I. (1992b, October). A survey of Austrian AA meetings. Paper presented at the Fourth Working Meeting of the ICSAA, Mexico City, Mexico.

Emrick, C.D. (1987). Alcoholics Anonymous: Affiliation processes and effectiveness as treatment. *Alcoholism: Clinical and Experimental Research, 11*(5), 416–423.

Emrick, C.D. (1989). Alcoholics Anonymous: Membership characteristics and effectiveness as treatment. In M. Galanter (Ed.), *Treatment research, Recent Developments in Alcoholism* 7 (pp. 37–53). New York & London: Plenum.

Emrick, C.D., Tonigan, J.S., Montgomery, H., & Little, L. (1993). Alcoholics Anonymous: What is currently known? In B.S. McCrady & W.R. Miller (Eds.), *Research on Alcoholics Anonymous: Opportunities and Alternatives.* New Brunswick, NJ: Rutgers Center of Alcohol Studies.

de la Fuente, J.R. (1991, January). Early detection of heavy alcohol drinkers. Paper presented at the International Symposium on Drug Dependence, Mexico City, Mexico.

Glaser, F.B. & Ogborne, A.C. (1982). Does A.A. really work? *British Journal of Addiction, 77,* 123–129.

Grant, Bridget F. (1992). Prevalence of the proposed DSM-IV alcohol use disorders: United States, 1988. *British Journal of Addiction, 87,* 309–316.

Helmersson, K. (1991, January-February). A.A. in Sweden. Paper presented at the Third Working Meeting of the ICSAA, San Rafael, California.

Kiviranta, P. (1969). *Alcoholism syndrome in Finland.* Helsinki: Finnish Foundation for Alcohol Studies.

Kurtz, E. (1979). Not-God: A history of Alcoholics Anonymous. Center City, Minn.: Hazelden.

Kurtz, E. (1988). *A.A.: The story.* San Francisco: Harper & Row.

Kurube, N. (1991a, January-February). The Link movement: A historical overview. Paper presented at the Third Working Meeting of the ICSAA, San Rafael.

Kurube, N. (1991b, January-February). Organizations and activities of Links. Paper presented at the Third Working Meeting of the ICSAA, San Rafael, California.

Lehto, J. (1991). Juoppojen professionaalinen auttaminen (Professional help for drunkards). Helsinki: National Board for Social Welfare and Health.

Levine, H. (in press). Temperance cultures: Concern about alcohol problems in Nordic and English-speaking cultures. In G. Edwards, M. Lader, & C. Drummond (Eds.), *The nature of alcohol and drug related problems.* New York: Oxford University Press.

Madsen, W. (1980). *The American alcoholic.* Springfield: Charles C. Thomas.

Mäkelä, K. (1989, October). Service structure of Alcoholics Anonymous in Finland. Paper presented at the Second Working Meeting of the ICSAA, Zaborow, Poland.

Mäkelä, K. (1991a). Social and cultural preconditions of Alcoholics Anonymous (AA) and factors associated with the strength of AA. *British Journal of Addiction, 86*(11), 1405–1413.

Mäkelä, K. (1991b, January-February). Preliminary results of a survey of Finnish A.A. meetings. Paper presented at the Third Working Meeting of the ICSAA, San Rafael, California.

Mäkelä, K. (1992, October). Alcoholics Anonymous as an international fellowship. Paper to be presented at the Fourth Working Meeting of the ICSAA, Mexico City, Mexico.

Miller, W.R. (1988). Including clients' spiritual perspectives in cognitive-behavior therapy. In W.R. Miller & J.E. Martin (Eds.), *Behavior therapy and religion* (pp. 43–56). Newbury Park: Sage.

Miller, W.R., Benefield, R.G., & Tonigan, J.S. (in press). Enhancing motivation for change in problem drinking: A controlled comparison of two therapist styles. *Journal of Consulting and Clinical Psychology.*

Niemelä, J. (1990). Viinasta vapautuminen ja retkahdusten torjuntakeinot uskoon tulleilla alkoholisteilla (How converted alcoholics seek to lead a liquor-free life and avoid backsliding). *Alkoholipolitiikka, 55*(6), 303–308.

Ogborne, A.C. & Glaser, F.B. (1981). Characteristics of affiliates of Alcoholics Anonymous. *Journal of Studies of Alcohol, 42*(7), 661–675.

Olafsdóttir, H. (1988). Lekmenn, alkoholisme og behandling (Laymen, alcoholism and treatment). *Alkoholpolitik, 5,* 83–90.

Olafsdóttir, H. (1991, January-February). Results from a survey on A.A. meetings in Iceland. Paper presented at the Third Working Meeting of the ICSAA, San Rafael, California.

Olafsdóttir, H. (1992, October). The AA meeting. Paper presented at the Fourth Working Meeting of the ICSAA, Mexico City, Mexico.

Peterson, J.H. (1992, October). Practicing the AA program. Paper presented at the Fourth Working Meeting of the ICSAA, Mexico City, Mexico.

Probst, R. (1980). The comparative efficacy of religious and nonreligious imagery for the treatment of mild depression in religious individuals. *Cognitive Therapy and Research, 4,* 167–178.

Rosenqvist, P. (1992, October). Common experiences, common identity? Gender relations in AA. Paper presented at the Fourth Working Meeting of the ICSAA, Mexico City, Mexico.

Rosovsky, H. (1989a, October). History and development of A.A. in Mexico. Paper presented at the Second Working Meeting of the ICSAA, Zaborow, Poland.

Rosovsky, H. (1989b, October). Characteristic features of A.A. in Mexico. Paper presented at the Second Working Meeting of the ICSAA, Zaborow, Poland.

Simpura, J. (Ed.). (1987). Finnish drinking habits. Helsinki: Finnish Foundation for Alcohol Studies.

Stenius, K. (1991). "The most successful treatment model in the world": Introduction of the Minnesota model in the Nordic countries. *Contemporary Drug Problems, 18,* 151–179.

Stewart, C., Didon, G. & Johnson, R. (1991). Self-help for alcoholics. *World Health Forum, 12*(2), 205–206.

Trice, H.M. & Roman, P.M. (1970). Delabeling, relabeling, and Alcoholics Anonymous. *Social Problems, 17*(4), 538–546.

Vourakis, C. (1988, August). The process of recovery for women in Alcoholics Anonymous: Seeking groups "like me." Paper presented at the First Working Meeting of the ICSAA, Helsinki, Finland.

Woronovicz, B. & Zielinski, A. (1992, October). Alcoholics Anonymous meetings in Poland. Paper presented at the Fourth Working Meeting of the ICSAA, Mexico City, Mexico.

Zink, M. (1990, July/August). The story of Creating a Sober World. *Sobriety News.*

CHAPTER 12

Ethnic Minority Groups and Alcoholics Anonymous: A Review

RAUL CAETANO

Alcoholics Anonymous (AA) has had tremendous growth in recent years. In the U.S., AA grew not only because of an increase in the number of registered groups, but also by having its view of alcoholism and 12-step ideology adopted by a majority of the alcohol treatment programs treating whites and ethnic minority groups. Yet, to date there is no information on the proportion of AA members who are part of ethnic minority groups, and little or nothing is known about the use of AA as a treatment resource by minorities in the U.S. population, about the structure of AA groups in minority communities, or about the effectiveness of AA as a treatment for minorities vis-à-vis the majority population with alcohol problems.

The objective of this chapter is to review the existing literature on the relationship between AA and ethnic minority groups in the U.S. More specifically, the study will: (1) review data on the acceptance of alcoholism as a disease by U.S. ethnic groups (acceptance of alcoholism as a disease, especially if it involves notions espoused by AA, is important for gauging AA acceptability among ethnic minority groups); (2) describe data on the utilization of AA by ethnic groups in the U.S. population and in health and social services agencies (these data cover national surveys conducted by the Alcohol Research Group [ARG] in 1979, 1984, and 1990 [Clark & Hilton, 1991; Clark & Midanik, 1982; Midanik & Clark, 1992], as well as data collected with comparable methods from agencies in a Northern California county); (3) review the alcohol literature on AA utilization by members of ethnic groups in the U.S.; and (4) provide suggestions for future epidemiological research on the use of AA by U.S. ethnic groups.

Support for the Disease Concept of Alcoholism

Data collected in the 1984 national survey of drinking patterns and alcohol problems among blacks and Hispanics provide information regarding acceptance of the disease concept by these two groups (see Caetano,

1989a, for a detailed description of methods). Agreement among whites, blacks, and Hispanics for items stating well-known AA tenets about alcoholism—"alcoholism is an illness," "without help problems get worse and worse" and "to recover alcoholics have to quit forever"—is almost unanimous (Table 1). This support is independent of sex, age, income, education, and frequency of drinking (Caetano, 1989a). There is less support for the three items that contradict AA tenets: "alcoholics can control their drinking again," "most alcoholics drink because they want to," and "alcoholics are morally weak." Support for these three items is lower among whites than among blacks and Hispanics. Within each ethnic group, subjects in lower income and education levels show more support than other subjects for these three items that contradict the disease concept. Differences across ethnic groups remain after controlling independently for education and income (Caetano, 1989a). However, there is inconsistency regarding the status of alcoholism as a disease among respondents of all three ethnic groups. Blacks and Hispanics are more inconsistent than whites: About 39% of the whites, 62% of the blacks, and 60% of the Hispanics who agree that alcoholism is an illness also agree that the alcoholic is a morally weak individual (Caetano, 1989a).

Data collected from Japanese Americans and Caucasians in Santa Clara, California, and from Japanese Americans in Hawaii also show strong support for the disease concept of alcoholism among these groups (Table 2) (see Clark & Hesselbrock, 1988, for details on methodology). At least 90% of respondents in these three groups agree that "alcoholism is an illness" and that untreated "alcoholism will get worse and worse." Support for the statement that "to recover alcoholics have to quit forever" is lower among Japanese Americans in Hawaii and Santa Clara than among Caucasians. As with whites, blacks, and Hispanics in the 1984 survey, there is less support among Japanese Americans and Caucasians for the items that contradict AA supported concepts such as "alcoholics can control their drinking again." Also, as in the results above, support for these three items is lower among Caucasians than among Japanese Americans.

These data suggest that the disease concept of alcoholism as proposed by AA is well accepted among whites, blacks, Hispanics, and Japanese Americans in Santa Clara, California, and Hawaii. Disagreement with these tenets should not be a barrier to AA utilization by these groups. Unfortunately no such data are available for other groups of Asian Americans and Native Americans.

AA Utilization by Ethnic Minority Groups in the General Population

This section describes survey data on AA use by ethnic groups in the U.S general population. Respondents in the 1979, 1984, and 1990 national

TABLE 1

Agreement with Items About the Disease Concept of Alcoholism among Whites, Blacks, and Hispanics in the U.S. General Population (in percent)

	MEN			WOMEN		
	White (*n* = 735)	Black (*n* = 712)	Hisp. (*n* = 599)	White (*n* = 1,029)	Black (*n* = 1,204)	Hisp. (*n* = 842)
Alcoholism is an illness	93	93	91	95	95	92
Without help, problems get worse and worse	95	95	93	96	96	97
To recover, alcoholics have to quit forever	83	80	88	93	88	94
Alcoholics taper off and control drinking again	24	48*	41*	22	42*	38*
Most alcoholics drink because they want to	56	73*	74*	61	70*	71*
Alcoholics are morally weak individuals	42	60*	56*	38	64*	65*

*Hispanic vs white and black vs white, $p \leq .5$, test of proportions.

TABLE 2
Agreement with Items About the Disease Concept of Alcoholism
among Japanese Americans and Caucasians in Santa Clara, California,
and Japanese Americans in Hawaii (in percent)

	Japanese Americans in Hawaii (n = 513)	SANTA CLARA	
		Japanese Americans (n = 516)	Caucasians (n = 511)
Alcoholics can decide whether to drink or not	64	58	63
Without help, problems get worse and worse	92	93	96
Alcoholism is an illness	92	90	88
Most alcoholics drink because they want to	48	36	49
To recover, alcoholics have to quit forever	67	68	81
Alcoholics taper off and control drinking again	26	16	14

surveys conducted by the Alcohol Research Group were asked whether they had ever been to AA and other health and social services agencies for a drinking problem.[1] Table 3 shows these data. By virtue of a methodological design based on the interviewing of probability samples of the U.S. general population, both the 1979 and the 1990 survey have a relatively small number of blacks and Hispanics. Rates derived for these and other ethnic groups in each of these surveys may be unstable, and should be seen with caution. The 1984 survey was designed to interview a national representative sample of blacks and Hispanics. Results from this survey are therefore more representative of the experience of service agency contact of these two populations.

In general, only a small proportion of respondents in each ethnic group reports ever using any service for an alcohol problem (Table 3). Among whites and blacks, utilization rates for almost all agencies are higher in 1990 than in previous years. For Hispanics, utilization rates in 1990 are lower than in 1984. AA is the resource most used by respondents. The proportion of whites and blacks who report ever contacting AA more than tripled between 1979 and 1990. Among Hispanics, the utilization rate of AA in 1990 is as high as that for blacks but lower than the rate for whites.

When only those respondents in the 1984 survey who reported ever having a problem are considered, the proportion of those who ever had

TABLE 3

Proportion of Whites, Blacks, and Hispanics in the U.S. Population Who Have Ever Gone to AA and Other Agencies About a Drinking Problem

	WHITES			BLACKS			HISPANICS	
	1979 (n = 1,487)	1984 (n = 1,777)	1990 (n = 1,570)	1979 (n = 165)	1984 (n = 1,947)	1990 (n = 261)	1984 (n = 1,433)	1990 (n = 150)
Alcoholics Anonymous	1.0	2.0	3.4	0.7	1.5	2.7	3.5	2.7
Other alcohol	0.7	1.0	1.9	0.2	0.5	2.3	2.0	0.5
General hospital	0.4	0.1	1.2	0	0.7	1.5	1.4	0.5
Health or mental program	0.5	0.7	1.4	1.2	0.2	1.1	1.5	0.5
Mental hospital	0.2	0.2	0.6	0	0	0	1.0	0.5
Medical group or private physician	0.5	1.0	1.3	0	0.6	0.4	2.0	1.6
Social welfare department	0	0.3	0	0	0.1	0.4	1.0	0.5
Vocational rehabilitation	0.1	0.3	0.6	0	0.4	0.8	2.0	0

TABLE 4
Utilization of Alcoholics Anonymous by Whites, Blacks, and Hispanics
in the U.S. Population Who Ever Had an Alcohol Problem: Adjusted
Odds Ratio (OR) and 95% Confidence Interval (CI)*

	WHITES		BLACKS		HISPANICS	
	OR	95% CI	OR	95% CI	OR	95% CI
Education (HS or more)	2.9	1.3-6.8	–	–	0.2	0.1-0.6
Heavier drinker	–	–	2.9	1.2-6.7	11.2	4.5-28.5
Marital status (unmarried)	–	–	–	–	3.2	1.3-7.6
Male	–	–	–	–	6.7	2.7-16.7

*ORs adjusted for all variables in the table plus age and income.

contact with AA for a drinking problem is higher than those in Table 3: 5% for whites, 5% for blacks, and 12% for Hispanics. Multivariate analysis can be used to ascertain the characteristics of these individuals in contrast to those who also report ever having a problem but do not report ever going to AA. Logistic regression was used for this purpose, and Table 4 shows the results of this analysis. The dependent variable is a dichotomy coded as 0 if the respondent did not go to AA and as 1 if the respondent went to AA. The predictors are also dichotomies, coded as follows: age: 18-39 = 0, 40 and over = 1; marital status: married = 1, single and separated or divorced = 2; education: less than high school = 1, high school or more = 2; annual income: less than $10,000 = 1, $10,000 or more = 2; heavier drinker: drinks once a week or more often and has five or more drinks at a sitting at least once a year = 1, all others = 0.[2]

Among whites, those with high school education or more have three times more chances of having been to AA than others. Among blacks the only attribute that increases respondents chances of ever having been to AA is heavier drinking. For Hispanics, the attributes are: being male, having less than high school education, being unmarried and being a heavier drinker. The goodness-of-fit chi square is not significant for any of the models. However, these results should be taken with caution. The number of respondents in some cells is small, and the estimators could therefore be unstable.[3]

Another way to gauge AA acceptability in the community is to assess whether survey respondents would recommend AA as a treatment for alcohol problems. Data collected in a 1989 survey of the general population in Contra Costa county, California, provide an answer for this question.[4] AA is the most frequently recommended resource to deal with an alcohol

TABLE 5
Proportion of Respondents Recommending Different Agencies
to Help With an Alcohol Problem by Ethnicity:
Contra Costa General Population, 1989

	Asian (*n* = 35)	White (*n* = 523)	Black (*n* = 64)	Hispanic (*n* = 38)	All (*n* = 680)
Alcoholics Anonymous	76	94	87	97	93
Private hospital program	47	68	61	63	65
Public alcohol program	71	59	57	72	60
Ordinary hospital	42	14	24	16	17
Psychiatrist/psychologist	39	42	62	57	44
Family doctor	63	53	63	59	55
Priest/minister/rabbi	53	46	70	58	49
Social worker/social service agency	58	43	55	66	46
Mental health center	29	33	51	34	34

problem across all ethnic groups (Table 5). More than two thirds of all Asian-Americans and about 90% of whites, blacks, and Hispanics would recommend AA to someone with a drinking problem. The second most frequently recommended resource among Asian Americans and Hispanics would be a public alcohol program. For whites the second choice would be a private alcohol program, and for blacks, a member of the clergy.

Similar results are found in an analysis of comparable data collected from Japanese Americans and Caucasians in Santa Clara county, California, and Japanese Americans in Hawaii (Clark & Hesselbrock, 1988) (Table 6). AA is the most frequently recommended agency for someone with a drinking problem, with at least 90% of respondents in each of the three groups making that recommendation. The pattern of responses is similar for Japanese Americans and Caucasians, the exceptions being the recommendations to use a social worker/social service agency, a health center, and relatives/friends. These resources are recommended less by Caucasians than by Japanese Americans.

The Contra Costa survey also presented respondents with vignettes describing different types of alcohol problems and asked what would be the "best place" to handle the problems. Table 7 shows the agency most frequently mentioned, the proportion of respondents who chose that agency, and the proportion who chose AA for four different problems, by ethnicity of the respondent. In general, there is agreements across ethnic groups regarding which is the best place to handle the described problems. Yet, the proportion of individuals in each ethnic group selecting any particular agency as the best is never overwhelming, ranging from 26% to 65%. A drug treatment program was the place of choice for the first vignette.

TABLE 6
Proportion of Japanese Americans and Caucasians in Santa Clara,
California, and Japanese Americans in Hawaii Recommending
Different Agencies to Help with an Alcohol Problem

| | Japanese Americans in Hawaii (*n* = 513) | SANTA CLARA | |
		Japanese Americans (*n* = 516)	Caucasians (*n* = 509)
Alcoholics Anonymous	87	92	94
Care unit	60	65	55
Ordinary hospital	26	20	27
Psychiatrist/psychologist	50	49	50
Family doctor	57	57	55
Priest/minister/rabbi	53	51	52
Social worker/service agency	54	51	40
Health center	54	56	41
Mental health center	36	30	42
Relatives/friends	43	46	38
Danshukai	65	69	NA

Note: NA = not applicable.

For the second vignette, the best place was an alcohol program. The third vignette was the most controversial, with white and Asian Americans preferring the police, blacks opting for an emergency room, and Hispanics choosing an alcohol program. The fourth vignette described a problem that the majority of whites, blacks, Hispanics, and Asians thought should be dealt with by an alcohol program.

The proportion of respondents who chose AA as the best agency is not high for any problem. Hispanics seem to be the ethnic group that gives most preference to AA. The problems described in the second and the fourth vignette (from top to bottom of the table) are those with the highest proportion of respondents suggesting that AA is the best agency to handle that problem.

Altogether the data from Tables 5 and 7 provide a different picture of the place of AA in responding to drinking problems. The data suggest that subjects' responses will vary considerably depending on the type of question being asked. The data in Table 5 come from answers to a general question where the drinking problem is not identified. AA is then the choice of most respondents. The data in Table 7 come from answers to questions describing specific types of problems. AA then is the place of choice for only a minority of respondents. These results suggest that AA is well known and is closely linked to alcohol problems in general by most individuals. However, when confronted with a specific problem and hav-

TABLE 7
"Best" Agency to Respond to Different Drinking Problems and Proportion Who Would Recommend AA: Contra Costa General Population, 1989 (in percent)

	White (n = 523)	Black (n = 64)	Hispanic (n = 38)	Asian (n = 35)
	Suppose you had a 24-year-old son who has been drinking heavily on weekends and has been using cocaine, too. But the son shows up and does okay on his job.			
Most frequent choice	Drug treatment 54	Drug treatment 62	Drug treatment 59	Drug treatment 26
AA	8	3	12	14
	A friend talks to you because she's very upset. She and her husband have been having marital problems. She blames them mostly on his drinking. He agrees that he drinks alot, but doesn't see it as a problem. He claims the only thing wrong is that she keeps hounding him.			
Most frequent choice	Alcohol program 48	Alcohol program 37	Alcohol program 36	Alcohol program 44
AA	26	18	33	14
	Someone walking past your house trips on a curb and falls pretty heavily. You check to see if he needs help, and you notice he's bleeding a little from scrapes and small cuts, but seems basically OK—except that he's very drunk, so drunk that he can't really get up and walk.			
Most frequent choice	Police 29	Emergency room 43	Alcohol program 26	Police 35
AA	8	11	17	4
	You have a grown son who's picked up for the second time on a drunk-driving charge. You know that he drives after drinking pretty regularly, but otherwise his life seems pretty together.			
Most frequent choice	Alcohol program 52	Alcohol program 53	Alcohol program 65	Alcohol program 41
AA	23	23	19	25

ing a number of agencies to choose from, the preferred agency varies by problem and is chosen in relation to characteristics of the problem being described. Unfortunately, none of the vignettes describes a situation that could be typically handled by AA (e.g., someone with drinking problems who had been to treatment and who needed long-term maintenance of sobriety). The vignettes were not designed to assess differences in AA use associated with ethnicity either. These could perhaps describe drinkers with the same pattern of problems but who would be of different ethnic groups.

Experience of AA Utilization by Ethnic Minority Groups in Health and Social Service Agencies

The Alcohol Research Group has collected alcohol-related data, including history of agency contact because of an alcohol-related problem, from samples in a variety of health and social service agencies in a Northern California county. The methods used in these studies have been described in detail elsewhere (see Room & Weisner, 1988; Weisner, 1991). The samples are all representative of the populations in these agencies, and the methodology for data collection (face to face interviews with standardized questionnaires) makes the data strictly comparable across studies.

In all these studies respondents were asked whether they had ever been to an AA meeting because of a drinking problem. Table 8 shows these data for whites, blacks, and Hispanics interviewed in eight agencies and in the general population in the same county. The samples in the table are ordered from top to bottom based on an increasing proportion of respondents who reported ever going to an AA meeting. Unfortunately, the number of Hispanics in the mental health, drug treatment, and alcohol treatment samples is too low for estimating a stable rate. Three clusters of samples can be seen in the table. The general population sample and those from primary health care agencies and emergency rooms have a relatively low proportion of individuals with AA experience. The experience of AA contact across the three ethnic groups in these samples is not very different, with one exception: blacks in the primary health care sample report a higher rate of AA contact than did whites and Hispanics. Individuals interviewed in mental health and welfare agencies, in the criminal justice system, and in drug treatment programs report higher rates of contact than did the previous samples, with rates varying between 20% and 50%. Whites have a higher rate of contact than do blacks and Hispanics, particularly in the welfare and drug treatment samples. Finally, both whites and blacks in alcohol treatment have a high rate of contact with AA, but the rate for whites is still higher than that for blacks.

AA's Adaptability and Expansion among Ethnic Minority Groups

A number of articles in the literature have discussed AA use by U.S. ethnic groups. This AA presence is documented in the description of

TABLE 8
Proportion of Whites, Blacks, and Hispanics in Health and
Social Service Agencies and in the General Population
Who Report Ever Going to an AA Meeting

	Whites	Blacks	Hispanics	All
General population (1987)	7	7	7	7
N	2,329	281	200	3,056
Primary health care (1989)	8	17	7	10
N	221	79	44	374
Emergency rooms (1984)	8	7	6	8
N	1,627	526	226	2,555
HMO emergecy room (1989)	4	2	4	4
N	722	153	82	1,031
Mental Health (1986)	22	24	9*	23
N	247	74	22	380
Welfare (1989)	37	19	20	27
N	312	326	65	743
Criminal justice (1988)	39	26	35	35
N	556	316	97	1,022
Drug treatment (1987)	47	31	12*	42
N	169	104	23	308
Alcohol treatment	93	80	23*	88
N	182	134	24	376

*Absolute number (proportion not estimated due to small number of respondents).

ethnic-specific alcohol programs in the literature (e.g., Harper, 1979; Slagle & Weibel-Orlando, 1986; Watts & Wright, 1988) and in other research (e.g., Caldwell, 1983; Gordon, 1981; Hudson, 1985; Jilek-Aall, 1981; Leland, 1976; Weibel-Orlando, 1985). There is also recognition by some of the lack of systematic information regarding AA use by U.S. ethnic groups (Delgado, 1989; Gilbert & Cervantes, 1987; Rodin, 1985). This section discusses the existing alcohol literature on AA utilization by ethnic groups. Articles are grouped by ethnic group: Native Americans, followed by blacks, Hispanics, and Jews. The use of AA by Asian Americans has not been documented in the published alcohol literature and this group is not included in this review.[5]

AA and Native Americans. Native Americans' use of AA has been documented by a number of studies. Many of these articles describe how AA has been adapted by Indians to fit their culture, suggesting that this was the main reason why AA was accepted as a resource to deal with alcohol problems. For example, Heath (1981) refers to a description by Joy Leland of AA meetings on an Indian reservation in Nevada which never have "drunkalogues," and where the conversation is built around stock-raising and range-management. Leland (1976) reports on the creation of an alcoholism program in a Paiute-Shoshone reservation that incorporated AA meetings in a "quite different format" from those in traditional AA. Jilek-Aall (1981) describes meetings among the Coast Salish Indians as follows:

> At Indian AA meetings, members come and go as they please. The meeting is constantly interrupted by people entering and leaving; mothers bring their babies and small children, teenagers their friends. Young people having private fun in a corner...AA speeches are being patterned by Indian traditional themes of death and rebirth.... To many Coast Salish with alcohol problems, Indian AA has become a substitute church, combining elements of the former guardian-spirit quest and the Catholic Church, as well as the Shaker religion. (pp. 154–155)

Slagle and Weibel-Orlando (1986) suggest that AA and the Indian Shaker Church have many characteristics in common in their approach to alcoholism. Weibel-Orlando (1985) proposes that Indian programs with higher rates of sobriety are those that integrate a variety of spiritual elements and activities in their interventions. In this framework AA membership is a representation of "sacred separation"; it is used to help separate the abstinence associated with several forms of religious experiences from profane activities associated with drinking. Of 26 Indian alcoholism programs studied by Weibel-Orlando, 17 were strongly affiliated with AA. Walker (1981) also describes an Indian alcohol program in Seattle that has successfully incorporated AA into its inpatient, intermediate care. Describing the characteristics of 72 patients admitted between January 1978 and July 1978, he state that 87% had had previous AA experience. Comparison of these patients with 1,030 alcoholics from Fort Logan, showed that Indians were more likely to seek AA. Finally, there has also been criticism of the effectiveness of AA as a treatment resource for Native Americans. Some have argued that it is useful for highly acculturated clients only, or that few Indians have been helped by non-Indian chapters of AA (Institute of Medicine, 1990; Lamarine, 1988; Lewis, 1982).

AA and blacks. Descriptions of AA meetings among blacks are lacking, in spite of suggestions that all black AA meetings are more beneficial to black alcoholics than racially mixed groups (Harper, 1976) and accounts dating the existence of the first AA black group back to 1945 (Hudson, 1985). Johnson (1987) suggests that if blacks-only groups exist, they are more hidden than those for Hispanics. He also suggests that all-black membership in AA groups would be due to their location in neighborhoods where most residents are black. The literature also seems to be more controversial regarding AA usefulness as a treatment for blacks and its adaptability to black culture than it is of AA use among Native Americans. AA supporters such as Hudson (1985) and Caldwell (1983) do not seem to see AA as having to be adapted to conform to black culture. Instead, they see black culture as sharing values espoused by AA. Thus, Caldwell (1983) characterizes black culture as one where: "(1) people place the highest value on interpersonal relationships; (2) epistemology is largely affected and based on symbolic imagery and rhythm; and (3) logic accommodates the union of opposites" (p. 91). Caldwell then argues that these characteristics are all present in AA ideology and that therefore it should be an effective resource for treating black alcoholics.

Hudson (1985) sees AA as working for black alcoholics "because of the nature of the disease and because of the nature of the process of recovery" (p. 28). Suggesting that alcoholism follows a uniform process in all individuals, Hudson reasons that black alcoholics have the same needs as all other alcoholics which therefore makes AA a useful treatment resource for them. For example, black alcoholics who are isolated and alienated due to their problems and in need of primary group relations, would have these needs satisfied by AA groups (Brisbane & Wells, 1989; Hudson, 1985).

Criticism of AA's applicability to the treatment of black alcoholics is based on the fact that it may be seen as foreign to black culture. Thus, in spite of characterizing black culture using exactly the same three descriptors used by Hudson (1985), above, Denzim (1987) thinks that AA's values have nothing in common with it. Harper (1976) and Bourne (1976) adopt a more guarded approach in their appraisal of AA effectiveness in the treatment of black alcoholism. They suggest that in some cases AA has been substantially modified to fit the needs of black clients, being shaped then by "ideas of Black identity and racial pride" (Bourne, 1976, p. 46). However, the extent of AA's impact as a treatment resource on black alcoholics remains an empirical question to be addressed by research (Harper, 1976, 1979).

AA and Hispanics. Discussions of AA use by Hispanic groups in the U.S. are limited. Some descriptions in the literature suggest that AA groups have also been adapted to reflect Hispanic culture. Gordon (1981, 1985) suggests that Guatemalan alcoholics have adopted AA quite successfully as a treatment resource. Among Guatemalans the AA group is part of a complex system of social relationships that extends into the community and reflects values espoused by the Guatemalan immigrant culture. Trotter (1985) mentions an AA Spanish group that has been in existence for 6 years in an alcohol program in the Lower Rio Grande Valley of Texas because the AA material has been linguistically modified to match border language and values. Eden and Aguilar (1989) also suggest that AA is a viable treatment modality for Hispanics. However, they also think that due to the influence of "machismo," Hispanic men would have difficulties in admitting that they cannot control their drinking and would therefore reject AA as a form of treatment.

AA and Jews. The published literature has few descriptions of the use of AA by Jews, and in most cases the evidence presented is very limited with regards to answering questions about AA utilization by this ethnic group. Master (1989) reports on data collected with a voluntary sample of 18 Jews who had attended AA meetings, all of whom seem to express positive experiences with AA. Cohen (1980) describes briefly the creation of an AA group at the International Synagogue at Kennedy Airport, but does not provide any information on group characteristics, structure, or membership.

Potential Explanations for Ethnic Minorities' Use of AA

AA has been described as a middle-class invention (Mäkelä, 1991) and as a product of Anglo-Saxon and Protestant culture with its deep preoccupation with self-control and restraint (Levine, 1990). AA ideology has also been described as rigid, espousing a view of alcoholism that is rooted on negative images of drinking usually associated with Temperance cultures, where people drink a large part of their alcohol as spirits, drunkenness is relatively frequent and drinking is disruptive (Levine, 1990).

This recognition of AA as a class- and culture-bond phenomenon triggers legitimate questions about its effectiveness in helping individuals from ethnic minority groups in the U.S. to achieve sobriety. Analyses of AA's eight membership surveys between 1977 and 1989 cannot be used to assess AA's membership among ethnic groups for these surveys have not collected data on members' ethnicity. Analysis of other demographic data suggests that there has been a change in the membership characteristics, with an increase in young people and women (Alcoholics Anonymous, 1991). Ethnicity is therefore treated differently from gender, age, and occupation by the organizers of the survey.

Evidence on the extent of ethnic groups' participation in AA is given by Maxwell (1982), and is probably outdated by now. Maxwell reports that in 1980 there were 130 Indian groups in the U.S. and Canada, and 300 Spanish-speaking groups in the U.S. Spanish-speaking groups had set up their own intergroup offices in Los Angeles, San Francisco, Chicago, Newark, New York, and San Juan. They also have held an annual Spanish-speaking national conference since 1972. Maxwell (1982) does not provide information about black groups, suggesting that "for the most part, Blacks belong to predominantly White groups." Gilbert and Cervantes (1987) writing in 1987 indicate the presence of 150 Spanish-speaking AA groups in Los Angeles county.

This presence of AA among ethnic groups in the U.S. is surprising, given the above descriptions of AA as a typical American middle-class, Protestant movement. However, further evidence of AA's ability to transcend the culture in which it was born comes from the recent worldwide expansion of the movement. This expansion has occurred not only in countries with Anglo-Saxon, Protestant cultures but also, and perhaps especially, in Catholic countries of Latin America from which U.S. Hispanics come. Thus, between 1965 and 1970 AA groups increased 170% in Mexico and Central America, 108% in South America, but 29% in the U.S. (Leach & Norris, 1977). Data reported by Mäkelä (1991) indicate that between 1965 and 1986 the number of AA groups in Latin American countries increased from 606 to 16,574. Mexico alone had an increase in the number of groups from 0 to 8,510.

Mäkelä (1991) has described AA characteristics. The text below discusses how these characteristics and others can perhaps explain AA's use by minority ethnic groups in the U.S. First, AA is based on an interaction system that is flexible so that the structure of group meetings varies considerably (Mäkelä, 1991). This, plus its cell structure with group autonomy and independence, makes it easy to reach different population groups. This flexibility is well reflected in the above review of the literature on AA utilization by U.S. ethnic groups and has been documented in the literature describing AA groups in general (Johnson, 1987). It is perhaps the most important factor explaining AA acceptability among U.S. ethnic minorities.

Second, although drinking problems can be shaped by the sociocultural environment of the drinker, there is a certain uniformity of problems in at least the countries of the Western world. To the extent that AA addresses the uniform consequences of chronic heavy drinking, it will find acceptability as a treatment intervention in different cultures.

Third, AA acceptability is also linked to the acceptance of a conceptual view of alcoholism as a disease. This view, which has been characterized by some as culture-bound (Room, 1985), has been widely adopted by the medical profession in the Western world. In Latin America, for instance, Jellinek's disease concept of alcoholism was until recently the main paradigm for understanding alcohol problems in clinical practice and research (Caetano, 1985). In the U.S., as discussed above, blacks, Hispanics, and Japanese Americans seem to accept as much as the white majority the view of alcoholism as a disease and the main tenets of AA's ideology.

Fourth, AA provides free help. There seems to be no pressure for money contributions. Members' standing in the group is not linked to occupation or financial position but is based on an informal prestige structure built around members' wisdom, life experience, work with people with problems, previous service engagement, and their oratorical skills (Mäkelä,

1991). These characteristics should be seen positively by ethnic minorities, who lack money or medical insurance to cover treatment and would be at a disadvantage in any structure based on socioeconomic status. Fifth, AA is polycephalous, with no central structure (Mäkelä, 1991) and no links to social welfare or health-related governmental agencies. This is also a plus for U.S. ethnic minorities, who have grown wary of and have learned to distrust government or other organizations built around a central structure isolated from its members. Lack of links with official agencies are especially attractive to U.S. Hispanics, given the pervasive avoidance and fear of immigration officials among many members of this ethnic group.

Sixth, AA does not advocate any theological or ontological beliefs (Mäkelä, 1991). Its roots are found in Christian and modern Protestant thinking. Catholicism has not been an impediment to AA expansion in traditionally Catholic countries and should not be so in the U.S. either. Levine (1990) explains the lack of resistance of Catholicism to AA by suggesting that there has been an accommodation of the Catholic church in the U.S. to Anglo and Protestant culture. This is certainly possible. It is also possible that U.S. cultural characteristics influence how Catholicism is practiced in the country.

Finally, Vaillant (1983) has proposed that AA's success as a treatment intervention can be linked to the following four characteristics: (1) offering the patient a nonchemical substitute dependency for alcohol; (2) reminding him ritually that even one drink can lead to pain and relapse; (3) repairing the social and medical damage that he has experienced; (4) restoring his self-esteem (p. 300). Sutro (1989) suggests that these AA characteristics are cross-culturally valid, helping to explain the development of an AA group in a Mexican Peasant-Indian village. However, Sutro's study is limited. It describes one group and presents no systematic evaluation of AA as a treatment intervention. Whether Vaillant's proposed characteristics are in fact the reasons why AA is effective in the U.S. or cross-culturally remains therefore an empirical question.

Conclusions and Suggestions for Future Research

This chapter reviewed two types of evidence on the utilization of AA as a treatment resource by U.S. ethnic minority groups: original data from general population surveys and data reported in the literature documenting AA use by clinical samples, AA's presence in treatment programs, and descriptions of the structure of AA groups in ethnic minority communities. Together this evidence suggests that AA and its view of alcoholism have been accepted by U.S. ethnic minorities. The survey data document direct use of AA by respondents and report whether respondents support AA's view of alcoholism, whether they would recommend AA, or think AA is an appropriate agency to deal with an alcohol problem. Some of these results are therefore hypothetical indicators of respondent's behavior regarding AA and should be seen as such. The published literature also has important limitations. There have been no large scale epidemiological surveys of AA membership in which members' ethnic identity has been recognized. Until such a study is conducted the evidence regarding the participation of ethnic minorities in AA will remain suggestive. There has been no systematic evaluation of AA's effectiveness as a treatment intervention. In that regard, the literature on ethnic groups is at par with much of the general literature on the evaluation of alcohol treatment in the U.S.

The published literature is for the most part ethnographic and describes AA use and the characteristics of group structure in special populations of Native Americans or Hispanics. While these articles provide important information, the generalizability of their findings is limited. Other studies discuss AA's fit to the culture of ethnic groups and AA's effectiveness as a treatment resource without being based on systematic data collection or hypothesis testing. These articles do not contribute much knowledge to the topic under consideration.

In the absence of systematic evaluations of AA's effectiveness as a treatment intervention, no conclusions can be drawn about this aspect of AA as it applies to U.S. minority groups. However, the main evaluation question to be asked is not whether AA is effective in helping U.S. ethnic minorities. The evidence of the utilization of AA as a resource by treatment programs catering for minority groups suggests that it probably helps at least some alcoholics. As proposed by Glaser and Ogborne (1982), the question needs to be more specific. Among ethnic groups such a question should address, for instance: (1) What types of adaptations in AA tenets, group interaction, and structure have occurred? (2) How are these adaptations, if any, related to AA effectiveness as a treatment intervention? (3) How do the adaptations interact with clients; that is, how can clients' characteristics be matched to intervention so that treatment can be made most effective? (4) What is the meaning of AA affiliation among ethnic groups? Do individuals join for meetings only, or are they active members performing 12-step work? (5) To what extent are findings reported for general samples of clients applicable to minority clients, for example, the positive relationship between some "participation" variables and positive drinking outcomes reported by Emrick et al. (1992)?

In answering these questions a variety of studies and methodologies are appropriate. In some cases the best methodology is ethnographic, with data being collected through participant observation, so that the characteristic pattern of interaction in a group is described. Such studies should strive to include more than one group, and possibly more than one ethnic group should be studied. This will create opportunities to highlight differences in structure and organization across ethnic groups that cannot otherwise be detected. AA effectiveness as a treatment resource needs to be evaluated in comparison with other types of interventions. The ideal methodology involves randomization of clients to treatment interventions. This method is, however, difficult to implement and maintain. Quasi-experimental designs may then be more appropriate.

In developing and implementing the research proposed above with ethnic minority groups, a number of important methodological steps must be observed: ethnic identification can be covered in a variety of ways. It may be based, for instance, on respondents' family of origin, the country most of the respondents' ancestors come from, country of birth, or self-identification. There is controversy as to what is the best method to assess respondents ethnicity and different methods may cover different dimensions of the construct. The U.S. census has used self-identification as the basic method to count ethnic groups in the U.S. Most researchers seem to agree that this is the method that best captures respondents' ethnicity.

Instruments designed to measure a number of important constructs in the majority population cannot be readily applied to ethnic groups. This involves constructs that are obviously culture bound such as depression, anxiety, and stress as well as other terms that perhaps have more universal use but are defined in different ways by different ethnic groups. Thus, the term "to drink" when translated into Spanish by the verb "tomar" acquires a significance that respondents do not associate with drinking in general but with heavy drinking. Careful translation and independent back translation of questionnaires and instruments by individuals not connected with the research team are necessary.

If instruments are going to be translated into languages other than English, it will also be necessary to have interviewers who are fluent in those languages. Many respondents who are bilingual prefer to be interviewed in their own language, and the fieldwork team must be prepared to offer this service. This means hiring bilingual interviewers, and conducting special training sessions with these individuals, who must be able to administer questionnaires both in English and in the other language in which they will be working. In the 1984 national survey conducted by the Alcohol Research Group (Caetano, 1989b) 43% of the Hispanic sample ($n = 1,453$) was interviewed in Spanish.

Acculturation to U.S. society and its relationship with alcohol use has been an important area of research with U.S. Hispanics. This should also be so with any ethnic group that has a history of recent migration to the U.S. and thus will have a large number of its members who are foreign born. It is therefore important to assess respondents' degree of acculturation to U.S. society. With regard to alcohol treatment, this variable alone may indicate basic characteristics of the services respondents are able to receive, as for instance the language spoken by staff. Acculturation, however, is a multidimensional construct, and as such it is difficult to measure. A number of scales have been developed for work with Hispanics (see Caetano, 1987; Cuellar, Harris, & Jasso, 1980; Delgado et al., 1990; Marin et al., 1987). The items in these scales cover topics such as language use (English versus Spanish), place of birth, time of residence in the U.S., ethnicity of friends and neighbors, and whether the respondents prefer food, music, TV and radio programs, books, newspapers that are more "Hispanic" or more "Anglo." There seems to be some overlap in topics being covered from one scale to another. However, there is also considerable controversy in the literature about the nature of the acculturation process. The discussion is around whether it is a unidirectional process that will invariably lead to loss of ethnic characteristics, or whether it is better understood as a bidirectional movement, leading to biculturalism.

Acknowledgment

Work on this chapter was partially supported by a National Alcohol Research Center grant to the Alcohol Research Group, Medical Research Institute of San Francisco, Berkeley, California.

Notes

1. The wording of the question in each survey is: "I am going to read you a list of community agencies and professions. For each one, please tell me if you have ever gone there about a drinking problem."
2. A drink is taken to mean 1 ounce of spirits, a 4-ounce glass of table wine or a 12-ounce can of beer, each of which contains approximately 9 grams of absolute alcohol.
3. This was the case with estimators for the variables identifying place of birth and acculturation among Hispanics. These variables were therefore excluded from the logistic regression. Crude odds ratios indicate that Hispanics who are acculturated and those who were born in the U.S. have 12 and 5 times more chances of having been to AA, respectively.
4. A total of 3,069 respondents were interviewed, constituting a probability sample of households in the county. The exact wording of the question was: "If a friend or relative in your community asked where they should seek help for an alcohol problem of their own, which of the following would you recommend?"
5. Kitano (1982) writing in 1982 mentions that a Japanese American AA group had just started in Los Angeles. Later Kitano et al. (1985), Kitano (1989), and Chi, Lubben, and Kitano (1989) mention the existence of "several" Japanese AA groups in Los Angeles, including a Japanese-speaking group.

References

Alcoholics Anonymous. (1991). *Comments on A.A.'s triennial surveys.* New York: Alcoholics Anonymous World Services.

Bourne, P. (1976). Alcoholism in the urban black population. In F.D. Harper (Ed.), *Alcohol abuse and black America* (pp. 39–46). Alexandria, VA: Douglass Publishers.

Brisbane, F.L., & Wells, R.C. (1989). Treatment and prevention of alcoholism among blacks. In T.D. Watts & R. Wright, Jr. (Eds.), *Alcoholism in minority populations* (pp. 33–52). Springfield, IL: Charles C Thomas.

Caetano, R. (1985). The diffusion of an idea: Jellinek's disease concept in Latin America. *International Journal of the Addictions, 20,* 1629–1641.

Caetano, R. (1987). Acculturation and drinking patterns among U.S. Hispanics. *British Journal of Addiction, 82,* 789–799.

Caetano, R. (1989a). Concepts of alcoholism among whites, blacks, and Hispanics in the U.S. *Journal of Studies on Alcohol, 6,* 580–582.

Caetano, R. (1989b). Drinking patterns and alcohol problems in a national sample of U.S. Hispanics. In D. Speigler, D. Tate, S. Aitken & C. Christian (Eds.), *Alcohol use among U.S. ethnic minorities* (pp. 147–162). NIAAA Monograph No. 18 (DHHS Publication No. ADM 87–1435). M.C. p. 397

Caldwell, F.J. (1983). Alcoholics Anonymous as a viable treatment resource for black alcoholics. In T.D. Watts & R. Wright, Jr. (Eds.), *Black alcoholism: Toward a comprehensive understanding* (pp. 85–99). Springfield, IL: Charles C Thomas.

Chi, I., Lubben, J.E., & Kitano, H.H.L. (1989). Differences in drinking behavior among three Asian-American groups. *Journal of Studies on Alcohol, 50,* 15–23.

Clark, W., & Hesselbrock, M. (1988). A comparative analysis of U.S. and Japanese drinking patterns. In L.H. Towle & T.C. Harford (Eds.), *Cultural influences and drinking patterns: A focus on Hispanic and Japanese populations* (pp. 79–98). NIAA Research Monograph No. 19 (DHHS Publication No. ADM 88–1563). Washington, DC: U.S. Government Printing Office.

Clark, W.B., & Hilton, M.E. (Eds.). (1991). *Alcohol in America: Drinking practices and problems.* Albany, NY.: State University of New York Press.

Clark, W., & Midanik, L. (1982). *Alcohol use and alcohol problems among U.S. adults: Results of the 1979 national survey.* In NIAAA, *Alcohol consumption and related problems,* alcohol and health monograph No. 1 (DHHS Publication No. (ADM) 82-1190). Washington, DC: U.S. Government Printing Office, pp. 3–52.

Cohen, E.J. (1980). A.A. at the International Synagogue, Kennedy Airport. In A. Blaine, (Ed.), *Alcoholism and the Jewish community* (pp. 321–325). New York: Commission on Synagogue Relations.

Cuellar, I., Harris, L.C., & Jasso, R. (1980). An acculturation scale for Mexican American normal and clinical populations. *Hispanic Journal of Behavioral Sciences, 2,* 199–217.

Delgado, J.L., Johnson, C.L., Roy, I., & Trevino, F.M. (1990). Hispanic health and nutrition examination survey: Methodological considerations. *American Journal of Public Health, Supplement, 80,* 6–10.

Delgado, M. (1989). Treatment and prevention of Hispanic alcoholism. In T.D. Watts, & R. Wright Jr. (Eds.), *Alcoholism in minority populations* (pp. 77–92). Springfield, IL: Charles C Thomas.

Denzim, N.K. (1987). *The recovering alcoholic.* Newbury Park, CA: Sage Publications.

Eden, S.L., & Aguilar, R.J. (1989). The Hispanic chemically dependent client: Considerations for diagnosis and treatment. In G.W. Lawson & A.W. Lawson (Eds.), *Alcoholism and substance abuse in special populations* (pp. 205–222). Rockville, MD: Aspen Publishers.

Emrick, C.D., Tonigan, J.S., Montgomert, H., & Little, L. (1992). Affiliation processes in and treatment outcomes of Alcoholics Anonymous: A meta-analysis of the literature (Typescript). Veterans Affairs Medical Center, Denver, CO.

Gilbert, M.J., & Cervantes, R.C. (1987). Alcohol services for Mexican Americans: A review of utilization patterns, treatment considerations and prevention activities. In M.J. Gilbert & R.C. Cervantes (Eds.), *Mexican Americans and alcohol* (pp. 61–93). Monograph 11. University of California, Los Angeles: Spanish Speaking Mental Health Research Center.

Glaser, F.B., & Ogborne, A.C. (1982). Does A.A. really work? *British Journal of Addiction, 77,* 123–129.

Gordon, A.J. (1981). The cultural context of drinking and indigenous therapy for alcohol problems in three migrant Hispanic cultures: An ethnographic report. *Journal of Studies on Alcohol,* Suppl. 9, 217–240.

Gordon, A.J. (1985). Alcohol and Hispanics in the Northeast: A study of cultural variability and adaptation. In L.A. Bennett & G.M. Ames (Eds.), *The American experience with alcohol: Contrasting cultural perspectives* (pp. 297–313). New York: Plenum Press.

Harper, F.D. (1976). Summary, issues and recommendations. In F.D. Harper (Ed.), *Alcohol abuse and black America* (pp. 187–200). Alexandria, VA: Douglass Publishers.

Harper, F.D. (1979). *Alcoholism treatment and black Americans.* National Institute on Alcohol Abuse and Alcoholism (DHEW Publication No. ADM 79–853). Washington, DC: U.S. Government Printing Office.

Heath, D.B. (1981). Determining the sociocultural context of alcohol use. *Journal of Studies on Alcohol,* Suppl. 9, 9–17.

Hudson, H.L. (1985). How and why Alcoholics Anonymous works for blacks. *Alcoholism Treatment Quarterly, 2,* 11–30.

Institute of Medicine. (1990). *Broadening the base of treatment for alcohol problems.* National Academy Press: Washington, DC.

Jilek-Aall, L. (1981). Acculturation, alcoholism and Indian-style Alcoholics Anonymous. *Journal of Studies on Alcohol,* Suppl. 9, 143–158.

Johnson, H. (1987). Alcoholics Anonymous in the 1980s: Variations on a theme. Unpublished doctoral dissertation. University of California, Los Angeles.

Kitano, H.L. (1982). Alcohol drinking patterns: The Asian Americans. In *Alcohol and Health Monograph No. 4, Special Population Issues* (pp. 411–430). (DHHS Publication No. ADM 82–1193). Washington, DC: U.S. Government Printing Office.

Kitano, H.L. (1989). Alcohol and the Asian American. In T.D. Watts & R. Wright, Jr. (Eds.), *Alcoholism in Minority Populations* (pp. 143–156). Springfield, IL: Charles C Thomas.

Kitano, H.L., Hatanaka, H., Yeung, W., & Sue, S. (1985). Japanese-American drinking patterns. In L.A. Bennett & G.M. Ames (Eds.), *The American experience with alcohol: Contrasting cultural perspectives* (pp. 335–357). New York: Plenum Press.

Lamarine, R.J., (1988). Alcohol abuse among Native Americans. *Journal of Community Health, 13,* 143–155.

Leach, B., & Norris, J.L. (1977). Factors in the development of Alcoholics Anonymous (A.A.). In B. Kissin & H. Begleiter (Eds.), *Treatment and rehabilitation of the chronic alcoholic* (pp. 441–543). New York: Plenum Press.

Lewis, R.G. (1982). Alcoholism and the Native American—A review of the literature. In Alcohol and Health Monograph No. 4, *Special Population Issues* (pp. 315–328) (DHHS Publication No. ADM 82–1193). Washington, DC: U.S. Government Printing Office.

Leland, J.H. (1976). *Firewater Myths.* New Brunswick, NJ: Rutgers Center of Alcohol Studies.

Levine, H.G. (1990, April). *Temperance cultures: Alcohol as a symbol of danger in Anglo and Nordic societies.* Paper presented at the Society for the Study of Addiction seminar on "Substance Misuse—what makes problems." Windsor, Great Park, England.

Mäkelä, K. (1991). Social and cultural preconditions of Alcoholics Anonymous (AA) and factors associated with the strength of AA. *British Journal of Addiction. 86,* 1405–1413.

Marin, G., Sabogal, F., Marin, B., Otero-Sabogal, R., & Perez-Stable, E.J. (1987). Development of a short acculturation scale for Hispanics. *Hispanic Journal of Behavioral Sciences, 9,* 183–205.

Master, L. (1989). Jewish experiences of Alcoholics Anonymous. *Smith College Studies in Social Work, 59,* 183–199.

Maxwell, M.A. (1982). Alcoholics Anonymous. In *Alcohol, Science and Society Revisited* (pp. 295–305). Ann Arbor: University of Michigan Press.

Midanik, L.T., & Clark, W.B. (1992). *The demographic distribution of U.S. drinking patterns in 1990: Description and trends from 1984.* Alcohol Research Group, Berkeley, CA, Working Paper F-299.

Rodin, M.B. (1985). Getting on the program: A biocultural analysis of Alcoholics Anonymous. In L.A. Bennett & G.M. Ames (Eds.), *The American experience with alcohol: Contrasting cultural perspectives* (pp. 41–58). New York: Plenum Press.

Room, R. (1985). Dependence and society. *British Journal of Addiction, 80,* 133–139.

Room, R., & Weisner, C. (1988). *Studying community responses to alcohol problems: An interim report.* Paper presented at the 14th annual alcohol Epidemiology Symposium, Keyttil Bruun Society, Berkeley, CA.

Slagle, A.L., & Weibel-Orlandon, J. (1986). The Indian Shaker Church and Alcoholics Anonymous: Revitalistic curing cults. *Human Organization, 45,* 310–319.

Sutro, L.D. (1989). Alcoholics Anonymous in a Mexican Peasant-Indian village. *Human Organization, 48,* 180–186.

Trotter, R.T., II (1985). Mexican American experience with alcohol: South Texas examples. In L.A. Bennett & G.M. Ames (Eds.), *The American experience with alcohol: Contrasting cultural perspectives* (pp. 279–296). New York: Plenum Press.

Vaillant, G.E. (1983). *The natural history of alcoholism.* Cambridge, MA: Harvard University Press.

Walker, R.D. (1981). Treatment strategies in an urban Indian alcoholism program. *Journal of Studies on Alcohol,* Suppl. 9, 171–184.

Watts, T.D., & Wright, R., Jr. (1988). Alcoholism and the urban black population. *City Medicine, 2,* 4–7.

Weibel-Orlando, J. (1985). Indians, ethnicity and alcohol: Contrasting perceptions of ethnic self and alcohol use. In L.A. Bennett & G.M. Ames (Eds.), *The American experience with alcohol: Contrasting cultural perspectives* (pp. 201–226). New York: Plenum Press.

Weisner, C. (1991, June). *Rates of problematic alcohol and other drug use in health and social service populations: Results from comparable epidemiologic studies.* Paper presented at the 1991 Research Society on Alcoholism Conference, Marco Island, FL.

CHAPTER 13

Alcoholics Anonymous and Gender Issues

LINDA J. BECKMAN

The state of our knowledge about women and Alcoholics Anonymous (AA) is comparable to what I stated in a 1975 review article about the dismal state of research on woman alcoholics at that time (Beckman, 1975):

> Few studies deal with the most effective treatment modalities for women who misuse alcohol. Many studies are not well designed, using inadequate or biased sampling procedures or inadequate control groups, or presenting only case history data. Although these studies provide a valuable first look at the problem of alcoholism in women, the need for better controlled research is evident.

To piece together a picture of possible gender issues among AA members that may affect recovery processes one has to rely on more general research (and theory) on sex-role socialization and gender differences; comments of key informants, women who are AA members; and a large dose of speculation.

In this chapter I will consider the limited research on gender and AA; discuss research on alcoholism in women and how women alcoholics differ from their male counterparts; and summarize more general research on gender differences that has implications for various aspects of AA membership for women versus men.

Gender Differences

It is generally assumed that differences between the sexes can be attributed to either biology or environment. When the underlying reason for such differences is biological they are referred to as sex differences, when the underlying causation is believed to be cultural, that is, to result from socialization, they are considered gender differences. However, it is very difficult to separate the influences of biology and environment because socialization begins at a very young age and most likely the differences that occur are the result of a complex interaction of psychological, socio-cultural, and biological factors (Basow, 1986). Because I believe the vast majority of the differences are largely environmentally determined, I usually use the term *gender differences*. Sex-role socialization, social roles, social status, power differentials, and gender schema all may contribute to gender differences in behavior. It is beyond my scope to discuss the origin of the these differences in detail. Underlying causes, however, have clear implications for the permanence of any differences and their malleability.

Some basic problems in examining research on gender differences arise because of two frequently made assumptions. I call these (1) the assumption of differences and (2) the assumption of male norms. One underlying assumption is that gender differences exist and are of practical as well as statistical significance (Basow, 1986). Since most journals publish only statistically significant findings, differences between the sexes receive undue emphasis in the research literature while similarities are ignored.

Most social and psychological differences between the sexes are of small to moderate magnitude (e.g., Eagly, 1987). The percentage of variability in the dependent variables explained by sex generally is below 10% and more frequently below 5% (Eagly, 1987). If Cohen's (1977) rough guidelines for size of effects in research are applied, most such differences fall in the small to medium range (.20 to .50 using the d metric) and are much smaller than physical sex differences in motor performance (Eagly, 1987; Hall, 1984) or differences in income.

Another problem is that it is assumed that male behavior is the norm. For instance, Kohlberg (1969) and his colleagues based their theory of moral development primarily on male subjects. When I looked through the titles of articles reviewed by Emrick, Tonigan, Montgomery, and Little (1992), I found there were four titles that mentioned women or female alcoholics, three that mentioned wives of alcoholics, two that mentioned male alcoholics, and none concerning husbands of alcoholics. Most studies of AA state nothing about the sex of subjects in their titles despite the fact that they frequently do not include women or include very few women. Thus, theory and research based primarily on males, usually white males, is presented to the academic community as if it applies to people in general.

The assumptions generally made about gender differences are congruent with a positive empiricist model of research that restricts analysis to a few clearly observable units of behavior (Unger, 1983). Unger suggests that such a model ignores the effects of social constructs such as social status and power on the research enterprise itself. She supports a much more reflexive model of research that involves understanding of the reciprocal and interactive relationship existing between the person and reality and, thus, between experimenter and subject. Such a model may be of direct relevance for research on spirituality and recovery processes that AA members experience.

Studies of AA

Whereas initially AA was an organization composed primarily of men and alcoholism was rarely perceived as a disease of women, recent triennial surveys conducted by AA consistently show that women compose more than 30% of the its total membership (Alcoholics Anonymous, 1990). It is puzzling, therefore, that the median sample size of males in the studies reviewed by Emrick et al. (1992) was 116, whereas the median number of females was nine. No matter what one believes about the relative prevalence of alcoholism in women and men, it is clear that women are underrepresented in studies on AA. This is consistent with the underrepresentation of women in studies of all types of alcoholism treatment reported by Vannicelli (1984).

What are the reasons for a research literature based primarily on men? First, research samples of AA members are overwhelmingly inpatient samples. Women alcoholics, because of their obligations to family, children, and employment (and perhaps their lower economic resources and insurance coverage for alcoholism), may be less likely to be in inpatient treatment than are men. The lack of economic resources is particularly critical for women of color. For instance, Amaro, Beckman, and Mays (1987) reported that African-American women alcoholics have lower incomes than white women. Moreover, they are much less likely to have insurance coverage for alcoholism treatment. Second, women may still feel more stigmatized by the label "alcoholic" and therefore may choose to avoid participation in situations where they are identified as alcoholic.

A third possibility, previously raised about alcoholism treatment outcome studies in general, is sexist bias. Vannicelli (1984) pointed out that there are differences in the ways in which female and male investigators have reported data on treatment outcome of alcoholics. When a woman was the first author, the proportion of women in the sample was larger, more attention was given to specifying the sample size by gender, there was a greater emphasis on prognostic characteristics that distinguish between women with good and poor outcomes, and there was a greater possibility that sex differences in treatment outcome would be reported.

My own search of the literature, which did not include doctoral dissertations, found only eight studies that considered affiliation with AA or AA as a treatment modality for women.

Affiliation

Two studies consider factors influencing women's affiliation with AA. The only community-based study I have found that examines influences on treatment entry for women and men who are AA members is Smith's (1986) examination of gender-related differences in pathways to alcoholism diagnosis and treatment. Her sample consisted of 20 self-identified recovering alcoholics who were volunteers from the membership of a private social club for members of AA. Smith offers some interesting suggestions about the nature of the denial system and the determining factors leading to diagnosis and entry into AA and/or other treatment modalities that are consistent with theories of gender socialization and sex-role stereotyping. Women are often the first to recognize their drinking problem while men are more likely to have confrontations, especially with authorities, that bring them involuntarily into contact with treatment caregivers. Women seek help from those upon whom they depend and consider stronger, but often such persons initially reject their concerns or refer them for psychiatric treatment. Women who finally reach treatment often do so because their survival instincts lead them to rebel against traditional sex-role behaviors.

Huselid, Self, and Gutierres (1991) studied factors affecting treatment completion for 30 female substance abusers in an AA-focused halfway house program. This study used a preexperimental design with no comparison group and a very small sample, some of whom were not primarily alcohol abusers (30%). Contrary to their initial prediction that self-serving attributional biases would be beneficial, they found that women who attributed recent negative events to stable and global causes were *more* likely to complete the program. Women who see recent negative events as caused by factors that influence many areas of their lives and are likely always to be present may be more likely to recognize the salience of negative events associated with drinking and admit they do not have control over alcohol. Therefore, they may find it easier to accept their dependence on a "higher power" in order to achieve sobriety. Indeed high levels of powerlessness may be a positive influence on affiliation with AA.

Women who received more social support from AA sponsors were more likely to complete the program. Such a result is congruent with non-gender-specific studies or male-only studies that have found having an AA sponsor is related to positive outcomes (see Emrick et al., 1992).

A high percentage of those who go to AA drop out of the organization (Alcoholics Anonymous, 1990). About 50% of attendees discontinue by the fourth month. Alford (1980), discussed further below, found that women attended AA more than did men after inpatient treatment.

Treatment Outcome

As I could not find any empirical studies that examined gender differences in the recovery process in AA, treatment outcome studies were next examined. The six studies found (Alford, 1980; Corrigan, 1980; Kammeier, 1977; Kammeier & Conley, 1979; Kammeier & Laundergan, 1977; Smith, 1975), all in-patient samples except for Corrigan, are listed in Table 1. All these studies have significant limitations.

Two of the studies compare women in AA to some type of control or comparison group of women. Smith (1975) compared women in a residential treatment program for women (n = 43) with a control group (n = 35) that only received inpatient detoxification. He found that 79% of the treatment group and 3% of the control group claimed abstinence throughout the follow-up period. Among the methodological problems were unequal durations of follow-up and unequal attrition for the two groups, and a strong likelihood that more motivated women self-selected the treatment group.

Corrigan's (1980) book on women in treatment (n = 116) provides data on abstinence and other treatment outcomes for women who self-selected into various forms of alcoholism treatment. While her results suggest that women attending AA have better treatment outcomes than those who do not attend, she notes that "because of the large number of women who at some point attended AA, the effect of AA on treatment results is examined and found to have minimal impact on abstinence if AA is the only form of treatment" (p. 132). Most members of her AA treatment group experienced non-AA forms of treatment before follow-up approximately one year later. Therefore, their superior outcomes on emotional health as well as attainment of abstinence cannot be clearly interpreted. Because AA is a component of most major treatment programs, it often is impossible to separate the effects of AA from those of other treatment modalities concurrently experienced.

Four studies examined gender differences in treatment outcome. Alford (1980) examined gender differences among 27 male and 29 female alcoholics who completed an in-patient treatment program based on AA principles and philosophy, finding substantially higher outcome rates for females than for males (61% of women and 30% of men were abstinent, productively functioning, and socially stable at one year follow-up). This study, despite its small sample, is somewhat more sophisticated methodologically than the studies previously reviewed in that it had three follow-up contacts, considered patients who could not be followed up as treatment failures, and obtained data from multiple collaborative sources concerning subjects' treatment outcomes. Alford notes possible reasons why women had better outcomes, including:

TABLE 1
AA Treatment Outcome Studies: Women

Author	Sample	Follow-Up Period	Measure	Outcome
COMPARISONS OF DIFFERENT TREATMENTS FOR WOMEN				
Corrigan (1980)	F = 116	13 months after admission	Drinking behavior, emotional health	AA group better? AA group better?
Smith (1985)	F = 43 (AA) F = 35 (control)	14–19 months after study entry	Drinking behavior, social & role	AA group better
COMPARISONS OF TREATMENT OUTCOME FOR WOMEN AND MEN				
Alford (1980)	M = 29 F = 27	6 months, 12 months 24 months after treatment	Drinking behavior, social & role	Women better
Kammeier (1977)	M = 402 F = 188	24 months after treatment	Drinking behavior, social & role	NS Women better
Kammeier & Conley (1979)	T = 1,291	12 months after admission	Drinking behavior, social & role	Women better
Kammeier & Laundergan (1977)	M = 1,083 F = 420	12 months after treatment	Drinking behavior, social & role	NS NS

Note: F = female, M = male, NS = not significant.

1. Twice as many men as women were lost to follow-up and thus considered treatment failures.
2. It is easier for the housewife alcoholic to drink surreptitiously and data for such women may overreport abstinence.
3. Acceptance of the AA philosophy, which requires acknowledgment of powerlessness over alcohol and admission that one cannot control his or her own behavior, is harder for men.
4. More women attended AA and they attended a greater number of AA meetings during follow-up than did men.

The last two possibilities are worthy of investigation in more tightly controlled studies. As Alford points out, the greater AA attendance of women does not mean that these meetings affected treatment outcome more positively for women. Alcoholics could have stopped attending AA when they returned to drinking.

Finally, there are three studies of large samples of patients admitted to the Hazelden Foundation treatment program, an AA-based 12-step program. One study (Kammeier & Conley, 1979, reported in Vannicelli, 1984) found women to have significantly better outcomes in all areas 12 months after admission. A second reported no differences in drinking behavior but noted better social and health outcomes for women at the two-year follow-up (Kammeier, 1977, in Vannicelli). A third found no gender differences (Kammeier & Laundergan, 1977, in Vannicelli). Since subjects in all three studies apparently participated in similar types of treatment, the conflicting results are puzzling.

The literature on gender differences gives limited evidence about the relative efficacy of AA for women versus men. The larger literature on gender differences in treatment outcome for alcoholism (Vannicelli, 1984) suggests few gender differences in treatment outcome and perhaps a slight tendency for women to experience better treatment outcomes. This chapter suggest that the tendency for women to experience better outcomes than men is more apparent for AA than for other treatment modes.

Studies of Women Alcoholics

The characteristics of women alcoholics that have implications for affiliation with and recovery in AA are present in Table 2. Previous research shows differences between female and male alcoholic patients in patterns of alcohol consumption, demographic characteristics, other diagnoses, and psychological characteristics. Women in treatment are more likely than men to show primary affective disorder and to experience greater marital and family instability. They are also more likely to have alcoholic spouses (for a review see Beckman, 1978a). Women with alcoholic spouses who are not in recovery and women with primary affective disorder that

TABLE 2
Gender Differences in Psychological
Characteristics and Social Behavior

In Alcoholic Samples
Affective disorder
Alcoholic spouse
Low self-esteem/powerlessness/external locus of control
Costs of treatment entry
Social opposition to treatment
Physical and sexual abuse
In Nonalcoholic Samples
Influenceable/conforming
More help seeking
Help giving?
Nonverbal communication
Different verbal communication patterns
Self-disclosure
Needs for affiliation/communion
Different group roles and interaction patterns

Note: Items indicate the characteristics and behaviors
more common in women.

is not treated may be poor candidates for AA. It is likely that failure to continue affiliation with AA may result from pressure from spouse in the first case and from depression that does not dissipate when drinking ceases in the second.

Low Self-Esteem, Powerlessness, External Locus of Control

Alcoholic women may have lower self-esteem than men (Beckman, 1978b) and they more frequently report that they drink when they feel powerless or inadequate (Beckman, 1980). Alcoholic women also have more stable attributions for failure than alcoholic men or nonalcoholic women (Frieze & McHugh, 1977). Hurlbert, Gade, and Fuqua (1983) found that among white and Native American alcoholics, males are more internal in locus of control than females. This pattern of traits is congruent with several steps of AA (e.g., Steps 1, 2, 4, 5, 6, and 7) that ask the alcoholic to admit inability to control alcohol use and past wrongdoings and require her to put her trust in "a power greater than ourselves" in order to attain sobriety.

Future research might consider:

1. Is it is easier for women than for men to "work" certain of the AA steps, because they are less likely initially to deny that they are powerless in certain areas of their lives?

2. Do women in AA who have more external locus of control or lower self-esteem have better or worse treatment outcomes, not only with respect to sobriety but also in social stability, interpersonal functioning, and psychological status than do other AA women?

Jean Kirkpatrick, the founder of Women for Sobriety (WFS) (Kirkpatrick, 1986; Kaskudas, 1989), contends that women drink because of feelings of inadequacy, loneliness, frustration, depression, and worthlessness. She believes that women need something in addition to or as an alterative to AA because they feel that they have failed in traditional female roles—as women, wives, daughters, and mothers—and they carry a great burden of guilt that men do not experience. Alcoholic women who have low self-esteem and lack self-confidence, she contends, do not need the heaviness of moral atonement included particularly in Steps 4 and 5 of the AA program. Moreover, many of these women's emotional problems are tied up in male-female relationships and rehabilitation via a mixed-sex organization is not appropriate at specific times. Kirkpatrick's program teaches 13 affirmations instead of the 12 steps. These affirmations emphasize positive thinking, believing one is competent, spiritual and emotional growth, and abstinence. The emphasis is on control (determining why you became dependent on alcohol) rather than powerlessness and on competence rather than humility. Group meetings are focused so as to provide a safe, noncompetitive environment for women and avoid the slogans and rhetoric common to AA meetings.

Comparisons of the treatment processes and outcomes of AA and other support groups such as WFS are important, as are studies of women who choose women-only versus mixed-sex groups. If AA is designed for those with selfishness and self-centeredness as the root of their problems, is it equally applicable to those who feel powerless and lack self worth? Do some women, for example, feminists or those with nontraditional sex roles, find it harder to accept AA? Comparison of women who have attained long-term sobriety in AA and those who have rejected AA and attained abstinence in other ways can began to answer the question of for whom is AA most beneficial.

Costs of and Opposition to Treatment

There is evidence that white women experience more personal and social costs in entering treatment than do white men. They encounter more opposition to treatment entry from family and friends than do men for whom such opposition is rare (Beckman & Amaro, 1986). It may be significant that agencies that provide treatment for children, child care and aftercare services and have a larger percentage of staff members who are professionals and a greater number of different supportive services also tend to serve a greater percentage of women (Beckman & Kocel, 1982). Women may have more limited financial resources than men and African-American women are particularly limited because of low financial resources and lack of insurance (Amaro, Beckman, & Mays, 1987). Although these social role and social structural factors seem counterbalanced by women's intrapersonal characteristics that may make them more accepting of AA, they are barriers that can prevent entry into AA or facilitate discontinuation. On the other hand, AA may be an easier form of alcoholism treatment for women to enter than most other forms because it is free and anonymous. Some women may attend AA, at least initially, without telling families, spouses, and friends who have tried to dissuade them from the idea that they are alcoholic.

Physical Abuse, Sexual Abuse, Sexual Harassment, and Presence of Multiple Sexual Partners

Alcoholic women are more likely to experience physical or sexual abuse or spousal violence than are alcoholic men (Wilsnack, 1984). They also are more likely than nonalcoholic women to state that when drinking they have had sex with persons they would not otherwise have had sex with (Beckman, 1980). Because of sex-role norms, men do not experience the same guilt or shame when admitting the presence of multiple sexual partners before a mixed-sex group as do women. Women may be more likely to admit and dwell upon their past mistakes and indiscretions, but it may be harder for them to state such indiscretions in a public meeting.

Another issue for some women, especially recent AA members, is unwelcome sexual advances or in some cases sexual harassment from male members. Men may approach women newcomers for a date when women are particularly vulnerable and not ready to deal with the situation.

Gender Differences in Samples Not Specific to Alcoholics

Data on gender differences in so-called general population samples (most usually white college students) that may be relevant to the behavior and experience of persons in AA are presented in Table 2. Interpretation of gender differences in the general population is an area fraught with methodological peril and political controversy. Therefore, rather than rely on individual studies I have put greatest weight on a number of meta-analyses of sex differences including decoding of nonverbal cues (Hall, 1978); non-verbal behavior (Hall, 1984); helping behavior (Eagly, 1987; Eagly & Crowley, 1986); influenceability (Eagly, 1987; Eagly & Carli, 1981); task and socioemotional behaviors in groups (Eagly, 1987);

and leadership in groups (Eagly & Johnson, 1990). In most of these areas situational factors or situational factors in interaction with gender appear to be major influencers of behavior (Basow, 1986).

Influenceability

The bulk of the literature supports the conclusion that women are more influenceable than men if a situation involves group pressure (Kaplan & Sedney, 1980), although they may not be more subject to influence in other types of situations. They also exhibit more visual field dependence on tests such as the Embedded Figures Test (Kaplan & Sedley, 1980) and in some studies more external locus of control, which may be associated with feelings of helplessness and fear of success. These findings are consistent with those previously reported for alcoholic women.

Does women's greater influenceability in social situations make them more accepting of the spiritual aspects of AA and the need to admit their own powerlessness? If women are more suggestible, one could hypothesize that they would be more likely to continue AA attendance, a prediction supported by Alford (1980). There are at least two reasons why it might be easier for women to undergo the cognitive shift in attitudes and values necessary for the AA member. First, they may already have values and beliefs systems closer to the AA philosophy, and second, they may be more suggestible and more easily influenced than men. Therefore, it is easier for them to have a conversion experience (Fowler, Chapter 7 of this volume) or to reconstruct the self (Brown, Chapter 8 of this volume) and adopt and practice the AA philosophy.

Help-Seeking and Giving

Women are more likely to seek help than men, but which group offers help more depends on the specific situation. In short-term interactions with strangers men help more than do women, probably because of the heroic or agendic nature of such helping. However, most quantitative analyses of gender differences exclude the types of helping that are carried out primarily by women within the family and other close and long-term relationships (Eagly, 1987). Moreover, willingness to seek and receive help is influenced by the gender and sex-typing of the help-seeker and helper (Basow, 1986).

What might differences in help seeking and help giving suggest about Steps 3 and 12, the accepting of help from "God, *as we understood Him*" and the giving of help to others by trying "to carry this message to alcoholics"? Extrapolating from the findings, one can hypothesize that women are more likely to seek help from AA, but, as we have seen, social and personal barriers may be greater for women. It would make sense, however, that women are represented in greater proportions in AA groups than in other forms of treatment. No AA member is going to tell a woman that her drinking problem is imaginary or is really a psychiatric or physical problem. The Step 12 involves help giving. If provision of help is seen as heroic (even though such a heroic act may not agree with the AA philosophy), men may find it easier to do, especially if the persons involved are not actively seeking help. If such help giving is in response to specific requests, women may find Step 12 easier to fulfill.

Communication Patterns

Gender differences in communication patterns, particularly nonverbal communication, are well established. Women appear to be better at sending and receiving messages nonverbally. In social situations they smile and laugh more, show more involvement with others, and are more emotionally expressive (Basow, 1986; Eagly, 1987). They are better at identifying the emotions of others if given either visual or auditory information. In verbal communications men and women may invoke different conversational schemas arising from their different social structures and experience. Men interrupt more, accounting for up to 90% of the interruptions, and tend to control conversations (Basow, 1986). Many of these gender differences are influenced by power and status differentials not specific to gender.

Self-Disclosure

It is generally believed that women have a greater willingness to accept and acknowledge emotions to others (Kaplan & Sedley, 1980), although observational studies most often show no differences between the sexes, suggesting that men defend against unpleasant feeling better. However, women appear more likely to disclose emotions and personal and intimate topics such as negative personality traits and body matters to others (at least to other women). Might this orientation make it easier for a woman to tell her story at AA meetings and/or hear the stories of others?

Affiliation and Communion

Many of the differences already discussed reflect women's interest in and concern about people. It is suggested that women show greater interest in affiliation and more positive feelings about social interactions (Basow, 1980). If women are more concerned about communion, emphasizing cooperation and receptivity, while men are more concerned about agency, promoting dominance, self-assertion, and ego enhancement (Bakan, 1966), then it follows that men and women may enter AA with different needs and different agendas and this is reflected in their behaviors as AA members.

Group Roles and Interaction

Basow (1980, p. 71) states that "peer interactions and expectations for competence tend to socialize males and females to play different roles in groups." Moreover, gender-typed behavior in groups appears determined by sex roles, not dominance. In groups (at least in groups of strangers), women appear more concerned with socioemotional behavior whereas men are more task-oriented (Eagly, 1987). Women are less assertive in mixed-sex groups and do not speak up as much, especially in structured groups. It is noteworthy that these gender differences may only occur for whites. African-American women appear more assertive and more dominant in such situations. Women adopt a more democratic leadership style than men (Eagly & Johnson, 1990) and in initially leaderless groups women less often emerge as leaders.

The social roles and patterns of behavior of women and men in AA groups most probably reflect differences in sex-role behavior that are found in other types of groups. Gender socialization and social roles may determine female-male differences among AA members in (1) type of AA responsibilities and tasks; (2) verbal and nonverbal behaviors during meetings and in social interactions with other AA members; and (3) level of comfort and frequency of speaking in a mixed-sex group, as previously mentioned. Much of the AA philosophy and the process of AA groups mirrors stereotypically feminine rather than stereotypically masculine behaviors. For instance, AA emphasizes decisions by consensus, democracy, and equality among members.

Conclusions and Recommendations

Gender differences in psychological characteristics and social behavior exist among alcoholics. A key question is whether these differences are large enough in magnitude and significant in their impact on recovery processes. The somewhat better outcomes of women in treatment suggests they are.

Gender differences in social roles, social status, and power still are endemic to our society. We need to ask how these differences, frequently based on inequities in power and resources, affect affiliation with AA and experiences within it.

The interactions of gender roles, experiences in AA, and processes of change provide an untapped but fruitful area for future research. For instance, do women and men work each of the 12 steps in exactly the same manner? Do their "stories" have similar themes? How are themes presented in their "stories" related to recovery? Are different issues involved for women and men in sponsoring and being sponsored? Do the sexes vary in the ways in which they act as sponsors? Many other research questions have been discussed above. The list goes on and on.

In the research to date, two key variables that may interact with gender also have been ignored. First, cultural differences in the nature and course of alcoholism and characteristics of encounters with the treatment system may be important in determining program affiliation and treatment outcome within AA. The studies discussed above have been studies primarily of whites and the results may not generalize to other ethnic groups. Second, the issue of multiple addictions is totally ignored in the literature. Women with multiple addictions may frequent not only AA but also other self-help groups.

To adequately capture the richness of this area it is not sufficient to describe differences between the sexes. We must explore the stability of these differences, the reasons they occur, and their relationship to treatment outcomes. Only through examination of the complex interactions of gender and other variables influencing behavior in small groups—helping behaviors and help seeking, mentoring, feelings of control, and other areas—will we truly understand the gender issues that impact Alcoholics Anonymous.

When I started out on the journey of discovery involved in writing this paper, as a feminist I probably would have agreed with Jean Kirkpatrick that women who have feelings of inadequacy, worthlessness, and powerlessness and are faced with different issues than men need same-sex support groups and treatments that emphasize competence and self efficacy, not powerlessness and humility. Moreover, women should not be overrepresented in AA compared to men. But having reviewed the literature and learned more about processes of change in AA, I am much less confident about these conclusions. I now believe that AA, a fellowship originally designed by and composed primarily of men, appears to be equally or more effective for women than for men. There is no clear empirical evidence to suggest that certain types of women would fare better in other types of alcoholism treatment.

References

Alcoholics Anonymous. (1990). *Comments on A.A.'s triennial surveys.* New York: Alcoholics Anonymous World Services.

Alford, G.S. (1980). Alcoholics Anonymous: An empirical outcome study. *Addictive Behaviors, 5,* 359–370.

Amaro, H, Beckman, L.J., & Mays, V.M. (1987). A comparison of black and white women entering alcoholism treatment. *Journal of Studies on Alcohol, 48,* 220–228.

Bakan, D. (1966). *The duality of human existence.* Chicago: Rand McNally.

Basow, S.A. (1986). *Gender stereotypes: Traditions and alternatives.* Pacific Grove, CA: Brooks-Cole.

Beckman, L.J. (1975). Women alcoholics: A review of social and psychological studies. *Journal of Studies on Alcohol, 36*(7), 797–824.

Beckman, L.J. (1978a). Psychosocial characteristics of alcoholic women. *Drug and Alcoholism Review, 1*(5/60), 3–12.

Beckman, L.J. (1978b). The self-esteem of alcoholic women. *Journal of Studies on Alcohol, 39*(3), 491–498.

Beckman, L.J. (1980). The perceived antecedents and effects of alcohol consumption in women. *Journal of Studies on Alcohol, 41*(5), 518–530.

Beckman, L.J., & Amaro, H. (1986). Personal and social difficulties faced by women and men entering alcoholism treatment. *Journal of Studies on Alcohol, 47*(2), 135–145.

Beckman, L.J. & Kocel, K. (1982). The treatment-delivery system and alcohol abuse in women: Social policy implications. *Journal of Social Issues, 38*(2), 139–151.

Brown, S.D. (1993). Therapeutic processes in Alcoholics Anonymous. In B.S. McCrady & W.R. Miller (Eds.), *Research on Alcoholics Anonymous: Opportunities and alternatives.* New Brunswick, NJ: Rutgers Center of Alcohol Studies.

Cohen, J. (1977). *Statistical power analyis for the behavioral sciences.* New York: Academic Press.

Corrigan, E.M. (1980). *Alcoholic women in treatment.* New York: Oxford University Press.

Eagly, A.H. (1987). *Sex differences in social behavior: A social-role interpretation.* Hillsdale, NJ: Lawrence Erlbaum Associates.

Eagly, A.H., & Carli, L.L. (1981). Sex of researchers and sex-typed communication as determinants of sex differences in influenceability: A meta-analysis of social influence studies. *Psychological Bulletin, 90,* 1–20.

Eagly, A.H., & Crowley, M. (1986). Gender and helping behavior: A meta-analytic review of the social psychological literature. *Psychological Bulletin, 100,* 283–300.

Eagly, A.H., & Johnson (1990). Gender and leadership style: A meta-analysis. *Psychological Bulletin, 108,* 233–256.

Emrick, C.D., Tonigan, J.S., Montgomery, M.S., & Little, L. (1992). Affiliation processes in and treatment outcomes of Alcoholics Anonymous: A meta-analysis of the literature. Prepublication manuscript.

Fowler, J.W. (1993). Alcoholics Anonymous and faith development. In B.S. McCrady & W.R. Miller (Eds.), *Research on Alcoholics Anonymous: Opportunities and alternatives.* New Brunswick, NJ: Rutgers Center of Alcohol Studies.

Frieze, I.H., & McHugh, M.C. (1977). Debilitating attributions of the woman alcoholic undergoing treatment. Paper presented at the annual meeting of the American Psychological Association, San Francisco, 1977.

Hall, J.A. (1978). Gender effects in decoding nonverbal cues. *Psychological Bulletin, 85,* 845–875.

Hall, J.A. (1984). *Nonverbal sex differences: Communication accuracy and expressive style.* Baltimore: Johns Hopkins University Press.

Hurlbert, G., Gade, E., & Fuqua, D. (1983). Sex and race as factors on locus of control scores with an alcoholic population. *Psychological Reports*, *52*(2), 517–518.

Huselid, R.R., Self, E.A., & Gutierres, S.E. (1991). Predictors of successful completion of a halfway-house program for chemically-dependent women. *American Journal of Drug Alcohol Abuse*, *17*(1), 89–101.

Kammeier, M.L. (1977). *Alcoholism is the common denominator: More evidence on the male/female question*. Hazeldon Papers No. 2. Center City, MN: Hazelden Foundation.

Kammeier, M.L., & Conley, J.J. (1979). Toward a system for prediction of posttreatment abstinence and adaptation. In M. Galanter (Ed.), *Currents in alcoholism, Vol. 6*. New York: Grune & Stratton.

Kammeier, M.L., & Laundergan, J.C. (1977). *The outcome of treatment: Patients admitted to Hazelden in 1975*. Center City, MN: Hazelden Publications.

Kaplan, A.G., & Sedley, M. (1980). *Psychology and sex roles: An androgynous perspective*. Boston: Little, Brown.

Kaskutas, L. (1989, summer). Women for Sobriety: A qualitative analysis. *Contemporary Drug Problems*, 177–200.

Kirkpatrick, J. (1977). *Turnabout: New help for the woman alcoholic*. Seattle: Madrone.

Kohlberg, L. (1969). Stage and sequences: The cognitive-developmental approach to socialization. In D.A. Goslin (Ed.), *Handbook of socialization theory and research* (pp. 347–380). Chicago: Rand McNally.

Smith, A.R. (1985). Alcoholism and gender: Patterns of diagnosis and response. *Journal of Drug Issues*, *16*, 407–420.

Smith, D.I. (1986). Evaluation of a residential AA programme for women. *Alcohol and Alcoholism*, *20*, 315–327.

Unger, R.K. (1983). Through the looking glass: No Wonderland yet (The reciprocal relationship between methodology and models of reality). *Psychology of Women Quarterly*, *5*, 645–653.

Vannicelli, M. (1984). Treatment outcome of alcoholic women: The state of the art in relation to sex bias and expectancy effects. In S.C. Wilsnack & L.J. Beckman (Eds.), *Alcohol problems in women: Antecedents, consequences, and intervention*. New York: Guilford.

Wilsnack, S.C. (1984). Drinking, sexuality and sexual dysfunction in women. In S.C. Wilsnack & L.J. Beckman (Eds.), *Alcohol problems in women: Anteceents, consequences, and intervention*. New York: Guilford.

How Can Change Be Measured?

CHAPTER 14

The Social Climate of Self-Help and Mutual Support Groups: Assessing Group Implementation, Process, and Outcome

RUDOLF H. MOOS, JOHN FINNEY, AND PEG MAUDE-GRIFFIN

Self-help and mutual support groups are an important resource in our society. They assist individuals in life transitions and crises by providing a forum in which to give and receive support and candid feedback, learn new coping skills, and enhance members' well-being and self-esteem. However, these groups are not homogeneous; they differ in their purposes and goals, in the types of people who are drawn to and remain active in them, in their social climate, and in their effectiveness.

In this chapter, we present a conceptual framework that provides a context for examining the characteristics and outcomes of self-help and mutual support groups. After describing the social climate perspective, we identify underlying dimensions of group climate, show how information about social climate can be used to measure the quality and implementation of groups, and then examine the determinants and outcomes of group climates. Because there has been little social climate research on Alcoholics Anonymous (AA) groups, we focus first on research involving other types of groups. We then draw some implications for self-study and research on AA and other 12-step groups.

A Guiding Conceptual Paradigm

In previous work, we described a conceptual paradigm informed by stress and coping theory and showed how it can guide evaluations of substance abuse and other intervention programs (Moos, Finney, & Cronkite, 1990). We will adapt that paradigm here to focus on self-help and mutual support groups and the factors that influence them.

The adapted paradigm shown in Figure 1 suggests that the outcome of participation in a group (Panel V) is influenced by an individual's resources prior to entering the group, including demographic and personality factors, aspects of functioning such as the severity of substance abuse,

FIGURE 1
A Conceptual Paradigm to Guide the Assessment and Evaluation of Self-
Help and Mutual Support Groups

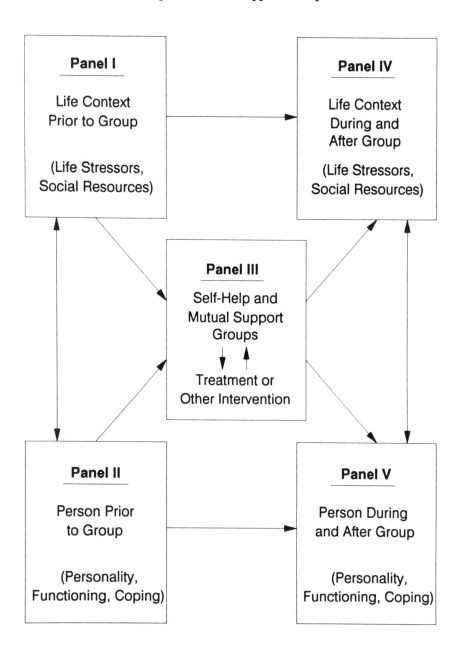

and coping skills (Panel II). Outcomes are also influenced by prior life context factors (Panel I) and those that occur during and after participation in the group (Panel IV), as well as by the individual's experiences in a group and in aspects of other associated interventions, such as a treatment program (Panel III). In addition, the paradigm depicts both personal and life context factors (i.e., variables in Panels I and II) as determinants of entry into a group and, in interaction with group climate and other group factors, of the amount and quality of an individual's participation in a group (Panel III).

This paradigm highlights three points to consider in evaluating the process and outcome of involvement in a self-help or mutual support group. First, it encourages the careful study of a group, including an assessment of how well the group is implemented and an examination of the association between specific aspects of the group and members' outcomes. Second, it clarifies the importance of linkages between a self-help or mutual support group and aspects of other associated intervention programs, such as the quality of a psychotherapy group or an overall treatment program. Finally, it considers factors external to a group and how they influence an individual's decision to participate in the group and the outcome of participation.

Self-help and mutual support groups are placed in Panel III in the model to illustrate their conceptual status as a type of intervention. However, they also can be placed into Panel I as salient aspects of individuals' social networks. In either case, it is important to consider self-help and mutual support groups in the framework of individuals' overall life contexts. The paradigm highlights the complexity of the process of change and places self-help and mutual support groups in context as one among many sets of factors that influence an individual's functioning and well-being.

The Social Climate Perspective

The social climate perspective assumes that each environment has a unique quality that gives it unity and coherence. Like people, some social environments are friendlier, more oriented toward self-discovery, or better organized than others. Individuals form global ideas about a group from their appraisal of specific aspects of it. These perceptions are based in part on reality; for example, a judgment of friendliness in a group might stem from whether members greet each other, help each other, participate in activities together, and so on.

Perceived social climates can be thought of in both personal and consensual terms. Not only does each individual have his or her own perception of the social characteristics of a group, but perceptions of the social environment may be shared by other group members. This latter, group-level construct typically has been operationalized by aggregating the individual perceptions of group members. As shown later, research on group social climate has been conducted at both the individual member and group levels of analysis.

Based on work in a range of settings, Moos (1987) identified three underlying sets of social climate dimensions. *Relationship* dimensions reflect the nature and intensity of interpersonal relationships in an environment. *Personal growth* or *goal orientation* dimensions reflect the basic directions along which personal growth or self-enhancement are encouraged. *System maintenance and change* dimensions assess the extent to which an environment is orderly and clear in its expectations, maintains control, and is responsive to change.

The Group Environment Scale

The Group Environment Scale (GES) is composed of 10 subscales that measure the social climates of groups—self-help and mutual support groups as well as psychotherapy, task-oriented, and social groups. The GES has three forms: the "real form" (form R) measures individuals' perceptions of actual group settings; the "ideal form" (form I) taps individuals' conceptions of ideal groups; and the "expectations form" (form E) assesses prospective members' expectations of a self-help, mutual support, or other group. Information about the development and psychometric characteristics of the GES are provided in the manual (Moos, 1986).

The 10 GES subscales assess relationship, personal growth, and system maintenance and change dimensions. Relationship dimensions are measured by the *cohesion, leader support,* and *expressiveness* subscales. These subscales tap members' commitment to the group and the friendship they show for one another, the help and concern the leader or chairperson shows for the members, and the emphasis on freedom of action and expression of feelings.

Personal growth or goal orientation dimensions are measured by the *independence, task orientation, self-discovery,* and *anger and aggression* subscales. These subscales assess how much the group encourages independent action and expression among members, the emphasis on practical problem-solving and learning specific skills, the orientation toward members' self-revelation and discussion of personal information, and how much the group welcomes members' open expression of negative feelings and disagreements.

System maintenance and change dimensions are measured by the *order and organization, leader control,* and *innovation* subscales. These subscales focus on the structure of the group and explicitness of rules and sanctions, the extent to which the leader or chairperson makes decisions and directs the group, and how much the group facilitates diversity and change in its functions and activities.

Many self-help and mutual support groups have designated leaders. In some groups, however, leadership rotates among the members and leaders are labeled facilitators, chairpersons, and the like. In this situation, the GES instructions may need to be adapted to specify that the items that tap leader support and leader control refer to the facilitator or chairperson.

Measuring Group Quality and Implementation

Information about group social climate can be used to describe and compare groups, indicate whether groups are adequately implemented, and monitor group maturation and change (for some examples, see Moos, 1986). We illustrate some of these applications here by describing how the GES has been used to assess the implementation of GROW International self-help groups and to monitor implementation and congruence of a treatment approach at the program and group levels.

Implementation of GROW International Self-Help Groups

Toro, Rappaport, and Seidman (1987) focused on the implementation of 32 self-help groups affiliated with GROW International, which sponsors structured weekly group meetings and other activities to help former mental patients develop support networks and adjust to community living. In order to clarify whether self-help groups develop a therapeutic social climate, the GROW groups were compared with psychotherapy groups.

As shown in Figure 2, the GROW self-help groups were more cohesive and had more active and supportive leadership than the psychotherapy groups. They also were more task-oriented and well-organized and somewhat higher on independence. The psychotherapy groups were oriented more toward the open expression of anger and showed more flexibility and innovation. These differences reflect the supportive, well-organized, task-focused approach of GROW International and an orientation toward catharsis and self-understanding in the psychotherapy groups. As Lavoie (1981) also noted, recovery groups tend to play down expressiveness and confrontation, which may be an adaptive orientation in groups that do not have a professionally trained leader.

In a study of 45 GROW groups in Australia, Young and Williams (1989) found that these groups establish a supportive social climate oriented toward members' personal growth. Compared with a normative sample of psychotherapy and mutual help groups, GROW groups were more cohesive and well-organized, directed more toward independence and task

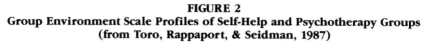

FIGURE 2
Group Environment Scale Profiles of Self-Help and Psychotherapy Groups
(from Toro, Rappaport, & Seidman, 1987)

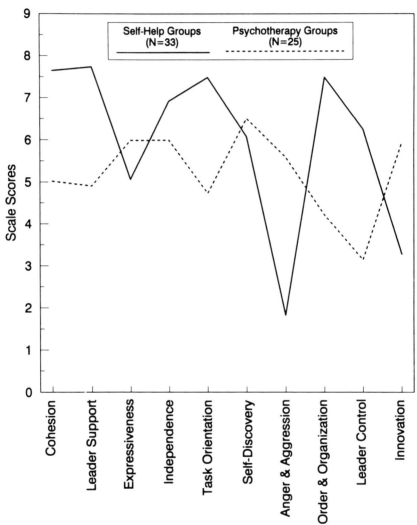

orientation, and higher on both leader support and leader control. They were similar to psychotherapy groups on expressiveness and self-discovery and tended to play down both the open sharing of anger and change. Taken together, these two studies show that the GROW philosophy is well-implemented in groups in both Australia and the United States.

Implementation of a Treatment Approach
at the Program and Group Level

Many mutual support and psychotherapy groups function in a broader setting, such as a residential treatment program. Such groups may or may not reflect the underlying philosophy of the overall program. To focus on this issue, Moffett (1991a) used the Community-Oriented Programs Environment Scale (COPES) to describe the social climate of a therapeutic community (Satori) for substance-dependent patients and the GES to describe three psychotherapy groups within the community. These assessments were made on 17 occasions over a 10-year interval.

The Satori program is designed as a highly structured therapeutic community oriented toward patients with personality disorders. It involves an extensive set of rules and a strong practical orientation as reflected by an emphasis on learning daily living skills and participation in part-time paid work. The program tries to facilitate patients' understanding of the causes of substance abuse while at the same time controlling their substance use and coping with their impulsivity and aggression.

The Satori community. Patients described the Satori program's social climate as quite consistent with the underlying treatment philosophy. In comparison with normative data, the program was somewhat above average in involvement and spontaneity; oriented strongly toward learning practical skills, self-disclosure, and the open expression of anger; and relatively high in staff control. However, it was somewhat below average in staff support, organization, and clarity. Strikingly, Satori's social climate was relatively stable over a ten-year period. It reflected a differentiated and well-implemented treatment approach. As intended by its designers, Satori was better organized and higher on staff control than a normative therapeutic community profile identified by Moos (1989).

Satori's psychotherapy groups. Satori patients described the social climate of each of the program's three psychotherapy groups quite similarly, indicating consistent implementation of the treatment philosophy. All three groups were task-focused and oriented toward self-discovery and the open expression of anger (Figure 3). They also were above the average of normative psychotherapy and mutual support groups on cohesion and leader support, as well as on organization and leader control. However, they were seen as less innovative.

The social climates of the therapeutic community program and its component psychotherapy groups were similar in their orientation toward practical problem-solving and learning task-related skills, self-discovery, the open expression of anger, and staff or leader control. These findings indicate that the overall treatment program and the three psychotherapy groups were implemented in a stable and consistent way.

FIGURE 3
Group Environment Scale Profiles of Satori Groups and Normative Psychotherapy and Mutual Support Groups (from Moffett, 1991a)

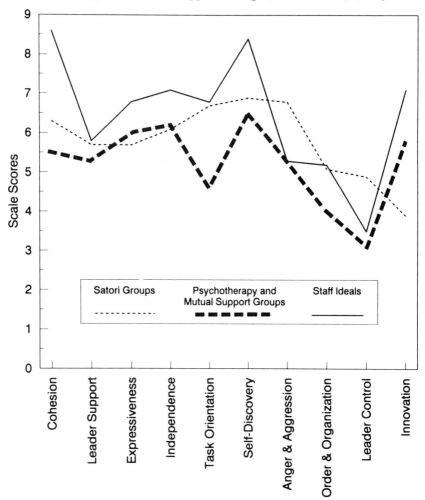

Ideal Climate Conceptions as an Implementation Standard

Members' and leaders' preferences can be used as another typically more stringent implementation standard. Moffett (1991a) asked a sample of Satori staff members to complete the ideal form of the GES to describe their conceptions of the social climates of optimal psychotherapy groups. Compared with the actual groups, staff wanted the Satori groups to be more cohesive, oriented toward self-discovery, and innovative; to de-emphasize the open expression of anger; and to exert less leader control. Thus, groups that appear to be well implemented by normative standards may still fall short of members' or leaders' ideals.

Determinants of Group Climate

Self-help and mutual support groups vary widely in the quality of relationships among members, the emphasis on independence and self-discovery, and the level of organization and structure. This variation raises important questions: Why do group climates develop in such disparate ways? For example, what leads to a strong emphasis on cohesion, or independence, or organization in one group but not in another? Following our model (Figure 1), how is a group's climate (Panel III) influenced by group structure and policies (other variables in Panel III), by members' personal and life context characteristics (Panels II and I), by leader training and behavior (Panel III), and by the interaction of leader and member behaviors and characteristics? To focus on these issues, we provide some examples of relevant research using the GES.

Group Policies and Procedures

Brock and Barker (1990) examined the social climate of a task-oriented staff group in a day hospital prior to a change in the format of the group meetings and twice thereafter. In the novel format, senior staff members shared the roles of chair and interviewer on a rotating basis, the consulting psychiatrist did not attend the meeting, and the size of the group was reduced from 10 to six members. According to the GES, expressiveness and independence increased in the novel format meetings, indicating that group members felt they had more freedom of action and encouraged each other more to express their thoughts and feelings (Figure 4). The open expression of anger and leader control declined, probably because leadership functions were shared equally among several staff members.

There also were striking differences in the amount and content of staff discussions. In the novel format, the leader talked 14% of the time, compared with 46% in the traditional format. Key staff members talked 69% of the time, compared with 40% prior to the change. The time spent on patients' psychosocial and practical problems increased under the new format, whereas the time spent discussing general management issues declined. This example illustrates how information about social climate can be used to monitor changes in group processes associated with changes in the structure and size of a group.

Members' experiences in the early phases of a group can be structured so as to facilitate more self-disclosure and promote group cohesion. In a

FIGURE 4
Group Environment Scale Profiles of Traditional and Novel Psychiatric
Treatment Team Meetings (from Brock & Barker, 1990)

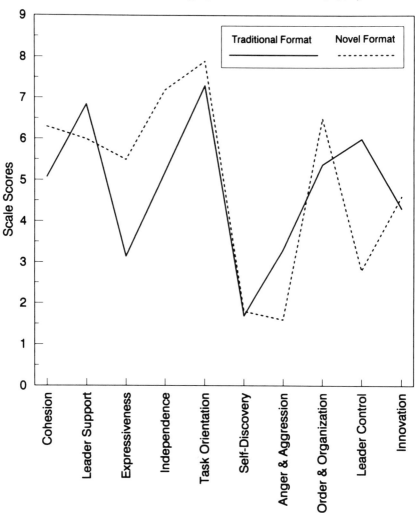

study of women participating in an experiential workshop, Rose and Bednar (1980) examined the influence of two kinds of structured pretraining
tasks: self-disclosure versus providing interpersonal feedback to another
group member, and communicating positive versus negative information.
Both types of structure were important determinants of group development. When group participants provided each other with structured feed-

back and discussed positive information about each other, interpersonal communication and group cohesion were higher than when they disclosed information about themselves and discussed negative information. The highest levels of intermember communication and group cohesion occurred when positive and negative information was mixed than in either all-positive or all-negative sequences, perhaps because mixed information is more credible and closer to reality. These findings imply that group leaders or facilitators should encourage feedback and try to promote the exchange of both positive and negative information among group members. Importantly, too much focus on negative feedback, as may sometimes occur during confrontation sessions, can hamper the development of group cohesion.

Members' Expectations and Interpersonal Orientations

Individuals' expectations and interpersonal orientations may help to predict their perception of the climate and behavior in a group. Melnick and Rose (1979) found that encounter group members who initially expected more interpersonal intimacy in their group subsequently saw the group as more cohesive than did those who initially expected less intimacy. Thus, individuals who had more positive expectations later perceived the groups more positively, perhaps because they were more actively involved in them. In addition, individuals who were more inclined to take interpersonal risks in socially ambiguous situations performed better in the groups; those who had high expectations for intimacy and were risk takers performed the best.

Training of Leaders

A leader can exert an important influence on the social climate of a group. One question of special relevance to self-help groups is whether indigenous leaders can create cohesive, self-directed, and well-organized groups. A related question is whether professional leadership alters the effective ingredients of self-help groups. Toro and his colleagues (1988) examined these issues by comparing the social climate of GROW groups that were led by an indigenous group member with those led by a mental health professional. GROW group leaders are usually drawn from the membership, but in some situations GROW's leaders invite professionally trained individuals to sponsor groups.

Overall, there was a striking similarity between the two sets of groups. The indigenous leaders' groups were as supportive, independent, task-oriented, and well organized as were the groups led by mental health professionals (Figure 5). In fact, members of the groups led by indigenous

FIGURE 5
Group Environment Scale Profiles of Self-Help Groups with Indigenous or Professional Leaders (from Toro et al., 1988)

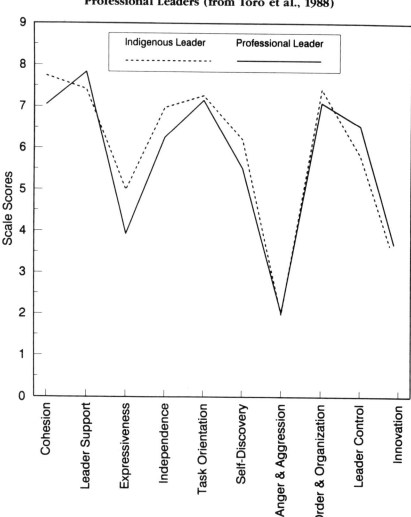

leaders reported somewhat more cohesion, open expression of feelings, and discussion of personal material. Based on behavioral observations, members of the indigenous leaders' groups also showed more instances of giving each other information and agreeing with each other.

These findings show that indigenous leaders can establish cohesive and well-organized groups and point to a somewhat more formal psychologically directed approach in the groups led by mental health professionals.

Similarly, in a study of community-based psychiatric programs, we (Moos, 1988) found that nonprofessional staff developed relationships among clients and between clients and staff that were comparable in quality to those developed by professional staff. Toro et al. (1988) note that some modeling may have occurred in these groups, since the leaders and members behaved similarly by, for example, showing few instances of agreement and discussion of mundane matters. Also, when the leader is a professional, group members may feel somewhat inhibited and thus be more passive.

Interaction of Member and Leader Characteristics

The composition of a group and characteristics of its leader jointly can affect a group's climate. Waltman (1984) examined the extent to which structuring the composition of counselor training groups based on the members' and the leader's willingness to openly discuss personal issues affected the group climate and the members' learning of helping skills.

Contrary to expectation, leaders who were more group-oriented did not establish more cohesive or supportive groups than leaders who were not. However, the interaction of leader and member characteristics influenced the group social climate. More specifically, when group-oriented leaders were matched with groups in which members were less willing to discuss personal issues, these groups were seen as more supportive and better organized than were similar groups matched with less group-oriented leaders. According to Waltman (1984), group-oriented leaders may be more committed and work harder to keep groups on task.

These findings on determinants of group climate provide some guidelines to assist group members as leaders to develop more cohesive groups. However, more information is needed on how members' characteristics and group structure and procedures affect the social climate of self-help and mutual support groups.

Outcomes of Group Climate

Only a few researchers have tried to link variations in self-help and mutual support groups' social climates to members' outcomes (that is, to examine connections between variables in Panels III and V of the model). However, some studies have focused on the social climate of mental health consultation and educational groups and members' outcomes, and on the prediction of group survival.

Self-Help Group Members' Satisfaction and Well-Being

In general, members of supportive, and well-organized groups that emphasize personal growth dimensions such as task-orientation and self-discovery tend to report more satisfaction and well-being and to show better out-comes (Moos, 1986).

Cohesive and well-organized groups. Maton (1988) studied three types of self-help groups: Compassionate Friends, Multiple Sclerosis, and Overeaters Anonymous, which is similar to AA in that it focuses on an addiction or problem of behavioral control. Members of better organized groups reported more benefits from and satisfaction with the group, as well as less depression and more self-esteem. Role differentiation (the extent to which different members' perform different task-related roles) and the capability of the group leaders were also related to better outcomes. Even in the Overeaters Anonymous groups, in which leadership is rotated among the members and the group process is highly structured, the leaders' abilities were associated with group effectiveness.

Maton (1989) also compared four high cohesion and four low cohesion self-help groups. Cohesion was related to members' reports of more support received and provided in the group, to the development of friend-ships with group members, and to less depression. Moreover, group cohesion had an especially positive effect among highly stressed individ-uals. Specifically, highly stressed members of the four high cohesion groups reported that they received more support and developed more friendships with other group members than did their highly stressed counterparts in the low cohesion groups. They also reported less depres-sion and more self-esteem.

Individual perceptions, participation, and outcome. Individuals with a more optimistic outlook may participate more actively in self-help groups and elicit more support from other members; as a consequence, they may become more integrated into the group and see it more posi-tively. In this respect, medical students who initially were more strongly motivated to attend self-help groups tended to appraise them later as more cohesive, expressive, task-oriented, and innovative (Goetzel, Croen, Shelov, Boufford, & Levin, 1984).

There are similar findings for patients in substance abuse treatment pro-grams. Clients who dropped out of a Salvation Army alcoholism treatment program had seen the program as less involving, supportive, clear, and well organized than those who remained in treatment (Moos, Mehren, & Moos, 1978). In contrast, Pratt, Linn, Carmichael, and Webb (1977) found that alcoholic patients who attended aftercare had seen more emphasis on autonomy, personal problem orientation, and the open expression of an-ger on the inpatient program in which they were initially treated than did patients who chose not to participate in aftercare.

Turning to treatment outcome, Fischer (1979) noted that alcoholic pa-tients who reported more personal problem orientation, open expression of anger, and clarity of rules in their program showed better treatment outcome. In a long-term follow-up, we found that alcoholic patients who viewed their residential treatment program more positively showed better treatment outcome 10 years later, even after controlling for their demographic characteristics and functioning at intake (Finney & Moos, 1992). Thus, whatever their source, members' perceptions of a group may provide important predictive information about their participation in the group and future adaptation.

Outcomes of Mental Health Consultation and Educational Groups

Hartsough and Davis (1986) asked members of mental health consultation groups about the group climate and their satisfaction with the group experience. Members of more cohesive and expressive groups that were high on leader support were more satisfied with the group consultant, with consultation in general, and with the group experience. Members of more task-oriented and well-organized groups also showed better outcomes. When Wilcox (1980) evaluated mental health consultation groups, she found that members of cohesive and task-oriented groups tended to have more positive attitudes toward the group experience.

Similar to self-help and mutual support groups, facilitative group learning environments aim to emphasize both interpersonal communication (affective outcomes) and task orientation and learning practical skills (cognitive outcomes). When Meredith (1987) evaluated the extent to which small educational groups met these dual objectives, he found that the groups were generally well implemented. Two group characteristics were salient predictors of student outcomes. Cohesion predicted students' reports of better overall evaluation of the content taught in the group, of more personal effort and commitment, and of personal growth and development. Leader support predicted student intellectual development and a positive evaluation of the group leader.

Member Satisfaction and Survival of Neighborhood Self-Improvement Groups

Neighborhood self-improvement or advocacy groups are akin to self-help and mutual support groups in that they usually are composed of indigenous leaders who are working together to try to improve conditions in their neighborhood. However, advocacy groups often have a stronger task focus. In a study of the social climate of such groups, Prestby and Wandersman (1985) found that members of more cohesive and supportive groups that were task-focused, well organized, and high on leader control were more satisfied with the progress of the group.

Eight of the groups were still active after one year, whereas nine had stopped meeting by that time. At the initial assessment, members of the surviving groups had viewed them as more cohesive, well organized, and task oriented than did members of groups that later became inactive. Members of active groups also saw their leaders as more supportive and structured. Thus, information about the social climate of a group may predict how well it is functioning one year later.

Applications to AA and Other 12-Step Groups

Implementation of AA and Other 12-Step Groups

Alcoholics Anonymous developed in the 1930s along the lines of the nondenominational, evangelical Oxford Group and is one of the oldest and largest self-help organizations (Trice & Staudenmeier, 1989). AA is a voluntary self-help fellowship for individuals who share a common problem; it also offers a comprehensive spiritually based program of recovery. Even though AA groups have existed for more than 50 years, and there are more than 73,000 AA groups with more than 1.56 million members (Trice & Staudenmeier, 1989), there is very little systematic information about the social climate of these groups.

We have shown that information about social climate can be used to assess how well self-help and mutual support groups are implemented and to focus on the determinants and outcomes of group climate. In this section, we note some potential applications of social climate assessments to AA and other 12-step groups. Members of 12-step groups can play an active role in understanding and improving group social climate. With information about their group's climate, members can learn about groups and how they work and contribute to the development of group unity and cohesion. (For a general overview of the use of social climate assessment and feedback in changing social settings, see Finney & Moos, 1984.)

By facilitating social climate assessments, AA groups can provide a model for how individual members can implement the type of self-anaylsis and self-disclosure involved in Steps 4 and 5 of the 12-step approach. More broadly, providing that it is consistent with "group conscience" (that is, that group members agree), AA can exemplify one key aspect of its approach by facilitating the self-study of AA groups.

Measure Group Quality and Implementation

As described earlier, social climate self-assessments can identify how well an AA group is implemented and monitor its stability and change over time. Given their goals and the 12 traditions (Alcoholics Anonymous,

1952), well-implemented AA groups should emphasize group unity and the members' common welfare (moderate to high cohesion and support). The groups have a broad sense of purpose and each group has a specific topic; thus, well-implemented groups should be relatively organized and have a moderate emphasis on task orientation. Because members relate their personal histories, there should be some emphasis on self-understanding. AA members seldom discuss their feelings about one another (cross-talk is discouraged); thus, expressiveness and the open display of anger should be moderate to low. Because the group secretary and chairperson rotate and are seen as servants rather than leaders, members should perceive control as relatively low. Finally, the structure provided by the 12 steps and the 12 traditions should inhibit innovation and keep independence at a moderate level.

When Montgomery, Miller, and Tonigan (in press) adapted the GES to assess four AA groups, they found a relatively high level of cohesion; moderate levels of expressiveness, independence, self-discovery, and organization; and very little emphasis on innovation. The four groups differed significantly in their levels of cohesion, organization, and the open expression of anger. Montgomery and his colleagues (1991) also added a spirituality dimension, which was relatively high in all four groups. A broader sampling of AA groups probably would identify substantial intergroup variation in all these dimensions.

Social climate implementation assessments of AA groups can go beyond a general characterization of groups, however. For example, one can compare the social climate of open versus closed meetings (including those for new versus those only for old members); discussion, 12-step study, and testimonial meetings; meetings chaired by different individuals or types of steering committees; and so on. At the individual member level, one can examine the extent to which members alter their appraisal of a group over time as they change their roles by, for example, obtaining a sponsor, becoming a sponsor, or being the chairperson, secretary, or elder statesman.

One important question is whether an emphasis on self-disclosure affects the quality of a group. In this respect, Shoptaw (1991) studied structured self-help groups and found a relatively low prevalence of high-risk self-disclosures. Moreover, such disclosures did not have a detrimental influence on group climate. It would be useful to focus on the association between self-disclosure and social climate in AA groups and to learn whether high-risk disclosures have different effects depending on members' or indigenous leaders' characteristics.

Feedback about group climate. Information about group quality and implementation can suggest ways to improve AA and other 12-step groups. One approach is to assess the actual and preferred social climate, as Waters and Gavin (1980) did with a couple's counseling group in an alcoholism treatment program. The members apparently saw the group as well implemented; they reported above average cohesion, leader support, and expressiveness, as well as independence, task orientation, self-discovery, and innovation. However, information about preferences showed that the members wanted less emphasis on expressiveness, independence, and self-discovery. When these findings were made available to the members, they led to a spirited discussion of how best to promote the purposes of the group.

Moffett (1991b) used information about group social climate as an adjunct to group therapy and in staff training. Group members were provided with individual feedback on their perceptions of the group. The information identified divergent perceptions, generated a discussion of why they occur, and enabled group members to focus more objectively on specific group interactions. This feedback process often leads to a focus on members' preferences and values and to a discussion of how they can take responsibility for and try to improve the group.

Important information may be obtained when group leaders or chairpersons are asked to predict how group members see the social climate. There are no published examples of this approach in self-help or mutual support groups; however, Archer and Amuso (1980) asked staff members in a psychiatric program to respond to the Ward Atmosphere Scale (WAS) under two conditions: self-ratings reflecting their own perceptions of the program and predictions of how the typical patient would respond. Staff tended to see the program more positively than patients did. More important, staff misjudged patients' reactions. They thought that patients would see the program as less clear and well organized and as higher on personal problem orientation and anger than patients actually saw it. Thus, staff learned that patients saw the program structure as adequate but that they expected more insight-oriented treatment and viewed the program as deficient in this area.

Monitoring and implementing change. More generally, information about social climate can be used to monitor and improve group climate. As described earlier, Brock and Barker (1990) monitored changes in staff group climate after a change in the format of the group meetings. Although there are no published examples of this approach in self-help groups, feedback about social climate has been used to improve alcoholism treatment programs.

When a treatment setting ceases to function effectively, information about the social climate can identify policies that need to be modified. For example, Verinis (1983) studied an alcoholism rehabilitation unit that had a high patient retention rate but experienced a sudden increase in irregular discharges. The WAS showed a concomitant decline in support, spontaneity, and clarity. After staff became aware of the decay in the program environment, they established a more therapeutic atmosphere with significant increases in independence, organization, and clarity. The number of irregular discharges declined to its prior level (for other examples, see Moos, 1988, 1989). Just as in this example of an overall treatment program, information about the social climate of self-help and mutual support groups can be used to improve them.

Determinants of Group Climate

AA and other 12-step groups that utilize traditions to govern group functioning face unique challenges as they try to adapt to the ever-changing demographic and ethnic structure of our society and the increasing diversity of alcoholic and problem-drinking individuals. A growing proportion of AA members are women and younger individuals. Moreover, there now are more members who have concomitant drug addiction and/or serious psychiatric problems. It is important to learn whether the resulting heterogeneous AA groups are well-implemented and, if not, to identify ways to enable them to become more cohesive and well organized. Other questions involve the social climate of larger versus smaller groups, of groups for women only, of groups composed of cognitively impaired individuals, of groups for adult children of alcoholics, and so on.

One hallmark of AA, embodied in the third tradition, is its status as a voluntary fellowship; the one requirement for membership is a desire to stop drinking. Yet many AA members attend meetings to comply with professional therapists' recommendations or because of court-mandated requirements. Mandated attendance is contrary to one of AA's fundamental principles. AA groups composed largely or entirely of resistant members or court-mandated members are likely to be less well-implemented than AA groups composed of voluntary and involved members. In this respect, randomized studies of the effect of AA on mandated members have shown that these individuals do less well than those who received no or other comparison interventions (Emrick, 1989; Walsh et al., 1991). Most important, social climate assessments can highlight emerging problems in groups composed of mandated members and can help identify specific individuals who are less well integrated into these groups.

Another hallmark of AA and many other self-help organizations is an emphasis on the autonomy of local groups, as embodied in the fourth tradition. Even so, consistent with the first tradition's emphasis on promoting group welfare and unity, AA could disseminate information about possible ways to facilitate the development of cohesive local groups. In this respect, the mutual exchange of both positive and negative information among group members may promote group cohesion and members' involvement more than does the self-disclosure of negative information that is so strongly emphasized in AA (Rose & Bednar, 1980). Other ways to facilitate cohesion involve developing positive expectations among prospective members, providing information about the value of self-disclosure, emphasizing the importance of cooperation and humor, and facilitating diversity to reflect the varied cultural contexts of local group members.

The Outcomes of Group Climate

Between 50% and 75% of new members apparently quit AA after only brief contact with it (Emrick, 1987). This fact has led to a number of studies that tried to identify the personal characteristics of individuals who were likely to affiliate with AA, such as those who were more sociable, dependent, middle-class, and the like. In a recent review, however, Emrick (1987, 1989; Emrick, Tonigan, Montgomery, & Little, 1993) concluded that there were no strong associations between individuals' demographic or personality characteristics and AA affiliation.

This line of research has focused almost exclusively on person variables; according to our model (Figure 1), however, it is important to consider the quality of AA group environments. New members who attend well-implemented groups probably have a better chance of establishing long-term affiliations with AA. On the other hand, strong, powerful environments, such as charismatic AA groups, are likely to both attract and repel individuals. Accordingly, there may be an optimal level of group cohesion and structure; too little may be associated with high drop-out rates due to members' lack of involvement, but too much may cause some individuals to disaffiliate due to the all-encompassing nature of the group.

At a broader level, most AA groups survive but some cease to meet and become defunct; Leventhal, Maton, and Madara (1988) found this to be true of 2.1% of AA groups in New Jersey that were followed after one year. Information about group climate can identify risk factors, such as lack of cohesion and organization that may predict the decline and death of AA groups.

Finally, it is important to identify the links between AA group climates and individual members' outcomes. In his reviews, Emrick (1987, 1989) concluded that individuals who maintain membership in AA are more likely to show better drinking-related outcomes (see also Emrick et al., 1993), but that it is not possible to predict the specific individuals who will do well and those who will not. Again, prior research has used solely a person-based approach; however, some AA groups probably are more successful than others. As suggested by our model (Figure 1), members of well-implemented AA groups are likely to expand their supportive social network, enhance their well-being, and show better drinking-related outcomes.

Because many individuals who join AA groups also participate in other intervention programs, it is important to examine the joint effects of AA and these programs. In this vein, Anderson and Gilbert (1989) conducted a behaviorally oriented skills-training program for alcoholic patients that effectively improved the self-analysis and self-disclosure skills involved in Steps 4 and 5 of the AA recovery program. A next step in this line of work is to examine whether trained patients actually perform better in AA groups and whether any such improved performance depends on the group climate. In addition, we need to focus on the continuity and discontinuity between AA and any other concomitant interventions to identify how their influences support or detract from each other (for example, see Galanter, Talbott, Gallegos, & Rubenstone, 1990; Muhleman, 1987).

To maximize members' personal growth as well as group welfare, AA groups must integrate their focus on task versus supportive functions and balance the relative emphasis on cohesion and autonomy. One issue involves how much to focus on the development of specific personal strengths versus self-understanding and the open disclosure of personal information and affect. The second and more basic issue is to strike a reasonable balance between the conformity that may be expected by a cohesive group and the independence some members may need to fully attain their personal potential. One effective resolution of these dilemmas may involve membership in both AA groups and in interactive therapy groups that function in a way that is consistent with AA principles (Matano & Yalom, 1991).

Future Directions

We have described the social climate perspective and shown how information about group climate can be used to monitor the quality and implementation of groups and to examine the determinants and outcomes of group climate. To improve the functioning and efficacy of self-help and mutual support groups, more longitudinal studies are needed of how they influence members' satisfaction, well-being, social network, and substance abuse and other aspects of functioning. Following the conceptual model shown in Figure 1, it also is important to focus on the personal and life context factors that intervene between self-help group processes and members' outcomes. To understand the influence of self-help and other types of mutual support groups, researchers should examine their interplay with the ongoing conditions of individuals' lives, such as stressful life circumstances and social network resources.

Self-help and mutual support groups now encompass more than six million participants annually in the United States alone and are likely to assume a more central role in the future delivery of mental health services

(Jacobs & Goodman, 1989). These groups often generate intense commitment and long-term participation among their members, facilitate members' self-improvement and personal growth, and contribute substantial benefits to society as a whole. As such, it is vital to learn more about self-help groups and to try to improve their effectiveness. In turn, information about the growth-enhancing processes of self-help and mutual support groups may contribute to the development of more effective indigenous and professionally organized intervention programs.

Acknowledgments

Preparation of the manuscript was supported by Department of Veterans Affairs Medical and Health Services Research and Development Service Research Funds and by NIAAA Grants AA02863 and AA06699. We thank Bernice Moos and Debbie Steinbaum for their help in the preparation of the manuscript and Martha Beattie and Robert Matano for their comments on an earlier draft.

References

Alcoholics Anonymous. (1952). *Twelve steps and twelve traditions.* New York: Alcoholics Anonymous World Services.

Anderson, J.G., & Gilbert, F.S. (1989). Communication skills training with alcoholics for improving performance of two of the Alcoholics Anonymous recovery steps. *Journal of Studies on Alcohol, 50,* 361–367.

Archer, R.P., & Amuso, K.F. (1980). Comparison of staff's and patients' perceptions of ward atmosphere. *Psychological Reports, 46,* 959–965.

Brock, D., & Barker, C. (1990). Group environment and group interaction in psychiatric assessment meetings. *International Journal of Social Psychiatry, 36,* 111–120.

Emrick, C.D. (1987). Alcoholics Anonymous: Affiliation processes and effectiveness as treatment. *Alcoholism: Clinical and Experimental Research, 11,* 416–423.

Emrick, C.D. (1989). Alcoholics Anonymous: Membership characteristics and effectiveness as treatment. *Recent Developments in Alcoholism, 7,* 37–53.

Emrick, C.D., Tonigan, J.S., Montgomery, H., & Little, L. (1993). Affiliation processes in and treatment outcomes of Alcoholics Anonymous: A meta-analysis of the literature. In B.S. McCrady & W.R. Miller (Eds.), *Research on Alcoholics Anonymous: Opportunities and Alternatives.* New Brunswick, NJ: Rutgers Center of Alcohol Studies.

Finney, J.W., & Moos, R.H. (1984). Environmental assessment and evaluation research: examples from mental health and substance abuse programs. *Evaluation and Program Planning, 7,* 151–167.

Finney, J.W., & Moos, R.H. (1992). The long-term course of treated alcoholism: II. Predictors and correlates of 10-year functioning and mortality. *Journal of Studies on Alcohol, 53,* 142–153.

Fischer, J. (1979). The relationship between alcoholic patients' milieu perception and measure of their drinking during a brief follow-up period. *International Journal of the Addictions, 14,* 1151–1156.

Galanter, M., Talbott, D., Gallegos, K., & Rubenstone, E. (1990). Combined Alcoholics Anonymous and professional care for addicted physicians. *American Journal of Psychiatry, 147,* 64–68.

Goetzel, R., Croen, L., Shelov, S., Boufford, J., & Levin, G. (1984). Evaluating self-help support groups for medical students. *Journal of Medical Education, 59,* 331–340.

Hartsough, C.S., & Davis, J.M. (1986). Dimensions of the Group Environment Scale. *American Journal of Community Psychology, 14,* 371–376.

Jacobs, M.K., & Goodman, G. (1989). Psychology and self-help groups: Predictions on a partnership. *American Psychologist, 44,* 536–545.

Lavoie, F. (1981). Social atmosphere in self-help groups: A case study. *Canada's Mental Health, 29,* 13–15.

Leventhal, G.S., Maton, K.I., & Madara, E.J. (1988). Systematic organizational support for self-help groups. *American Journal of Orthopsychiatry, 58,* 592–603.

Matano, R.A., & Yalom, I.D. (1991). Approaches to chemical dependence: Chemical dependency and interactive group therapy—a synthesis. *International Journal of Group Psychotherapy, 41,* 269–293.

Maton, K.I. (1988). Social support, organizational characteristics, psychological well-being, and group appraisal in three self-help group populations. *American Journal of Community Psychology, 16,* 53–77.

Maton, K.I. (1989). Community settings as buffers of life stress? Highly supportive churches, mutual help groups, and senior centers. *American Journal of Community Psychology, 17,* 203–232.

Melnick, J., & Rose, G. (1979). Expectancy and risk-taking propensity: Predictors of group performance. *Small Group Behavior, 10,* 389–401.

Meredith, G.M. (1987). Attributes of group atmosphere as predictors of students' satisfaction in seminar format classes. *Psychological Reports, 61,* 79–82.

Moffett, L.A. (1991a, August). Social climates of a therapeutic community for substance dependent veterans. Presented at the American Psychological Association Convention, San Francisco, CA.

Moffett, L.A. (1991b). Using the Group Environment Scale in training and in therapy. Palo Alto, CA: Psychology Service, Department of Veterans Affairs Medical Center.

Montgomery, H.A., Miller, W.R., & Tonigan, J.S. (in press). Differences among AA groups: Implications for research. *Journal of Studies on Alcohol.*

Moos, R. (1986). *Group environment scale manual* (2nd ed.). Palo Alto, CA: Consulting Psychologists Press.

Moos, R. (1987). *The social climate scales: A user's guide.* Palo Alto, CA: Consulting Psychologists Press.

Moos, R. (1988). *Community-oriented programs environment scale manual* (2nd ed.). Palo Alto, CA: Consulting Psychologists Press.

Moos, R. (1989). *Ward atmosphere scale manual* (2nd ed.) Palo Alto, CA: Consulting Psychologists Press.

Moos, R., Finney, J., & Cronkite, R. (1990). *Alcoholism treatment: context, process, and outcome.* New York: Oxford University Press.

Moos, R., Mehren, B., & Moos, B. (1978). Evaluation of a Salvation Army alcoholism treatment program. *Journal of Studies on Alcohol, 39,* 1267–1275.

Muhleman, D. (1987). 12-Step study groups in drug abuse treatment programs. *Journal of Psychoactive Drugs, 19,* 291–298.

Pratt, R., Linn, M., Carmichael, J., & Webb, N. (1977). The alcoholic's perception of the ward as predictor of aftercare attendance. *Journal of Clinical Psychology, 33,* 915–918.

Prestby, J., & Wandersman, A. (1985). An empirical exploration of a framework of organizational viability: Maintaining block organizations. *Journal of Applied Behavioral Science, 21,* 287–305.

Rose, B.S., & Bednar, R.L. (1980). Effects of positive and negative self-disclosure and feedback on early group development. *Journal of Counseling Psychology, 27,* 63–70.

Shoptaw, S.J. (1991). Functions of risky disclosures in programmed self-help groups. Doctoral dissertation, University of California-Los Angeles, 1990. *Dissertation Abstracts International, 51,* 5591B.

Toro, P.A., Rappaport, J., & Seidman, C. (1987). Social climate comparisons of mutual help and psychotherapy groups. *Journal of Consulting and Clinical Psychology, 55,* 430–431.

Toro, P.A., Reischl, T.M., Zimmerman, M.A., Rappaport, J., Seidman, E., Luke, D.A., & Roberts, L.J., (1988). Professionals in mutual-help groups: Impact on social climate and members' behavior. *Journal of Consulting and Clinical Psychology, 56,* 631–632.

Trice, H.M., & Staudenmeier, W.J. (1989). A sociocultural history of Alcoholics Anonymous. *Recent Developments in Alcoholism, 7,* 11–35.

Verinis, J.S. (1983). Ward Atmosphere as a factor in irregular discharge for an alcohol rehabilitation unit. *International Journal of the Addictions, 18,* 895–899.

Walsh, D.C., Hingson, R.W., Merrigan, D.M., Levenson, S.M., Cupples, L.A., Heeren, T., Coffman, G.A., Becker, C.A., Barker, T.A., Hamilton, S.K., McGuire, T.G., & Kelley, C.A. (1991). A randomized trial of treatment options for alcohol-abusing workers. *New England Journal of Medicine, 325*(11), 775–782.

Waltman, D.E. (1984). Counselor training groups: The effects of group composition, trainer characteristics, and trainer/group arrangements on members' perception of the group environment and their acquisition of helping skills. Doctoral dissertation, Kent State University, 1983. *Dissertation Abstracts International, 44,* 2985A.

Waters, J.E., & Gavin, A.B. (1980). Social ecology: A method for evaluating groups. *International Journal of Social Psychiatry, 26,* 272–279.

Wilcox, M.R. (1980). Variables affecting group mental health consultation for teachers. *Professional Psychology, 11,* 728–732.

Young, J., & Williams, C. (1989). Group process and social climate of GROW, a community mental health organization. *Australian and New Zealand Journal of Psychiatry, 23,* 117–123.

CHAPTER 15

Perspectives on Longitudinal Studies of Alcohol-Related Problems

Don Cahalan

It is very hard to study the effectiveness of Alcoholics Anonymous (AA) because so many variables must be taken into account in dealing with a modality that commonly is intertwined with a great variety of pressures being exerted toward or against the client's recovery from alcoholism. Other chapters in this book (especially chapters 4, 10, 11, 12, and 13) have made it abundantly clear that if we wish to establish the effectiveness of AA, either in aggregate terms or in relation to AA's interaction with various modes of treatment, we must control for a wide range of variables in host-agent-environment interactions. For example, if we want to see how effective a specific type of treatment is when combined with AA participation, we must define the nature of the specific AA setting (at least the type of group and the general environment); the nature and extent of pressures toward and opposed to participating in AA (such as court orders to participate or influences against participating); the length and character of participation of the individual in AA; the age, sex, and social status of the individual; and the individuals' attitudes and values about drinking. Considering the number of factors that must be taken into account in such an endeavor, we should accord a high priority to a research approach like meta-analysis to evaluate not only the effectiveness of AA but also what it is and who it serves.

The crucial importance of longitudinal studies in dealing with AA is obvious because past studies—particularly the two RAND reports (Armor, Polich, & Stambul, 1976; Polich, Armor, & Braiker, 1980)—have shown that effectiveness can vary a great deal depending upon the time span involved: whether follow-ups on improvement are conducted after only a few months or several years after the initial assessment of the individual's condition.

Almost 30 years ago, Knupfer (in 1963) prepared a succinct definition and critique of longitudinal studies for publication in Jellinek's *Encyclopedia of Problems of Alcohol,* which unfortunately never saw print. In it she made many trenchant observations about longitudinal studies that have been well borne out by subsequent experience. She begins by saying:

> A longitudinal study can be defined as a study which uses repeated observations on the same individual subjects (not necessarily persons) at different points in time. This definition covers a wide range, of course, including such varied types of investigations as the positions of the planets at different times, the determination of the boiling point of a chemical substance, laboratory studies on the effects of a stimulus, the prediction of "success" in marriage, and the stability of intelligence quotients from ages 3 to 30. Even if we confine the discussion to the use of the method in the social sciences there are many differences in types, depending on variations in the elements of the design. (p. 1)

Drawing upon Fillmore's thoroughgoing discussions in her book *Alcohol Use Across the Life Course* (1988), longitudinal studies can include relating data on alcohol use and problems obtained from respondents' self-reports to independent historical data on the respondent's family background and other environmental influences, as well as observations and judgments from other informants (such as family members, friends, or health or social welfare sources), and linkage of any of the above to morbidity or death records. Research can be called longitudinal if there are two or more measurements of any type of data related to the same individual as measured at two or more points in time. This broad and loose definition of longitudinal used here is implicit in Fillmore's incisive and clarifying discussions but also in the books by Vaillant (1983) and Goodwin, Van Dusen, and Mednick (1984).

The pioneering longitudinal studies of drinking behavior and problems launched by my colleagues and me at Berkeley and George Washington University in the 1960s and continuing into the present have provided many valuable learning experiences about the advantages and limitations of longitudinal surveys. In these general population national probability surveys, the initial waves included a broad range of questions about environmental and personality correlates of drinking behavior as well as the nature and extent of drinking problems; the second waves (conducted after too brief two- or three-year intervals) measured self-reports of changes in drinking behaviors and problems. Our series of analyses of changes in drinking behavior and problems after these short time spans brought into question the established Jellinekian hypothesis that there exists a hierarchy of types of problems ranging from less intractable to more intractable in nature, which the potential alcoholic is likely to adopt in a predictable pattern in his or her sinking into alcoholism. However, our analyses demonstrated that while the *number* of types of drinking problems reported in the first interview was helpful in predicting the number of types of problems reported in the second interview, there was little relationship between the *types* of problems reported in the first interview and their ability to predict a worsening of problems over the span of several years (Cahalan, 1986; Cahalan & Roizen, 1974; Clark, 1976; Clark & Cahalan, 1976; Roizen, Cahalan, & Shanks, 1978). These findings, as well as analyses that demonstrated that young men were more likely to report sporadic drinking problems while middle-aged men—more typical of the age range of clinical alcoholics—were more likely to report chronic problems, helped to establish the need to distinguish between alcohol problems per se and the addictive aspects of alcoholism (Cahalan & Room, 1974; Fillmore & Midanik, 1984). Such early longitudinal studies thus made a contribution to the development of more eclectic, empirical perspectives for the study of the dynamics involved in the onset and cessation of drinking problems and alcoholism.

These early longitudinal surveys had rather obvious inherent defects. One was that our U.S. surveys were confined to an "historical moment" and to just the American culture; disentangling cohort effects could not be done properly with these design limitations. Another shortcoming was that our questionnaires borrowed rather heavily from the now outmoded Jellinekian hierarchy of drinking problems. We did this primarily to be able to test the validity of the Jellinek hypotheses themselves; but it did burden our questionnaires with much detail that then was carried on to the follow-up questionnaires in order to measure changes, with some loss in efficiency of before/after comparisons. Another shortcoming was that these changes in drinking behavior and problems were measured only through respondents' self-reports and thus were subject to distortion through denial and forgetting. Another inherent limitation, discussed in Knupfer's helpful unpublished paper (1963), is the fact that each wave of a survey occasions some inevitable attrition of respondents, so that even if one attains the fairly high completion rate of 80%, one is left with 64% at the end of the second wave and of not more than 51% at the end of a third wave—or hardly more than half the initial sample, leaving very questionable representation. While we managed to approach a 90% completion rate in each wave for most of our longitudinal surveys, the necessarily high expense of conducting so many attempts at finding missing respondents naturally reduced the sizes of samples we were able to afford within our limited budgets.

The ongoing meta-analytic cross-cultural longitudinal surveys of drinking behavior being reanalyzed by Fillmore and colleagues are making significant contributions to a better understanding of how various factors interact to affect changes in behavior. The findings of these many general population surveys from 15 predominantly European or North Atlantic countries, as set forth in the preliminary papers published recently in the

British Journal of Addiction (Fillmore, Hartka, Johnstone, Leino, Moto-yoshi, & Temple, 1991), provide abundant warnings on the need to take into account not only individual-level characteristics (such as age, sex, ethnic background, and social status) in studying changes in drinking behavior, but also such factors as differences in age cohorts (e.g., different drinking norms under differing conditions of alcohol taxes and other constraints). The beauty of the meta-analysis approach is that, when raw data from multiple studies are utilized, it permits the analysts to disentangle more clearly the influence of a wide range of variables (such as aging, differences in cohorts, and major historical trends, as well as the familiar variables of age, sex, and social status).

The necessity for cross-cultural studies of AA as a phenomenon was also underscored by Mäkelä's discussion (chapter 11 of this volume) of the differences that now exist among the AA movements in various cultures and subcultures.

In studying the effectiveness of AA, it must be kept constantly in mind that participation in AA is ostensibly voluntary and also is usually intertwined with treatments of (or influences upon) drinking behavior; therefore we must study not only the character and presumed effects of AA but also the many other influences that can affect treatment outcomes. Also, study of the effects of AA and other influences hardly can be conclusive unless based on random samples of the populations of concern. Some such studies should begin with random samples of the general population to determine which individuals are exposed to AA experience. These large-scale surveys would be followed by random subsamples of individuals among subsets of first-attenders at AA meetings, chosen among stratified subsamples of various types of AA groups in different localities, and conducted among adequate subsamples of the subgroups that the early general population studies have found to differ a great deal in their drinking behavior and their exposure to AA and other key influences on drinking. Again, in all these samplings attention should be focused on the effects not only of AA but also of other significant forces bearing upon the drinking behavior of the individuals and of their key reference groups.

The complexity of the interrelationship among background variables and drinking behavior and problems evident in the studies of Fillmore and colleagues, and in the tenor of much other research during the last generation, certainly underscores the necessity, in studying the effectiveness of AA, of beginning with precise definitions of samples and adherence to closely controlled randomized designs. But if one wishes to start with a truly random sample of AA first-time attenders, a random sample of the U.S. adult population would have to be a huge one in order to yield sufficient numbers of qualified respondents. While AA has long been the leading modality utilized in deterring alcoholism, only a relatively tiny proportion of the general public has ever been associated with AA. Weisner, Greenfield, and Room (1991) found, in assessing trends from 1979 to 1990 in respondent self-reports of ever undergoing any type of alcoholism "treatment," only a little more than 3% of the general adult population reported *ever* having had "treatment" through AA. Room and Greenfield (1991), working with a national sample of 2,058 persons aged 18 or older, found that only 9% reported that at some time in their life they had attended an AA meeting, and only 3.4% reported attending within the last year—and even this small percentage did not necessarily consist only of actual AA members or first-time attenders.

While AA is one of the least expensive and most widely applied modalities associated with recovery from alcoholism, almost all alcohol specialists will agree with Miller and Hester (1986) that there is at yet little solid proof as to its effectiveness. Longabaugh (1991), in his overview of the state of the art in alcohol research, emphasized that there is still insufficient evidence of AA's effectiveness. He also observed:

> Alcohol treatment research has come of age: Current research embodies rigorous designs capable of detecting treatment differences. However, while we are now able to conceptualize and implement rigorous designs, one of the facts that doesn't leave us is how difficult it is to do treatment outcome studies. One particular fact that has become clear is that otherwise well designed studies of the past have suffered from inadequate statistical power. Chief among the reasons for this is that our sample sizes have been too small. Consequently, we have probably underdetected true differences between different treatments. (p. 1)

Accordingly, we should be on our guard about drawing hasty conclusions from such individual studies as the recent one by Walsh et al. (1991). That study of 227 participants in an individual employee assistance program, randomly assigned to one of three groups, yielded the most favorable results with the group that got a combination of hospitalization *and* AA participation; those allowed to choose their own program had intermediate outcomes, while those assigned to AA alone (but who might not have participated) had the least favorable outcomes. Findings of this small-sample study, which had the additional limitation of being conducted only on a single employee assistance program base, have been seized upon by those providing long-term hospital alcoholism treatment as "proving" that lengthy hospital care combined with AA is the most effective mode of treatment. Obviously, many such studies with many varied types of population bases, and truly controlled modes of treatment, accompanied by adequate qualitative studies that could enlighten us on the rationales back of the interactions of various modes and combinations of treatments, will be necessary before we can know anything conclusive about which treatments are most cost-effective under what sorts of circumstances.

Clearly, there is urgent need for increased coordination of treatment-relevant research in analysis of past and future longitudinal data, to bolster and supplement attempts by the National Institute on Alcohol Abuse and Alcoholism (NIAAA) to synthesize the findings on drinking behavior and problems from the wide variety of national and localized surveys conducted from the 1960s by a variety of agencies. These should include our own Berkeley–George Washington Social Research and Alcohol Research Groups funded by NIAAA, the surveys on drinking and other drug use conducted by the University of Michigan under the auspices of the National Institute on Drug Abuse (NIDA), and studies under a number of other auspices. To these should be added the growing inclusion of drinking and drug and alcoholism treatment questions in the periodic massive National Center for Health Statistics (NCHS) national household surveys cosponsored by NIAAA. In just one of these studies, in 1988, as reported in Schoenborn (1991), a total of 43,809 adults aged 18 and older were interviewed, with a response rate of 90% of eligible respondents and about 85.5% of the total National Health Interview Survey (NHIS) sample. This report concentrated on familial exposure to alcoholics. Other large-scale NCHS surveys have covered in separate surveys in 1977 and 1983 (Schoenborn & Cohen, 1986) such issues as trends in smoking, alcohol consumption, and other health practices. Because these NCHS national surveys cover a wide range of health and nutritional issues, and because the affiliated Health and Nutrition Examination Surveys (HANES) can provide data on the association between drinking and morbidity, the NCHS data files provide an excellent opportunity for further longitudinal follow-up surveys of subsamples to measure changes in drinking behavior and treatments and their correlates, as well as morbidity/mortality data on selected subgroups with varying drinking practices and treatment experiences.

It is beyond the scope of this chapter to present a detailed plan for coordinating reanalyses and follow-ups based on the recent vast accumulation of individual surveys on drinking behavior conducted from the 1960s into the 1990s. But it looks obvious from the payoffs thus far achieved by Fillmore and her colleagues (1991) with their analysis of the raw data from cross-national and cross-historical alcohol studies, that there should be great promise in a series of meta-analytic studies pooling those cross-national studies with perhaps a dozen U.S. national or regional surveys of drinking behavior and exposure to various modes of treatment as well as less formal influences. Such a meta-analysis would establish which should be the key control variables needed to provide a firmer base for planning subsequent controlled studies of alternative modes of alcoholism treatments.

I asked Fillmore to read this paper, and her informal memo of January 19, 1992, offered additional suggestions for a research strategy:

A quick note on how one might assess A.A. "effectiveness" (or other treatment "effectiveness" for that matter) through the back door. First, we know that there are many treatment evaluation studies out there which are, of course, longitudinal but these studies typically suffer from small and/or biased samples as well as historical effects (e.g., the changing nature of the clientele being served and even the "treatment" rendered). Second, the great majority of these studies ask the respondents about their usage of A.A. at followup as well as previous exposure to A.A.

Now, what if one brought these studies together using the research synthesis or meta-analytic approach? In this "mega-sample," one has data on (a) those who did not attend A.A. but had some treatment of some sort and (b) those who did attend A.A. and had some treatment of some sort. One codes on the individual level for the type of treatment and the extent of treatment (number and duration) and the garden variety of individual-level variables we typically look at (e.g., age—which is, of course confounded by cohort and history, sex, extent and nature of problems). As well, one codes on the aggregate level or the study level for historical factors (e.g., when treatment occurred), cohort effects, treatment availability, problems with the sample (e.g., "representativeness," loss at followup).

In this "mega-sample," we would ask the basic question: Under what historical, cultural, treatment and personal conditions did the presence of A.A. in a person's life and the degree of exposure to A.A. influence a change in the person's drinking pattern? This would be a contextual-level analysis in which your predictors are not only the characteristics of the person (e.g., age, sex, referral source, criminality, and other drug use) but also the characteristics of the period of history in which the "treatment" occurred, the nature of the "other" treatments in which the persons were exposed and any other aggregate-level variables you want to throw into the model (for instance, from a sociological point of view, I would be more interested to look at the "threshold" for treatment, i.e., the *mean* number of problems or the *mean* volume of drinking of those entering treatment in differing historical epochs).

Well, that's nice, you must be saying. But there is a great big hole in this evaluation and that concerns those people who never went to "formalized" treatment. This is where your multiple general population longitudinal samples come in. You would "pool" these samples to the extent that they are all coded to the same constructs. But, they are coded with respect to their own study-level characteristics as you have done with the treatment studies (e.g., when they took place, where they took place, sample loss, mortality, etc.) as well as the individual-level characteristics of the people under study. These samples fill out the picture because you have essentially three broad groups: (a) those with other treatment and no A.A., (b) those with other treatment and various doses of A.A., and (c) those with no other treatment and various doses of A.A.

Now, the nice thing about this "little" scheme is that you will have varying lengths of followup. Oops, you say to me, That's bad, isn't it? No, it isn't, I reply. Because you can "determine" the duration of the effectiveness of the exposure to A.A. under a variety of conditions. It is because the length of followup can be entered as a predictor variable in your model to predict outcome on the individual level.

So, in summary, I think that to get to the "heart" of this matter is to use contextual-level models in which the slippery nature of the beast (both A.A. and treatment) can be understood in the context of its time and culture as well as by the individual-level characteristics of those exposed to either A.A. and/or other treatment. Otherwise, if you don't take these "larger" influences into account, about the time you think you have a hold on what's going on, history or findings from another culture are going to kick sand in your face.

Of course, the analysis staffs in the NIAAA are well aware of the need for more ambitious approaches to the coordination and integration of drinking studies that already have been conducted. As summarized in a January 17, 1992, letter from Mary C. Dufour, chief of the Epidemiology Branch of the NIAAA Division of Biometry and Epidemiology, NIAAA has invested significant amounts of their contract budgets in various NCHS studies over the years, including alcohol supplements in the 1983 and 1988 National Health Interview Surveys, the 1980 and 1988 Maternal and Infant Interview Surveys, and the NHANES (National Health and Nutrition Examination Survey) Epidemiologic Follow-Up Study. NIAAA currently has a heavy investment in the development of the 1993 National Mortality Followback Survey and also helped by consultation on the 1986 National Mortality Followback Survey.

However, while the NIAAA has been able to mount a limited number of contracts for the development of statistical and computing methodology for large complex sample surveys (Annual Report FY91, Division of Biometry and Epidemiology), NIAAA has not as yet been provided the funding and other incentives to undertake more elaborate analyses that go much beyond presenting the results of the individual surveys with limited attention to arriving at any consensuses. While the NCHS staff puts a commendably high priority on making their data available for further analyses upon request, their own reports consist primarily of bare-bones presentations of the basic findings of individual surveys, with limited resources being available to deal with more of the subtleties of the findings and their implications for further research.

Thus far, there has not been much in the way of really large-scale U.S. probability sample studies of the correlates and presumed effects of various types of alcoholism and other alcohol-problem treatments, even though such studies obviously could be helpful in planning future controlled studies of treatment. The supplementary follow-up interviews to collect data on treatments experienced among subsamples of respondents covered in a number of the NIAAA- and NCHS-sponsored surveys mentioned above could enable us to have a better understanding of the role of treatment in respondents' lives, as well as to pinpoint special groups of varying treatment experiences who should be reinterviewed an additional time—and also checked in morbidity and mortality records—to help in arriving at a better understanding of long-term treatment effectiveness.

However, I recognize that it will take considerable lobbying to develop more adequate incentives to mine the rich resources of alcohol surveys already conducted. In some 50 years of experience in commercial or government-sponsored surveys, I have found that administrators are much more inclined to fund surveys that are carried only through presentation of summaries of the main findings than they are to spend relatively small additional suns for reanalysis of the data or follow-up studies. It will take a lot of persuasion to convince administrators that the true test of the value of research is *the yield in highly useful and conclusive facts*, and not the sheer volume of superficial data accumulated.

References

Armor, D., Polich, J., & Stambul, H. (1976). *Alcoholism and treatment.* Santa Monica, CA: RAND.

Cahalan, D. (1968, June). *Correlates of change in drinking behavior in an urban community sample over a three-year period.* Unpublished Ph.D. dissertation, Department of Psychology, George Washington University.

Cahalan, D., & Roizen, R. (1974, December 12–18). Changes in drinking problems in a national sample of men. Paper presented at the annual meeting of the North American Congress on Alcohol and Drug Problems, San Francisco.

Cahalan, D., & Room, R. (1974). *Problem drinking among American men.* New Brunswick, NJ: Rutgers Center of Alcohol Studies.

Clark, W. (1976). Loss of control, heavy drinking and drinking problems in a longitudinal study. *Journal of Studies on Alcohol, 37,* 1256–1290.

Clark, W., & Cahalan, D. (1976). Changes in problem drinking over a four-year span. *Addictive Behaviors, 1,* 251–259.

Dufour, M.C. (1992, January 17). Letter to Don Cahalan on research program of the Epidemiology Branch, National Institute on Alcohol Abuse and Alcoholism.

Fillmore, K.M. (1992, January 19). Memo to Don Cahalan.

Fillmore, K.M. (1988). *Alcohol use across the life course: A critical review of 70 years of International longitudinal research.* Toronto: Addiction Research Foundation.

Fillmore, K.M., & Midanik, L. (1984). Chronicity of drinking problems among men: A longitudinal study. *Journal of Studies on Alcohol, 45,* 228–236.

Fillmore, K.M., Hartka, E., Johnstone, B.M., Leino, E.V., Motoyoshi, M., & Temple, M.T. (1991). The collaborative alcohol-related longitudinal project: Preliminary results from a meta-analysis of drinking behavior in multiple longitudinal studies. *British Journal of Addiction, 86,* 1203–1210.

Goodwin, D., Van Dusen, K., & Mednick, S. (1984). *Longitudinal research in alcoholism.* Boston/The Hague: Kluwer-Nijhoff Publishing.

Longabaugh, R. (1991, November 13). Alcohol treatment research: Present and future. Presentation to the American Public Health Association, Atlanta, Georgia.

Mäkelä, K. (1993). Implications for research of the cultural variability of Alcoholics Anonymous. In B.S. McCrady & W.R. Miller (Eds.), *Research on Alcoholics Anonymous: Opportunities and alternatives.* New Brunswick, NJ: Rutgers Center of Alcohol Studies.

Miller, W.R., & Hester, R. (1986). The effectiveness of alcoholism treatment: What research reveals. In W.R. Miller & N. Heather (Eds.), *Treating addictive behaviors.* New York: Plenum.

National Institute on Alcohol Abuse and Alcoholism. (1991). *Annual report FY91: Division of Biometry and Epidemiology.* Rockville, MD: NIAAA.

Polich, J., Armor, D., & Braiker, H. (1979). *The course of alcoholism: Four years after treatment.* Santa Monica, CA: RAND.

Roizen, R., Cahalan, D., & Shanks, P. (1979). "Spontaneous remission" among untreated problem drinkers. In D. Kandel (Ed.), *Longitudinal research in drug use: Empirical findings and methodological issues.* Washington DC: Hemisphere Press.

Room, R., & Greenfield, T. (1991). Alcoholics Anonymous, other 12-step movements and psychotherapy in the U.S. population. Berkeley, CA: Alcohol Research Group [undated; ARG Paper F281].

Schoenborn, C.A. (1991, September 30). Exposure to alcoholism in the family: United States, 1988. National Center for Health Statistics, No. 205.

Schoenborn, C.A., & Cohen, B.H. (1986, June 30). Trends in smoking, alcohol consumption, and other health practices among U.S. adults, 1977 and 1983. National Center for Health Statistics, No. 118.

Vaillant, G. (1983). *The natural history of alcoholism: Causes, patterns, and paths to recovery.* Cambridge, MA: Harvard University Press.

Walsh, D.C., Hingson, R.W., Merrigan, D.M., et al. (1991). A randomized trial of treatment options for alcohol-abusing workers. *New England Journal of Medicine, 325*(11), 775–782.

Weisner, C., Greenfield, T., & Room, R. (1991). Trends in treatment for alcohol problems in the U.S. general population, 1979–1990. Berkeley: Alcohol Research Group [undated; ARG Paper F277].

CHAPTER 16

Evaluating Individual
Difference Dimensions

G. ALAN MARLATT, WILLIAM R. MILLER, AND JOHN S. BAER

Survey research conducted by Alcoholics Anonymous (AA) itself has focused on outcomes only at the aggregate level, and because of anonymity constraints, the same individuals cannot be identified at multiple time
points in these studies (Alcoholics Anonymous, 1990). Outcome research
customarily includes evaluation of individual status at follow-up in relation to pretreatment measures. This raises the question of which individual difference dimensions should be evaluated, and how these dimensions
can be assessed. Our focus here will be on individual difference measures
pertinent to the evaluation of outcomes. Potential predictor variables for
outcomes within AA are discussed by Emrick and Glaser in Chapters 4
and 21 of this volume.

One major domain of importance in outcome assessment is alcohol/
drug use and its consequences. At least five dimensions are relevant here:
(1) alcohol and other drug use, (2) negative consequences of use,
(3) symptoms of dependence, (4) biomedical impairment, and (5) neuropsychological impairment. Direct examination of consumption and its
sequelae, however, does not tell the whole story. A broader assessment of
an individual's status would include evaluation of: (6) social and psychological factors specifically associated with alcohol and drug use, (7) other
life adjustment dimensions (e.g., employment, relationships) not necessarily related to alcohol/drug use, (8) personality, (9) other psychological
problems, including diagnosable disorders, (10) motivation for change and
maintenance of change, and (11) personal models of addiction and change.

Use and Its Consequences

Alcohol Consumption

Although for some purposes it may suffice to ask merely about the
presence or absence of drinking at follow-up, a more careful assessment
takes into account the topography of alcohol consumption, including its

frequency, quantity, and patterning. There are three major approaches to such quantitative assessment.

The *quantity/frequency* approach asks a series of brief questions about drinking during a specified period of time (e.g., Cahalan, Cissin, & Crossley, 1969). The dimensions queried always include frequency (on how many days) and quantity (amount consumed on a typical drinking day), which may be asked for alcohol beverages in general, or separately for classes of beverages (beer, wine, spirits). An advantage of this approach is its brevity, as well as its feasibility within a self-report questionnaire format. The simplicity of the quantity/frequency approach may also be its weakness. Reporting a typical or average day's consumption may underestimate the occurrence of heavy drinking. For this reason, some questionnaires have added specific questions about the frequency of heavy drinking days (e.g., Saunders & Aasland, 1987).

The complexity of drinking patterns has led to the development of other structured interview formats, employing more detailed strategies for eliciting self reported alcohol use. One such strategy has been to construct typical *pattern grids* by asking the respondent to describe alcohol consumption during an average week, quantifying drinking for morning, afternoon, and evening intervals for each day (Miller & Marlatt, 1984, 1987). To account for variability, the interviewer then asks about and quantifies episodes of heavier drinking. Data derived from this approach can be used to report consumption as a number of standard drink units (Miller, Heather, & Hall, 1991). Blood alcohol concentration (BAC) estimations can also be derived from grid data (Markham, 1992; Matthews & Miller, 1979) to yield dependent variables such as peak BAC during a given period or the percentage of hours above a specified BAC point. The grid method also has its limitations. As previously used, it does not capture well spans of abstinence within drinking periods, and its averaging approach may not adequately characterize the variability of drinking. It also does not provide real-time dating of events as needed for certain purposes, such as survival analysis.

A third alternative is the *time-line follow-back* approach (Sobell, Maisto, Sobell, Cooper, Cooper, & Saunders, 1980), which uses a calendar to reconstruct drinking day by day throughout the period of interest. When completed, the calendar contains the client's drinking status for each day of the period, usually characterized as abstinence, light, medium, or heavy drinking. Consumption data at this level, however, are not readily converted into standard drink units or BAC estimates. Furthermore, despite the memory-aid value of the calendar, a day-by-day reconstruction can tax a client's memory and patience with intervals longer than 30 days.

Most recently, a team of researchers working within NIAAA's Project MATCH developed a hybrid of the grid and time-line methods (Miller,

1991). Dubbed "Form 90," this structured interview uses the strong calendar-based format of the time-line method and the grid approach to more efficiently reconstruct large blocks of drinking days. The calendar format is also used to locate and quantify other outcome variables of interest, including employment, AA attendance, health care utilization, institutionalization, and other drug use.

The relative validity of these alternative approaches to alcohol quantification is currently unknown. They differ in ease and time of administration, specificity of data provided, and types of variables yielded for analysis.

A relatively simple check on self-report, at least at the time of interview, is breath alcohol testing. Other biomedical verification procedures under development are a saliva "dipstick" and a tamper-proof sweat patch for sampling alcohol. In addition, collateral reports, that is, reports of drinking patterns and problems by those who know the individual, can serve as important means of data verification. Interviews with family members not only provide additional data but also serve to improve the validity of self report by clients themselves; the knowledge that others are reporting leads to more honest responses.

Other Drug Use

The quantification of other drug use has focused most often on the presence/absense or frequency of use during a specific period. Assessing the quantity of use is more complex for drugs other than alcohol. Rough indices of quantity may be obtained through the number of subjective units used (e.g., joints, lines), the cost of drugs consumed, or judgments of strength and purity through subjective effects.

A starting point is to ascertain the general classes of other drugs used at least once during the period in question. This may be done efficiently by a card sort method in which clients place cards naming major drug classes into two piles—those used and those not used (Miller & Marlatt, 1984; Miller, 1991). The frequency of use can then be determined for each category used. As noted above, a calendar-based method may be used to reconstruct drug use over time. Quantity may be assessed by inquiring about the typical amount of each drug used in one day of use. Random or routine urine screening has also been used to corroborate self-reported abstinence from or use of drugs.

Negative Consequences

Whether heavy or risky use constitutes *problem* use is determined by the presence and degree of adverse consequences related to use. Several methodological problems arise here: (1) Common measures of problem severity such as the Michigan Alcoholism Screening Test (MAST; Selzer, 1971) confound a variety of factors including life problems, prior treatment experiences, AA exposure, and alcohol dependence symptoms. We believe it is wise to assess such dimensions separately. (2) Certain symptoms overlap these dimensions. The occurrence of alcohol blackouts, for example, might be considered both a negative consequence and an indication of dependence. Continued use despite adverse consequences is considered a diagnostic sign of alcohol dependence (American Psychiatric Association, 1987). (3) It is not always a straightforward matter to determine whether life problems are the result of drinking. (4) Measures of *lifetime* problem accumulation such as the MAST, often used at intake, do not provide a proper baseline against which to compare the point prevalence of problems at follow-up.

The most common assessment approach is to review a laundry list of possible alcohol-related problems, scoring each as present or absent (either currently or ever). Some scales (e.g., MAST) weight problems differentially based on their perceived seriousness. A variety of such problem lists is available (e.g., Fillmore, 1987; Hilton, 1987). Miller (1990) has developed a Drinker Inventory of Consequences (DrInC), intended to assess alcohol-related problems as a dimension distinct from alcohol dependence, including consequences often of concern to women but usually omitted from problem lists (e.g., impact on parenting, weight, appearance). An initial psychometric study with 299 drinkers revealed internal reliability (Cronbach alpha = .92 for problems "ever," and .90 for problems during the past three months). Correlations with Skinner and Horn's (1984) Alcohol Dependence Scale (.58 for ever and .56 for past 3 months) and with quantity/frequency of consumption (.37 and .47, respectively) suggest that problem score as measured by the DrInC is related but not identical to these dimensions. Yet another approach is to survey a list of broad life problem areas to determine their occurrence (e.g., Marlatt & Miller, 1984), then to inquire whether each is (in the client's view) at least partially related to alcohol use.

Alcohol Dependence

Alcohol dependence is currently described in DSM-III-R as a diagnostic entity encompassing tolerance, withdrawal syndrome, and related behaviors (American Psychiatric Association, 1987). One assessment approach is to determine the presence or absence of each of the nine symptoms from the DSM-III-R list, or from another list (e.g., Hilton, 1987). Skinner has developed a psychometrically sound Alcohol Dependence Scale (Skinner & Horn, 1984), closely related to dependence measures from the Alcohol Use Inventory (Horn, Wanberg & Foster, 1990). A variety of other alcohol dependence measures have been used in outcome research (e.g., Miller & Marlatt, 1984; Stockwell, Hodgson, Edwards, Taylor, & Rankin, 1979; Sullivan, Sykora, Schneiderman, Naranjo, & Sellers, 1989).

Biomedical Impairment

Knowledge of a person's level of alcohol consumption, consequences, and dependence does not allow confident prediction of the extent of biomedical impairment from drinking. Physical damage to organ systems and changes in function represent an important assessment domain. Such measures also can serve, to a limited extent, as checks on the accuracy of self-report.

Serum assays of liver function have been the most common indices of alcohol-related biomedical impairment. Among those frequently used are SGOT (AST), SGPT (ALT), GGT, and total Bilirubin. Changes in mean corpuscular volume, uric acid, alkaline phosphitase, and high density lipoprotein (HDL) cholesterol have also been included in treatment outcome research. Shifts in GGT levels from one follow-up point to another may be useful as a check on self-reports of abstinence.

Neuropsychological Impairment

Another evaluation dimension, at best modestly related to other domains described above, is the client's neuropsychological functioning. There is a relatively consistent pattern of impairment associated with heavy drinking, and improvement in functioning is often observed over the first year or more of recovery (Miller & Saucedo, 1985). Measures commonly impaired in clinical alcoholics include the Digit-Symbol, Block Design, and Object Assembly performance subscales of the Wechsler Adult Intelligence Scale, and the Categories, Tactual Performance, Finger Oscillation, and Trail-Making tests from the Halstead-Reitan Neuropsychological Test Battery for Adults. Impairment and recovery on such measures are highly variable, however, leading to the suggestion that cognitive deficits observed in alcoholics may, at least in part, be an antecedent rather than the result of heavy drinking. For this reason, neuropsychological measures may not be strong correlates of favorable outcome on other dimensions.

Other Individual Differences

The evaluation of outcome after participation in anonymous programs should not be limited to alcohol or drug use indices. Treatment can affect more than alcohol or drug use. More general psychosocial functioning certainly is important in its own right and is often related to risk of re-lapse to addictive disorders.

Social and Psychological Factors Associated with Alcohol or Drug Use

A variety of social and psychological factors have been associated with the process of changing addictive behavior patterns. Individuals vary in the beliefs they hold about the effects of alcohol (Goldman, Brown, & Christiansen, 1987). Termed *expectancies,* these belief systems have been shown to relate to drinking patterns of young people and adults. Because these belief systems are thought to be one aspect of motivation to drink, considerable work has been directed at changing expectancies through treatment. Successful outcomes through program participation should be accompanied by changes in one's expectancies about alcohol's effects. Ex-pectancies about alcohol or drug effects can be assessed with several dif-ferent scales (see Leigh, 1989, for a review).

People have also been shown to have varying degrees of confidence, or self-efficacy, in their ability to maintain sobriety (or other behavior changes; Bandura, 1982). Ratings of self-efficacy are sometimes the best predictor of relapse processes after addictive behavior change (c.f., Baer, Holt & Lichtenstein, 1986). Individuals can be overconfident as well; cli-ents entering treatment with higher confidence sometimes do more poorly after treatment (Burling, Reilly, Moltzen, & Ziff, 1989). Efficacy can be assessed in a variety of ways. The most common scale in alcohol research is the Situational Confidence Questionnaire (Annis, 1988). This scale asks respondents to rate their degree of confidence in their ability to refrain from drinking in a variety of common drinking situations. Scores from this scale not only reflect generalized confidence, but may also pro-vide indices of low confidence in specific situations.

The actual situations that individuals encounter also can relate to suc-cessful outcomes. Individuals can rate their degree of temptation in situ-ations (c.f., DiClemente, Gordon, & Gibertini, 1983) and describe the situations where they are tempted (Marlatt & Gordon, 1985). Helen Annis has developed an Inventory of Drinking Situations (Annis, 1982) that can be used to rate the likelihood of drinking in different situations. This scale can also be used to rate likelihood of temptation in different situa-tions. Successful changes in addictive behavior patterns should be accom-panied by reduced temptation and fewer situations where temptation is experienced.

Life Adjustment Not Directly Related to Alcohol/Drug Use

Research on outcomes following treatment for addictions often suggests that factors associated with the environment of the recovering person, such as family functioning, stressful life events, and economic difficulties, are more associated with successful recovery than are characteristics of the type of treatment or characteristics of the individual patient (Moos, Finney, & Cronkite, 1990). Demographic indices, such as marital status, children, income, and legal complications, should also be routinely assessed. Moos, Fenn, Billings, and Moos (1989) have recently described a comprehensive instrument for assessing life stressors and social resources, the LISRES. This scale measures eight domains of adjustment: physical health, home/neighborhood, financial, work, spouse, children, extended family, and friends. Scores on this measure have been shown to relate to maintenance of treatment gains.

Each of these domains can be assessed with more detail as a function of research interest. For example, types of employment can be assessed through scales that reflect the autonomy, control, and income associated with particular occupations (i.e., the Job Diagnostic Survey; see Hackman & Oldham, 1975). Social support and family functioning are critical aspects of individual adjustment. Considerable controversy surrounds the role of a person's spouse and other family members in the recovery process. A number of authors have suggested that family members suffer from codependency syndromes and exacerbate drinking and drug use problems (i.e., Beattie, 1987). On the other hand, family members can be considered as a primary means of social support and stability, therefore facilitating recovery processes (Gottlieb, 1988).

Life stress is related to social functioning and can be assessed as a function of significant life events (i.e., Sarason, Johnson, & Siegel, 1978), daily hassles (Folkman & Lazarus, 1985), or more general perceptions of tension or control (Cohen, Kamarck, & Mermelstein, 1983). A complete review of the research literature on the assessment of stress is beyond the scope of this chapter. Other life problems, assessed more generally, reflect a person's adjustment and perhaps happiness. Problems can be assessed with a variety of methods. The card sort from the Comprehensive Drinking Profile (noted above, Marlatt & Miller, 1984) is one simple technique for subjects to list and rate difficulties in personal relationships, employment, economics, etc. The General Health Questionnaire (Goldberg, 1972) is one standardized scale to assess physical and psychological problems. General psychological adjustment can also be assessed using the standard psychiatric screening instruments reviewed below.

Personality

Although often considered to be stable traits, personalty patterns can change over time, particularly when psychological treatments are involved and significant behavioral changes are observed. For example, certain scales of the MMPI (scale 2, depression; scale 7, anxiety) often change over the course of treatment. Thus, assessment of personality functioning is important for characterizing changes in behavior not specifically related to drinking and for characterizing persons who respond most significantly from program participation.

The most commonly used scale to assess personality is the Minnesota Multiphasic Personality Inventory (MMPI; Hathaway & McKinley, 1982). Although there appears to be no MMPI profile specifically associated with addiction problems (Sobell, Sobell, & Nirenberg, 1988), elevations of certain subscales (such as scale 4) may be related to risk of addiction (Cox, 1987). Behavior patterns of impulsivity, sensation seeking, and harm avoidance are commonly associated with addiction problems (Windle, 1990).

More recent research approaches to personality assessment offer a more comprehensive and data-based approach to personality. The five-factor model (NEO-PI-R) of Costa and McCrea (1992) is commonly used in psychological research; application to AA participants would allow for comparisons across problems and treatment populations. Other more research-based approaches to personality assessment, such as the Multidimensional Personality Questionnaire (Tellegen & Waller, in press) and the Millon Clinical Multiaxial Inventory-II (Millon, 1990) could be used as well.

Other Psychological Problems

Persons with addiction problems sometimes experience other significant psychological distress (Institute of Medicine, 1990). Assessment of several aspects of psychological functions can provide a more general and accurate characterization of outcomes after program participation. For example, symptoms of depression (low mood, problems with sleep, changes in appetite, thoughts of suicide) often accompany addictive problems. This pattern of distress often remits when addictive patterns of use are changed. Yet some persons with addiction problems remain depressed even after achieving stable sobriety and depressive problems can be related to risk of relapse.

Diagnostic interviews, based on the Diagnostic and Statistical Manual of the American Psychiatric Association (DSM-III-R; American Psychiatric Association, 1987), are the most common means of assessment of concurrent psychological problems. The most commonly used interviews are the Diagnostic Interview Schedule (DIS; Robins, Helzer, Croughan, & Ratcliff, 1981) and the Structured Clinical Interview for DSM-III-R (SCID; First, Gibbon, Williams, & Spitzer, 1990). These structured interviews lead both interviewer and client through a series of questions that systematically test for the presence of major psychiatric disorders. The psychiatric scale of the Addiction Severity Index (McLellan, Luborsky, Woody, & O'Brien, 1980) also provides screening questions for psychological problems. Measures of psychiatric symptomatology, such as the Symptom Checklist 90 (SCL-90; Derogatis, Lipman, & Covi, 1973), reflect a broad array of adjustment difficulties that do not specifically match diagnostic schemes. However, such checklists can suggest clinical syndromes. For example, the SCL-90 contains scales that reflect symptom clusters of depression, anxiety, psychoticism, etc.

Several psychiatric syndromes are most likely to be noted in those in treatment for addiction problems. Depression is most common (reviewed briefly above). In addition, post-traumatic stress disorders are often accompanied by alcohol or drug-use problems. Many treatment programs with veteran's populations see considerable numbers of those suffering from this type of disorder. Alcohol is also commonly used to manage anxiety syndromes.

A subset of those with alcohol and drug problems also suffer from severe problems such as psychoses. These patients, often labelled "dual diagnosis," usually carry diagnoses of schizophrenia or schizoid, schizotypal, or borderline personality syndromes. Those with psychoses who are also in contact with organized mental health treatment programs often participate in anonymous programs. Their outcome status may vary significantly from those of participants without other complicating psychological disorders.

Motivation for Maintenance of Change

Motivation to change addictive behavior is an important yet illusory concept. Typical traitlike interpretations of motivation assume that some individuals are simply more willing to make changes while others are not. From this perspective, little can be done to enhance and maintain motivational states. Miller (1985) has suggested that motivation is best understood as a state, one that is responsive to life events and the behavior of therapists, assessors, and significant others. For example, individuals are likely to become more motivated to stop drinking if they feel supported by others, believe they are capable of changing, and believe they will be happy in a sober lifestyle. Such motivation most often fluctuates through the recovery process and can be an important measure of functioning after treatment.

Miller and Rollnick (1991) suggest two techniques of assessing statelike motivation. First, decision-balance sheets are useful tools in determining the content and number of positive and negative consequences of changing (or maintaining) a behavior. With a line running down a sheet of paper, the individual is asked to list on opposite sides of the paper all the pros and cons of changing addictive patterns (or for follow-up, maintaining changes can be rated). The relative number of entries, as well as the rated importance of the entries, can be taken as a measure of motivation. A second approach in the assessment of motivation asks the person to rate their willingness or readiness to change. As noted above, such a general question will naturally involve several dimension of cognition: perceived need, possibility, efficacy, and intentions to change. Nevertheless, responses to such general questions sometimes are related to addictive behavior changes.

Prochaska and DiClemente's (1984) model of stages of change provides one approach to such assessment. This model describes different coping processes typically utilized in different stages when people change addictive behavior patterns. Individuals are thought to first contemplate change before actually trying it, then actively work to change, then enter a maintenance stage. Coping strategies tend to vary across these stages. After and during participation in AA, for example, people are likely to vary in the degree to which they see themselves actively working to stop drinking as opposed to maintaining a sober status. Slips or lapses in abstinence can also affect a person's stage. Some individuals go back to contemplating change, while others become more active in changing. Scales developed by Prochaska and DiClemente (the URICA for behavior in general and SOCRATES for alcohol and drug use more specifically; Montgomery, Miller, Tonigan, Meyers, Hester, Abbot, & Delaney, 1990) may also provide utility in assessing individuals' perceptions of their efforts to change behavior. These processes may be related to longer term drinking outcomes and patterns of service utilization.

Personal Models of Addiction and Change

Finally, individual models of addiction and change are not uniform (Brickman, Rabinowitz, Karuza, Coates, Cohn, & Kidder, 1982; Institute of Medicine, 1990). For example, people vary in the degree to which they feel responsible for addiction problems and the degree to which biological factors are considered causal. People clearly vary in their own personal spirituality and the way in which they perceive spiritual issues relating to recovery processes (Gorsuch, Chapter 17 in this volume). Treatment programs offer a variety of explanations about how problems have developed and what is necessary for change. Seldom are patients' understanding of this information measured. Thus, it is not clear if understanding of program principles change over time or are necessary for successful recovery. Assessment of these dimensions allows for better understanding of how treatment affects individuals. The important and/or necessary components of individual understanding of addictive problems can be studied.

Assessment: An Individualized Integrative Approach

In this chapter, we have surveyed a wide variety of assessment and diagnostic measures. Our intent here is to provide a broad sampling of different assessment domains that could be considered in evaluating the impact of AA. We are not recommending that every study of AA effectiveness employ all of these various measures. Selection of which measures to employ depends on the purpose of your task. Research on treatment outcome typically employs more measures than clinical diagnosis because good research casts a "wide net" to pick up any changes that may be related to treatment process and outcome. As a result, treatment outcome studies usually select a critical set of key variables from each of the areas we have reviewed above. Measures to assess these variables are then administered to all subjects at the same time periods, from pretreatment to follow-up.

In contrast to outcome research, the purpose of clinical diagnosis is to provide an individualized, integrative assessment of the client's problems and the life context in which they occur. Addiction problems are multifaceted and require assessment within a comprehensive biopsychosocial framework of etiological and prognostic factors (Donovan & Marlatt, 1988). This information can then be used in several ways to help the client. Treatment matching can be facilitated by a clear assessment of relevant client characteristics. Clients can be referred to the best treatment match available, whether it be Alcoholics Anonymous, Rational Recovery, professional treatment, etc.

Second, assessment information can be used to provide motivational feedback to the client. Areas of strength can be identified as well as points of vulnerability. Feedback on risk factors, treatment progress, and general lifestyle change is a critical component of both motivational interviewing (Miller & Rollnick, 1991) and relapse prevention (Marlatt & Gordon, 1985).

The individualized assessment approach outlined in this chapter goes against the grain of traditional AA clinical lore and legend. As one AA slogan goes, "Keep it simple, stupid!" In AA parlance, alcoholism is a progressive disease and you either have it or you don't. If you have it, you always will have it, whether you drink or not (you are still "recovering"). From this perspective, assessment is a dichotomous category: alcoholism, present or not, perhaps further subdivided into three stages: early, middle, or late-stage alcoholism. Treatment outcome studies, on the other hand, require a broader stroke in assessing a variety of individual factors that are relevant regardless of the particular ideology adopted by a specific treatment modality. Most outcome measures are multivariate (unlike the univariate disease model) and continuous (unlike the dichotomy of the disease model). This latter distinction becomes critical in the assessment of drinking rates following treatment intervention. In traditional disease ideology, any drinking (no matter how much or how little) is equated with relapse, since it is assumed that even a single drink will trigger loss of control. Treatment outcome researchers, on the other hand, attempt to measure individual differences in drinking behavior to assess relative degrees of change over time: less drinking is less dangerous than more drinking based on the principles of harm reduction (Marlatt & Tapert, in press). Only future research can help us resolve some of our theoretical disagreements and spur us on to develop more effective alternatives to help people with alcohol and other drug-related problems.

References

Alcoholics Anonymous. (1990). *Alcoholics Anonymous 1989 membership survey.* New York: Alcoholics Anonymous World Services.

American Psychiatric Association. (1987). *Diagnostic and statistical manual of mental disorders* (3rd ed. rev.). Washington, DC: Author.

Annis, H.M. (1982). *Inventory of drinking situations.* Toronto: Addiction Research Foundation.

Annis, H.M. & Graham, J.M. (1988). *Situational Confidence Questionnaire.* Toronto: Addiction Research Foundation.

Baer, J.S., Holt, G., & Lichtenstein, E. (1986). Self-efficacy and smoking reexamined: Construct validity and clinical utility. *Journal of Consulting and Clinical Psychology, 54,* 846–852.

Bandura, A. (1982). Self-efficacy mechanism in human agency. *American Psychologist, 37,* 122–147.

Beattie, M. (1987). *Codependent no more: How to stop controlling others and start caring for yourself.* New York: Harper.

Brickman, P., Rabinowitz, V.C., Karuza, Jr., J., Coates, D., Cohn, E., & Kidder, L. (1982). Models of helping and coping. *American Psychologist, 37,* 268–284.

Burling, T.A., Reilly, P.M., Moltzen, J.O., & Ziff, D.C. (1989). Self-efficacy and relapse among inpatient drug and alcohol abusers: A predictor of outcome. *Journal of Studies on Alcohol, 50,* 354–360.

Cahalan, D., Cissin, I.H., & Crossley, H.M. (1969). *American drinking practices: A national survey of behavior and attitudes.* New Brunswick, NJ: Rutgers Center of Alcohol Studies.

Cohen, S., Kamarck, T., & Mermelstein, R. (1983). A global measure of perceived stress. *Journal of Health and Social Behavior, 13,* 99–125.

Costa, P.P., & McCrea, R.R. (1992). *The NEO-Personality Inventory-R.* Lutz, FL: Psychological Assessment Resources.

Cox, W.M. (1987). Personality theory and research. In H.T. Blane & K.E. Leonard (Eds.), *Psychological theories of drinking and alcoholism* (pp. 55–89). New York: Guilford Press.

Derogatis, L.R., Lipman, R.S., & Covi, L. (1973). The SCL-90: An outpatient psychiatric rating scale. *Psychopharmacology Bulletin, 9,* 13–28.

DiClemente, C.C., Gordon, J.R., & Gibertini, M. (1983, August). *Self-efficacy and determinants of relapse in alcoholism treatment.* Paper presented at the 91st annual convention of the American Psychological Association, Anaheim, CA.

Donovan, D.M., & Marlatt, G.A. (Eds.) (1988). *Assessment of addictive behaviors.* New York: Guilford Press.

Fillmore, K.M. (1987). Prevalence, incidence and chronicity of drinking patterns and problems among men as a function of age: A longitudinal and cohort analysis. *British Journal of Addiction, 82,* 77–83.

First, M.B., Gibbon, M., Williams, J.B.W., & Spitzer, R.L. (1990). Structured clinical interview for DSM-III-R (SCID). North Tonawanda, NY: Multi-Health Systems, Inc. and American Psychiatric Press.

Folkman, S., & Lazarus, R.S. (1985). If it changes it must be a process: Study of emotion and coping during three stages of a college examination. *Journal of Personality and Social Psychology, 48,* 150–170.

Goldberg, D.P. (1972). *The detection of psychiatric illness by questionnaire: A technique for the identification and assessment of nonpsychotic illness.* London: Oxford University Press.

Goldman, M.S., Brown, S.A., & Christiansen, B.A. (1987). Expectancy theory: Thinking about drinking. In H.T. Blane & K.E. Leonard (Eds.), *Psychological theories of drinking and alcoholism* (pp. 181–226). New York: Guilford.

Gorsuch, R.L. (1993). Assessing spiritual values in Alcoholics Anonymous research. In B.S. McCrady & W.R. Miller (Eds.), *Research on Alcoholics Anonymous: Opportunities and alternatives.* New Brunswick, NJ: Rutgers Center of Alcoholic Studies.

Gottlieb, B.H. (Ed.) (1988). *Creating support groups: Formats, processes and effects.* New York: Sage Publications.

Hackman, J.R., & Oldham, G.R. (1975). Development of the Job Diagnostic Survey. *Journal of Applied Psychology, 60,* 159–170.

Hathaway, S.R., & McKinley, J.C. (1982). Minnesota Multiphasic Personality Inventory: User's guide for the Minnesota Report. Minneapolis: University of Minnesota Press.

Hilton, M.W. (1987). Drinking patters and drinking problems in 1984: Results from a general population survey. *Alcoholism: Clinical and Experimental Research, 11,* 167–175.

Horn, J.L., Wanberg, K.W., & Foster, F.M. (1990). *Guide to the Alcohol Use Inventory.* Minneapolis, MN: National Computer Systems.

Institute of Medicine. (1990). *Broadening the base of treatment for alcohol problems.* Washington, DC: National Academy Press.

Leigh, B.C. (1989). In search of the seven dwarves: Issues of measurement and meaning in alcohol expectancy research. *Psychological Bulletin, 105,* 361–373.

Markham, M. (1992). *The blood alcohol concentration computation system (BACCuS).* Computer software program, University of New Mexico.

Marlatt, G.A., & Gordon, J.R. (Eds.). (1985). *Relapse prevention: Maintenance strategies in the treatment of addictive behaviors.* New York: Guilford Press.

Marlatt, G.A., & Miller, W.R. (1984). *Comprehensive drinker profile.* Odessa, FL.: Psychological Assessment Resources, Inc.

Marlatt, G.A., & Tapert, S.F. (in press). Harm reduction: Reducing the risks of addictive behavior. In J.S. Baer, G.A. Marlatt, & R. McMahon (Eds.), *Addictive behaviors across the lifespan.* Newbury Park, CA: Sage Publications.

Matthews, D.B., & Miller, W.R. (1979). Estimating blood alcohol concentration: Two computer programs and their applications in therapy and research. *Addictive Behaviors, 4,* 55–60.

McLellan, A.T., Luborsky, L., Woody, G.E., & O'Brien, C.P. (1980). An improved diagnostic evaluation instrument for substance abuse patients: The Addiction Severity Index. *Journal of Nervous and Mental Diseases, 168,* 26–33.

Miller, W.R. (1985). Motivation for treatment: A review with special emphasis on alcoholism. *Psychological Bulletin, 98,* 84–107.

Miller, W.R. (1990). *The Drinker Inventory of Consequences.* Unpublished instrument, University of New Mexico.

Miller, W.R. (1991). *Form 90: Structured assessment interview for drinking and related behaviors.* Unpublished manual for Project MATCH, National Institute on Alcohol Abuse and Alcoholism.

Miller, W.R., Heather, N., & Hall, W. (1991). Calculating standard drink units: International comparisons. *British Journal of Addiction, 86,* 43–47.

Miller, W.R., & Marlatt, G.A. (1984). *Manual for the Comprehensive Drinker Profile.* Odessa, FL: Psychological Assessment Resources.

Miller, W.R., & Marlatt, G.A. (1987). *Comprehensive Drinker Profile manual supplement for use with Brief Drinker Profile, Follow-up Drinker Profile, Collateral Interview Form.* Odessa, FL: Psychological Assessment Resources.

Miller, W.R., & Rollnick, S. (1991). *Motivational interviewing: Preparing people to change addictive behavior.* New York: Guilford Press.

Miller, W.R., & Saucedo, C.F. (1985). Assessment of neuropsychological impairment and brain damage in problem drinkers. In C.J. Golden, J.A. Moses, Jr., J.A. Coffman, W.R. Miller, & F.D. Strider (Eds.), *Clinical neuropsychology: Interface with neurologic and psychiatric disorders* (pp. 141–195). New York: Grune & Stratton.

Millon, T. (1990). *Millon's Clinical Multiaxial Inventory–II.* Minneapolis, MN: National Computer System.

Montgomery, H.A., Miller, W.R., Tonigan, J.S., Meyers, R.J., Hester, R.K., Abbott, P.J., & Delaney, H.D. (1990, November). SOCRATES *as presage: Validation of a new instrument for assessing motivation for behavior change in problem drinkers.* Paper presented at the annual meeting of the Association for Advancement of Behavior Therapy, San Francisco.

Moos, R.H., Fenn, C.B., Billings, A.G., & Moos, B.S. (1989). Assessing life stressors and social resources: Applications to alcoholic patients. *Journal of Substance Abuse, 1,* 135–152.

Moos, R.H., Finney, J.W., & Cronkite, R.C. (1990). *Alcoholism treatment.* New York: Oxford University Press.

Prochaska, J.O., & DiClemente, C.C. (1984). *The transtheoretical approach: Crossing traditional boundaries of therapy.* Homewood, IL: Dow Jones/Irwin.

Robins, L.N., Helzer, J.E., Croughan, J., & Ratcliff, K.S. (1981). National Institute of Mental Health Diagnostic Interview Schedule: Its history, characteristics, and validity. *Archives of General Psychiatry, 38,* 381–389.

Sarason, I.G., Johnson, J.H., & Siegel, J.M. (1978). Assessing the impact of life changes: Development of the Life Experiences Survey. *Journal of Consulting and Clinical Psychology, 46,* 932–946.

Saunders, J.B., & Aasland, O.G. (1987). *WHO collaborative project on identification and treatment of persons with harmful alcohol consumption. Report on Phase I: Development of a screening instrument.* Geneva: World Health Organization.

Selzer, M.L. (1971). The Michigan Alcoholism Screening Test: The quest for a new diagnostic instrument. *American Journal of Psychiatry, 127,* 1653–1658.

Skinner, H.A., & Horn, J.L. (1984). *Alcohol Dependence Scale (ADS): User's guide.* Toronto: Addiction Research Foundation.

Sobell, L.C., Sobell, M.B., & Nirenberg, T.D. (1988). Behavioral assessment and treatment planning with alcohol and drug abusers: A review with an emphasis on clinical application. *Clinical Psychology Review, 8,* 19–54.

Sobell, M.B., Maisto, S.A., Sobell, L.C., Cooper, A.M., Cooper, T., & Saunders, B. (1980). Developing a prototype for evaluating alcohol treatment effectiveness. In L.C. Sobell, M.B. Sobell, & E. Ward (Eds.), *Evaluating alcohol and drug abuse treatment effectiveness: Recent advances* (pp. 129–150). New York: Pergamon Press.

Stockwell, T.R., Hodgson, J.R., Edwards, G., Taylor, C., & Rankin, H.J. (1979). The development of a questionnaire to measure severity of alcohol dependence. *British Journal of Addiction, 74,* 79–87.

Sullivan, J.T., Sykora, K., Schneiderman, J., Naranjo, C.A., & Sellers, E.M. (1989). Assessment of alcohol withdrawal: The revised clinical institute withdrawal assessment for alcohol scale (CIWA-Ar). *British Journal of Addiction, 84,* 1353–1357.

Tellegen A., & Waller, N.G. (in press). Explaining personality through test construction. In S.R. Briggs & J.M. Cheek (Eds.), *Personality Measures: Development and Evaluation, vol. 1.* Greenwich, CT: JAI Press.

Windle, M. (1990). Temperament and personality attributes of children of alcoholics. In M. Windle & J.S. Searles (Eds.), *Children of alcoholics* (pp. 129–167). New York: Guilford Press.

CHAPTER 17

Assessing Spiritual Variables in Alcoholics Anonymous Research

RICHARD L. GORSUCH

Despite the importance of spirituality in Alcoholics Anonymous' (AA) 12 steps, addiction research has seldom measured spirituality (Miller, 1991). The purpose of this chapter is first to examine several definitions of spirituality that might be important for measuring this facet of AA. The empirical relationships of these measures to alcohol abuse will then be summarized and the theoretical relationship of spirituality to addiction and AA will be explored from a psychological perspective. Finally, a methodological point will be made that is essential if spirituality as an intervention is to be properly evaluated.

What Is Spirituality?

Since approximately 1950, a considerable body of empirical research on religion and spirituality has developed. This section provides a brief overview of major trends in that literature (for more detailed overviews see Gorsuch, 1984, 1988; Spilka, Hood, & Gorsuch, 1985, chap. 2). This line of research has been less toward general spirituality and more toward Christianity as a form of spirituality. The emphasis is only partly on Christianity because many of the investigators are Christian; instead, the primary reason for this focus is because the majority of our culture views spirituality from a Christian perspective.

Christian Spirituality

There are numerous scales available for measuring religious beliefs, but most are of little value. Indeed, if the scale is said to be measuring "orthodoxy" or "beliefs," then it is most likely to be rather unsophisticated. Scales with these labels typically are a hodge-podge of different psychological variables mixed together in random proportions. They may include what a more technical definition of beliefs might include, but they also contain affect, values, and even reported behavior. Beware of such scales because they are theoretically vacuous.

The most prominent tradition of measurement in the psychology of religion has been that of the intrinsic/extrinsic (I/E) motivation distinction introduced by Allport (e.g., Allport & Ross, 1967) and reviewed by Donahue (1985). Intrinsicness is defined as being religious for the sake of being religious and not to fulfill any other need or value. Extrinsicness is defined as being religious for some other reason, such as to develop social relationships or to gain personal comfort in a time of crisis. The original scales by Allport and others had some of the same problems mentioned above regarding "belief" scales: they were not clearly motivational. The Allport and Ross (1967) scale, for example, contained several reports of behavior along with motivational items. For that reason, the scales have been rewritten so as to measure directly intrinsic and extrinsic motivation and only the motivation itself (Gorsuch & McPherson, 1989).

Note that I/E scales measure the motivation for one's personal religion. They do not say what that person's religion is—neither its beliefs nor the nature of its deity, if any. However, the traditional I/E measures are slanted toward religions where "worship services" is a meaningful term; hence, they apply most readily, in this form, to Christian motivation.

Another popular way of measuring religious commitment—and by implication spirituality—is to ask for reported behaviors. The range of measures used to evaluate religious and spiritual behavior has been wide. At the weakest level, investigators have simply asked for the religious preference (e.g., Protestant, Catholic, Jew, none, or other). Those who had a religious preference would be compared against those with none. Probably the most surprising conclusion from evaluations of psychology of religion research has been that this preference measure has worked as well as it has. For example, it was the prime measure used in over 20 studies of how people came to abuse an illicit drug for the first time (Gorsuch & Butler, 1976) and showed that those with a religious preference abused drugs significantly less than those with no religious preference. An actual question regarding the spiritual behavior of direct interest is, of course, considerably better than something as vague as "religious preference."

Numerous studies have used church attendance as a measure of behavior. While this is considerably better than religious preference, there are still some cautions in using this particular measure. It is important to adhere closely to the traditional way of wording the question (as found in, e.g., Gorsuch & McFarland, 1972). The problem that can otherwise occur is that one can, for example, ask about the number of times of worship per week without recognizing the fact that the opportunity for worship varies widely from one denomination to another. A Catholic could attend mass seven days a week or more whereas in many mainline Protestant denominations the maximum number of worship services one could attend is one per week. Of course, religious attendance at general worship services is again an indirect measure of the spirituality referred to in the 12 steps, and a particularly Christian definition of it.

Application of measures of Christian spirituality are rather straightforward and can be done effectively. If only a basic measure of religiousness is needed, then several of the classical items in the psychology of religion literature do quite well. Normally these would include reported attendance and participation in worship services as well as self-rated importance of religion (see below). Each of these is measured quite effectively by a single-item scale (Gorsuch & McFarland, 1972). They measure what might be considered the general Christian factor of spirituality and do it sufficiently well for studies with religion as a *nonfocal* topic. If motivation is of a primary concern, then the intrinsic/extrinsic-revised scales referenced above are appropriate. If spirituality defined as mystical experiences is the primary focus, then Hood's measures are appropriate. Several of these are used if religion is a focus of the study. Morgenstern's (1993) factor about God appears useful, particularly if used with the above scales so we can understand how it fits in with the other measures.

In addition, there is another approach to measuring Christian religion's impact upon life that, while more outside the area of spirituality than the above, may still be of considerable interest because it is concerned with coping. Pargament et al. (1988) have identified several different measures of how one uses or does not use religion in coping. Those measures of coping that identify the person as using both their own resources and their spiritual resources are generally related positively to measures of psychological health (Hathaway & Pargament, 1990) and are based on religious beliefs and motivation (Schaefer & Gorsuch, 1991). Hence one would expect that AA's encouraging spirituality would be manifest through these coping styles and then would lead to a more effective life. Schaefer and Gorsuch (Schaefer, 1992) have revised these scales so they can be used on a state as well as a trait basis.

General Spirituality

As noted above, most of the psychology of religion literature has been concerned with Christian spirituality. Several of these measures can be readily generalized to a more general spirituality. For example, the attendance measures can be revised so as to work with any religious group that has participation in group services. These would be more independent of the Christian focus per se but would, to varying degrees, concentrate upon participation in some type of religious life.

Pay close attention to Mäkelä (1993) and the international data on organized religion. It is less in many other countries. But then how do those people interpret their spiritual aspects of the 12 steps? One item widely used refers just to one's own religion, regardless of whether it is Christian or not. It is the self-rated importance of religion in one's own life. It is a good single item measure of spirituality defined by the respondents' own definition of religion. The exact wording is in Gorsuch and McFarland (1972).

The intrinsic/extrinsic distinction is now being tested for its application cross-culturally and across religions as a measure of motivation for spirituality. Gorsuch, Mylvaganam, Gorsuch, and Johnson (1991) had items that were written exclusively to measure I/E without regard to Christianity per se. The set of items was tested by comparing a traditional Christian sample with two samples from Asia, one Christian and one non-Christian. The analyses showed the revised I/E scales function well in all three groups and hence measure spiritual motivation for religions that include Christians with their focus upon a theistic God and Buddhists with no focus on a single theistic deity.

Spirituality as a term is, however, used in a considerably broader sense than that discussed so far. Spirituality in this sense appears to be referring to people who are concerned with metaphysical issues as well as their day-to-day lives. It need have no belief in God. Little research has been done with this construct and so there is no real tradition of measurement with it. This does not mean, however, that it should be ignored. From a general definition of spirituality there may well be a number of people who could be classified as spiritual but not within one of the traditional religions. Shafranske and Gorsuch (1984) found that half of the psychologists they surveyed felt spirituality was important but were not involved in institutional religion. Since psychologists have one of the lowest rates of involvement in traditional religions, this group is, in contemporary American culture, one of the more likely reservoirs of such people.

But what is this spirituality if it is entirely outside of a traditional religious focus, and does this spirituality relate to the Alcoholics Anonymous' "Higher Power"? Casual conversation suggests that spirituality might mean being thoughtful or engaging in meditation or just a general concern for metaphysical issues. This does not seem to be too fruitful without more systematic theoretical development.

Spirituality can have a clearer definition than those noted above. Berenson (1990) suggests that "spirituality, as opposed to religion, connotes a direct, personal experience of the sacred unmediated by particular belief systems prescribed by dogma or by hierarchical structures of priests, ministers, rabbis, or gurus" (p. 59). While this is idealistic—no experience is uninfluenced by one's past, personal belief systems, and expectations—it does clearly recognize a transcendent element not tied to one particular religion. This distinction does have an operation measure already in existence: Hood's scales of mystical experience. Ralph Hood (Spilka et al., 1985) has developed measures of religious experience. The M-Scale is for reporting whether one has had mystic experiences by direct questioning and the Religious Experience Episodes Measure (Hood, 1975) evaluates the degree to which one has mystical experiences, whether they be from nature or from an experience with a deity. People who score high are those who have more integrative experiences where they feel they are part of a broader and more powerful whole. This appears to have a clear relevance to the concern with and dependence on a "Higher Power."

Spirituality can also be defined specifically with regards to AA. Brown and Peterson (1991) developed a questionnaire deliberately including items from the AA literature. "Spiritual practices" are included within the questionnaire. The authors, however, rightfully refer to their questionnaire as a "recovery process inventory," not a spirituality questionnaire, for it includes more than just spirituality. Nevertheless, it may be possible to score a subset of items as a spirituality scale, a scale that would be AA-based.

As can be seen from the above, there is an excellent selection of measuring instruments for spirituality. Some are simple one-item measures. Some are Christian specific. Some are experience oriented and independent of any one religion. Those attempting to measure spirituality should use one or more of these scales; new scales are not needed until more is known about how these established scales relate to AA. (For those tempted to develop a new scale, see Gorsuch, 1984.)

Past Research: How Does Spirituality Relate to Alcohol Use?

The discussion above provided a brief overview of different ways that it is currently possible to measure spirituality. Not all of those have been used in studies relating to alcohol or AA. Those used generally have been used in associational studies that survey a sample at a given point in time. The sample includes a wide range of people who use or abuse alcohol in different degrees. The dependent variable then is a measure of alcohol use or alcohol abuse. These studies at least provide a background for understanding what spirituality variables may be of importance for further theory and evaluation of treatment programs regarding alcohol abuse.

Global measures of Christian involvement have been found to be definitely related to a lack of alcohol use and abuse in samples from general populations. These studies, reviewed in detail in Gorsuch (1976, 1988), have replicated on numerous occasions this particular relationship. The relationship would be even clearer except for the lack of understanding of spirituality shown by some investigators, or at least their lack of experience with a variety of religious traditions. A number of the studies have included in their measure of alcohol use whether or not a person "ever drinks" and classify those who say "yes" as moderate drinkers. That fails, however, in evaluating spirituality because by that measure those in a variety of religious traditions are always drinkers. The reason is because wine is, for historical reasons, used in the religious ceremony. The amount of wine might, as in some Protestant denominations, be no more than what a small piece of bread can absorb, but these people would still have to answer yes to that question for they consume alcohol at least once a week. It seems strange to group those whose only alcohol consumption is a trivial amount in religious ceremonies with people who actually consume a fair amount of alcohol.

Despite measurement limitations, being an active member of any U.S. religious tradition—Jewish to Catholic to Protestant—has been shown conclusively to be related to less alcohol consumption. The results are clearest when the definition of "drinking alcohol" excludes that taken in religious ceremonies. If one is willing to accept the interpretation that those who are active in any of the religious traditions in the United States are more spiritual than those who are not, this then would be interpreted as obvious evidence that spirituality prevents alcohol abuse.

Use of intrinsic/extrinsic measures of motivation for religious commitment also relates to a lack of alcohol consumption, just as religious participation in general. The number of times one attends worship services and the importance of one's personal religion for one's self—the single-item measures mentioned above as highly useful when religion is not a focal part of research—generally correlate negatively with alcohol abuse.

It was noted above that belief traditionally has been a poor measurement category in the psychology of religion. A "religious belief" scale might contain anything—from some particular doctrinal beliefs, to attitudes or values regarding institutions or beliefs thereof, to reports of personal experiences and religious behaviors. But belief becomes a meaningful category *if* the term is related to the norms of a particular religious tradition. "Does your denomination believe all drinking of alcohol is a sin?" is a worthwhile belief question for AA research.

The religious norms for alcohol—which are indeed different across religious groups—have implications for alcohol, its consumption, and abuse. Such norm differences do, by common observation, exist and do, by research, relate to people's practices. The followers of Bacchus, for example, were noted for their alcohol use and abuse. Moslems and American conservative Christians have strong norms against alcohol consumption. Liberal Christians have strong norms against alcohol abuse, but not against consumption. Hence, the norms of the reference group for spirituality—

TABLE 1
Percentage Alcohol Abuse in U.S. Christian and Non-Christian Groups

Religion Worship Attendance	Heavy drinkers	
At least once a week	10%	
Nonattenders	22%	

Religious Affiliation	Heavy alcohol users	Percentage of alcohol users who abuse
Conservative Protestant	7%	13%
Liberal Protestant	13%	16%
Catholic	19%	23%
No religion	20%	25%

Source: Adapted from Cahalan, Cisin, and Crossley (1969).

classically the person's Christian denomination in psychological re-search—have major implications for the relationship of spirituality and alcohol.

The relationship of religious denomination's norms to alcohol consumption is reviewed in more detail elsewhere (Gorsuch, 1976, 1988) and so will only be summarized here. The conclusion is simple: *the more anti-alcohol the religious tradition, the less its people drink and the less alcohol is abused.* Since the conclusion is so clear, I shall spend little time or space in developing it further, but I do wish to underscore that this is indeed *a major, strong, and well-replicated conclusion.* An illustration is presented in Table 1.

One of the earliest studies, which has been widely quoted, came to a different conclusion, namely that of those who drink, those reared in an antialcohol-use tradition abuse alcohol more than those raised in other traditions. *This result has never been replicated,* despite attempts to do so. The other references that might be included in a list of references in support of that proposition are, in my experience, just quoting the *one* data set.

The results typically found are illustrated by Table 1. Cahalan, Cisin, and Crossley (1969) used a national sample and attempted to replicate the earlier finding. The results are consistent with the general conclusion given above and support the conclusion that Christianity is a bulwark against alcohol abuse at all levels and stages. If antialcohol Christians do drink, they are less likely to abuse alcohol than non-Christians who drink.

Noting that different norms among religious traditions lead to different behaviors is important and has been a "back door" approach to defining norms in more detail so that the different orientations toward spirituality can be taken into account. Spirituality per se is only part of the story, for the nature of the spirituality must be known to adequately understand the behavior. We have no theory or data that suggest that spirituality in the abstract relates to alcohol abuse or the effects of AA unless the norms of that spirituality are taken into account. This is probably the reason moral development in children (Gorsuch & Arno, 1979) has been unrelated to attitude toward alcohol abuse. The level of moral development does indeed identify a style of thinking; it is independent of the content of that thinking. Behavior is always content laden.

If the religious institution's alcohol norms are important, how then, a reader might ask, do we explain the well-replicated fact that involvement in any religious tradition means less alcohol or drug abuse? The explanation is twofold. First, that theory has been tested only with the Judeo-Christian/Moslem religious cultures, all of which are against alcohol abuse and many of which are against any alcohol use. Hence, those data do not separate out spirituality according to different beliefs toward alcohol consumption, as would be necessary to use these data to support that hypothesis. Second, spirituality in a general sense often is related to the general thoughtfulness of the individual, and it is likely that our common observation of spiritual people being less prone to abuse alcohol is due to the fact that these are also people who think and consider their actions carefully, and, in particular, think in terms of long-range consequences of alcohol abuse.

The foundations of alcohol use and abuse using both measures of religiousness and measures of reasoned action elements combined by a multivariate belief-motivation theory are currently being examined. Cole-Cabrera (1990) used college students as subjects and collected data on their religious motivation, their denomination's position on drinking, their beliefs about the consequences of drinking, the affect generated by those consequences, and how they valued those consequences. General alcohol use/abuse and the amount of alcohol they consumed over the weekend following the testing were the dependent variables. The results of that study were in keeping with past studies in that religious motivation did predict less alcohol use/abuse. It is important to note that the study also confirmed the results of past studies that the religious tradition's position on drinking was also important, even after individual beliefs, spiritual commitment, values, and other such variables were taken into account.

The study also suggests one other light in which spirituality could be considered, as value judgments rather than personal attitudes. Measures of values as defined from a philosophical perspective as moral obligation correlated .91 with a person's attitude toward consumption of alcohol. But would an emphasis explicitly with values in a traditional moral sense conflict with the AA emphasis on the physiological factors of alcohol as an illness? The de-valuing, illness emphases of some alcohol interventions have been releasing because they have helped the person step outside the moral condemnation that has "frozen" them in their behavior, and they have given them the hope that a fresh approach gives. That point is well taken but applies to the category of "moral guilt" rather than to the category of values. There is evidence in psychology that moral guilt is unrelated to value commitment. For example, the superego strength factor on the 16PF correlates virtually zero with the 16PF guilt proneness factor (Gorsuch & Cattell, 1967). Because these two are linked in the lay mind and need to be broken apart, there has been the feeling that moral judgments must be one of the problems. But might it not be that the true problem is a feeling of lack of power to carry out one's values rather than one's values per se? It appears that AA's "reliance on a Higher Power" is a message that a power exists to enable living of the values that are important.

It is interesting to note that in Cole-Cabrera's dissertation we found a multiple correlation that is within .01 of the highest multiple correlation between psychological variables and alcohol use/abuse that we were able to find in the psychological literature. This was our first attempt in using this multivariate belief-motivation model in this particular domain. The high correlation was only possible because we recognized spirituality defined as religious motivation and values and also by taking the degree of antialcoholism of the person's own spiritual tradition into account.

From past research we can conclude that religious spirituality is indeed an important variable related to alcohol abuse. The results are systematic, conclusive, and show a strong associational relationship. Hence, both the degree of traditional religious commitment to spirituality along with the norms of the religious tradition toward alcohol should always be included in every research study of alcoholism. If spirituality is not a focal point of the study, these measures should still be included because they can, through partialling, reduce the error term of statistical tests, thus making the tests of other variables more sensitive.

Possible Roles of Spiritual Factors in Alcoholics Anonymous

Alcoholism as the Failure of Spirituality

From the literature noted above, it is conclusive that the classical religions of our culture—Catholic, Jewish, and Protestant—have been a major bulwark against alcohol abuse. What then of the religion of people who still become alcoholic?

It is obvious that either (a) the alcoholic person has not had the same relationship with American religion that the nonalcoholic has had or (b) other factors have been so overwhelmingly strong that the antialcoholic impact of spirituality has been negated. Without research it is difficult to know which of these two explanations might be explanatory for which people.

Both from casual reports and systematic interviews by J.W. Fowler (1993), alcoholics consistently report a judging, condemning, vindictive deity. This is most interesting because alcoholics' concept of God differs so widely from the Christian culture that they are supposed to have been a part of. Christianity stresses forgiveness and love, not judgment and vengeance. "Repentance" is called for, but an exacting translation of the New Testament Greek term is "to turn around." Jesus told the parable of the son who took his inheritance and squandered it (the alcoholic), and yet was forgiven and accepted by his father (God) when he "turned around," acknowledging he was wrong. Paul writes in his letter to the Romans that we are saved by grace, not by works, and so nothing other than "turning around" is needed for forgiveness. Indeed, a major theological problem Paul faced in writing the letter was why Christians, being already forgiven by grace, should not sin in any and every way they pleased! Even those Christian traditions that seek to convince people of their sins do so, in that tradition's eyes, in order that those people might realize the strength of God's love toward them since God loves us while we are yet sinners, who would then repent and accept God's love and forgiveness.

The non-AA alcoholic has not yet repented and so may be alienated from God. But the act of joining AA and admitting that one is an alcoholic is exactly the repentance that the church has classically seen as reestablishing the relationship with God, if one is willing to accept God's unconditional love.

Unfortunately, many alcoholics are convinced of the wrongness of alcohol abuse and have "turned about," but still have missed the point that God loves them even before that repentance, is delighted at the alcoholic's participation in AA, and has forgiven them. Since this forgiveness is by grace and not what the alcoholic does, the forgiveness is unconditional. Theologically, the problem is that the alcoholic is not really convinced that God loves them personally.

In terms of psychological research, God concept studies show traditional Christians see God as kind, loving, and benevolent—but the alcoholics completely miss this. They would score high on another God concept factor: wrathfulness, *which is unrelated to the classical concept of the Christian God* (Spilka et al., 1985). Hence, psychologically as well as theologically the "Christianity" of alcoholics is not the Christianity of most other American Christians.

Alcoholics have a non-Christian view of God. How could this have come to be? Christianity can be inadequately developed for a number of reasons. Since the majority of people in our culture are not active Christians, it is likely that many alcoholics have not been truly exposed to it. Other factors such as no experience with unconditional love or parents who used a God of their own creation to control a child may be at work. A congregation with members who themselves have not really felt God's love could be at fault. Dropping out of the church before reaching cognitive maturity would mean that their only concept of God would be a childish one (which, from moral development theory, would focus on rewards and punishments instead of relationships). The person may be more judgmental of themselves than God is of them, but being unable to forgive themselves means they find it hard to really feel forgiven by God.

These or other causes may be at work, and that is a question for psychological research. The point for AA and its evaluation is that *alcoholics are primarily those who have failed to be encultured in the Christian faith.* Theirs is a theologically immature faith, and because it is immature, it is also ineffective.

Proper incorporation of spirituality in AA (and its evaluation) must recognize that for most Americans alcoholism is a failure of the classical American Christianity to take root and grow. That is why alcoholics abuse alcohol and feel God is vengeful despite the fact that Christians are seldom alcohol abusers and see God as loving. If alcoholics' development had paralleled that of most Christians, they would see God as loving and forgiving while not abusing alcohol.

The Possibility of Spirituality in AA Programs

As noted in the research on religion and use of alcohol, churches have been successful in enculturating against alcohol abuse. Hence, it is logical to feel that spirituality in AA should also produce such socialization. Unfortunately, we know little as to how the church produces such enculturation, but this is certainly a point worthy of further research.

Regardless of the pathway that a person has followed into alcohol abuse, there is one element necessary for a person to change the habits and patterns that involve alcohol abuse and to explore better ways of meeting their needs: hope. Without hope the individual quickly gives up attempting to stop alcohol abuse. The element of hope in the AA 12 steps comes from the reliance upon a higher power, for a spiritual conversion includes the sense of power to radically change one's life. William James in his *Varieties of Religious Experience* (1902/1985) noted that the sense of being empowered to change and hope for the future was a major element that resulted from religious involvement.

Modern psychological terms for hope and empowerment include "internalized locus of control," "self-efficacy," and "acceptance of responsibility." Bridgman and McQueen (1987) provide a conceptual analysis that locus of control is indeed central to the AA message of reliance upon a higher power but Miller (1991) correctly notes that spirituality is more than locus of control since it involves a transcendent element, which is the basis for hope. Spirituality is the event that produces hope and internalized locus of control. Hence, the spirituality aspects of AA should become manifest in evaluations utilizing locus of control measures.

The above paragraphs contain a few very brief comments regarding how spirituality might be involved to help reduce alcohol abuse. Brown, Peterson, and Cunningham (Brown & Peterson, 1989, 1990a, 1990b, 1991; Brown, Peterson, & Cunningham, 1988a, 1988b, 1988c) have devised several ways of involving spirituality broadly defined in AA. Their writings reflect an in-depth knowledge of AA not found in the general psychological literature noted above. The elements identified in these papers as well as elements in the general psychological literature are implicit in the AA steps and so are important for evaluating AA programs. However, to what degree do the AA groups in a particular project truly use spirituality and higher power?

In my perspective there is a difference between "lip service" spirituality and involving spiritual resources in a program. Seeking to lay the groundwork for an evaluation of spirituality in alcoholic treatment programs, Lai (1982) interviewed 13 facilities in the Los Angeles area regarding both "lip service" to and the use of spirituality in their treatment programs. Some interview questions asked about the importance of spirituality, others asked for their knowledge of spirituality of their staff and patients, and others asked about the use of religion and spirituality as a working basis for treatment. Almost all programs *said* spirituality was important. But of the 13 programs, nine reported no awareness of the religiousness of their clients and staff. If the program expects to involve spirituality to help the individual client, it would seem that such knowledge would provide a basis from which to work with that particular alcoholic. It also seems strange, if spirituality is to be encouraged in a program, that the leadership of the majority of programs had little knowledge of the spirituality of the staff. It is difficult to believe that the staff could be utilizing spirituality as an active tool in alcoholic rehabilitation without such knowledge at least accidentally occurring.

Lai's programs showed the same sense of ambiguity regarding spiritual institutions that are found in AA and its programs: a rejection of institutional religion and an acceptance of spirituality. Thus, we found that 10 of the 13 programs had leaders who suggested a negative impact of religion on alcoholism and treatment. These respondents principally felt that churches and religion produced detrimental feelings of guilt; they only invited religious leaders to participate in their program if they emphasized spirituality and not religion per se. Given the above discussion on alcoholism as the failure of the alcoholic's personal form of spirituality, it seems that the professionals of these programs were following their clients rather than leading them.

The same ignoring of truly spiritual aspects in alcohol treatment programs is also found in research. Miller (1991) has noted that spirituality has been "virtually unstudied." When it has been studied, the operational definitions have made spirituality so broad that the transcendent aspect has been ignored despite AA's focus on a higher power. Spirituality needs to be in both the programs and in the evaluations (following the methodological note below) for its true impact to be evaluated.

The tension between religious institutions and spirituality is well known in Christian circles. It is common to make a strong distinction between these two because of the numerous instances where people in the church have not lived up to their high ideology. This is made explicit in the communions that have a confession of sin as a formal part of most worship services. Of course, in the New Testament Jesus is constantly stressing the difference between living with love for others versus following legalistic practices on an institutional basis. Almost every monastic movement and religious denomination arose explicitly to offset institutionalism with spirituality. Those who treat alcoholics are hardly new in making this distinction between being religious and being spiritual, and will find most Christian leaders in strong agreement.

The distinction between religious institutions and spirituality does, however, seem to be oversimplified. Every human institution—including treatment programs for alcoholics—falls short of its ideologies. But the implication that imperfect religious institutions and their representatives are not helpful in treating alcoholics may be shortsighted for two reasons. First, it fails to recognize that, as noted in the literature above, the classical religious institutions of our culture have been a strong bulwark against alcohol abuse. To deny that is so—either in word or attitude—is to reject the empiricism upon which AA research and evaluation is based. Second, the classical religious institutions are still the place where the greatest knowledge regarding spirituality occurs within our culture. Fichter (1982) notes a number of special retreats for alcoholics that are aimed at spirituality and have grown out of the religious institutions. Hence, making such a strong split between classical religious institutions and spirituality encourages people to ignore the ready resources of their own traditions that could truly help in their spiritual development.

It seems to me that the split between religion and spirituality has at least two bases. The first basis is that AA is, of course, nondoctrinal. Being nondoctrinal should mean, in terms of AA and spirituality in the 12 steps, that the emphasis is placed upon getting in touch with one's own spiritual roots in the tradition of one's choice. Second, AA attracts the people for whom the classical religious institutions have not had the impact they have had with other people. If the AA people had been appropriately socialized into such institutions, they would not be alcoholics. Hence, there is a failure in the socialization, either due to no religious background ever having been involved or because somehow the person has not yet experienced that religious tradition in its full depth. No place is this clearer than in the feeling that religious institutions are unforgiving and judgmental against alcoholics, whereas at the heart of the Christian faith at least is the notion of forgiveness and acceptance. While those who run AA programs are seldom qualified themselves to deal with such major spiritual issues, there are professionals within most religious traditions who can competently deal with such issues. Involvement of or referral to clergy, selected from within the alcoholic's religious tradition and for their sensitivity to the problems of alcoholics, would probably be highly beneficial.

The difficulty in ignoring relevant doctrinal issues—that is, relevant to alcoholism as a function of a person's spirituality—can be seen if one conceptualizes the impact of spirituality being, in part, producing better religious coping styles as defined by the Pargament et al. (1988) scales noted above. Schaefer and Gorsuch (1991) demonstrate that the Multivariate Belief-Motivation Theory of Religiousness does indeed provide underpinnings for religious problem-solving styles. Spirituality is generally conceived of in terms of religious motivation, and so that study's finding that religious motivation is relevant is as expected. In addition, religious beliefs were also important. This study limited itself to Christians and it was found that viewing God as false, deistic, and worthless led to coping styles that were correlated positively with anxiety. Believing God was benevolent and caring correlated positively both with coping styles identified by Pargament et al. (1988) as more adaptive and with reduced anxiety. While the emphasis within AA on respecting each person's own spiritual tradition is, from my perspective, an important one, it has to be carefully presented so that it does not deny the relevance of the beliefs of that religious tradition. To deny that the beliefs are important is to leave unexamined beliefs that may be a handicap in recovery.

Based upon our cultural traditions, there are many ways that spirituality could become truly manifest within AA programs and therefore could test whether the spirituality in the steps are helpful. Several come immediately to mind:

1. Providing for each AA participant to be also a participant in a spiritually oriented organization of their choice simultaneously with involve-

ment in AA. The participant would be urged to attend worship services, participate in bible studies, meet with a mentor for spiritual guidance, and to otherwise become actively engaged in that particular tradition. Prayer meetings where they *experience* the love and forgiveness at the heart of Christian faith would be important. This would help them to relate to a higher power, to develop new habits in a non-alcohol subculture, and to develop the internalized locus of control which relates from feeling the power of a higher being.

2. Including the expectation of personal participation in personal spiritual exercises as an explicit part of AA. Depending upon the tradition of the individual, these would include personal meditation with appropriate written material, such as the bible, and personal prayer. People would be taught these as a spiritual discipline, be expected to practice them on a daily basis, and to share reports of doing so.

3. Encouraging participation in special retreats, with spirituality as the prime goal of the meetings. The history of spirituality has always contained a strong thrust toward building one's resources by stepping back from one's culture for a limited period of time. The retreat is generally directed by those who are highly involved in spiritual practices themselves and the retreat provides a time to reflect, grow, and change. AA could be a recruiter for organizations providing such retreats.

Only when spirituality is truly used within the AA programs will it be possible to evaluate those aspects of the 12 steps that involve spirituality per se. An evaluation of these steps needs to first establish that the programs have clearly *changed the spirituality* of the participants. The dependent variables should then be those most sensitive to the goal of the particular spirituality targeted by the practices of the AA group. This would explicitly recognize the cultural differences in what is meant by spirituality across cultures and across groups within a culture.

Methodological Note

Note that an associational (correlational) research design is inappropriate for evaluating the impact of spirituality on people involved in AA. Such an associational design would incorrectly survey current AA people as to their traditional spirituality practices and then relate those to their success in reducing consumption of alcohol or how long they remain abstinent. Who would be the spiritual person who becomes alcoholic but those for whom spirituality had failed in the past? Since it had failed in the past, there is no rationale for predicting that it would succeed in the present. A comparison of such people with those who are not alcoholics to see why spirituality had failed would be important, but comparison of spiritual practices long engaged in with no success in preventing or reducing alcohol abuse would be inappropriate. Instead the *change* in spiritual practices need to be related to alcohol abuse reduction. Only those who had made major *new* attempts to become more spiritual and who reported changes in spiritual experiences would be expected to be able to build upon that spirituality to reduce their alcohol intake.

Fichter (1982) shows the appropriate way to measure spirituality. He interviewed clergy alcoholics to determine whether a spiritual experience or awakening had occurred *during their recovery from alcoholism.* Subjects with such experiences during recovery reported that their therapy experience had included more emphasis on spiritual recovery than those who had not had such an awakening. Those who were spiritually awakened reported greater absolute improvements—since they had more blackouts and poorer job performance before treatment—than those without a spiritual awakening and they also reported major improvements in the quality of their work and interpersonal relations.

The problem of evaluations ignoring changes over time is also shown in this study; Fichter (1982) notes that there were no differences in remission rates among the more and the less spiritual (p. 141), but then notes later that those who were spiritually awakened had been significantly worse off than nonawakened both in blackouts and job performance (p. 160). Hence, the change showing improvement was much greater among those with a spiritual awakening, but he did not find that in his initial analysis because the question was asked without reference to change. So it seems that *change* in spirituality related to the *change* in alcohol abuse is the appropriate test.

References

Allport, G.W., & Ross, J.M. (1967). Personal religious orientation and prejudice. *Journal of Personality and Social Psychology, 5,* 432–443.

Berenson, D. (1990). A systematic view of spirituality: God and twelve-step programs as resources in family therapy. *Journal of Strategic and Systemic Therapies, 9*(1), 59–70.

Bridgman, L.P., & McQueen, W.M., Jr. (1987). The success of Alcoholics Anonymous: Locus of control and God's general revelation. *Journal of Psychology and Theology, 15*(2), 124–131.

Brown, H.P., Jr., & Peterson, J.H., Jr. (1989). Refining the BASIC-ISs: A psychospiritual approach to the comprehensive outpatient treatment of drug dependency. *Alcoholism Treatment Quarterly, 6*(3/4), 27–61.

Brown, H.P., Jr., & Peterson, J.H., Jr. (1990a). Rationale and procedural suggestions for defining and actualizing spiritual values in the treatment of dependency. *Alcoholism Treatment Quarterly, 7*(3), 17–46.

Brown, H.P., Jr., & Peterson, J.H., Jr. (1990b). Values and recovery from alcoholism through Alcoholics Anonymous. *Counseling and Values, 35,* 63–68.

Brown, H.P., Jr., & Peterson, J.H., Jr. (1991). Assessing spirituality in addiction treatment and follow-up: Development of the Brown-Peterson Recovery Progress Inventory (B-PRPI). *Alcoholism Treatment Quarterly, 8*(2), 21–51.

Brown, H.P., Jr., Peterson, J.H., Jr, & Cunningham, O. (1988a). A behavioral/cognitive spiritual model for a chemical dependency aftercare program. *Alcoholism Treatment Quarterly,* 5(1/2), 153–166.

Brown, H.P., Jr., Peterson, J.H., Jr, & Cunningham, O. (1988b). An individualized behavioral approach to spiritual development for the recovering alcoholic/addict. *Alcoholism Treatment Quarterly,* 5(1/2), 177–192.

Brown, H.P., Jr., Peterson, J.H., Jr, & Cunningham, O. (1988c). Rationale and theoretical basis for a behavioral/cognitive approach to spirituality. *Alcoholism Treatment Quarterly,* 5(1/2), 47–59.

Cahalan, D., Cisin, I.H., & Crossley, H.M. (1969). *American drinking practice: A national study of drinking behavior and attitudes.* New Brunswick, NJ: Rutgers Center of Alcohol Studies.

Cole-Cabrera, N. (1990). *Moral obligations and religiousness in alcohol use.* Unpublished doctoral dissertation, Graduate School of Psychology, Fuller Theological Seminary, Pasadena, California.

Donahue, M.J. (1985). Intrinsic and extrinsic religiousness: Review and meta-analysis. *Journal of Personality and Social Psychology,* 48(2), 400–419.

Fichter, J.H. (1982). *The rehabilitation of clergy alcoholics: Ardent spirits subdued.* New York: Human Sciences Press.

Fowler, J.W. (1993). Alcoholics Anonymous and Faith development. In B.S. McCrady & W.R. Miller (Eds.), *Research on Alcoholics Anonymous: Opportunities and alternatives.* New Brunswick, NJ: Rutgers Center of Alcohol Studies.

Gorsuch, R.L. (1976). Religion as a major predictor of significant human behavior. In W. Donaldson (Ed.), *Research in mental health and religious behavior* (pp. 206–221). Atlanta, GA: Psychological Studies Institute.

Gorsuch, R.L. (1984). Measurement: The boon and bane of investigating religion. *American Psychologist,* 39(3), 228–236.

Gorsuch, R.L. (1988). The psychology of religion. *Annual Review of Psychology,* 39, 201–221.

Gorsuch, R.L., & Arno, D. (1979). The relationship of children's attitudes towards alcohol to their value development. *Journal of Abnormal Child Psychology,* 7(3), 287–295.

Gorsuch, R.L., & Butler, M. (1976). Initial drug abuse: A review of predisposing social psychology factors. *Psychological Bulletin,* 83(1), 120–137. Reprinted in S.B. Sells (Ed.), *The effectiveness of drug abuse treatment,* Vol. IV. Cambridge, MA: Ballinger, 1976; in H. Shaffer (Ed.), *Myths and realities: A book about drug realities.* Hinghow, MA: Project Turnabout, 1977.

Gorsuch, R.L., & Cattell, R.B. (1967). Second stratum personality factors defined in the questionnaire realm by the 16PF. *Multivariate Behavioral Research,* 2, 211–224.

Gorsuch, R.L., & McFarland, S. (1972). Single vs. multiple-item scales for measuring religious values. *Journal for the Scientific Study of Religion,* 11(1), 53–64.

Gorsuch, R.L., & McPherson, S.E. (1989). Intrinsic/extrinsic measurement: I/E-Revised and single-item scales. *Journal for the Scientific Study of Religion,* 28(3), 348–354.

Gorsuch, R.L., Mylvaganam, G., Gorsuch, K., & Johnson, R. (1991). *Generalization of the I/E scales to Asian cultures.* Paper presented at the meeting of the Society for the Scientific Study of Religion.

Hathaway, W.L., & Pargament, K.I. (1990). Intrinsic religiousness, religious coping, and psychosocial competence. A covariance structure analysis. *Journal for the Scientific Study of Religion,* 29(4), 423–441.

Hood, R.W., Jr. (1975). The construction and preliminary validation of a measure of reported mystical experience. *Journal for the Scientific Study of Religion, 14*, 29–41.

James, W. (1985). *The varieties of religious experience.* Cambridge, MA: Harvard University Press. (Original work published 1902)

Lai, J.A. (1982). *Impact of religion in the treatment of alcoholism.* Unpublished master's project, Fuller Theological Seminary, Graduate School of Psychology, Pasadena, California.

Mäkelä, K. (1993). Implications for research of the cultural variability of Alcoholics Anonymous. In B.S. McCrady & W.R. Miller (Eds.), *Research on Alcoholics Anonymous: Opportunities and alternatives.* New Brunswick, NJ: Rutgers Center of Alcohol Studies.

Miller, W.R. (1991). Spirituality: The silent dimension in addiction research. The 1990 Leonard Ball oration. *Drug and Alcohol Review, 9,* 259–266.

Morgenstern, J., & McCrady, B.S. (1993). Cognitive processes and change in disease-model treatment. In B.S. McCrady & W.R. Miller (Eds.), *Research on Alcoholics Anonymous: Opportunities and alternatives.* New Brunswick, NJ: Rutgers Center of Alcohol Studies.

Pargament, K.I., Kennell, J., Hathaway, W., Grevengoed, N., Newman, J., & Jones, W. (1988). Religion and the problem-solving process: Three styles of coping. *Journal for the Scientific Study of Religion, 27*(1), 90–104.

Schaefer, C.A. (1992). *Situational and personal variations in religious coping style.* Unpublished doctoral dissertation, Fuller Theological Seminary, Graduate School of Psychology, Pasadena, Calif.

Schaefer, C.A., & Gorsuch, R.L. (1991). Psychological adjustment and religiousness: The multivariate belief-motivation theory of religiousness. *Journal for the Scientific Study of Religion, 30*(4), 448–461.

Shafranske, E.P., & Gorsuch, R.L. (1984). Factors associated with the perception of spirituality in psychotherapy. *Journal of Transpersonal Psychology, 16*(2), 231–241.

Spilka, B., Hood, R.W., & Gorsuch, R.L. (1985). *The psychology of religion: An empirical approach.* Englewood Cliffs, NJ: Prentice-Hall.

SECTION V

How Could Studies of Alcoholics Anonymous Be Designed?

CHAPTER 18

How Could Studies of Alcoholics Anonymous Be Designed? Evaluation Within Treatment Contexts

J. CLARK LAUNDERGAN

Examining the questions of how studies of Alcoholics Anonymous (AA) could be designed within a treatment context requires a brief consideration of the variety of available alcoholism treatment modalities. Some treatment modalities use the AA steps and traditions as primary adjuncts of treatment, while other modalities have little conceptually or operationally in common with AA. It could be asserted that the most effective way to design studies of AA from a treatment context would be to study former patients from treatment programs that either use AA as a primary adjunct in treatment or as a standard aftercare referral.

If this assertion is accepted, behavioral treatment would seem to be an unlikely modality from which to attempt a study of AA and its role in recovery from alcoholism. The disease concept of alcoholism found in AA and the behavioral understanding of alcoholism with its etiological emphasis on learning represent differences that may help explain why AA is not a standard aftercare referral for behavioral treatment (Ward, 1983). Although there are not always conceptual consistencies between treatment and care after treatment, studying AA from a behavioral treatment context does not seem to be productive because of the likelihood that most clients will not attend AA following treatment.

The wide range of therapies that may be included in the psychotherapy modality could either allow a heavy AA emphasis or have no inclusion of AA whatsoever. Studying AA from the context of treatment for clients receiving psychotherapy for the treatment of alcoholism would be a methodological challenge because of the variety of orientations toward AA found within this modality. Such research, if the methodological obstacles could be overcome, would provide a potentially valuable contribution to the literature where AA affiliation could be examined in relation to antecedent AA orientation in psychotherapy.

The treatment modality most amenable to carrying out studies of AA is the Minnesota Model, known also as chemical dependency (CD) treatment or comprehensive treatment. Chemical dependency treatment, the term used within the Minnesota Model to refer to treatment of alcoholism and harmful dependence on other mood-altering drugs, does not make distinction by drug of choice for assignment to rehabilitation, although patient uniqueness is considered in individual treatment planning. The Minnesota Model of treatment for alcoholism represents a blending of behavioral science and AA that developed over 40 years through an interplay of trial and error, pragmatic assessment, and utilization of AA's program in bringing about client changes that serve as the foundation for recovery. This treatment approach uses recovering alcoholics working their own 12-step programs as focal counselors and comembers of a multidiciplinary treatment team. AA is also interwoven into treatment in different ways: use of bibliotherapy including the books *Alcoholics Anonymous* and *Twelve Steps and Twelve Traditions*, repeated recitations of the Serenity Prayer, and group meetings where AA thinking either guides the discussion or where specific AA group skills are practiced, such as step groups and in-house AA meetings.

Minnesota Model treatment is not just an introduction and orientation to AA, but consists of a variety of individual assessments, individualized treatment plans, and monitoring of client progress. Three generally held goals of treatment are (1) abstain from alcohol or other mood-altering chemical use, (2) attend Alcoholics Anonymous, and (3) use available resources, including AA, to improve social and psychological functioning.

The thoughts presented here on designing studies of AA from a treatment context will utilize Minnesota Model treatment as the modality under consideration. This is done for two reasons: (1) the Minnesota Model seems to be the most logical treatment context from which to study AA by reason of the above stated assumption, and (2) this writer's 20 years of evaluation-outcome research have been exclusively with the Minnesota Model, thereby providing a experiential base from which to consider the question of designing studies of AA from a treatment context. The latter reason may be considered as both a strength and weakness of this chapter, but to the extent that the comments made here generate discussion and possible debate because they are couched in the framework of a single treatment modality, the intended purpose will have been accomplished.

Purpose

The purpose of the present chapter is twofold: (1) to discuss three large alcoholism treatment outcome study databases that have asked questions about AA participation and (2) to consider future research directions that may be more productive than the common past practice of limiting AA inquiry to frequency of attendance.

Treatment outcome study databases are: (1) DAANES (Drug and Alcohol Normative Evaluation), a format for reporting client characteristics and treatment follow-up supported by the Minnesota Department of Human Services; (2) CATOR (Comprehensive Assessment and Treatment Outcome Research), a treatment outcome evaluation service that has worked with more than 100 treatment facilities nationwide; and (3) Hazelden/Hazelden Evaluation Consortium (HEC), an alcoholism treatment outcome evaluation service that serves Hazelden and has contracted to carry out treatment outcome evaluation for more than a dozen treatment centers located throughout the United States. Each of these databases provides a different format for assessing the role of AA in client recovery and therefore serves to illustrate some of the ways AA has been studied through treatment outcome research. Some additional research developed out of Hazelden follow-up data will also be discussed as preliminary attempts to explore AA from a treatment context.

The second purpose of the chapter is to explore potentials for carrying out research, identify areas of inquiry, and raise possible obstacles that should be considered in formulating new research into AA from a treatment context. The thoughts presented are not framed as prescribed questions or detailed methodological recommendations. Rather, the thoughts reflect a loosely organized compilation of observations formulated during 20 years of chemical dependency treatment process and outcome evaluation research that may be useful in charting a course of new research into AA.

Limitations and Biases

The treatment modality served by the three client follow-up approaches used in this discussion is largely, although not exclusively, of the Minnesota Model type. The Minnesota Model may appear at first glance to be a single program of rehabilitation for alcoholics and drug abusers. In fact, there is considerable variation in programs that may be classified as being within the Minnesota Model. Some treatment programs have a strong spiritual emphasis, whereas other stress spirituality far less. Some treatment programs attempt to empower patients by nurturing group skills and promoting internalization of the AA perspective, while other treatment programs rely on counselors to instruct patients about what they should know and do so that they may recover. Within a single treatment setting there may be variation between treatment groups and between counseling style of individual counselors. Acknowledging this variability within the Minnesota Model does not detract from this form of alcoholism treatment, but it does introduce a host of research variables that may influence client's post-treatment AA behavior.

Who goes to Minnesota Model treatment? There are a number of selection factors that may bias the composition of the client populations in this type of treatment setting. Treatment at a Minnesota Model rehabilitation facility may be influenced by residential location, orientation of the referral source, source of third-party payment, and similar structural and process factors. These factors may be illustrated by the example of a town in western Nebraska that had a locally well-known alcoholic begin his recovery in the Minnesota Model treatment program. Public officials were so impressed that this former active alcoholic began recovering that they committed funding for other alcoholics to be treated in Minnesota Model programs. As more Minnesota Model alumni accumulated in the community, AA became stronger. The local AA drop-in location was in the back room of a liquor store where impromptu AA discussions were held while participants sat on beer cases and drank coffee. If an alcoholic went to treatment from this town or vicinity, it became highly probable that he or she went to a Minnesota Model program.

In addition to treatment variability and treatment selection, there are a number of factors that may be viewed as limitations and biases in attempting to study AA from a treatment evaluation context. Clients may have past involvement in AA, current participation in AA, or no prior AA experience. Local and regional AA fellowships may view treatment for alcoholism apart from attendance at AA meetings as unnecessary or may be highly supportive of alcoholism treatment programs and a major source of treatment referrals. AA may provide the basis for friendship networks and social activities or may be limited to weekly meetings with little other inclusion in the member's life. There is also the intriguing question of whether there are AA nonattenders who are working their own AA programs. These issues of limitation and biases will be returned to in the later discussion of future directions in researching AA from a treatment context.

Three CD Treatment Evaluation Systems

The three CD treatment outcome evaluation systems serve as evaluation service/contractors for a number of treatment programs. The treatment programs evaluated include inpatient and outpatient, hospital-based and free-standing, and for profit and nonprofit programs. In some of the treatment programs the costs are predominately paid by insurance or the clients, while other treatment programs have a large share of public paid clients. With the exception of the state-supported database (DAANES), CD treatment programs have contracted for their treatment outcome evaluation services. Each of the three systems uses its own forms for abstracting information from client records, gathering information from clients directly and following up clients after discharge. DANNES relies on treatment programs to telephone discharged clients six months after treatment. With a few exceptions, Hazelden/HEC is responsible for follow-up data gathering through mail questionnaires and telephone interviews, CATOR relies on telephone interviews that are done by their staff.

DAANES

In 1983 the Minnesota Department of Human Services, Chemical Dependency Program Division, introduced the Drug and Alcohol Normative Evaluation System (DAANES). Chemical dependency treatment programs throughout the state receiving state funds were required to use DAANES for maintaining records of client characteristics and services as well as collecting follow-up information from clients. In 1988, new Minnesota legislation, referred to as the Consolidated Chemical Dependency Treatment Fund, expanded the requirement for use of DAANES or comparable system resulting in a nearly sevenfold increase in client files from 2,870 to 20,464 (McMahon, 1989). DANNES is available to public and nonpublic alcoholism and drug treatment facilities at no cost to the program for the data-gathering forms or the computer processing and supplying of printouts back to the facilities where the information originated. Treatment programs invest staff time in putting client information on forms and contacting clients at six months after treatment for a follow-up telephone interview.

A tremendous amount of information has been gathered, processed, and summarized in the years of DAANES operation. The early years were plagued with inaccuracies resulting from getting the information entered into computer files, but most of those problems have been addressed. Treatment providers also experienced delays in receiving information back from the centralized data processing location in St. Paul, although that turnaround time has been considerably improved.

DANNES data runs are sent back to treatment programs quarterly. A treatment program can receive as much as a six-inch stack of paper annually in computer printouts for each form of treatment (inpatient, outpatient, etc.). Much of the information returned to treatment providers is quickly reviewed and placed in a file rather than being used as a tool to improve programming or assess treatment. Ignoring these data is not surprising in that treatment providers are overwhelmed by the volume of information, they feel no ownership of the data system, and because they are originating the data (completing forms and contacting clients at follow-up) they think that they have a sense of what the tabulated results report.

The intake/admission information gathered using the DAANES system asks two AA questions: "Has client ever participated in AA or other support groups?" (yes, no); "If so, how often did he/she attend AA or other CD support group in the six months prior to treatment?" Response categories to the second question range from "more than once a week" to "less than once a month." The obvious limitation of these questions is the combination of AA with other chemical dependency support groups, thereby making meaningful interpretation confused. This same confusion does not carry over to the discharge information where it is asked whether the "client is being referred to AA support group?" (yes, no). About 80% of clients from treatment programs using DAANES are referred to AA.

The client follow-up survey also asks specifically about AA: "How often have you attended AA support group(s) during the 6 months since treatment?" One of the major limitations of DAANES is that follow-up contact with the former client is the responsibility of the treatment program. Because counselors and other staff have many demands on their time and most programs do not have personnel specifically assigned to follow up, DAANES has a 22% response rate from clients statewide (McMahon, 1990). Given the limitation of this unacceptable response rate, 55% of the contacted former clients were attending AA at least once a week. During the six months after discharge, 68% of the treatment completers attending AA were abstinent and 53% of the treatment dropouts attending AA were abstinent (Harrison, 1992).

Non-AA attenders were likely to be under 25 years of age or over 65, high school dropouts, minority persons, and unemployed. Treatment completers who *did not* attend AA had a 52% rate of abstinence and treatment noncompleters who *did not* attend AA had a 36% abstinence rate. Again, selectivity resulting from low response to follow-up and a higher response from treatment completers make these findings questionable.

If the DAANES findings are questionable, why mention them at all? The state of Minnesota is reassessing its investment in this large database and is planning to develop a follow-up evaluation approach where the state would sample treatment programs and do an intensive follow-up of clients. The decision to use this alternative approach will produce much higher quality findings and may provide a new opportunity to study AA within a treatment context. Specific questions could be included in the new evaluation format that could serve as a test for some of the ideas that will emerge from this conference. Future directions in researching AA should seek to take advantage of opportunities to tie into state-funded efforts to monitor the effectiveness of alcoholism and drug treatment.

CATOR

Identifying itself as the largest independent chemical dependency evaluation service in the United States, CATOR has collected data on 50,000 adult and 10,000 adolescent clients since 1980. Recently, CATOR experienced a major organizational change by leaving its affiliation with St. Paul Ramsey Medical Education and Research Foundation, a unit of the St. Paul Ramsey Medical Center, and becoming a division of New Standards, Inc. Norman Hoffman continues as CATOR's executive and scientific director.

Abstinence and AA attendance of 900 former inpatients (71% follow-up of 1,272 total admissions) followed up at six months after chemical dependency treatment discharge by CATOR were reported on in a 1983 study (Hoffman, Harrison, & Belille, 1983). During the six-month follow-up, 69% attending AA several times a month were abstinent and 73% who were attending weekly were abstinent from alcohol and drugs. A significant difference in abstinence was found between these participators and infrequent and nonattenders. Weekly AA attendance was reported by 48% and 33% were nonattenders.

More recently, Hoffman (1991) reported on abstinence and AA attendance of 4,166 inpatients (57% follow-up rate) and 898 outpatients (63% follow-up rate) one year after chemical dependency treatment. For one year following treatment, 46% of the inpatients were regular AA attenders with 75 percent abstinent and 51% of the outpatients were regular AA attenders with an abstinence rate of 82%. Although the follow-up response rate is lower for the 1991 study, the consistency in the pattern of the 1983 findings and the findings reported in 1991 is important to note. More complete analysis of AA patterns from the CATOR data set is reported by Lull (1988).

Lull carried out secondary analyses of a sample from the CATOR III inpatient database. The total database contained 9,922 client records and the sample consisted of 2,950 client records. Four follow-up intervals were considered: six months, 12 months, 18 months, and 24 months after treatment discharge. Bivariate and multivariate analyses were carried out, looking at AA attendance and aftercare in relation to sobriety. Biodemographic and outcome variables were also considered in the analysis.

The chi-square analysis found a moderately strong relationship between AA attendance and sobriety at each of the follow-up time intervals. Cross-lagged correlations were then done: "the data suggest that AA attendance had a greater impact on subsequent sobriety in this sample, than the reverse situation in which established sobriety influenced subsequent AA attendance" (Lull, 1988, pp. 158–159). Stepwise multiple regression identified AA as the independent variable of most importance in explaining variance associated with sobriety, however the majority of the variance was unexplained. Sobriety was the only outcome variable statistically associated with AA attendance. Age, marital status, type of substance abused, and previous CD treatment were all statistically associated with sobriety, but none of these variables had a statistically significant relationship to AA attendance; only education in three of the four time periods was associated with AA attendance.

Secondary analysis of large data sets such as CATOR maintains is another way that AA can be studied from a treatment context. Opening its data set for analysis by graduate students demonstrates a generosity on CATOR's part and should be encouraged for large alcoholism treatment data sets. The primary shortcoming of the CATOR data set in studying AA is that no greater detail about AA participation is gathered other than frequency of meeting attendance. Further revisions of the CATOR evaluation instruments should consider expanding AA-related questions.

Hazelden/Hazelden Evaluation Consortium

Outcome evaluation began at the Hazelden Foundation Treatment Center located in Center City, Minnesota, as the result of a 1969 Northwest Area Foundation grant. Experience with its own outcome evaluation studies resulted in the early 1980s in the formation of the Hazelden Evaluation Consortium, which provided contract outcome evaluation for other alcoholism treatment centers. Recently, Hazelden divested itself of the Hazelden Evaluation Consortium and these services are now being provided by Data Lock, a private company based in St. Paul, Minnesota.

The format of AA questions used in the Hazelden outcome questionnaires has been more extensive than that found in DAANES or CATOR. Respondents have been asked about whether they have led a meeting, told their story, done 12th-step work, sponsored a member, made frequent use of Step 10, continued working on Steps 6 through 12, and the extent that AA has been helpful in bringing about improvement in life. Questions are also asked about AA as a resource if relapse has occurred and the place of AA in helping keep in touch with a Higher Power. As might be expected, former patients who attend AA are more likely to respond affirmatively to the detailed questions about AA activities.

The detailed AA activities questions have not been shown to have much explanatory power, although they have not received extensive analytical attention. The relationship between Higher Power and AA attendance was identified as important, however. In a 1982 publication analyzing treatment follow-up questionnaires from former Hazelden patients, regression and path analysis were used to identify those variables that explained successful outcome. Successful outcome was defined as attending AA, not using alcohol or other chemicals, and improvement in sociopsychological functioning (Laundergan, 1982). Using multiple regression, increased prayer and meditation were the strongest explainers of variance in the prediction of AA attendance. Increased prayer and meditation emerged in the path analysis as having a strong relationship with both AA attendance and improved sociopsychological functioning. AA attendance showed a moderately strong association with abstinence and abstinence had a strong relationship with improved sociopsychological functioning.

The point of bringing up this analysis when considering studying AA from a treatment context is that the spiritual aspects of life as exercised through prayer, meditation, or some alternative form cannot be separated from AA. Often social science researchers are reluctant to study spirituality, but without research designed to explore the interplay between AA and spiritual dimensions, the essence of AA as a factor in recovery from alcohol and drug addiction will not be productive. Higher Power may take "God as we understand him" forms or refer to a group such as an AA group. One former patient described how he would sit on a hillside facing a large communications tower on the neighboring hillside and, acknowledging that the tower was larger than he was, openly speak his thoughts and feelings. He was not praying to the tower but instead used the hillside tower setting to set the stage for his relationship to "that which is greater than I am."

For many clients, treatment is a time to reassess spiritual concerns. Active alcohol and drug use seem to both fill and widen the spiritual void people feel. Appreciation for nature and the awakening of senses of smell and sight are often experienced in treatment, along with recognition of the power of human concern and the release provided by open sharing of feelings. Patients are told and begin to accept that these renewed sensations and appreciations are their Higher Power working in their lives to help them recover. AA is seen as a spiritual program that works through a fellowship, but the fellowship does not work without the "Higher Power" part.

How do researchers measure spirituality? An indicator such as increased prayer and meditation may be used, but to better understand the role of spirituality in recovery, a multiple indicator approach must be developed. Developing such a spiritual assessment and exploring how spirituality relates to AA involvement and recovery will require more exploratory studies using in-depth interviews, diaries, and other personal expressions of individualized and shared understandings of Higher Power.

The relationship between AA attendance and abstinence has been supported by the Hazelden and Hazelden Evaluation Consortium data sets, although consistent plotting of this pattern has not been done in recent years. In fact, the treatment outcome information contained in these data sets has been reported as simple frequencies and percentages that seem to be an uneconomical return on what has to be a major investment for Hazelden and the treatment facilities included in the consortium.

During the six months after discharge, 52% of the consortium aggregate inpatients who responded to the Alcoholics Anonymous/Narcotics Anonymous meeting attendance question reported attendance of once a week or more (Baeumler, 1991). This AA attendance rate dropped to 43% at the 12-month follow-up point. The pattern of post-treatment attendance identified in the three large databases (DAANES, CATOR, Hazelden/HEC) shows a consistency, but there needs to be exploratory work done to add substance to the bare outline of percentage AA attendance. Longer timeframes than the 6- and 12-month or up to 24-month follow-up should also be considered. Using follow-up databases to identify prospective participants for exploratory and longer timeframe studies is another way that the treatment context may contribute to the study of AA.

In 1982 an unpublished exploratory study was done by this writer of former Hazelden patients; it consisted of a convenience sample of 1976 and 1977 inpatients five years after their treatment. The former clients in this study had responded to a 6-, 12-, and 18-month mailed questionnaire and lived in the greater Twin Cities area of Minneapolis and St. Paul. Some had used alcohol and drugs after treatment and some had been abstinent for the entire 18-month period. A questionnaire was sent at five years after treatment discharge and the former clients were asked to respond to questions about their lives for each of the past four years. Questions included alcohol and drug use, reason for resumed chemical use if any, additional treatment, other therapy, AA attendance, marital changes, job changes, frequency of Higher Power contact, rating of sociopsychological functioning, and important positive or negative highlights of each year. At the end of the five-year questionnaire, former clients were asked if they would be willing to be interviewed. If they were willing, a face-to-face interview was conducted where the interviewer asked for elaboration of the questionnaire responses and sought to identify the respondent's personal network of friends and support or nonsupport.

The findings illustrate how patterns of AA involvement identified may provide further insight into AA and how it works in people's lives. A few brief examples will show the data yield from this exploratory methodology:

Example 1: Respondent is a 38-year-old male. Prior to treatment he drank a case of beer daily and used street drugs. He has been abstinent since treatment. During the first three years of recovery he attended AA six times weekly and then attendance began to drop off as he began to understand the program. He now attends AA three times a week and sometimes more. He admits that he increases his attendance when he is hurting about something like the end of a relationship. He has led meetings, sponsored members, and done 12-step work. He reads most AA materials and really studies them. *Twenty-Four Hours a Day,* the "Big Book" and "12 × 12" help to pinpoint areas of change in terms of behavior and attitudes. He admits that the steps work for him and that AA has become a lifestyle for him. Presently, he is working the last three maintenance steps, regular contact with God, self-inventory, and taking the message to others. He states that in terms of literature, all he really needs is the "Big Book," that all other self-help material makes life too confusing.

Example 2: Respondent is a 47-year-old male. Prior to treatment he was a binge drinker, but drank heavily every day for the eight months before entering treatment. He tried AA six months before going into treatment. For nine months after treatment he was abstinent, he then drank for six months with quantity increasing until he was drinking the same as before treatment; he stopped drinking and has remained abstinent. He says that he was assigned an AA sponsor when he left treatment but did not get along well with the sponsor. The AA group he began to attend was an "old timers group" and had very little regard for treatment. He stopped attending AA and admits that he really didn't understand AA. He thought about it as a rules game—if you followed the rules things would work out—but now he recognizes that it doesn't work that way. After treatment, he still had a lot of resentment and that contributed to his dislike of AA. While in treatment he had trouble accepting the first step of AA, he was able to admit that he was powerless over alcohol but says that he couldn't accept that he was powerless. Presently, he is active in AA, has done a lot of 12th step work in his work place, is involved in Intergroup, takes new AA members to an introductory meeting, and has been a squad leader. Also, he has been on the board and is active in his Alano Club, which is a separate organization from AA that owns property where AA and Al-Anon meetings are held. He met a person during his brief attendance at aftercare and this person later became important in his return to AA and abstinence.

Example 3: Respondent is a 50-year-old female. Her drinking behavior was binging for three days, followed by ten days dry and then a repeated binge. She was admitted into treatment following a shooting episode where she was inside her garage shooting repeatedly into the wall until the police responded. She went to AA three times after treatment but does not attend AA presently. Her main reason for not attending AA is that she works rotating shifts and is not always sure of her work schedule. She feels that if a person is lonely, AA is a good source of support. Despite not attending AA, she does consciously work Steps 4 and 5 most of the time. She also does her own 12th-step work and there isn't a day that goes by when she doesn't think of AA. The 12 steps have become a way of life for her and made her "gloriously happy."

The three examples illustrate three of many patterns of AA involvement. Example 1 shows what might be termed "conversion-emersion," where AA has been continuously central in the respondents life. Example

2 may be characterized as that of a "rejector-acceptor" where AA involvement has been begrudgingly embraced as a better alternative than continued drinking. Example 3 illustrates a "nonattender-program of living" pattern, where the AA 12 steps are worked but no AA meeting participation occurs. By documenting the way former clients work or don't work AA programs, it should be possible to use the treatment context as a window into AA experience that may otherwise not be open to the researcher.

Possible use of the three treatment outcome systems will be explored next. Other similar alcoholism treatment follow-up evaluation systems may hold similar promise for future AA research. Because follow-up systems already have working relationships with treatment providers, it is reasoned that they provide the best access and lowest cost route for future AA research from a treatment context.

Consideration for Future AA Research

The three alcoholism treatment follow-up evaluation systems (DAANES, CATOR, and Hazelden/HEC) may become structures from which to study AA from the context of treatment. All of these follow-up systems service a number of treatment facilities and therefore represent a large total client population. Similarity in repeated descriptive findings reported by each of these outcome data systems over a period of years clearly indicate that in an era of tight resources and changing expectations there is a need to rethink past practice and attempt to address a more challenging set of questions.

DAANES is undergoing modification prompted by its inadequate follow-up response rate. Select research questions will be examined for specified populations following treatment with the goal of achieving a 80% or better response rate. Follow-up data gathering will be done by a contracted research organization rather than by treatment facilities. This revised approach appears to be potentially responsive to addressing questions such as AA and its role in chemical dependency recovery.

States other than Minnesota are looking at their alcohol/drug client tracking systems and questioning whether there are better ways to accomplish data collection and processing. With technology changes, large mainframe computer systems are being replaced with microcomputers and low-cost software can give treatment providers immediate access to data files. Computer literacy and greater use of information systems in treatment management set the stage for new opportunities for looking at questions related to AA. The challenge for utilizing these treatment program specific databases is how to access them and network with them? Here the states could play an important role in linking researchers to treatment programs that would cooperate in research ventures using their client records and adding questions of interest such as AA attendance/nonattendance.

CATOR has revised its data gathering at least four times since its inception. The analyses done by Lull (1988) used CATOR III and the Stockholm paper delivered by Hoffman (1991) used CATOR IV. With CATOR's new corporate identity there may be even greater interest in revising instruments and permitting secondary analysis of CATOR data sets. Public and private foundation money could be used as incentives for including questions of research interest in future CATOR revisions and in attracting graduate students and professionals to undertake analysis of the resulting information. Treatment facilities would continue to pay the major cost associated with originating and maintaining the database, but they would get more for their investment if the data were subject to more analyses.

Hazelden will continue to manage the follow-up evaluation of its clients but will no longer provide this service to other treatment programs. Data Lock, the newly created private company, will contract with many of the treatment centers in the former Hazelden Evaluation Consortium. Both Hazelden and Data Lock are using similar follow-up questionnaires and procedures, but it is expected that both will be considering changes in the next few years. Hazelden has been tracking clients for 20 years and is due for an assessment of its procedures and future evaluation strategy. Data Lock is a new organization that has been created out of the former Hazelden Evaluation Consortium. Their challenge will be to maintain the evaluation services and innovate to make itself competitive in the changing marketplace of the treatment industry. Both Hazelden and Data Lock should be receptive to incorporating new questions about AA in their client record and follow-up instruments.

The use of treatment centers as a source of clients for exploratory studies should be considered as a part of the discussion about structural implications for studying AA. Former clients who have participated in exploratory studies show an eagerness to share their experiences, both positive and negative. For the most part, they appear candid, as evidenced by statements such as "my wife doesn't even know ..." or "I've never told anyone before that ...." Questions and probing of AA participants on AA and spirituality can provide researchers some of the insight necessary to frame research questions that may be used to develop indicators of the AA phenomenon. Without sufficient exploratory investigation, our discovery potential will be limited and we run the risk of being hampered by current incomplete paradigms.

There is another structural limitation that may be encountered in attempting to study AA. Several years ago, a study was attempted by this writer and an associate using guests at Hazelden's renewal center as voluntary informants describing their chemical dependency recovery. The guests who stay at the renewal center from two to five days have to be working a 12-step recovery program and may chose to participate in available group sessions or engage in private contemplation during their stay. Guests were asked to complete an open-ended questionnaire where they identified factors contributing to their recovery program or threatening recovery. Some guests were dealing with recovery problems and others had a stable recovery and were working to maintain it by taking time for a program such as the renewal center. After several months of gathering information, the project was terminated because of the dominance of "motto" responses. "First things first," "one day at a time," "let go, let God," and other AA mottos were repeated as the guests expressed their understanding of their own recovery process. Jellinek (1960, p. 38) acknowledged this problem in studying AA in his *Disease Concept of Alcoholism* when he cautioned the reader to recognize the progression of Gamma alcoholism as a possible artifact of socialization in AA. AA formats the alcoholic experience for the alcoholic in the fellowship as well as providing a program of living with this chronic condition. It is not surprising, therefore, that the experience of recovery is framed in mottos and other conventional wisdom that makes up the AA culture.

Is AA a fellowship, a program of living, or both of these? When questions are asked about post-treatment AA attendance, it is anticipated that AA members work their programs through the fellowship of AA attendance. The possibility that AA may function as a program of living without AA attendance needs to be examined. Many in AA key in on certain steps that they find particularly helpful at certain points in their lives. In the same manner, there may be times when increased AA attendance is felt to be necessary and other times when working an AA program does not seem to require meeting attendance. Some people may not openly acknowledge that they are working an AA program but admit to using a daily meditation that reflects AA thinking or reading the Serenity Prayer located on the bathroom wall each morning as they start their day.

AA may restructure personal networks as members disengage from family and friends whose activities are centered on drinking and using. Some former friends may wish to distance themselves from the nondrinking/using person who has affiliated with AA. New personal networks may not be confined to AA meetings but may include family outings, meeting for breakfast sharing sports interests, and indirectly integrating a support system into daily activities. AA networking outside of meetings may be seldom, only for organized activities such as an annual round up, or may include occurrences such as job referral and dating. The array of personal networks that interconnect AA with other aspects of social life cannot be ignored.

The treatment program link to AA is complex but cannot be neglected. Treatment programs that seek to empower participants with group skills, provide an intensive exposure on applying AA to restructure world view, and nurture spiritual connectedness may have differences in client transition from treatment to AA member than treatment programs that are more instructional, with an inclusion of AA and a low emphasis on spiritual concerns. Aftercare planning, the fit between the patient and the designated sponsor, and the receptivity of the designated AA group may all contribute to post-treatment AA attendance.

Social and behavioral scientists seem to have a reluctance to studying spirituality. The social science literature on spirituality ranges from inquiries sponsored by organizations such as the Institute of Noetic Sciences (Grof, 1987) to examinations of organizational aspects of religion. Spirituality should be a legitimate topic for social and behavioral science. In fact, if scientific research on AA is going to be undertaken, the aversion to using the tools of science in the study of spirituality will have to be overcome. AA involves a spiritual conversion (Wilson, 1963). However, the spiritual conversion may be dramatic or incremental, may involve a transcendental awakening or rediscovery of God as defined in some tradition of religious teaching, or may be the realization of "not God" described by Kurtz (1979). As the alcoholic referred to in Example 2 commented, AA was first seen as a rules game where if the rules were followed things would work out. His struggle was to accept powerlessness, which means the acceptance of some power outside of himself. This something may be termed "Higher Power" and can be manifest in many forms. The acceptance of powerlessness is an act of conversion but it is the acceptance of a personal concept rather than the adoption of a preset dogma. AA fellowship represents collective spirituality centering on diverse Higher Power understandings. Science can study this phenomenon, but first it must inventory its reluctance for using empiricism to study that which may be considered not observable. To paraphrase the sociologist W.I. Thomas, "If something is believed to be true, it's true in its consequences," and science can study both the beliefs and the consequences.

The example that was given of the community in Nebraska raises the question of researching AA not only as a fellowship but as part of a community dynamic. AA may be better understood within the community than as a self-contained social system. The liquor store that served as an AA drop-in location is perhaps unique to the small Nebraska town, but other communities make their own adaptations to AA. How do the helping professions, the courts, the churches, and other community subsystems relate to AA and either nurture it or thwart its purpose? Is Intergroup active in involving participants or is there a small core of dedicated workers that keep things going? These are just samples of questions that should be considered in community studies of AA.

Referral to AA may come in the form of a friend helping a friend, a treatment expectation for "aftercare," a court-required condition of probation, or a former member referring back to the fellowship. Each of these paths of referral may establish a different dynamic of meeting experience and commitment to continued participation. If people feel that they can identify with what is shared in a meeting and they experience acceptance, they are likely to participate. But reaching the point of belonging may take time during which the participant may experience discomfort that works against continued participation. How referral originated and how the adjustment period in AA is experienced needs to be studied.

Analysis of ratings of treatment components indicate that those who found group or "collective activities" beneficial were more likely to attend AA (Laundergan, 1982). This may be related to why greater education has been identified as a predictor of AA attendance. Other research has indicated greater education explains ease of establishing new relationships (Fischer, 1982, p. 251). Use of the Big Book, other literature, and speaking in AA meetings may also be a negative selection factor for persons with low educational attainment. Certainly education and AA needs to be researched further.

Available AA groups may play a part in selective attendance. Some AA groups are termed "old timer" groups and are likely to resist polydrug users, treatment graduates, and others who don't fit their image of what AA should be like. Large communities provide many options of AA format because of the numerous available meetings. Step groups, large or small groups, and nonsmokers groups make up just part of the variety that may be found in large cities. Small communities may not offer these options, with the result that some potential participants refuse to attend. Some communities are just too small to have AA meetings without sacrificing the anonymity of participants. Native Americans have voiced a concern about AA on reservations where lack of anonymity can be a deterrent to attendance.

Conclusion

A variety of methodologies will be required to research the many characteristics that should be examined in research on Alcoholics Anonymous. Exploratory and descriptive modes should be utilized where appropriate. It is important not to let the sophistication of controlled explanatory designs limit access to the multifaceted reality known as AA. The future of AA research includes refined measurement and multivariate statistical analysis, but this must be preceded by sufficient acquaintance knowledge so as to build appropriate measures. Awareness of this concern should influence decision making by researchers and funding agencies alike if the essence of AA is to be satisfactorily understood from a scientific perspective.

Treatment programs can play a role in carrying out research on AA, but there are obstacles. Many treatment facilities wish to maintain the status quo and therefore would consider scientific inquiry into AA as disruptive. Also, treatment facilities that depend on goodwill and cordiality with AA would not want to risk alienating AA by straining this relationship relative to Tradition 6 and Tradition 8. Tradition 6 cautions against endorsing or lending the AA name to any outside enterprise and Tradition 8 asserts that 12-step work should remain nonprofessional. This results in a potentially precarious situation for treatment facilities that are identified as using an AA approach (although not officially endorsed by AA) and utilizing peer counselors, referred to as "two hatters," whose twelve-step program recovery is part of their employment credentials. Treatment programs may be reluctant to assume a major AA research function that gives the appearance of displacing AA's research when AA has been able to directly or indirectly control much of the research that has been done on AA. Most treatment facilities would likely be prudent and seek at least an opinion on their cooperation in AA research from the General Service Office in the same way that the organizers of the "Research on Alcoholics Anonymous: Opportunities and Approaches" conference did prior to holding the conference. These obstacles may be minor and easily dealt with or may have the effect of sidetracking coordinated research efforts.

During the decade of the 1990s, the treatment industry will face many problems tied to the organizational crises in health care delivery and how to pay for services. Additionally, some critics are questioning whether treatment for alcohol and drug problems has a sufficient cost benefit. These social forces are generally viewed negatively by treatment administrators, but the conditions of the 1990s are not going to disappear. Instead, creative ways need to be found to respond to changing conditions. One direction that could be further explored by the treatment industry is developing greater collaboration with the scientific community. Proprietary evaluation of treatment programs will not provide the credibility that the treatment programs need in this era of scarcity. Forming alliances with scientific investigations into AA could provide the beginning of greater cooperation between alcoholism researchers and treatment providers.

References

Baeumler, R., Bakke, J., Collins, F., Curtis, C., Duryee, T., Hughes, S., & Newman, M. (1991). *1991 Annual Report: Hazelden Evaluation Consortium combined data from consortium member treatment centers.* Center City, MN: Hazelden Foundation.

Fischer, C.S. (1982). *To dwell among friends: Personal networks in town and city.* Chicago: University of Chicago Press.

Grof, S. (1987). Spirituality, alcoholism and drug abuse: Transpersonal aspects of addiction. *ReVision, 10,* 3–4.

Harrison, P.A. (1992, February). Personal communication related to the Minnesota Department of Human Services in-house report, "Aftercare programs and post treatment support groups: DAANES, 1988–1989."

Hoffman, N.G., Harrison, P.A., & Belille, C.A. (1983). "Alcoholics Anonymous after treatment: Attendance and abstinence." *International Journal of Addictions, 18,* 311–318.

Hoffman, D.G. (1991, June). *Treatment outcomes from abstinence-based programs.* Paper presented at the International Institute on the Prevention and Treatment of Alcoholism, Stockholm.

Jellinek, E.M. (1960). *The disease concept of alcoholism.* New Brunswick, NJ: Rutgers Center of Alcohol Studies.

Kurtz, E. (1979). *Not God, A history of Alcoholics Anonymous.* Center City, MN: Hazelden Educational Materials.

Laundergan, J.C. (1982). *Easy does it: Alcoholism treatment outcomes, Hazelden and the Minnesota Model.* Center City, MN: Hazelden Foundation.

Lull, D.C. (1988). *Alcoholics Anonymous attendance, aftercare, and outcome: A secondary analysis of two years post hospitalization data.* Unpublished doctoral dissertation, University of Minnesota.

McMahon, M.J. (1989, April). "Alcohol and other drug use among clients admitted to treatment, 1983–1988." In *Minnesota, State Epidemiology Work Group Proceedings.* St. Paul, MN: Department of Human Services.

McMahon, M.J. (1990, October). "Alcohol and other drug use among clients admitted to treatment, 1983–1988." In *Minnesota, State Epidemiology Work Group Proceedings.* St. Paul, MN: Department of Human Services.

Ward, D.A. (1983). *Alcoholism: Introduction to theory and treatment* (rev. 2nd ed.). Dubuque, IA: Kendall/Hunt.

Wilson, W.G. (1963, January). Letter to Dr. Jung. *Grapevine.*

CHAPTER 19

Assessing the Effectiveness of Alcoholics Anonymous in the Community: Meeting the Challenges

ALAN C. OGBORNE

As a community-based fellowship, Alcoholics Anonymous (AA) presents many challenges to its evaluation as a therapeutic resource. Unlike many of the other "treatments" evaluated by social scientists, AA's philosophy seems unscientific and its ways incompatible with the dominant paradigm of controlled experimentation (Vaillant, 1983). Moreover, the AA tradition of anonymity and the reluctance of some groups to permit research at meetings seem to present unsurmountable barriers to the conduct of studies that meet current standards.

To some extent these challenges have been overcome in a number of published research studies, and as shown by Emrick (1987; Emrick, Tonigan, Montgomery, & Little, 1992) and other reviewers (e.g., Institute of Medicine, 1989; McCrady & Irvine, 1988), the accumulated results challenge claims of AA's remarkable potency and superiority to other forms of treatment (e.g., Hudson, 1985; Sheeren, 1988). However, many of these studies have significant shortcomings and we are far from having a clear understanding of AA's strengths and limitations. Without further high-quality research, it will not be possible to provide sound advice concerning AA to alcoholics seeking help. Also, those seeking to secure and maintain funds for professional treatment services will be unable to counter frequently heard statements that AA is the only thing that works and, best of all, it requires no government funds.

This chapter considers some of the challenges to evaluating AA as a therapeutic resource and suggests ways in which these challenges might be met in future studies.

Challenges to the Evaluation of AA

One of the greatest challenges in the evaluation of Alcoholics Anonymous stems from the fact that the movement does not offer a fixed form of treatment. On the contrary, those involved with AA may be exposed to experiences that vary with the groups they attend and the characteristics and motivations of sponsors (McCrady & Irvine, 1988). Unlike the standardized, quality-controlled interventions that many treatment researchers consider prerequisite for outcome evaluations, AA is a purposefully "unorganized," nonexclusive, open-ended movement that relies on untrained, unpaid, and unsupervised individuals engaged in a loosely defined, mutual self-help process. Simple questions concerning AA effectiveness (e.g., Does it work?) ignore the inevitable and demonstrable variations in the experiences of those exposed to the movement. Also these variations will be masked by simple measures of AA involvement, such as the number of meetings attended. What actually happens to individuals attending these meetings is by no means guaranteed. Rather, it can be assumed that their experiences differ markedly with respect to therapeutic appropriateness and effectiveness.

AA's open doors also challenge evaluators because they invite a heterogenous population of potential beneficiaries. Unlike many formal treatment programs, AA does not screen out those who are unsuitable due to poor motivation, legal charges, mental health problems, low social stability, or inability to pay. Those who relapse are welcome to return as are successful abstainers seeking to prevent relapse. The outcomes of similar AA-related experiences are thus likely to vary with the characteristics of those involved. This suggests that a fully comprehensive evaluation of AA will require many types of studies, including studies involving very large samples.

The challenges to the evaluation of AA posed by its unstandardized and open-ended nature are compounded by the influence of self-selection in exposure to AA-related experiences. Thus, both new and experienced members may attend as many meetings as they wish and also determine their level of participation in these meetings and other events. Some may choose to sit quietly through many meetings, to have few contacts with other members, and to reject the attentions of sponsors. Others may speak regularly, seek out a sponsor, sponsor new members, and become enthusiastic participants in social events.

These choices are likely to vary with the characteristics of those concerned. For example, socially inhibited people may be reluctant to speak at meetings or to establish a relationship with a sponsor. The outcomes of various AA-related experiences may be determined as much by these characteristics of those involved as by the experiences themselves. Interactions involving individual and AA-related factors are also likely. For example, those who respond well to highly directive interventions may do better in highly task-oriented groups than in groups that are less focused. The potential importance of such interactions complicates the evaluation process and they will be missed or underestimated if evaluative studies are not planned to take them into account.

The AA tradition of anonymity has been cited as a barrier to evaluation. The tradition partly reflects the concern that members avoid self-centeredness and personal aggrandizement, but in practice it means that AA members do not use their full names when speaking at meetings and that attendance lists are either not kept or incomplete. Also, members are not supposed to report on each other's activities either for research or other purposes.

Although some studies have used AA attendance lists and information obtained through membership networks (e.g., Bill C., 1965), the tradition of anonymity makes these information sources of limited value. Also, current ethical standards will not permit researchers to seek information from collateral sources without the signed consent of the target case.

Some AA groups have permitted the distribution of short questionnaires at meetings or allowed researchers to act as participant or nonparticipant observers. However, it is not clear if AA groups would tolerate the distribution of lengthy questionnaires or permit detailed evaluative studies focused on specific individuals. Therefore, among other challenges to the evaluation of AA may be the reluctance of some groups to permit use of critical research tools.

Negative attitudes to evaluation among some AA members and professionals can also impede evaluative research. As McCrady and Irvine (1988) point out, AA offers experiential, faith-based, recovery processes. This had led to many members, and some professionals, to conclude that AA does not require objective evaluation. Rather, AA is promoted as something that always works for those who totally embrace its traditions and steps. By the same token, failure in AA is not viewed as a reflection of the movement's philosophy or operations but as a sign of failure in compliance.

These attitudes may limit researchers' ability to involve AA members in studies. Also, research that fails to show AA in a positive light may be rejected by the movement and by others who believe that AA is neither "evaluable" nor in need of scientific validation. This will add to the friction that exists between some AA groups and the professional treatment-research community and could jeopardize further studies.

Finally, things that happened to those who go to AA are simply events in complex lives. Many interacting factors may mediate the impact of AA-related experiences and it is difficult to isolate the effects of these experiences per se. This challenge is posed in the evaluation of all forms of treatment and there are limits to the extent to which it can be overcome using either experimental or statistical methods.

Meeting the Challenges

Unlike those seeking membership in AA, those who wish to assess AA's effectiveness do not need to admit that they are "powerless" in the face of the many challenges inherent in the task. On the contrary, experienced social researchers have many skills and resources equal to these challenges. However, it is important to recognize that the evaluation of AA requires attention to complex processes that must be represented by an appropriate paradigm. Such a paradigm is needed to help develop appropriate research questions and studies.

A Paradigm for Research on AA

Critical reviews of quantitative evaluations of AA (e.g., Emrick et al., 1992; McCrady & Irvine, 1988) show that these evaluations rarely consider what happens to individuals who participate in AA. The influence of external social influences and their interactions with AA-related experiences have also generally been ignored. Indeed, with few exceptions most qualitative studies of AA might be characterized as "black-box" studies in which AA has been treated as a fixed treatment that different individuals experience to a greater or lesser extent. Thus, those who enter and stay in AA have been compared with those who stay away or drop out. However, little attention has been paid to specific AA-related experiences or, indeed, to other events in the lives of those studied.

The limitations of black-box research have been clearly elaborated by Moos and Finney (1982), who called for a paradigm shift in addiction treatment research. A new paradigm proposed by Moos and Finney emphasizes the importance of formative research to document treatment experiences and draws attention to extra-treatment factors that interact with the treatment process and influence outcomes.

When the Moos-Finney paradigm is used to represent processes centered on specific treatment programs, AA-related experiences are included among the other extra-treatment factors to which subjects might be involved. However, when AA-related experiences are given center stage, other treatment experiences would be viewed as parts of the complex environment in which AA experiences take place. This will be evident from the schematic model in Figure 1, which is based on the model originally proposed by Moos and Finney. It identifies and shows linkages between factors that research and experience suggest should be considered when attempting to assess the effects of AA-related experiences. Specifically, personal and environmental factors which predate, follow, or coexist with involvements in AA; specific AA-related experiences to

FIGURE 1
A Process-Oriented Paradigm for the Evaluation of Alcholics Anonymous

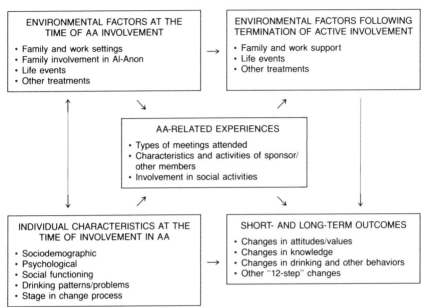

Note: Based on a model by Moos and Finney (1982).

which participants might be exposed; and the various emotional, cognitive, and behavioral changes that involvement in AA might facilitate or impede.

In Figure 1, the extent to which those who go to AA engage in each of the 12 steps is portrayed as an outcome. This is because these steps concern changes in attitudes and behaviors that are expected to follow exposure to the process identified in the central box (information, role models, social support). This assumption is central to AA's model of change. Its validity can be established by comparing 12-step attitudes and behaviors among otherwise similar people with different rates of exposure to specific AA-related experiences. Both quantum-leap and more gradual changes might be expected (Miller, 1990).

A second assumption in AA's model of change is that of a positive relationship between 12-step attitudes and behaviors and other outcomes. This can also be tested by correlating 12 behaviors with changes in drinking and in other life areas. A few studies (reviewed by Emrick et al., 1992) have shown these correlations to be positive for some specific 12-step behaviors, and abstinence. However, these studies have not generally controlled for preexisting differences between those who are more or less active in 12-step work. This, and the fact that many alcoholics become sober without going to AA or doing 12-step work, clearly challenges the proposition that 12-step work is both necessary and sufficient for the maintenance of sobriety.

Implications for Research

As shown in Figure 1, it is clear that the question "Does AA Work?" fails to respect the complexities of the treatment/rehabilitation process in which AA-related experiences may play a part. The question is far too simplistic and needs to be expanded to reference-specific components of the paradigm and the change process it represents. Some examples:

- What are the characteristics and circumstances of those exposed to various AA-related experiences?
- What conditions facilitate or impede affiliation with AA?
- Under what circumstances do 12-step changes occur?
- Are employed, white-collar, middle-aged males threatened with job loss due to excessive drinking more likely to achieve long-term abstinence following referral to AA than following compulsory hospitalization?

A variety of studies will be necessary to answer these questions. Process studies, featuring both quantitative and qualitative methods, would address (1) questions concerning the characteristics of affiliates and dropouts, (2) critical components of the overall AA experience, (3) the situational context in which AA experiences take place, and (4) the immediate and short-term changes associated with these experiences. Process studies will help us to understand AA and why it might work or fail for particular individuals or in particular circumstances.

Outcome studies would consider the longer term effects of exposure to AA, particularly with respect to the use of alcohol. These studies might also include both qualitative and quantitative measures. Also, both non-experimental and experimental designs will be possible under certain circumstances. However, the utility and credibility of outcome studies will be increased if they also document the experiences (AA-related and other) to which subjects were exposed. As previously noted, a count of the number of AA meetings fails to take account of the variety of experiences that might or might not have occurred at these meetings. Unless these and other experiences are documented, outcome studies will be difficult to interpret and failure to detect the expected changes might erroneously be attributed to AA when, in fact, the experiences never took place.

Specific Variables to Consider

The literature on AA, and the more general treatment research literature, suggests a number of individual and environmental factors that
should be considered in future process and outcome studies. However,
more needs to be done to identify critical components of the AA experience and to develop measures to be used in all types of studies.

Characteristics of those exposed to AA. In general, the prognosis of
treated problem drinkers is influenced by conceptual levels, neuropsychological impairments, severity of alcohol-related problems, problems in
other life areas, locus of control, perceived choice in treatment method,
and goals and stage of change (Miller & Hester, 1986a). Studies of AA
suggest that drinking styles, spiritual activity, and early childhood experiences may also correlate with AA involvement and influence outcomes
(Emrick et al., 1992).

Measures concerning many of these characteristics are discussed elsewhere in this volume and by Miller (1976) and Lettieri, Nelson, and Sayers (1985). These measures should be used in future studies of AA
including studies of people with different types of AA-related experiences
(e.g., dropouts versus long-term affiliates) and studies of individual differences in reactions to these experiences.

Clinical experience suggests that stage of change may be especially important in the evaluation of AA. Consistent with the common view of AA,
some clients report going to meetings at times of crisis—when they
reached a new "rock bottom" and have nowhere to go but up. However,
many others go to AA attempting to consolidate gains achieved by other
routes, including gains made in treatment programs. Some clients also report going to AA when they fear relapse or during a relapse episode. Of
course, many precontemplative drinkers go to meetings with no intention
of changing their drinking habits. These include heavy drinkers required
to attend AA by the courts and others pressured to attend by family members, physicians, and therapists.

These differences suggest several possible short-term relationships between AA involvement and changes in drinking patterns. For example,
precontemplators who use AA as a primary treatment resource may continue to drink yet move closer to active and successful attempts to
change. Ongoing drinking might also characterize those who return to AA
during periods of relapse. Significant pre-post changes in drinking could
be expected if AA is a successful treatment for alcoholics, but these
changes would be less dramatic when AA is used as a form of aftercare.
Pre-post and comparison group studies that fail to control for differences
in change status may thus mask or underestimate differences in the various positive effects that AA might have on different people.

Environmental influences. The treatment research literature also suggests a variety of situational factors that may directly or indirectly affect the outcomes of involvement in AA. These include support provided by friends and family members (including family members involvement in Al-Anon), legal pressures, involvement in other treatments, and stressful life events (Moos & Finney, 1982; Ogborne, Sobell, & Sobell, 1985). Measures relevant to those factors are discussed elsewhere in this volume and the two references cited above.

Outcomes. The potential outcomes of specific AA-related experiences include both short- and long-term changes in cognitions, attitudes, and behavior. These include changes in self-efficacy, actual drinking behaviors, functioning in other life areas, as well as changes reflected in AA's 12 steps. Changes in spirituality would be of special interest given AA's emphasis on spiritual renewal (Miller, 1990). Other specific outcomes and relevant measures are discussed elsewhere in this book and by Glaser and Ogborne (1982), Ogborne (1984), and Sobell et al. (1987).

When outcome questions are appropriate, both proximal and distal changes should be considered. If all changes are in the expected direction, this provides support for AA's theory of change. If only proximal changes are significant, and in the expected direction, this could show that AA-related changes are short lived or undermined by other factors. In this case, those referred to AA may need additional ongoing support from other resources.

Specific AA-related experiences. AA's treatment methods—the specific therapeutic influences to which its members are exposed—are in many ways similar to those used by psychotherapists (Bean-Bayog, 1991; Brown, 1985) and behavior therapists (Bassin, 1975; Burt, 1975; McCrady & Irvine, 1988). These include providing information about alcoholism and recovery, the use of role models, role playing (e.g., "fake it until you make it"), and social support and reinforcement for abstinence. In various ways AA members are taught new coping skills and new ways to think about themselves and their problems and are provided with opportunities to develop new communication skills. Of course, the movement also provides opportunities to make new friends and, for some members, the religious aspects of AA are very important (Kurtz, 1982).

The specific therapeutic experiences to which AA members are exposed can be expected to vary in type, quality, and intensity. Types of AA-related experiences and the quality of these experiences will be influenced by the characteristics of sponsors and other members, while the intensity is likely to be influenced by the characteristics of both providers and receivers. For example, an eager and helpful sponsor might nonetheless be avoided by a shy or unmotivated novice. In contrast, sponsors might be actively sought out by those highly committed to change.

Reviews of previous descriptive studies of AA and additional qualitative and quantitative studies are needed to elaborate critical features of the AA involvement and disengagement process and to develop relevant indices and scales. These measures can then be used by observers or research subjects in larger scale studies designed to learn more about what happens in different AA groups and about the ways in which specific experiences affect different people.

Existing measures of the atmosphere of group experiences and reactions to therapists (Moos, 1974) may also provide valuable insights into the workings of AA and the ways in which various aspects of the movement are experienced by its members.

Recruiting Subjects

Subjects involved in both process and process-outcome studies should represent drinkers in the community who become exposed to the AA movement. However, the heterogeneity of AA members and groups makes it likely that the results from specific studies will have limited ability for generalization. There is thus a need for a series of studies involving different AA groups but using similar instruments and procedures.

Several methods for recruiting subjects can be envisaged, each with the potential to engage cases representing important subgroups of those who ever attend meetings.

From those seeking help from professional. A large proportion of all those who attend AA are, at various times, involved with professionals. Many professionals refer their alcoholic clients to AA. Studies involving such cases would thus engage an important subgroup of AA attenders and the results could have significant implications for the ways professionals respond to people with drinking problems.

Professionals are in a good position to monitor and evaluate the experience of clients referred to AA because comprehensive assessment and case management are essential components of professional care. It is therefore regrettable that few professionals have capitalized on the opportunities available to them. At a minimum, professionals who refer clients to AA could conduct and report systematic case studies. These will provide useful insights into the recovery process and identify issues to be investigated on a larger scale. Meta-analyses of large numbers of similar case studies may also yield results that can be generalized.

Professionals are also well placed to implement larger scale prospective studies, including those featuring experimental designs (see below). Professionals can ensure that their clients are fully informed about these studies and provide signed consents to participation. Studies involving drinkers attending outpatient services should have the highest priority because previous studies involving AA referrals from professionals have usually involved discharges from residential programs (Emrick et al., 1992).

Studies involving media-recruited subjects. Media-recruited subjects have been used in a number of studies designed to evaluate treatments (Pearlman, Zweben, & Li, 1989). In principle, it should therefore be possible to recruit research subjects with AA-related experiences through newspaper and other notices. These notices would describe a study designed to evaluate AA. No such studies have been reported and it is possible that some AA members will object to such notices. However, nothing in the AA traditions seems to conflict with individual members' participation in such studies. Also, other studies involving media recruited subjects have involved subjects who attend AA and who have been asked about this experience.

Heavy drinkers and those at risk identified in surveys. Heavy drinkers and those at risk for drinking problems have been identified in many surveys. Over time a high proportion of such people appear likely to have some contacts with AA (Vaillant, 1983). With their consent, such people could be recruited for longitudinal studies involving multiple assessment interviews and possibly other monitoring tools such as mailed questionnaires and diaries. Items concerning changes in drinking and other behaviors, experiences with AA, other life events and their consequences would be monitored with these instruments. With large samples, good rates of research compliance, and long-term follow-up such studies have the potential to provide extremely valuable information concerning AA and the influence of formal treatments and other factors on drinking and other behaviors.

Subjects recruited at AA meetings. AA meetings provide an obvious source of subjects for longitudinal studies and, by definition, those who ever attend AA groups will be representative of the AA-using population. Recruitment could be done informally by researchers who approach randomly selected individuals at the end of meetings. Alternatively, some AA groups might permit researchers to speak at meetings to explain their plans and to ask for volunteers. A few studies involving subjects recruited by this method have been reported (e.g., Bill C., 1965).

Experimental Studies—Are They Really Necessary?

Many questions concerning the evaluation of AA neither require nor are amenable to research involving random assignments. For example, random assignments would not be required to address questions about the characteristics of AA members, questions about the engagement-disengagement process, or questions about the fate of self-referrals. Also, the availability of multivariate data analysis methods has to some extent reduced the need to regard random assignment as the only means to control for factors that compound the effects of social interventions.

Certainly, AA has many features that are incompatible with the conditions considered ideal for field experiments involving random assignment (Cook & Campbell, 1979; Denis & Boruch, 1989). I refer specifically to the lack of a fixed program of recovery and the importance of self-selection in exposure. The ability to generalize studies involving only cases who agree to randomization and other conditions of research may also be limited.

Experimental studies of all kinds can be compromised by negative or compensatory reactions of those assigned to less attractive treatments. This may be a serious problem among subjects selected from cases seeking help from professionals. Although many of these cases may have previous exposure to AA, they and others may be disappointed if they are assigned to AA for research purposes. This could result in decreased motivation to change or attempts to subvert the research protocol.

Experimentation per se does not, of course, rule out the reactive effects and other measurement problems or placebo effects. Also, random assignment does not guarantee that a study has the technical feasibility to detect effects that are nonetheless present. For example, the sample size may be sufficient to detect small effects or interactions.

In spite of these difficulties and limitations, experimental studies concerning AA should not be ruled out completely. The alternative—nonexperimental studies—are also fraught with difficulties in implementation, analysis, and interpretation. Studies of all kinds have limitations, but this does not necessarily mean that the results are invalid. Experiments, for all their problems, do at least control for preexisting differences among those exposed to different types of intervention. Other methods for controlling these differences assume that factors confounding assignment to treatment conditions have been measured. Questions invariably remain about the extent to which this is the case.

Three experimental studies involving AA have been reported (Brandsma, Maultsby, & Walsh, 1980; Ditman et al., 1967; Walsh et al., 1991) and in no case did they show AA to advantage. However, in none of these studies were cases referred to AA screened for potential suitability and in all cases it is doubtful that subjects' circumstances made them appropriate candidates for a self-help fellowship. In two cases all or most subjects were required to attend AA by the courts, while in the Walsh study subjects were in an employee assistance program and threatened with the loss of jobs.

In none of these experiments were subjects' AA-related experiences monitored nor were subjects asked about the influence of AA, other treatments, or other life events. Thus, these experiments do little to help us to understand why AA (or the other treatments) might have worked or failed for those involved.

Further experimental studies of AA would be of value if they gave more attention to the specific events to which subjects were exposed and did more to optimize the chances that AA could be shown to be helpful (e.g., by matching subjects with sponsors). This would only be possible with the cooperation of subjects and AA sponsors and the results might not generalize to all referrals or sponsors. Also, the number and type of AA groups involved in any one study would be limited. However, if the study was otherwise sound, and included both qualitative and quantitative assessments of the factors discussed above, the results would illuminate the processes of change in AA and in the other interventions considered and show the particular advantages of each, at least for the types of subjects involved.

One Possible Experiment

An outline for an experimental study involving AA has been proposed by Glaser and Ogborne (1982). With a number of refinements, such a study could provide useful information concerning benefits of AA to selected referrals from professionals.

The study would involve subjects seeking help from a professional agency. All those seeking help would be assessed across a variety of dimensions using standardized methods and instruments and those considered suitable for AA would be asked to consent to follow-up and to identify collateral sources to validate self-reports. Agreements to use self-monitoring forms and diaries would also be sought. Criteria for selection would include belief in the need for complete abstinence and the absence of gross psychopathology.

Those selected as potential candidates for AA and agreeing to the research follow-up procedures would then be told about the procedures, benefits, cost, and risks associated with AA and other programs in the agency or the community. The description of AA would include the conditions of referral established for the study (e.g., introduction to a sponsor of similar age, gender, social class, and interests). Subjects would then be asked to rate AA and each of the other programs with respect to attractiveness, expected benefits, and disadvantages.

Those having no strong preferences for particular forms of assistance would then be asked to take part in an experiment involving random assignment to AA or another program with similar goals. The investigator would explain that the experiment was needed to resolve genuine doubts about the relative effectiveness of different types of help and give details of the assignment process and other aspects of the study. Those agreeing to those conditions would then be randomly assigned to AA or to other programs.

Those in the AA condition would each be matched with an AA sponsor of the same gender, of a similar age, and, if possible, with similar interests. Sponsors would be recruited from those known personally and professionally to research staff. They would be selected from those who are confident in their own sobriety and prepared to accept that AA is not for everyone. Although some professionals seem to doubt that AA members can be so open-minded (Tournier, 1979), the author's experience is quite to the contrary.

Those assigned to the AA condition would be asked to accompany their sponsors to at least one AA meeting and, thereafter, to attend AA and engage in other AA-related activities as often as they wish. However, they would also be advised that they may find some groups more attractive than others and to attend several different groups. They would also be told that research shows that those who attend AA more frequently and become active in the movement do better than less frequent or less active members.

Both sponsors and clients would be asked to keep records of AA attendance and other relevant activities and events. Both would be interviewed at regular intervals over the follow-up period. This would be explained at the time of subject recruitment and both subjects and sponsors would sign the appropriate consent forms.

Interviews, questionnaires, and records and diaries kept by subjects and collaterals in both the AA and the control conditions would be used to keep track of AA related experiences, other life events, and of drinking and other behaviors over the follow-up period. This should be as long as possible but for at least 12 months. Those considered good candidates for AA, who agreed to follow-up but declined randomization and were thus given their treatment of choice, could also be followed up as comparison groups for those randomly assigned to AA or other interventions.

Over the follow-up period some of those in the control condition are likely to become involved with AA. However, the experiment would only be seriously compromised if the nature and extent of involvement with AA is comparable across all study conditions. One study suggests that, at least in the short term, this may be unlikely (Sisson & Mallams, 1981). This study involved the use of random assignment to two ways of making referrals to AA. In one condition subjects were simply given information about local AA groups and encouraged to attend. In the other condition counselors telephoned a local AA or Al-Anon member and let them speak to subjects about AA. The AA or Al-Alon member also offered to meet subjects, to telephone them before the next AA meeting, and to provide a lift to the meeting. The results showed that within one week, 100% of the experimental group attended at least one AA meeting, compared with none of the control group.

More studies are needed to monitor attendance rates of AA referrals and others over longer periods and, if these rates are similar, experiments involving assignments to AA and other conditions could use matched pairs of cases. If the results show that a control case has more involvement in AA than the matched experimental case, both cases would be dropped from the analysis.

What might be learned from such an experiment? Certainly, if AA is an effective therapeutic resource for referrals from professionals, the results should show this to be the case. The experimental group involves subjects expected to affiliate with AA and benefit from the experience. Short- and long-term outcomes comparable to those treated by other means should therefore be expected. Also, a cost-effectiveness analysis involving comparisons between the AA group and those provided professional treatments should be in AA's favor. However, even if the overall results are inconclusive, the study will still generate a great deal of information concerning the role of AA-related experiences and other factors in the recovery process. If the study involves a large number of heterogeneous cases, it should also tell us more about the benefits of matching cases to AA and the other programs studied.

Should such a study have high priority? Not to the exclusion of other types of studies and certainly not without pilot studies to assess the feasibility of the proposed methods. In particular, pilot studies are needed to determine the extent to which assisted referrals to AA (i.e., those introduced to matched sponsors) engage in the movement and the extent to which an experimental study would be compromised by control group members who become involved in AA. However, if the proposed study (or some variant) can be successfully implemented, additional studies using similar procedures could be used to evaluate AA as a primary or secondary resource for clinical subjects recruited at different sites (outpatient, residential, workplace).

Conclusion

The complexities of AA and the diversity of alcohol-related problems are such that no one study can be expected to do more than move us a few steps closer to a full understanding of this remarkable movement. Many more studies are needed, especially multidisciplinary, process, and process-outcome studies involving different AA groups and drinking populations. The value of these studies could be increased if investigators used similar methods and instruments, and opportunities for large-scale, multisite studies should therefore be explored.

The research community should also make every effort to foster acceptance for AA's evaluation among members of the general service board and members of local groups. Although the results of evaluative studies are likely to be mixed, there seems little doubt that AA is very helpful for some people. Thus, the movement has nothing to fear from studies that seek to learn more about the conditions in which its effects may be optimal.

It is also important to note that, with few exceptions, all the research methods and designs described in this chapter have been used in previous studies. There is no question that they represent feasible alternatives that do not conflict with AA traditions. It is especially noteworthy that these methods and designs do not conflict with the AA tradition of anonymity. This is because "the preservation of participants privacy and confidentiality is a stringent requirement for all current evaluative studies" (Sobell & Sobell, 1979).

Notes

This chapter concerns only studies that seek to assess the effectiveness of AA for specific individuals. Excluded are population studies that correlate AA membership rates with per capita consumption and rates of alcohol-related problems (Smart, Mann, & Anglin, 1989; Mann, Smart, & Anglin, 1988). The results of these studies are consistent with the proposition that the growth of AA in North America has contributed to recent declines in alcohol consumption, liver cirrhosis, and alcohol-related offenses. These are intriguing results, but further studies are needed to assess their generalizability and the extent to which the observed correlations reflect causal relationships.

The views expressed in this chapter are those of the author and do not necessarily represent those of the Addiction Research Foundation.

References

Bassin, A. (1975). Red white and blue poker chips: An A.A. behaviour modification technique. *American Psychologist, 30,* 695–696.

Bean-Bayog, M. (1991). The Lay Treatment Community. In P.E. Nathan, J.W. Langenbucher, B.S. McCrady, & W. Frankenstein (Eds.), *Annual review of addictions research and treatment, Vol. 1.* New York: Pergamon Press.

Bill, C. (1965). The growth and effectiveness of Alcoholics Anonymous in a southwestern city. *Quarterly Journal of Studies on Alcohol, 26,* 279–284.

Bradley, A.M. (1988). Keep them coming back: The case for a valuation of Alcoholics Anonymous. *Alcohol Health & Research World, 12,* 192–198.

Brandsma, J.M., Maultsby, M.C., & Walsh, R.J. (1980). *Outpatient treatment of alcoholism: A review and comparative study.* Baltimore, MD: University Park Press.

Brown, S. (1985). *Treating the alcoholic: A developmental model of recovery.* New York: Wiley.

Burt, D.W. (1975). A behaviourist looks at A.A. *Addictions, 22,* 56–69.

Cook, T.D., & Campbell, D.T. (1979). *Quasi-experimentation: Design and analysis issues for field settings.* Chicago: Rand McNally.

Dennis, M.L., & Boruch, R.F. (1989). Randomized field experiments for planning and testing projects in developing countries: Threshold conditions. *Evaluation Review, 13,* 292–309.

Ditman, K.S., Crawford, G.G., Forgy, E.W., Moskowitz, H., et al. (1967). A controlled experiment on the use of court probation for drunk arrests. *American Journal of Psychiatry, 124,* 160–163.

Emrick, C.D. (1987). Alcoholics Anonymous: Affiliation processes and effectiveness as treatment. *Alcoholism: Clinical and Experimental Research, 11,* 416–423.

Emrick, C.D., Tonigan, J.S., Montgomery, H., & Little, L. (1992, February 11–13). *Affiliation processes in and treatment outcomes of Alcoholics Anonymous: A meta-analysis of the literature.* Paper presented at conference on the evaluation of AA. Alburqueque, New Mexico.

Glaser, F.B., & Ogborne, A.C. (1982). Does AA really work? *British Journal of Addiction, 77,* 123–129.

Hudson, H.L. (1985). How and why Alcoholics Anonymous works for blacks. *Alcoholism Treatment Quarterly, 45,* 946–947.

Institute of Medicine. (1989). *Prevention and treatment of alcohol problems: Research opportunities.* Washington, DC: National Academy Press.

Kurtz, E. (1982). The intellectual significance of Alcoholics Anonymous. *Journal of Studies on Alcohol, 43,* 38–80.

Lettieri, D., Nelson, J.E., & Sayers, M. (Eds.). (1985). *Alcoholism treatment assessment research instruments.* Rockville, MD: National Institute on Alcohol Abuse and Alcoholism.

Mann, R.E., Smart, R.G., & Anglin, L. (1988). Are decreases in liver cirrhosis rates a result of increased treatment for alcoholism? *British Journal of Addiction, 83,* 683–688.

McCrady, B.S., & Irvine, S. (1988). Self-help groups. In R.K. Hester & W.R. Miller (Eds.), *Handbook of alcoholism treatment approaches: Effective alternatives.* New York: Pergamon Press.

Miller, W.R. (1976). Alcoholism scales and objective assessment methods: A review. *Psychological Bulletin, 83,* 649–674.

Miller, W.R. (1990). Spirituality: The silent dimension in addiction research—the 1990 Leonard Ball oration. *Drug and Alcohol Review, 9,* 259–266.

Miller, W.R., & Hester, R.K. (1986a). Matching problems with optimal treatments. In W.R. Miller & N. Heather (Eds.), *Treating addictive behaviours: Processes of change.* New York: Plenum Press.

Miller, W.R., & Hester, R.K. (1986b). The effectiveness of alcoholism treatment: What research reveals. In W.E. Miller & N. Heather (Eds.), *Treating addictive behaviours: Processes of change.* New York: Plenum Press.

Moos, R.H. (1974). *The social climate scales.* Palo Alto, CA: Consulting Psychologists Press.

Moos, R.H., & Finney, J.W. (1982). New directions in program evaluation: Implications for expanding the role of alcoholism researchers. *Future Directions in Alcohol Abuse Treatment Research Monograph #15,* U.S. Dept. of Health and Social Services, Washington, DC.

Ogborne, A.C. (1984). Issues in follow-up. In F.B. Glaser, H.M. Annis, H.A. Sinner, S. Pearlman, et al. (Eds.), *A system of health care delivery, Vol. 3.* Toronto: Addiction Research Foundation.

Ogborne, A.C., Sobell, M.B., & Sobell, L.C. (1985). The significance of environmental factors for the design and the evaluation of alcohol treatment programs. In M. Galizio, and S.A. Maisto (Eds.), *Determinants of substance abuse.* New York: Plenum Press.

Pearlman, S., Zweben, A., & Li, S. (1989). The comparability of solicited versus clinic subjects in alcohol treatment research. *British Journal of Addiction, 84,* 523–532.

Sheeren, M. (1988). The relationship between relapse and involvement in Alcoholics Anonymous. *Journal of Studies on Alcohol, 49,* 104–106.

Sisson, R., & Mallams, J.H. (1981). The use of systematic encouragement and community access procedures to increase attendance at Alcoholic Anonymous and Al-Anon meetings. *American Journal of Drug and Alcohol Abuse, 8,* 371–376.

Smart, R.G., Mann, R.E., & Anglin, L. (1989). Decreases in alcohol problems and increased Alcoholics Anonymous membership. *British Journal of Addiction, 84,* 507–514.

Sobell, M.B., Bruchu, S., Sobell, L.C., Roy, J., et al. (1987). Alcohol treatment outcome methodology state of the art 1980–1984. *Addictive Behaviours, 12,* 113–128.

Sobell, M.B., & Sobell, L.C. (1979). Comments on paper by Tournier. *Journal of Studies on Alcohol, 40,* 320–322.

Tournier, R.E. (1979). Alcoholics Anonymous as treatment and as ideology. *Journal of Studies on Alcohol, 40,* 230–239.

Vaillant, G. (1983). *The natural history of alcoholism.* Cambridge, MA: Harvard University Press.

Walsh, D.C., Hingson, R.W., Merrigan, D.M., Levenson, S.M., et al. (1991). A randomized trial of treatment options for alcohol-abusing workers. *New England Journal of Medicine, 325,* 775–78.

CHAPTER 20

Process Research Perspectives in Alcoholics Anonymous: Measurement of Process Variables

LARRY E. BEUTLER, JASNA JOVANOVIC, AND REBECCA E. WILLIAMS

Participation in meetings of Alcoholics Anonymous (AA) is, undoubtedly, the most frequently prescribed treatment[1] for alcohol-dependent individuals. Most practitioners and participants alike seem to consider it to be an effective group intervention and typically prescribe it in preference to conventional group therapies (Flores, 1988). Because it enjoys this prominence in the alcohol-treatment field, AA represents the standard against which all conventional alcohol treatments must be judged. Yet, paradoxically, the efficacy of AA as a group treatment method has not been systematically established, precluding the presence of an accurate baseline against which either to evaluate the effects of other treatments or to assess advancements.

Comparative research has been hampered both by constraints imposed by the doctrine and philosophy of AA and by features of its treatment format. The 12-step and conventional psychotherapy programs propose a different set of constructs by which they explain how change occurs. As a consequence, the format and methods through which change is accomplished in AA are quite different from the formats and techniques that are ordinarily used in group psychotherapies. While there are likely to be similarities as well as differences in the processes of change in the two methods, it is not known if the processes which contribute to changes via AA and conventional psychotherapy methods actually arise from a common set of variables or if they can be attributed to methods that are unique to each treatment. Concomitantly, the measures that are used to assess the processes of change in group treatment methods are not readily adaptable to some AA formats and do not address many of the concepts that are considered to be central to change within this philosophy. These constraints add to the many problems that already face those who do research on group methods and arise because of the complexity of identifying and measuring group processes.

357

As the foregoing suggests, a central concern in any research on AA is the identification of a suitable comparison group. For a variety of ethical, methodological, and practical reasons, a comparison of AA and conventional group psychotherapies is advantageous. However, in order to compare AA to conventional group therapy methods, it may be necessary to identify the variety and distinctiveness of treatment processes to which change is attributed in the two approaches.

The treatment implications of identifying the relationships between processes and outcomes in AA and conventional group methods are manifold. Most obvious among these is the observation that if 12-step and conventional therapies exert their effects through similar mechanisms, then they may be assigned as alternative, interchangeable interventions. In this event, the two treatments can be considered to be logical equivalents and be assigned in order to fit the varying circumstances and the preferences of different clients and clinicians. Alternatively, if these two forms of treatment exert effects through separate and distinctive mechanisms of action, then they must be assigned either as complementary and coexisting treatments or, discriminatively, as a function of the empirically derived indicators and contraindicators presented by different patients.

In order to develop methods that will address the important questions of therapeutic mechanisms, this chapter will outline some of the constraints imposed on research both because of the distinctive philosophies of AA as compared to conventional group psychotherapy methods and because of the methodological weaknesses that characterize contemporary treatment research more generally. Specifically, we will (1) identify the philosophical assumptions and misconceptions that distinguish the mechanism through which change is assumed to occur in AA, (2) introduce some postulated mechanisms of change that AA may share with group therapy, (3) compare the varying formats used to evoke change processes by 12-Step and group therapy models, (4) outline some of the more practical methods of measuring group processes, and (5) propose some methods for evaluating the relationship between therapeutic processes and outcomes that both characterize and distinguish AA relative to other group methods.

Mechanisms of Change in AA

AA provides its members with a strong sense of support and identification, which is characteristic of most helpful groups. However, AA promotes its own unique ideology, which contrasts with more conventional psychotherapeutic theories. This philosophy has spurred considerable controversy that, in turn, has resulted in an unbreachable rift between the professionals and lay professionals who work with alcoholics. Indeed, as Flores (1988) points out:

> Alcoholics Anonymous, in the eyes of many professionals and researchers, is a much maligned, beleaguered and misunderstood organization. Many of AA's harshest critics... fail to understand the subtleties of the AA program and often erroneously attribute qualities and characteristics to the organization that are one-dimensional, misleading, and even border on slanderous. (p. 203)

Perhaps because alcoholism has rendered such a devastating effect on the personal and family lives of so many and because its treatment has been accepted as the province of medicine, religion, law, psychology, and public health, to name a few, opinions about its nature have been exceptionally diverse and the adherents to its various treatments have come to espouse their views with more religious-like fervor than with scientific restraint. Alcohol dependence has variously been attributed to moral, situational, characterological, and temperamental factors, usually depending more upon the background of the proponent than upon the nature of the alcoholic. As the most visible of the treatments, and as one whose stated philosophies embody both medical, religious, and psychological concepts, AA has congealed as the focus for much of the controversy in the field. Because of the intensity of the feelings and beliefs that characterize both its advocates and adversaries, it is critically important to understand the philosophy of AA and to identify the mechanisms that are thought to facilitate change in this approach. Only then can these mechanisms be subjected to empirical study and contrasted with those that operate in conventional group methods.

Flores (1988) argues that there are a number of common misconceptions regarding AA. Dispelling these misconceptions is, perhaps, necessary if the process of AA is to be better understood. Among the most prominent of these misconceptions are the beliefs that:

1. *AA promulgates a simplistic, naive disease concept of alcoholism.* Flores observes that quite the opposite is true. AA considers alcoholism as a "four-fold disease," incorporating mental, physical, emotional, and spiritual components.
2. *AA ignores psychological etiological factors.* It is only the first step of the AA program that addresses drinking, the remaining eleven steps are dedicated to what AA calls "the removal of character defects" (Flores, 1988).
3. *AA is a substitute dependency.* This viewpoint may have been born out of a popular psychology that devalued anything less than complete autonomy and independence. Flores (1988) maintains that "what gets

passed off as dependency by AA's critics is actually the alcoholic's investment of him/herself in relationships with the AA fellowship" (p. 216).

4. *AA forces members to admit to being alcoholic.* In principle, the responsibility of identifying whether or not one is "alcoholic" is that of the individual rather than that of others. The only requirement for membership is a desire to stop drinking (AA, 1955). An individual is only an alcoholic if he or she elects to define himself or herself in this way.

5. *AA rejects controlled drinking on purely ideological grounds.* While AA members have strong convictions regarding an alcoholic's ability to control his or her drinking, Flores (1988) suggests that these convictions are not due to ideological beliefs as much as to members' own histories of failure in maintained controlled drinking.

6. *AA is a religious organization.* The term "God" is either used or referred to in five of the 12 steps. However, God is defined as a "higher power" and, ostensibly, can be extracted from a religious context and taken to be natural forces other than deity. Flores (1988) points out that it is up to AA members to come to their own personal understanding of the meaning and significance of this higher power.

Both Flores (1988) and Thune (1977) provide an alternative conception of AA in which alcoholism is a lifestyle in which the misuse of alcohol is only one component. Cessation of drinking is only the necessary first step in the adoption of a new way of life and a new sense of self-worth and self-respect (Flores, 1988).

The recipe for altering an alcoholic lifestyle is outlined in AA's 12 steps (see Table 1). The 12 steps establish the principles of spiritual change. If practiced, it is assumed that these steps expel obsessions to drink and enable the sufferer to become happily and usefully whole (Alcoholics Anonymous, 1952).

Antze (1976) explains the nature of this 12-step program by highlighting five essential points of AA's philosophy. First, the nature of alcoholism is viewed as a disease, one over which the alcoholic has no control. Second, AA teaches that recovery can only begin after the alcoholic experiences complete despair ("hitting bottom") and is compelled to the realization that he or she is not in control. Third, the emphasis on the existence of "a power greater than oneself" must be accepted. Fourth, AA teaches that recovery can only be achieved through the steps of confession, forgiveness, and amends toward others. Finally, it is assumed that only other alcoholics can help alcoholics. Through this tradition of "12th-stepping" members learn that they can make a difference and be of importance to someone else (Flores, 1988).

Although noting the saliency of this ideology, Antze (1976) concludes that the primary therapeutic function of AA is dispelling a member's

TABLE 1
The 12 Steps of Alcoholics Anonymous[2]

1. We admitted we were powerless over alcohol—that our lives had become unmanageable.

2. Came to believe that a Power greater than ourselves could restore us to sanity.

3. Made a decision to turn our will and our lives over to the care of God as we understood Him.

4. Made a searching and fearless moral inventory of ourselves.

5. Admitted to God, to ourselves and to another human being the exact nature of our wrongs.

6. Were entirely ready to have God remove all these defects of character.

7. Humbly asked Him to remove our shortcomings.

8. Made a list of all persons we had harmed, and became willing to make amends to them all.

9. Made direct amends to such people wherever possible, except when to do so would injure them or others.

10. Continued to take personal inventory and when we were wrong promptly admitted it.

11. Sought through prayer and meditation to improve our conscious contact with God, as we understood Him, praying only for knowledge of His will for us and the power to carry that out.

12. Having had a spiritual awakening as the result of these steps, we tried to carry this message to alcoholics, and to practice these principles in all our affairs.

"sense of agency" (p. 332) while providing the member with the ability to accept personal limitations. This function is facilitated by feelings of being in the group. That is, AA group meetings and relationships break the cycle of interpersonal isolation and provide members with a place for testing new ways of dealing with their emotions and problems (Flores, 1988). In these respects, the functions and philosophies of AA appear to share much with other group methods. Hence, it is important to explore the possible relationships between the curative factors of group therapy methods and the processes that take place in AA.

Shared Processes of Change

Self-help groups or peer group organizations that do not rely on theoretically driven clinical practices but demonstrate consistent successes have been studied broadly by psychotherapy researchers as avenues to understanding therapeutic processes of groups (Antze, 1976; Bond, Borman, Bankoff, Lieberman, Daiter, & Videka, 1979; Lieberman, 1975, 1990a, 1990b; Lieberman & Borman, 1976; Yalom, 1985). Antze (1976), for example, suggests that self-help groups achieve their results through the use of simple social-psychological processes such as confession, catharsis, and mutual identification. Similarly, Lieberman (1990a) highlights three basic elements shared by all self-help groups: intensity of need, the requirements to share something personal, and the real or perceived similarity in members' suffering.

The focus on a common predicament or problem that is shared among all members is considered to be a powerful precipitant of change for all self-help groups, including AA. However, this quality is not unique to this modality but is rather a common factor in many formal group therapies.

Pratt, the founding father of group therapy, posited that factors such as reeducation, camaraderie, healthy emulation (modeling and imitation), instillation of a spirit of hope, raising morale, suggestion, persuasion, correcting destructive habit patterns, stirring and redirecting emotions, instilling common sense, and the development of new habits of thought were active in the group process. Subsequently, Yalom (1970, 1985), in his extensive work with groups, identified 12 curative factors operating in group psychotherapy: altruism, catharsis, existential factors, group cohesiveness, guidance, identification, instillation of hope, interpersonal input, interpersonal output, insight, recapitulation of the primary family, and universality.

Such curative factors are similar to the forces postulated to be effective in AA. Indeed, Flores (1988) suggests that although AA and other group therapy formats may differ in the mechanisms used to instigate change, the effective processes are similar. Yalom (1985), however, contends that some of the primary curative factors in group therapy are more active than others in the AA format, raising the possibility that different patterns of factors may be at work in the two treatment models. He suggests that the most active factors in AA include: instillation of hope, imparting information, universality, altruism, and some aspects of group cohesiveness.

In a review of the literature on AA, Emrick, Lassen, and Edwards (1977) identified the direct and indirect references to variables that could be linked to Yalom's 12 curative factors. They assumed that the frequency with which various factors were mentioned in the literature was an index of the importance of the role each factor played in AA. A summary of the frequencies with which each of Yalom's curative factors was referenced in Emrick et al.'s (1977) review is presented in Table 2. Based on their review, these authors concluded that interpersonal learning-output, catharsis, insight, and family reenactment operate in AA groups in a similar way as they do in other groups. However, Emrick et al. (1977) did observe distinctive qualities among those who participated in AA. When compared to those in traditional treatments, AA participants were more "responsive to peers, drawn towards a spiritually-oriented approach, com-

TABLE 2
Frequency of Publications Referring to Curative Factors Operative
in Alcoholics Anonymous Groups

Curative Factors	Number of Publications (*N* = 26)
Altruism	21
Group cohesiveness	20
Identification	14
Instillation of hope	12
Guidance	12
Universality	10
Catharsis	8
"Insight"	6
Interpersonal learning, "output"	2
Family reenactment	1
Interpersonal learning, "input"	0
Existential awareness	0

Source: Emrick, Lassen, & Edwards (1977)

fortable talking about their alcoholism in front of large groups and enjoy socializing with reformed alcoholics" (p. 138).

As this brief review will attest, the paucity of research on the process of AA has made it difficult to evaluate the role of the curative factors. One of the major obstacles to this effort is similar to that which faces research on other group treatment methods; namely, the role of various processes are difficult to determine if the methods used to effect change are unclear. In this case, an assessment of the curative factors in AA depends on understanding the nature of the procedures that are used to both convey philosophical information and to promote change.

AA vs. Group Therapy Formats

Both within and across communities, considerable variation exists in the groups operated by and in the name of Alcoholics Anonymous (Thune, 1977). The size of AA groups range from small, intimate meetings to large, lecture hall meetings. Moreover, attendance is inconsistent. Members are not "required" to attend a specific number of meetings; some members attend meetings sporadically while others may go to two or three meetings in one day. Slogans such as "keep coming back" or "90 meetings in 90 days" for newcomers are very much embedded in the AA program. All these variations are compounded by the adoption of the

12-step philosophy by professionally run treatment programs that often require attendance, utilize professional leaders, and structure the nature of meetings.

Broadly speaking, there are two distinct types of group formats within the AA structure—the "speaker meeting" format and the "discussion meeting" format. Both are distinguished from traditional group therapy methods by the proscription against cross-talk in the group interaction. In the speaker meeting format, veteran members tell of their struggles with alcohol, usually by reviewing their "life histories." Each speaker, in turn, presents his or her scenario of drinking and recovery. Thune (1977) concludes that these life history confessions are a key element in AA's practice and theory.

In contrast and with the exception of interactive cross-talk, the discussion format more closely approximates traditional group therapy formats (Thune, 1977). The meeting revolves around a topic usually suggested by the chairperson, and these topics range from a focus on personal problems (e.g., How does one deal with anxiety?) to theoretical and philosophical issues (e.g., Have I had my last "drunk"? or What do we mean by a "higher power"?). Occasionally, members suggest a discussion topic that is only indirectly related to drinking (e.g., procrastination) and individual members speak about his/her sobriety as it relates to the topic at hand.

AA groups also vary along other dimensions. Some meetings are open to anyone who wishes to attend, while others are closed (i.e., the same individuals attend each meeting). There are "newcomer meetings," where newly sober individuals are encouraged to attend; smoking and nonsmoking meetings; same sex meetings; and gay and lesbian meetings. There are also meetings called "Step Study" where a particular one of the 12 steps is chosen and the discussion is restricted to this topic. These latter meetings sometimes assume a format that is similar to a school classroom.

The mutual vulnerability that arises from the presence of a shared problem among self-help groups is enhanced somewhat uniquely in AA by an emphasis on public self-disclosure in all or most of the meeting formats. This self-disclosure is considered to be one of the most powerful healing mechanisms of AA (Kurtz, 1982). In order to stimulate self-disclosure, AA group leaders are invariably "sober" or recovering alcoholics who provide additional testimony of downfall and salvation. Yalom (1985) posits that the use of ex-drinkers as group leaders provides members with living models and inspiration, which is, perhaps, one of AA's greatest strengths.

Unlike self-disclosure in group therapy, alcoholics in AA are encouraged to express (or confess) their powerlessness over their problem (Flores, 1988). The explicit emphasis upon confessing helplessness contrasts with the emphasis on empowerment and self-determination that characterizes most theories of psychotherapy.

AA meetings focus on behaviors and situations external to the group that constitute danger or promote abstinence. This is in contrast to traditional therapy groups that tend to focus more on here-and-now interactions. Anderson (1982) observes that the formats and methods of AA are designed to gratify dependency needs, while the formats and procedures of group psychotherapy do so only enough to keep the client in treatment. As a result of their contradictory meta-messages, however, clinicians often observe that, in group therapy, AA members seem unable to relinquish an AA focus and tend to avoid openness and self-exploration (Brown & Yalom, 1977).

Clearly, there are a number of problems in applying concepts of group therapy process research to the AA format. Some of the more notable include the wide variability in format, lack of precisely defined methods, variations in group size, inconsistency of attendance in meetings, issues of confidentiality, and member willingness to self-disclose. All these problems add to the complexities of assessing the role of the philosophical underpinnings of AA and makes the task of evaluating this group process quite difficult.

Assessing Group Process in Alcoholics Anonymous

If identifying and measuring the processes that are important in individual psychotherapy are difficult, then identifying and measuring group processes are compounded several fold. Potentially, each dyad in the group, each triad, each quatrad, etc., exerts a distinct and synergistic effect on each member of the group. The group format assumes that indirect, vicarious, and secondary experiences are as important to the healing process as the direct interactions occurring between a therapist and a client.

The selection of an appropriate strategy to assess group process is a difficult task (Lieberman, Yalom, & Miles, 1973), made all the more complex because the curative factors and formats used in AA are at variance with those processes for which measures are readily available. While none tap all the dimensions that may characterize both AA and group therapy, there are many group process measures that have been used by researchers to examine components of applicable and diverse group environments. A representative list of group process measures that have been developed by researchers to examine varying components of the group environment is presented in Table 3.

As indicated in Table 3, there are two basic assessment formats used in process research: observational methods and self-report/phenomenological methods. Observational methods frequently involve the training and ratings of independent clinicians, although occasionally therapists and other group participants serve as the observers for the application of

TABLE 3
Group Process Measures

Measure	Reference	Focus	Format	Scales/Scores	Reliability
Behavior Scores System	Borgatta, 1963	Peer behavior assessments	Observational—peer and self assessments	1. Neutral assertions 2. Assertions 3. Antagonistic acts 4. Withdrawal acts 5. Supportive acts 6. Assertive supportive acts	Not indicated
Critical-Incident Form	MacKenzie, 1983	Anecdotal data of important issues at session rated for critical incidents	Self-report—answers rated by objective clinicians	1. Self-understanding 2. Self-disclosure 3. Learning from interpersonal actions 4. Instillation of hope 5. Vicarious learning 6. Acceptance 7. Universality 8. Altruism 9. Catharsis 10. Guidance	Kappa coefficient for interrater reliability, .28 to .35.
Curative Factors in Group (Rankings)	Rohrbaugh & Bartels, 1975	Participants perceptions of importance of curative factors	Q-Sort 60 items	Yalom's (1970) 12 curative factors	Demonstrated construct validity
Group Climate Questionnaire—Short Form	MacKenzie, 1983	Interpersonal behavior as perceived by group members	Self-report	1. Engaged 2. Avoiding 3. Conflict	Interscale correlations, −.18 to −.44

Instrument	Author	Focus	Method	Dimensions	Reliability
Group Environment Scale	Moos, 1986	Group climate	Self-report	1. Cohesion 2. Leader support 3. Expressiveness 4. Independence 5. Task orientation 6. Self discovery 7. Anger/aggression 8. Order/organization 9. Leader control 10. Innovation	Internal consistency, .62 to .86. Test-retest reliabilities, .65 to .87
Group Interaction Profile	Anchor, 1973	Quantitative measure of self-disclosure	Observational—participants' statements categorized into four areas: personal material, impersonal material, related to group, unrelated to group	Statements categorized into four areas: 1. Personal 2. Material 3. Related to group 4. Unrelated to group	Interrater reliability, .89; coefficient of agreement, $k = .81$
Group Rating Schedule	Cooper, 1977	Stress- or growth-related effects on experimental learning	Observational—rated by trained observers using Likert-type items	Five factors: 1. Process orientation 2. Social atmosphere 3. Trainer involvement 4. Relationship between trainer and participant 5. Participant emotional cohesiveness	Interrater reliabilities, .75 to .81

TABLE 3
(continued)

Measure	Reference	Focus	Format	Scales/Scores	Reliability
Helping Processes Questionnaire	Wollart, 1986	Perceived freqency of helping activities	Self-report	27 activities are rated on a 5-point scale where 1 = "an inaccurate description" to 5 = "a very accurate description"	.87 correlation between item means across two studies reported as evidence of reliability
Hill Interaction Matrix	Hill, 1965	Content and style of group interactions to determine therapeutic quality	Tape-recorded transcriptions coded by trained raters	Interactions coded into a Content/Style × Work/Style matrix. Contents categories are: 1. Topic 2. Group 3. Personal 4. Relationship Work categories are: 1. Responsive 2. Conventional 3. Assertive 4. Speculative 5. Confrontive	70% rater agreement
Interaction Process Analysis	Bales, 1950	Task and social-emotional behavior (emphasis on problem solving behavior)	Observational—trained observers use an interaction recorder	Interactions coded into 12 categories: 1. Shows solidarity 2. Shows tension release	Interrater reliabilities, .75 and .95

				3. Agrees 4. Gives suggestion 5. Gives opinion 6. Gives orientation 7. Asks for orientation 8. Asks for opinion 9. Asks for suggestion 10. Disagrees 11. Shows tension 12. Shows antagonism	
Personal Anticipations Questionnaire	Lieberman, Yalom, & Miles, 1973	Expectations about value of group experience	Self-report	Total score indicating high or low expectation level	Not indicated
Process Analysis Scoring System	Gibbard & Hartman, 1973	Member-leader relationships and member-member elements	Observational	Four categories are rated: 1. Hostility 2. Affection 3. Power relations 4. Ego states	Not indicated
Self-Reference Content Analysis	Reisel, 1978	Styles of self-disclosure	Tape-recorded transcriptions	Frequencies tallied in three "thought units" categories: 1. Self exclusively 2. Self as affected by group 3. Self as affecting group	Not indicated

TABLE 3
(continued)

Measure	Reference	Focus	Format	Scales/Scores	Reliability
Self-Reported Change Mechanism	Lieberman, 1983; Lieberman, Yalom, & Miles, 1973	Anecdotal data of what was important to participant	Self-report—responses coded by raters	22 categories including: positive/negative feelings, self-disclosure, feedback, experiencing intense emotions, cognitive events/experiences, communion/similarity, altruism, spectatorism, involvement, advice getting, modeling, experimentation, inculcation of hope, reexperiencing the group as a family	Not indicated
Wisconsin Relationship Orientation Scale	Danish, 1971	Relationship between leader and member as perceived by member	Ratings of leader by group leader	Score indicating how willing a member is to self-disclose to group leader	Not indicated

Source: Adapted in part from Fuhriman & Packard (1986).

these procedures. Lieberman (1983) observes that an advantage to observational methods is that they allow for the recognition of behaviorally embedded transactions and can provide assessments of the intensity and frequency of certain classes of behavior that may not be captured by a participant's self-report. However, Lieberman, Yalom, and Miles (1973) concede that observer ratings may not capture a participant's experience of intense emotion if it is not manifested in a behavior that is discernible to an observer. For example, "universality," expressed as the awareness that there are many others like oneself, is not assumed to be manifest in any particular set of behaviors (Lieberman, 1983). Hence, for observers, the task is to learn to consistently extrapolate a common or core quality from idiosyncratic behaviors and assess its intensity relative to that experienced by others. This is not an easy task in the absence of external criteria of intensity. The selection, rating, and training of raters becomes critically important. Beutler and Hill (1992) have provided some guidelines for this process. These include the following:

1. *Use an adequate number of raters.* Generally, at least two raters should be used when the scale is ordinal and three judges are recommended for nominal scales. For measures with low reliability, more raters should be used because adding raters and pooling their data increase the reliability of all such measures.

2. *Select raters carefully.* Giving potential raters a chance to rate a sample task is a useful selection device. The ability to do this trial task will provide an approximation of how adequately raters will perform the actual task. Once selected, it may be useful to select more raters than will be needed, with the expectation that some will drop out and others will need to be dropped because of unreliability.

3. *Reduce the effects of rater bias.* Since all observer ratings are partially influenced by their own standing on the dimensions being rated (Hill, O'Grady, & Price, 1988), reliability estimates could be improved by selecting raters who are homogeneous on personality or history dimensions. However, this would introduce a systematic bias in the direction of the homogeneity. A reasonable solution to the bias problem is to choose a group of raters who cover a range on the problematic personality characteristics. This will tend to yield lower interrater reliabilities than the foregoing procedure, but the validity of the ratings can be expected to be improved. Increasing the number of raters may be necessary to offset this problem.

4. *Provide raters with systematic training.* In general, the more abstract the ratings, the longer the training will need to be to achieve desired levels of reliability and validity. Establishing interrater agreement and comparing ratings against those of a standard calibration sample of group work helps to ensure that the ratings reflect constant levels of magnitude as well as rank order.

5. *Keep the ratings independent.* After raters are trained in regard to criteria, all data should be judged independently by judges prior to discussion. Reliability estimates should be calculated on these independent judgments, even if the ratings are combined or if consensus ratings are used in the data analysis. Similarly, if not all raters will be rating every piece of data, rating teams should be rotated so that the error associated with each rater gets spread around.

6. *Provide controls for correcting rater drift.* With increasing time on task, raters tend to become less attuned to nuances in the data and make snap judgments. One way to maintain group morale, to reduce rater drift, and to prevent raters from developing idiosyncratic ways of interpreting items is to have regular meetings at which ratings are reviewed and discussed. Criteria of reliability should be rechecked and the calibration tapes used in initial training should be reused at randomly prescribed intervals in order to maintain criteria levels for magnitude ratings.

As these guidelines would suggest, observational measures are very time consuming and expensive. However, self-report measures, while quick and reliable, suffer from idiosyncratic response tendencies, are subject to falsification, and fail to tap experiences with which the subject is unfamiliar or untrained to observe. Therefore, some combination of self-report and observational methods will be required to adequately assess the effects of AA. Unfortunately, measures that utilize both observational and self-report formats to assess the same dimensions frequently have low reliabilities. Hence, it may currently be necessary to utilize different scales and to evaluate slightly different dimensions with self-report and observational measures. Among the most promising, at least in terms of coverage and reliability, are instruments like the Group Interaction Profile and the Group Rating Schedule, which provide observational measures, and the Group Environment Scale, which is a self-report measure.

Discussion and Recommendations

Due to the complex, divergent nature of the structure and format of Alcoholics Anonymous groups, the inaccessibility of conducting research within this group structure, and the predicament of locating and developing appropriate instruments for assessment of group process, there seem to be no definitive answers as to whether the factors that affect group therapy are also at work in AA. Moreover, it is not clear whether the common or specific factors are actually at work within AA. Research on this topic is critically needed.

Designing a study that includes an assessment of the group processes that characterize and distinguish Alcoholics Anonymous is not simple.

The format of AA meetings—large groups, inconsistent attendance, and anonymity—present researchers with logistical problems. In order to assess processes of change, Emrick and his colleagues (1977) advocated a randomized clinical trials comparison of psychotherapy and AA groups using Yalom's instrument for measuring members' perceptions of the curative factors.

Our review, to this point, suggests that process evaluations must not only include an assessment of dimensions that are considered to be common to helping groups, as proposed by Emrick et al. (1977), but must also include other measures as well. Relationships with the therapist, attachment to other group members, and identification with the group must be included along with aspects of the group process that promote emotional expression, behavioral enactment and change, insight, reconceptualization, and hope. Accordingly, Emrick et al. (1977) suggested that research be directed to an exploration of the variables on which clients may be matched to different treatments. They suggest that this match be focused, at least in part, upon the personality characteristics that may predispose subjects to be differentially suited either to AA or to professional care.

In addition, process evaluation must taken into account the qualities and variables that are considered to be unique to AA. Specifically, an assessment of the degree of adherence to and belief in the 12 steps is necessary in order to determine the particular ways in which AA may operate. At the same time, a comparison with group therapy must include an assessment of the degree to which demand characteristics (i.e., the responses evoked or required by the methods) distinguish the philosophies of group therapy from those in self-help groups. Doing so, however, will probably mean that considerable research attention be devoted to instrument development, since there are currently no methods that assess processes that appear unique to AA and that can readily be applied across a variety of psychotherapeutic formats.

In developing these measures, one must be sensitive to the various formats and techniques used to effect change within, as well as between AA and group therapies of various types. The influences of concomitant therapies, including the possibility that AA members attend various types of groups at the same time, must also be considered. Group structure, variation of member participation, attendance rates, leader characteristics, and other member composition must all be taken into account as covarying factors of the format and process. This means that process evaluations must not depend upon the continuing availability of any subject, requiring that many of these ratings will be observer-based rather than self-reports.

When ratings are applied to the formats of treatment, special problems are encountered. In psychotherapy research it has become conventional to manualize the targeted treatment in order to reduce the idiosyncratic effects of therapists. Accordingly, manuals have been developed for different populations and modalities (Lambert & Ogles, 1988). However, AA formats cannot be manualized easily because of their variable structure, the presence of philosophical opposition, and their (often) leaderless style. Hence, the qualities of the group process that are considered to be essential to the method must be identified and ratings made of the degree to which the leader or the group complies with these criteria. This will help the investigator determine the relationship between key ingredients of the AA process and treatment effects.

We believe that longitudinal studies of participating individuals through systematic $N = 1$ study designs are necessary to evaluate the effects of AA and will supplement group designs. This may include post hoc analyses of individuals who benefit, or fail to benefit, from different treatments as well as prospective, multiple baseline and replication studies of single individuals over time. The use of individual analyses is necessary because of the wide inconsistency and lack of uniformity of attendance that characterizes AA participation and because the nature of relevant processes is still too unclear to identify variables toward which current measurement procedures might be targeted. Systematic $N = 1$ studies allow a close inspection of idiosyncratic processes and may serve as a means of clarifying the nature and identity of processes that are relevant to AA.

Multivariate correlational methods such as P-technique factor analysis (Cattell, Cattell, & Rhymer, 1947) provide a way to examine intraindividual change. In P-technique, one person's responses or measurements on many variables are intercorrelated across many occasions and factor analyzed (Roberts & Nesselroade, 1986). Such a factor analysis of $N = 1$ data provides a description of the pattern of covariation over the set of variables and occasions involved (Cattell, 1963). This description is in the form of factors that index the complexity of change processes across the measured time period. The patterning of the factors indicates the structure or nature of those changes (Jones & Nesselroade, 1991).

Mintz and Luborsky's (1970) description of a male college freshman's course of psychotherapy serves as a clear example of the power of P-technique. Transcripts from nine of the 12 treatment sessions from one patient were segmented into therapist and patient statements. These segments were then coded by three raters on a series of 16 variables. The resultant data generated a correlation matrix that was then factor analyzed, and four factors emerged: "patient health," "therapist natural," "patient involvement," and "therapist empathic." Factor scores for each of the factors were examined for trends over time. As a result of this analysis, Mintz and Luborsky (1970) found that of the four factors only patient health and patient involvement exhibited significant changes across time.

Clearly, a multivariate, single-subject, repeated measures design P-technique study could be instrumental in elucidating the change mechanisms involved in AA. When applied to broadly based measures that both combine rating sources and are maintained at reliable levels, such strategies may yield a basis for systematic, clinical trials. Progressive investigations that apply increasingly standardized treatments, representing varieties both of AA and psychotherapy formats, may be particularly helpful in ferreting out the differences between AA and psychotherapy outcomes.

Acknowledgments

Work on this chapter was partially supported by grant no. RO1-AA08970 from the National Institute on Alcohol Abuse and Alcoholism to Larry E. Beutler. Jasna Jovanovic was the project coordinator and Rebecca E. Williams was a graduate research assistant on the project. Theodore Jacob and Varda Shoham-Salomon from Stanford University and the University of Arizona, respectively, served as co–principal investigators.

Notes

1. Although AA does not accept the term *treatment* to describe its activities and objectives, attendance at meetings is frequently "prescribed" by caregivers and often is required as part of a comprehensive treatment program. Hence, we have used the term treatment throughout this chapter in order to draw attention to the significance of AA meetings and philosophy in the treatment arena. Nonetheless, the reader should be aware that controversy revolves around such prescriptive and required participation in AA.
2. "The Twelve Steps are reprinted with permission of Alcoholics Anonymous World Services, Inc. Permission to reprint the Twelve Steps does not mean that A.A. has reviewed or approved the contents of this publication, nor that A.A. agrees with the views expressed herein. A.A. is a program of recovery from alcoholism—use of the Twelve Steps in connection with programs and activities which are patterned after A.A., but which address other problems, does not imply otherwise."

References

Alcoholics Anonymous. (1952). *Twelve steps and twelve traditions.* New York: Alcoholics Anonymous World Services.

Alcoholics Anonymous. (1955). *The story of how many thousands of men and women have recovered from alcoholism.* New York: Alcoholics Anonymous World Services.

Anderson, S.C. (1982). Group therapy with alcoholic clients: A review. *Advances in Alcohol and Substance Abuse, 2,* 23–40.

Anchor, K.N. (1973). *Interaction processes in experimental massed and spaced group experiences.* Paper presented at Midwestern Psychological Association, Chicago, Ill.

Antze, P. (1976). The role of ideologies in peer group organizations: Some theoretical considerations and three case studies. *Journal of Applied Behavioral Science, 12,* 323–346.

Bales, R.F. (1950). *Interaction Process Analysis: A method for the study of small groups.* Cambridge, MA: Addison-Wesley.

Beutler, L.E., & Hill, C.E. (1992). Process and outcome research in the treatment of adult victims of childhood sexual abuse: Methodological issues. *Journal of Consulting and Clinical Psychology, 60,* 204–212.

Bond, G.R., Borman, L.D., Bankoff, E., Lieberman, M.A., Daiter, S., & Videka, L. (1979, January/February). Mended hearts: A self-help case study. *Social Policy,* 50–57.

Borgatta, E.F. (1963). A new systematic interaction observation system: Behavior scores system. *Journal of Psychological Studies, 14,* 24–44.

Brown, S., & Yalom, I. Interactional group therapy with alcoholics. *Journal of Studies on Alcohol, 38,* 426–456.

Cattell, R.B. (1963). The structuring of change by P-technique and incremental R-technique. In C.W. Harris (Ed.), *Problems in measuring change* (pp. 167–198). Madison: University of Wisconsin Press.

Cattell, R.B., Cattell, A.K.S., & Rhymer, R.M. (1947). P-technique demonstrated in determining psycho-physiological source traits in a normal individual. *Psychometrika, 12,* 267–288.

Cooper, C. (1977). Adverse and growthful effects of experimental learning groups: The role of the trainer, participant, and group characteristics. *Human Relations, 30,* 1103–1129.

Danish, S.J. (1971). Factors influencing changes in empathy following a group experience. *Journal of Counseling Psychology, 18,* 262–267.

Emrick, C.D., Lassen, C.L., & Edwards, M.T. (1977). Nonprofessional peers as therapeutic agents in effective psychotherapies. In G.E. German & A. Rozin (Eds.), *The therapist contribution to effective psychotherapy: An empirical assessment.* Elmsford, NY: Pergamon Press.

Flores, P.J. (1988). *Group psychotherapy with addicted populations.* New York: Haworth Press.

Fuhriman, A., & Packard, R. (1986). Group process instruments: Therapeutic themes and issues. *International Journal of Group Psychotherapy, 36,* 399–425.

Gibbard, G.S., & Hartman, J.J. (1973). The oedipal paradigm in group development: A clinical and empirical study. *Small Group Behavior, 4,* 305–354.

Hill, C.E., O'Grady, K.E., & Price, P. (1988). A method for investigating sources of rater bias. *Journal of Counseling Psychology, 35,* 346–350.

Hill, W.F. (1965). *Hill Interaction Matrix* (rev. ed.). Los Angeles: Youth Studies Center, University of Southern California.

Jones, C.J., & Nesselroade, J.R. (1991). *The multivariate, replicated, single-subject repeated measures designs and P-technique factor analysis: A review of intraindividual change studies.* Unpublished manuscript, Pennsylvania State University.

Kurtz, E. (1982). Why AA works. The intellectual significance of Alcoholics Anonymous. *Journal of Studies on Alcohol, 40,* 230–239.

Lambert, M.J., & Ogles, B.M. (1988). Treatment manuals: Problems and promise. *Journal of Integrative and Eclectic Psychotherapy, 7,* 187–204.

Lieberman, M.A. (1975). Some limits to research on T-groups. *Journal of Applied Behavioral Science, 11,* 241–249.

Lieberman, M.A. (1983). Comparative analyses of change mechanisms in groups. In R.R. Dies & K.R. MacKenzie (Eds.), *Advances in group psychotherapy: Integrating research and practice* (pp. 191–208). New York: International Universities Press.

Lieberman, M.A. (1990a). A group therapist perspective on self-help groups. *International Journal of Group Psychotherapy, 40*(3), 251–278.

Lieberman, M.A. (1990b). Understanding how groups work: A study of homogeneous peer group failures. *International Journal of Group Psychotherapy, 40*(1), 31–52.

Lieberman, M.A., & Borman L.D. (1976). Self-help groups. *Journal of Applied Behavioral Science, 12,* 261–463.

Lieberman, M.A., Yalom, I.D., & Miles, M. (1973). *Encounter groups: First facts.* New York: Basic Books.

MacKenzie, R.K. (1983). The clinical application of a group climate measure. In R.R. Dies & K.R. MacKinzie (Eds.), *Advances in group psychotherapy: Integrating research and practice* (pp. 159–170). New York: International Universities Press.

Mintz, J., & Luborsky, L. (1970). P-technique factor analysis in psychotherapy research: An Illustration of a method. *Psychotherapy: Theory, Research, and Practice, 7,* 13–18.

Moos, R. F. (1986). *Group Environment Scale Manual* (2nd ed.). Palo Alto, CA: Consulting Psychologists Press.

Reisel, J. (1978). *A search for behavior patterns.* Unpublished doctoral dissertation, University of California, Los Angeles.

Roberts, M.L., & Nesselroade, J.R. (1986). Intraindividual variability in perceived locus of control in adults: P-technique factor analyses of short-term change. *Journal of Research in Personality, 20,* 529–545.

Rohrbaugh, M., & Bartels, B.D. (1975). Participants' perceptions of "curative factors" in therapy and growth groups. *Small Group Behavior, 6,* 430–456.

Thune, C.E. (1977). Alcoholism and the archetypal past: A phenomenological perspective on Alcoholics Anonymous. *Journal of Studies on Alcohol, 38*(1), 75–88.

Wollart, R.W. (1986). Psychosocial helping processes in a heterogeneous sample of self-help groups. *Canadian Journal of Community Mental Health, 5,* 63–76.

Yalom, I.D., Block, S., Bond, G., Zimmerman, E., & Qualls, B. (1978). Alcoholics in interactional group therapy. *Archives of General Psychiatry, 35,* 419–425.

Yalom, I.D. (1970). *The theory and practice of group psychotherapy.* New York: Basic Books.

Yalom, I.D. (1985). *The theory and practice of group psychotherapy* (3rd ed.). New York: Basic Books.

CHAPTER 21

Matchless? Alcoholics Anonymous and the Matching Hypothesis

FREDERICK B. GLASER

Whether or not specific individuals with particular kinds of alcohol problems will benefit differentially from an association with Alcoholics Anonymous (AA) cannot be determined at the present time. The requisite data are not available. An effort of substantial magnitude, extending over a prolonged period of time, will be required to produce the data, and a parallel effort of at least comparable magnitude in restructuring the service delivery system will be required to render the data clinically useful. Faced with a need to invest much in terms of time, energy, and resources in order to resolve this issue, at least two questions must be asked. First, is it likely that characteristics of individuals and of their problems with alcohol can be identified that will predict affiliation with AA and a consequent successful outcome? Second, even if such characteristics can be identified, is the achievement likely to be worth the effort?

Are Matching Effects to AA Likely?

Several objections to the likelihood of successful matching to AA have been raised and must be carefully and seriously examined. If they are persuasive, persisting with matching research on AA may not be prudent.

As many commentators have observed, the probability that matching effects can be identified depends upon the heterogeneity of the population to be matched, including both the individual characteristics of its members and the characteristics of the problems that they manifest. If the targeted individuals do not differ from one another, and if their problems are also fundamentally the same, it is possible that a single therapeutic approach may prove effective for all. Under such circumstances a strenuous attempt to validate and implement a matching strategy might be superfluous. Two current objections to matching to AA deal with the fundamental issue of heterogeneity.

The first of these objections accepts heterogeneity as a reality but denies that it is relevant. Perhaps the only eponymic law of alcohol studies,

Keller's Law, holds that "the investigation of any trait in alcoholics will show that they have either more or less of it" (Keller, 1972). Keller's overall conclusion, however, is that "alcoholics are different in so many ways that it makes no difference." This view was reiterated a decade later in a study of treatment outcomes of a program based on the principles and practices of AA:

> Practically, differences that do not make any difference are not differences. It does not seem warranted at our present level of therapeutic knowledge to develop separate programs for different categories of alcoholics.... Within a single treatment approach it is possible to acknowledge and deal with individual differences, thereby treating both the common problem of alcoholism-chemical dependency and the problems unique to individual patients. (Laundergan, 1982, p. 36)

These are prima facie assertions and, as is characteristic of the genre, prima facie assertions can also be made in the opposite direction. That differences between individuals and between their problems do have a significant bearing upon treatment selection and outcome generically is not a new idea. One of its earlier proponents was Hippocrates, whose efforts in the fifth century B.C. enshrined differential diagnosis and specific treatment as the cornerstone of medical practice. Neither is matching a new idea in the treatment of alcohol problems specifically; in one of the earliest of modern works on the subject (1804), Thomas Trotter commented that "in treating these various descriptions of persons and characters, it will readily appear to a discerning physician, that very different methods will be required" (Jellinek, 1941, p. 587). Because matching approaches have been deployed in a multiplicity of areas, including education, corrections, psychology, psychiatry, and the treatment of drug problems (cf. Glaser, 1980), "matching in the treatment of alcohol problems is appropriately viewed not as a unique and idiosyncratic development but as a particular application of a general strategy in human therapeutics" (Institute of Medicine, 1990, p. 280).

More than a score of studies of treatment for alcohol problems that meet reasonable methodological criteria provide evidence that matching effects do occur in this particular area of therapeutics and can be predicted by such indicators as demographic variables, psychiatric diagnosis, personality factors, severity of alcohol problems, and antecedent factors (Institute of Medicine, 1990, pp. 282–283, modified from Annis, 1988). The principal conclusions from an exhaustive review of recent outcome studies in the alcohol treatment field were that

> The provision of appropriate, specific treatment modalities can substantially improve outcome.... There is no single superior approach for all persons with

alcohol problems.... Reason for optimism about alcohol treatment lies in the range of promising alternatives that are available, each of which may be optimal for different types of individuals. (Institute of Medicine, 1990, p. 537)

Ultimately, whether differences between individuals and their problems make a difference with regard to the efficacy of particular treatment approaches is an empirical question and calls for empirical testing rather than a prima facie response. Studies of treatment outcome utilizing a rigorous methodology directed at examining matching effects are required for the question to be answered. A combination of six specific features has been suggested for such studies. These include (1) a reliable predictor variable on which at least two types of individuals and/or problems can be objectively defined; (2) at least two distinct, well-differentiated treatment conditions; (3) assignment (preferably random) of each type of individual and/or problem to each treatment condition; (4) sufficient sample size across study conditions to detect a moderate effect; (5) an adequate post-treatment follow-up period; and (6) objective, reliable measures of therapeutic impact (Annis, 1988).

While variant methodologies to test for matching effects may evolve, they will ideally come within hailing distance of Annis' paradigm. Until many such studies are done, matching will remain an hypothesis in this field (cf. Glaser, 1980). The possible objection that, even if matching is applicable to other interventions dealing with alcohol problems, it may not be applicable to Alcoholics Anonymous, seems unlikely to be true. For various reasons, however, such as the requirement of anonymity, attendance at multiple groups, and so forth, it may prove more difficult to elucidate matches to AA than to other interventions. Potential ways around these difficulties have been suggested (Boscarino, 1980; Glaser & Ogborne, 1982).

The second major objection to matching to AA also deals with the fundamental issue of heterogeneity. Instead of affirming its reality, as in the instances discussed above, it takes the opposite tack; the existence of heterogeneity is questioned. While noting that "early research" did suggest "that alcoholics who affiliated with AA were not representative of the total population of alcoholics who received treatment" (see Emrick, 1987, p. 416), Emrick's detailed review concluded that "more recent data on the processes of affiliation with AA raise serious doubts about the existence of systematic distinctions between AA and non-AA members, at least among these alcoholics who receive conventional alcoholism treatment" (pp. 417–418). This assertion strikes at the heart of the notion of matching and accordingly requires careful examination.

An interesting feature of this particular review is that quite dissimilar conclusions from those noted above are reached at a subsequent point:

Given the variant nature of alcohol-dependent individuals, it seems prudent to view AA as most appropriate at certain times for particular individuals while professionals may provide a more helpful response to other alcoholics or at different times in the course of the disorder and its treatment. Still for others, or at certain times, a combination of AA and professional treatment may prove to be the most beneficial. (Emrick, 1987, p. 421)

To this general statement is added a particular one, which the author identifies as "an exception to the notion that AA is a suitable consideration for every alcoholic. Those alcohol-dependent individuals who are committed to reducing (controlling, moderating) their drinking are not likely to be attracted to, or maintain involvement with, AA given its goal of total abstinence" (p. 421).

These later statements in the same paper affirm rather than question heterogeneity and, as a consequence, the potential for successful matching. But the initial statement is of sufficient concern to require separate examination (see Emrick, 1987, Table 1, p. 417). A close examination, both as a group and as individual studies, of the studies said to cast serious doubt upon heterogeneity, will serve to illustrate many of the methodological difficulties that have thus far bedeviled studies of AA. To anticipate the conclusions of this analysis: while the cited studies do enhance our knowledge of AA in some ways, they are sufficiently flawed that they can tell us little about matching and less about AA in general than we need to know.

To begin with, none of the studies cited approach the prospective, experimental methodology suggested by Annis (1988). Rather, principal reliance in drawing conclusions about matching is placed on correlational data. Although they may be quite useful in generating testable hypotheses, correlational data do not provide satisfactory answers to questions of causality. An intriguing gloss upon this general principle is provided in one cited paper (Boscarino, 1980). Data forms completed by AA members in current attendance at 10 different groups were first analyzed in terms of the stability or instability of their affiliation. Alternate statistical procedures were then utilized to explore whether nine additional variables culled from the literature and from clinical experience were predictive of stability of affiliation. A correlation matrix revealed a positive association for only four of the nine variables. A multiple regression analysis showed an association for only three.

Finally, a principal components factor analysis with varimax rotations was performed, yielding two factors upon which the measure of stability of affiliation loaded differentially. It was found that "the size and/or direction of the factor loadings *for all nine independent variables* now support the original hypothesis" (Boscarino, 1980, p. 845, emphasis added).

The results of the prior statistical analyses, including the correlational analysis, were felt by the author to be misleading, and probably attributable to "the complex way in which [these variables] are intercorrelated. . . . These kinds of intercorrelations are suggestive of complex "suppressor" effects between some of the variables. . . . In an univariate analysis, these will conceal the relationships between variables. . . . If this is true . . . more complex multivariate techniques must be used" (pp. 843–844).

In this instance, the author of the original paper was satisfied that his study *had* demonstrated differential affiliation with AA. But portions of his data were cited in the review paper (Emrick, 1987) to show the opposite. What were cited were data from the univariate analyses rather than from the multivariate analysis, an interesting decision considering the original author's well-founded insistence upon the superior validity of the multivariate analysis. In a parallel manner, many of the other data cited in the review are from studies in which the original authors concluded that differential affiliation with AA and/or differential outcome *was* likely (Kolb, Cohen, & Heckman, 1981; Ogborne & Glaser, 1981; O'Leary, Calsyn, Haddock, & Freeman, 1980; Vaillant, 1983). Each study did indeed find some variables to be unrelated to affiliation or outcome. But other variables were found that *did* correlate with affiliation and/or outcome, and the original authors were persuaded by them.

Another kind of methodological problem is represented by the inclusion of a paper by Alford (1980). Although this paper is claimed by its original author to be an empirical outcome study of Alcoholics Anonymous, close inspection suggests that such a claim is wide of the mark. Rather, the focus of the study is an inpatient treatment program strongly influenced by AA, which is not quite the same thing. For example, although group therapy was provided (p. 361), no AA meetings were held within the program; because "program rules prohibited patients from leaving the grounds of the unit" (p. 360), no external AA meetings were attended. Alcoholics Anonymous has officially warned against considering such programs as a part of their efforts:

> *We cooperate, but we do not affiliate.* We wish to work with treatment facilities programs, administrators and staff, but we do not wish to be merged with them in the minds of administrators, clients, staff, or the public. A.A. is available to treatment facilities, but public linking of the A.A. name can give the impression of affiliation. Therefore, an A.A. meeting or group that meets in a treatment facility should not bear the name of the facility. Nor should the facility imply affiliation with Alcoholics Anonymous. (Alcoholics Anonymous, 1991, p. 1)

Although Alford's study is thus not an outcome study of AA, it does provide some data on its subjects' affiliations with AA after discharge from the inpatient unit. A higher proportion of female patients than male patients affiliated with AA subsequent to their inpatient experience; the proportions varied at the three separate follow-up times but increased to 46% of females as contrasted with 19% of males at the 24-month follow-up. Perhaps because of its counterintuitive nature, the finding was subjectively impressive and is specifically mentioned twice in the text (Alford, 1980, pp. 366, 369). Neither a statistical test of the significance of the finding nor the sex-specific attrition data required to test it is given in the original paper, but the author has kindly provided the information that the composition of the 24-month follow-up sample was 20 males and 23 females (Alford, 1991). The finding misses statistical significance at the .05 level by a whisker. Presenting these data as showing *no* relationship seems too summary a judgment under the circumstances.

A further pertinent methodological point is that, while the studies relevant to matching that are cited in the review do deal with a large number of variables (39), the list is not exhaustive. In particular, there is a paucity of test-measured variables, such as locus of control, field dependence, personality pattern, cognitive style, and others. There is evidence that these variables may differentially predict affiliation with and/or outcome from AA (cf. Ogborne & Glaser, 1981). Certainly the evidence is not conclusive and requires further testing. But in the absence of additional studies of these variables, it may be premature to conclude that there are no systematic differences between those who affiliate with AA and those who do not.

Another general methodological point has to do with the temporal relationship to AA affiliation of the variables examined. Many of the studies cited are retrospective; that is, the subjects were recruited *after* they had already affiliated with AA. In some studies that are cited members attending meetings were the subjects (e.g., Boscarino, 1980), while in others a past history of involvement in AA was utilized (e.g., O'Leary et al., 1980). It is not unreasonable to assume that individuals may change in at least some ways following their affiliation with AA. In a sense, that is the whole idea. If this does happen, at least some variables that are measured following affiliation may not have the same value they would have had prior to affiliation. Therefore, studies of AA members who have already affiliated present problems in interpretation with regard to the process of affiliation.

An example is a study that found higher scores on the Purpose-In-Life test and lower (more internal) scores on a measure of locus of control among AA members than among a comparison group of persons in treatment for alcohol problems but not involved with AA (Gianetti, 1981). These results seem most parsimoniously understood as effects of AA— that is, that subsequent to AA affiliation scores on the Purpose-in-Life test increased and scores on locus of control decreased—though admittedly this is an inference (cf. McCrady & Irvine, 1989). That low scores on the Purpose-in-Life test and high (more external) locus of control scores might predict AA affiliation is a plausible and testable hypothesis that could be drawn from the study. But it cannot realistically be claimed that the study critically tests the hypothesis—only that it is consistent with it. The example underlines the need for prospective and longitudinal studies of AA in which the relevant variables are gathered prior to affiliation and serially measured thereafter. This may help not only to elucidate outcome but also the process whereby the outcome is effected.

Of the 39 variables used to predict affiliation with AA that are identified in the review, 10—or more than one-quarter of all the variables examined—are said to be *inconsistently* related to AA membership. That is, in some of the cited studies a variable was related to affiliation and in others it was not. In the light of the final conclusions drawn, it appears that an inconsistent relationship was ultimately viewed as no relationship. However, it is possible that many (or even all) variables that might predict affiliation or outcome might do so partially, rather than fully. For example, age and sex may not fully predict AA affiliation, since there are young people and women in AA. But AA is predominantly male and predominantly older; the 1989 triennial survey of a large (ca.12,000) random sample of U.S. and Canadian members showed that 65% were male, 78% were 31 or older, and 97% were 21 or older (Alcoholics Anonymous, 1990). Thus, age and sex may add in some degree to the accuracy of predictions of affiliation.

An algorithm that takes multiple variables into account, weighing them carefully in order to arrive at a final prediction of affiliation, may be what is required. This kind of decision rule is frequent in human therapeutics generally (Wasson, Sox, Neff, & Goldman, 1985) and has also been used in the alcohol treatment field (Glaser et al., 1984, vol. III, pp. 143–154; Ogborne, Annis, & Miller, 1982). Enthusiasm for the use of algorithms in clinical decision making is not universal, and they are sometimes disparaged as poor substitutes for clinical judgment (Ingelfinger, 1973). But there may well be a place in therapeutics for both algorithms and clinical judgment (cf. Blois, 1980), and the rapidly expanding availability of computers makes the use of even complex decision algorithms a practical possibility in virtually all treatment settings. As components of such an algorithm, the variables that are described in the review as inconsistently related to prediction of affiliation may find a significant measure of utility.

In sum, to conclude from Emrick's secondary analysis (Emrick, 1987) that serious reservations should be entertained about systematic differences between those who affiliate with AA and those who do not, and consequently about the cogency of a research effort directed at matching to AA, seems to go too far, as indeed is suggested from other conclusions drawn later in the same paper (see above). With regard to predictor variables for affiliation with AA of demonstrated validity the Scotch verdict— not proven—seems more appropriate. There are, however, grounds for optimism in the range and variety of potential predictors that have been suggested and have received some support, though admittedly not enough support for practical application at the present time. It is heartening to note that a more recent review paper having the same senior author (Emrick, Tonigan, Montgomery, & Little, 1992) and basing its results upon a meta-analysis of existing data reaches conclusions favorable to the possibility of matching: "The results of this meta-analysis indicate that systematic distinctions between AA affiliates and non-affiliates can be identified ... distinctions drawn from this analysis can contribute to treatment-patient matching decision strategies" (p. 14).

Beyond the specific issue of matching, the studies cited in this review yield important lessons about methodological problems to be avoided in future research on AA. None are experimental controlled trials of the sort advocated by Annis (1988) as a critical test of matching. While there is certainly room for alternative designs in studying treatment, such experimental studies are crucially necessary and considerable caution should be exercised in the interpretation of those studies that are less rigorously designed. A related point is that a rigid adherence to conventional statistical cutoffs constitutes overkill when analyzing studies that do not employ powerful experimental designs; such studies are principally useful in suggesting hypotheses for future study, and obscuring patterns and trends in the data through the overly strict application of standard analyses limits their utility for this purpose. As well, many such analyses are univariate, accepting but not stating openly the assumption that a single variable will ultimately prove critical in matching individuals to AA. In fact, it is likely that a constellation of variables will be required to produce this and other effective matches, and multivariate and interactional statistical methods will accordingly be required to examine them. Indeed, many variables that may be critical to matching have as yet received inadequate examination and final conclusions should be reserved until sufficient testing has been done. In drawing conclusions about Alcoholics Anonymous it is crucial that AA itself be examined, rather than programs that are "based on AA principles." In drawing conclusions about affiliation with AA, individuals must be examined prior to their affiliation with the organization; examination of the characteristics of affiliated members runs the risk of confusing effects of AA with predictors of affiliation, though it may produce leads as to relevant variables to study in a prospective manner.

That it is possible to conduct informative research on AA itself, in spite of the many methodological difficulties that may be experienced, and to produce valuable information relevant to matching, may be seen from a more recent study. Researchers at the University of New Mexico have explored empirically the issue of what might be called the entitivity of AA (Montgomery, Miller, & Tonigan, in press). Is an individual's experience in AA likely to be sufficiently homogeneous that one can think in terms of matching to AA as an entity? Its pervasive and potent philosophy suggests that it may be. Practices that are common in AA, however, such as advising initiates to attend a multitude of groups in order to find one that is comfortable for them, suggest some level of perceived heterogeneity of AA experience. By administering an appropriate instrument to AA attendees, the authors have provided some valuable empirical data. In brief, they have found elements of both homogeneity and heterogeneity of the AA experience in their study population. Different AA groups were rated by their members as like each other in some respects and different from each other in other respects.

From a matching standpoint, this is both good news and bad news. The good news is that a considerable level of commonality appears to exist between different AA groups, so that general factors predicting a match to AA may be identifiable. It is also good news that a degree of variety obtains within the AA experience; the variety might, if systematically exploited, increase the acceptability of AA to a greater number of individuals. (Encouraging "shopping around," while prudent under present circumstances, may not be sufficiently systematic to maximize the desired result.) The bad news is that the matching task may be more complex than had been supposed, since specific predictors for a match to particular types of experiences within AA may have to be developed. We have been warned before that matching might be a complex phenomenon (Finney & Moos, 1986); here is evidence that the warning was well considered.

Is Matching to AA Worth the Effort?

Based on the foregoing, one seems entitled to maintain an optimistic view about the possibility of matching individuals and their problems differentially to Alcoholics Anonymous. Convincing evidence that this cannot be done has not yet surfaced. A consensus has developed that it may be possible, though there is no unanimity of opinion. Nevertheless it seems that such matching is likely to prove complex, and that a great deal of effort may be required to demonstrate finally that it can be done.

A long series of methodologically sound studies, utilizing Annis' paradigm or a reasonable approximation thereof, will need to be conducted. The series will necessarily be long, both because any such study takes approximately five years from its inception to its completion and because a variety of variables may be required to predict outcome; a single study can take into account only a limited number of variables. The standard R01 grant application procedure seems too piecemeal to sustain a research agenda of the sort necessary to deal with this question. Introduction of the multisite cooperative study as a framework for research is a major advance, bringing complex studies within the pale of possibility. Such a study is currently under way on the general issue of matching and is investigating (among other possibilities) the feasibility of matching to self-help groups. But multisite studies are as yet the exception rather than the rule. A possible alternative (or supplement) would be the establishment of a special, solidly funded clinical research facility or facilities capable of addressing such long-term, complex treatment issues. Regrettably, we seem very far indeed from such a possibility in the United States, where health services research has not yet achieved a high priority (cf. Wallen, 1988).

Even if in some way the research task could be accomplished, major revisions in the way services are delivered would be necessary in order to use the resultant information effectively. By definition, predictor variables would need to be measured prior to treatment in order to maximize their effect. This implies two structural innovations in patterns of service delivery: (1) at least some level of control of access to treatment, and (2) comprehensive pretreatment assessment.

If access to all treatment programs is uncontrolled, as is currently the case, people will take the most direct route into treatment, trusting to their unaided judgment to find the most appropriate modality. Or they may depend upon the judgment of caregivers, which may at times be objective but which may also be strongly biased by such considerations as financing (Hansen & Emrick, 1983) or ideology (Savitz, File, & McCahill, 1973). The high levels of attrition that have regularly been reported from AA (Brandsma, Maultsby, & Welsh, 1980; Emrick, 1987) as well as other treatment interventions suggest that such an approach does not work well. Many relevant matching variables are not available to unguided self-inspection but must be elicited by competently trained assessors (or their surrogates, such as appropriately programmed computers) in a carefully structured manner. For this and other reasons, thoughtfully designed, well-staffed, aggressively supervised, and financially and ideologically independent assessment and referral units through which all persons seeking other than emergency treatment for alcohol problems should pass are an essential element in the widespread implementation of matching. Indeed, what is really required is a comprehensive system of care, since additional elements, including especially routine outcome studies and the feedback of outcome information into decision algorithms, are also needed.

While unlikely, such a system is not an impossibility. A detailed blueprint has been prepared (Institute of Medicine, 1990). One state in the United States (Minnesota) has legislatively limited the access of persons seeking treatment to publicly funded programs, requiring both an independent (if limited) assessment prior to treatment and outcome studies following treatment. One province in Canada (Ontario) has had extensive experience with assessment-referral centers; it has been a generally positive experience, although the 33 centers reported upon had not yet had a major impact on service delivery patterns (Ogborne & Rush, 1990). A dozen programs in both countries had developed at least elements of the system that the Institute of Medicine felt was desirable, though only one program was using all the elements (Institute of Medicine, 1990, p. 336). If the proposed reorganization of the federal structure in the alcohol and drug field in the United States is realized, a new organizational entity devoted exclusively to applied research, including research on service delivery, will emerge and might over time impact these issues significantly.

Is the prize, however, worth the toss? Even if all of this were to come about, would it be worthwhile to go to this extent to "get the goods," so to speak, on the friendly fellowship that has done very nicely, thank you, on its own, determinedly eschewing all outside aid—as well as avoiding thereby all outside interference? Who needs it?

All of us who are interested in the future of treatment research need it. A principal goal of treatment research is to investigate the efficacy of treatments in a sufficiently persuasive manner that the results will gain clinical application. A probable determinant of clinical application is that judgments of efficacy be viewed as fair. A judgment of efficacy based on results in a population that is highly unlikely to benefit from the treatment under study is not fair. This is a problem for the two principal randomized controlled trials of the efficacy of Alcoholics Anonymous that have been reported to date (Brandsma, Maultsby, & Welsh, 1980; Ditman, Crawford, Forgy, Moskowitz, & MacAndrew, 1967). The subjects in both studies were chronic drunkenness offenders. While the studies illustrate that AA, like other interventions, is not universally effective (cf. Institute of Medicine, 1990), they do not fairly test the overall efficacy of Alcoholics Anonymous, since no treatment intervention is known to be outstandingly successful with this particular population. A fair test of the efficacy of AA would be to examine to what degree affiliation is associated with positive outcomes for individuals who are likely, or at least not unlikely, to benefit from it.

That is, the concept of matching should be taken into account in the design of efficacy studies and, at the very least, the study should not utilize as subjects those who are unlikely to benefit from the intervention (cf. McCrady & Irvine, 1989, who make, inter alia, the same point at pp. 165–66). A further example of this principle that is relevant to AA arises from a study that determined the reading level required for comprehension of the "Big Book," a fundamental AA text (Alcoholics Anonymous, 1955), was that of a beginning seventh grader (Mills, 1989). Testing the efficacy of bibliotherapy with this text would accordingly be unfair in a population that read at levels significantly below the seventh grade.

Those who are interested in the future of treatment need to assure that research on matching goes forward. Unless an element of precision can be introduced into treatment, the likelihood that ongoing funding will be available for it will continue to diminish exponentially. We are already too familiar with repeated efforts to exclude treatment for alcohol problems from health insurance coverage. The reasons for its exclusion are complex, but among them is a deep-seated conviction that such treatment is ineffective, a conviction that is strongly reinforced by intransigent insistence upon the suitability of each program for all persons with alcohol-related problems. If a systematic and successful effort is made to match individuals and their problems to AA and to other interventions, it will illustrate a healthy interest in a more efficient and effective mode of operation. We have already seen the baleful effects of insistence upon inpatient treatment as a necessary prelude to any treatment episode. The baby has been thrown out with the bathwater, and inpatient treatment is already extinct as a viable option in many areas of the country, even for those who really need it. We cannot afford to have this pattern repeated.

All of us need this approach, including professionals in the field. Consumer activism is increasing in all service areas, and the provision of treatment services to persons with alcohol-related problems is no exception. Professionals are increasingly being held accountable for the results of their referral decisions. Litigation has already become a pathway for those who wish to fight back. In Maryland an avowed atheist, John Norfolk, having been apprehended for drunk driving, was ordered by the state alcohol authority to attend AA. (Sending a militant atheist to AA is an intriguing application of the matching hypothesis.) He sued the state authority and was represented by an attorney for the American Civil Liberties Union. His petition was supported by a number of AA members who felt it was inappropriate for any individual to be forced to join the fellowship against their will. Mr. Norfolk won the case on appeal, though on the grounds of the general unreasonableness of the decision rather than because of a violation of the constitutionally mandated separation of church and state. Damages were not assessed against the state authority in the Norfolk case. But it is not difficult to foresee that if, for example, a professional were to make a referral to AA as a matter of course (rather than as the logical and defensible consequence of a comprehensive individual evaluation) and if that referral were followed by a failure to affiliate, despair that the "only effective treatment" had not worked, and a consequent suicide, damages of a high order might be awarded. It is not as unrealistic a scenario as one might hope (cf. Emrick, 1989, p. 9).

We need this cautious, incremental, and empirically based approach to treatment, including those among us who manifest alcohol-related problems. A graphic illustration is sorely needed that there are alternatives to AA, not only in terms of other 12-step programs like Women for Sobriety and the Secular Organization for Sobriety, but in terms of the many completely different approaches that, with AA and other like approaches, constitute the present therapeutic armamentarium. No one should feel that if they fail to affiliate with AA their future is devoid of hope. Yet this is all too often the case.

All of us need this kind of approach, including Alcoholics Anonymous itself. AA is a remarkable natural resource. In common with such resources, it often seems as if it will be with us forever, no matter what. But such a perception is misleading, as we should by now have learned from sad experience with other natural resources. Yes, AA has survived for 56 years; but, as Wilson Mizner reminded us, "Life's a tough proposition, and the first hundred years are the hardest." AA is potentially vulnerable and, like other "givens" such as the air we breathe and the water we drink, could be indiscriminately overused to a point at which its availability would be significantly impaired. Consider the following statement issued by the trustees of the organization:

> In recent years, an ever-growing number of people have been referred to A.A. by treatment centers, court programs and other agencies, resulting in some confusion about what A.A. is and is not. . . . A.A. does not wish to be exclusive, but experience indicates that we cannot remain effective if we attempt multipurpose activities. Experience also indicates that nonalcoholic persons, including drug addicts, do not get the long-term help or support they need from Alcoholics Anonymous. (Alcoholics Anonymous, 1991, p. 1)

By learning how to match individuals and their alcohol problems to AA, we will ultimately preserve a cherished element—perhaps the single most important element—of our therapeutic approach. Certainly there will be less than unanimous enthusiasm about taking an approach of this kind, because it does involve surrendering the notion that AA is for everyone with alcohol-related problems; although this seems now to have been accepted by the AA leadership, at least to some degree (see above), it has not necessarily filtered down to the membership. But to say that AA is not for everyone is to say nothing that cannot be said of any other kind of intervention. Those of us who admire AA stand in particular respect of the unflinching honesty that members of the fellowship exercise in the conduct of their programs and their lives. The ultimate test of this honesty will be to apply it to the program itself.

What Do We Do in the Meanwhile?

Until research provides us with more valid matching guidelines for AA, and until the service delivery system is restructured in such a way that this kind of information can be readily utilized, how should we proceed in clinical situations? Two principles suggest themselves. First, because we do not know what constitutes a mismatch, no one should be *required* to attend AA.

The same principle, of course, should also be followed with respect to any treatment program for which valid matching guidelines are unavailable. That is, no one should be coerced into a treatment program unless there is solid empirical evidence that a positive outcome is highly probable. A recent comprehensive review of the issue of coercion in treatment for alcohol-related problems concluded in part:

> There are ... complex ethical issues regarding coercion that must be addressed by the alcohol field. One concerns the ethics of coercing someone to enter treatment when the effectiveness of that treatment is unknown. ... individuals who enter treatment under pressure from one institution or another should not lose their rights; they should have alternatives to choose from, including an alternative to treatment itself. A second ethical issue relates to informed consent and the importance of providing the person with a full understanding of the proposed treatment program, as well as what is known about its efficacy. For both of these issues, it seems reasonable to extend the same protections as are granted individuals involved in research projects to persons entering treatment, especially when a person is entering treatment for reasons other than his or her own choosing. (Weisner, 1990)

The second principle is that, because we do not know what constitutes a match, everyone should be encouraged to *try* AA. It is widely available, there are no financial barriers, and many persons who have dealt successfully with their alcohol-related problems have found it helpful. Moreover, as with most treatment interventions, AA is difficult to evaluate secondhand. Attendance at a few meetings will provide a much better idea of the fellowship than any indirect description. If it simply confirms that no match exists between the individual and the fellowship, that confirmation is of value in future treatment planning.

Never require, always encourage. It is not a bad interim strategy, nor is it a simple one. For example, many existing treatment programs are based solely and exclusively on AA principles (cf. Alford, 1980). But if, as increasingly seems to be confirmed by empirical research, the population with which we are dealing is truly heterogeneous, diversifying treatment will be required in order to provide effective service for all. It is past time that we made a full spectrum of treatments available to all who seek help.

Acknowledgments

The author would like to thank Chad D. Emrick, Ph.D., who read an earlier draft of this chapter and made many valuable suggestions. Thanks are also due to the editors, Barbara McCrady, Ph.D., and William Miller, Ph.D., whose enterprise not only occasioned this chapter but whose perspicacity greatly improved it.

References

Alcoholics Anonymous. (1955). *Alcoholics Anonymous: The story of how many thousands of men and women have recovered from alcoholism* (rev. ed.). New York: Alcoholics Anonymous World Services.

Alcoholics Anonymous. (1990). *About AA: A newspaper for professionals.* New York: Alcoholics Anonymous World Services.

Alcoholics Anonymous. (1991). *About AA: A newspaper for professionals.* New York: Alcoholics Anonymous World Services.

Alford, G.S. (1980). Alcoholics Anonymous: An empirical outcome study. *Addictive Behaviors, 5,* 359–370.

Alford, G.S. (1992, January 16). Personal communication.

Annis, H.M. (1988). Patient-treatment matching in the management of alcoholism. In L.S. Harris (Ed.), *Problems of drug dependence.* NIDA Research Monograph #90. Washington, DC: U.S. Government Printing Office.

Blois, M.S. (1980). Clinical judgment and computers. *New England Journal of Medicine, 303,* 192–197.

Boscarino, J. (1980). Factors related to "stable" and "unstable" affiliation with Alcoholics Anonymous. *International Journal of the Addictions, 15,* 839–848.

Brandsma, J.M., Maultsby, M.C., Jr., & Welsh, R.J. (1980). *Outpatient treatment of alcoholism: A review and comparative study.* Baltimore, MD: University Park Press.

Ditman, K.S., Crawford, G.C., Forgy, E.W., Moskowitz, H., & MacAndrew, C.W. (1967). A controlled experiment on the use of court probation for drunk arrests. *American Journal of Psychiatry, 124,* 160–163.

Emrick, C.D. (1987). Alcoholics Anonymous: Affiliation processes and effectiveness as treatment. *Alcoholism: Clinical & Experimental Research, 11,* 416–423.

Emrick, C.D. (1989) Overview. In M. Galanter (Ed.), *Recent developments in alcoholism, volume 7: Treatment research.* New York: Plenum Press.

Emrick, C.D., Tonigan, J.S., Montgomery, H., & Little, L. (1992) Affiliation processes in treatment outcomes of Alcoholics Anonymous: A Meta-analysis of the literature. Prepublication draft.

Finney, J.W., & Moos, R.H. (1986). Matching patients to treatments: Conceptual and methodological issues. *Journal of Studies on Alcohol, 47,* 122–134.

Gianetti, V.J. (1981). Alcoholics Anonymous and the recovering alcoholic: An exploratory study. *American Journal of Drug & Alcohol Abuse, 8,* 363–370.

Glaser, F.B. (1980). Anybody got a match? Treatment research and the matching hypothesis. In G. Edwards & M. Grant (Eds.), *Alcoholism treatment in transition.* London: Croom Helm.

Glaser, F.B., Annis, H.M., Skinner, H.A., Pearlman, S., Segal, R.L., Sisson, B., Ogborne, A.C., Bohnen, E., Gazda, P., & Zimmerman, T. (1984). *A system of health care delivery.* Three volumes. Toronto: Addiction Research Foundation.

Glaser, F.B., & Ogborne, A.C. (1982). Does A.A. really work? *British Journal of Addiction, 77,* 123–129.

Hansen, J., & Emrick, C.D. (1983). Whom are we calling "alcoholic"? *Bulletin of the Society of Psychologists in Addictive Behaviors, 2,* 164–178.

Ingelfinger, F.J. (1973). Algorithms, anyone? *New England Journal of Medicine, 288,* 847–848.

Institute of Medicine. (1990). *Broadening the base of treatment for alcohol problems.* Washington, DC: National Academy Press.

Jellinek, E.M. (1941). An early medical view of alcohol addiction and its treatment: Dr. Thomas Trotter's "Essay, Medical, Philosophical, and Chemical, on Drunkenness." *Quarterly Journal of Studies on Alcohol, 2,* 584–591.

Keller, M. (1972). The oddities of alcoholics. *Quarterly Journal of Studies on Alcohol, 33,* 1147–48.

Kolb, D., Cohen, P., & Heckman, N.A. (1981). Patterns of drinking and AA attendance following alcohol rehabilitation. *Military Medicine, 146,* 200–204.

Laundergan, J.C. (1982). *Easy does it: Alcoholism treatment outcomes, Hazelden, and the Minnesota Model.* Center City, MN: Hazelden Foundation.

McCrady, B.S., & Irvine, S. (1989). Self-help groups. In R.K. Hester & W.R. Miller (Eds.), *Handbook of alcoholism treatment approaches: Effective alternatives* (pp. 153–169). New York: Pergamon Press.

Mills, K.R. (1989). Readability of Alcoholics Anonymous: How accessible is the "Big Book"? *Perceptual and Motor Skills, 69,* 258.

Montgomery, H.A., Miller, W.R., & Tonigan, J.S. (in press). Differences among A.A. groups: Implications for research. *Journal of Studies on Alcohol.*

Ogborne, A.C., & Glaser, F.B. (1981). Characteristics of affiliates of Alcoholics Anonymous: A review of the literature. *Journal of Studies on Alcohol, 42,* 661–675.

Ogborne, A.C., Annis, H.M., & Miller, W.R. (1982). Discriminant analysis and the selection of patients for controlled drinking programs: A methodological note. *Journal of Clinical Psychology, 38,* 213–216.

Ogborne, A.C., & Rush, B.R. (1990). Specialized addictions assessment/referral services in Ontario: A review of their characteristics and roles in the addiction treatment system. *British Journal of Addiction, 85,* 197–204.

O'Leary, M.R., Calsyn, D.A., Haddock, D.L., & Freeman, C.W. (1980). Differential alcohol use patterns and personality traits among three Alcoholics Anonymous attendance level groups: Further considerations of the affiliation profile. *Drug and Alcohol Dependence, 5,* 135–144.

Savitz, L.D., File, K., & McCahill, T.W. (1973). Referral decision-making in a multimodality treatment system. In *Proceedings of the fifth national conference on methadone treatment.* New York: NAPAN.

Vaillant, G.E. (1983). *The natural history of alcoholism: Causes, patterns, and paths to recovery.* Cambridge, MA: Harvard University Press.

Wallen, J. (1988). Alcoholism treatment service systems: A health services research perspective. *Public Health Reports, 103,* 605–611.

Wasson, J.H., Sox, H.C., Neff, R.K., & Goldman, L. (1985). Clinical prediction rules: Applications and methodological standards. *New England Journal of Medicine, 313,* 793–799.

Weisner, C.M. (1990). Coercion in alcohol treatment. In Institute of Medicine, *Broadening the base of treatment for alcohol problems.* Washington, DC: National Academy Press.

Appendix

ALL PARTICIPANTS in the conference were asked to respond, both verbally and in writing, to 10 core questions. Their responses reflect the richness and diversity of thinking represented within the conference. The ideas generated through this process are transcribed here with minimal editing to reduce redundancy, from both the participants' written responses and the conference recorder's notes from open discussion periods. The 10 questions were:

1. What are the most important questions that need to be addressed by future research on AA?
2. How could researchers gain access to and cooperation of AA groups?
3. What special issues arise with regard to anonymity, and how can these be addressed?
4. What constitutes "true AA," and how can researchers avoid obtaining a distorted picture of AA?
5. What alternatives are there for identifying and selecting AA samples for research?
6. What outcome measures should be employed in AA research?
7. What would be promising predictor measures for AA studies?
8. What alternatives are available for conducting follow-up in longitudinal studies of AA?
9. What special issues are likely to arise in the review process of proposals for research on AA?
10. What other ideas, opportunities, or alternatives should be considered for AA research that are not covered by the preceding questions?

1. What Are the Most Important Questions That Need to be Addressed by Future Research on AA?

- What happens to AA members over time? If members stop attending, what happens to them?
- How does AA participation affect desire to drink, and the topography of relapse?
- For whom is AA most effective, and why?
- Which elements within AA are most important (in terms of member compliance) in predicting favorable outcomes?
- How is sobriety/serenity different from mere abstinence?
- How can we capture and characterize the diversity among AA groups? Are there definable types of groups that are similar to each other and different from other types?
- Operationalize hypotheses implicit in AA's central writings.
- Via surveys, model the perceptions of AA among professionals.

- What patterns of alcohol consumption occur among those who do drink, in AA versus other approaches?
- What is the impact of AA on drug use other than alcohol?
- What is the impact of AA (versus other approaches) on alcohol expectancies, self-efficacy, etc.?
- If AA is a program of living, there is a need to study people living the program but not currently attending AA meetings.
- How can professionals help facilitate affiliation with 12-step groups? What makes an appropriate referral?
- Large demographic surveys to better understand current members.
- Surveys to better understand what aspects of AA encourage affiliation and with what groups.
- Better understanding of spiritual components of AA.
- Focus on community-based groups, not treatment-center meetings.
- What were individual members' ideas of "hitting bottom"?
- What happens to those who quit attending? Why do individual members stop going to AA?
- Who needs more treatment than just referral to AA?
- Explore the family's attitude, reaction, involvement toward AA. Does this affect affiliation and outcome?
- What is the best role for a therapist to take when a client is involved in AA?
- What is the underlying value of faith processes, conversion experiences, reconstitution of self that occur in AA? Are there gender or ethnic differences in these processes of change? What are the steps involved in these change processes?
- The above questions deal with cognitive changes in beliefs, attitudes, values, and changes in personality states. What about social interaction in AA groups? What are the rules that govern verbal and nonverbal behavior in groups? Are there gender or ethnic differences in group interaction? How do differences in the rules of the group *and* individual differences in social interaction patterns influence treatment outcome?
- What is the relative effectiveness of community-based AA versus other treatment modalities for diverse subgroups of alcoholics (gender, other substances abused; pre-existing psychiatric disorders, etc.)? How can we best match patients to treatments?
- How can spirituality best be conceptualized? Can it be measured?
- What are the specific processes and behaviors in AA associated with different dimensions of recovery (e.g., sobriety, emotional growth, interpersonal relations)? Working the steps? How does this vary for different cultural groups?
- What are pulls on people external to AA (e.g., family) that affect patterns of participation in AA?
- Does AA work, how, for whom, if not why not, who *doesn't* go and why?
- How can professional treatment providers get more sophisticated at collaborating with and referring to AA (i.e., deficits in clinical training)?
- The best information would be prospective, long-term, population based: Who goes where when they have alcoholism. This is prohibitively expensive to fund; perhaps easier in Denmark where there are church records to follow people.
- What impact have changes in insurance coverage for alcoholism treatment had on AA use?
- What about the lock that AA has on thinking in the treatment field, and how does this affect outcome research?
- Pathways into and out of AA.
- AA meetings as speech events.

- Dynamics of group splitting and the establishment of new groups.
- How do individual members learn the core of AA that is based on oral tradition?
- Experimental studies of specific tools and techniques used by AA members.
- What do different members mean by "spirituality"?
- To what extent do AA members believe that spirituality is an effective ingredient of AA, and how does that belief relate to outcome?
- How can AA reduce its dropout rate? Do AA members who drop out actually show worse outcome than those who stay in? Do dropouts after several years of attendance fare differently from those who drop out early?
- Does one have to label oneself "alcoholic" in order to become sober and be in recovery?
- Does one need to "surrender" and believe (and continue to believe) that one cannot control one's drinking?
- What are the characteristics of AA groups? How much do they vary in their policies and practices? Is this variation related to members' outcomes?
- What are the basic similarities and differences between AA and other 12-step groups?
- What constitutes standard practice in AA, and what are the principal deviations from standard practice? That is, how heterogeneous is AA? How stable are its practices?
- Are there variables that predict AA affiliation in general, or only those that predict affiliation with particular groups, or are there both?
- From an operational perspective, how important is the spiritual element in AA— that is, to what degree does it contribute to positive outcome? Indeed, to what degree is positive outcome a reflection of acceptance of AA ideology, and the acceptance of the behavior of individuals in AA as models?
- To what extent would the study of drug-free therapeutic communities illuminate our understanding of AA? They were derived from AA and have a similar history.
- How does working the 12 steps relate to outcome?
- What are effective methods that clinicians can use to encourage AA involvement?
- What are the cognitive and affective processes that change as a result of AA participation?
- Does AA participation result in "structural" change from a dynamic perspective?
- What individual personality characteristics or spiritual orientation factors are predictive of AA success?
- Are there characteristics that would preclude successful affiliation with AA?
- What is the role of sponsorship? Are there other ways people can "get the program"? How important is having a sponsor?
- How does the use of AA tools relate to subjective well-being?
- How does AA involvement alter spiritual processes in the individual's life?
- Researchers have much to learn in order to be prepared to study AA. Researchers should study the implications and the objectives (obvious as well as latent) of AA, through such sources as this monograph. Also researchers should attend AA meetings to see what actually happens there.
- There should be more research among behavioral scientists and practitioners to see what misconceptions and legitimate "beefs" there are about AA policies, practices, and communications. Many social scientists scientists are agnostics or skeptics, and terms such as *higher power* and *God* tend to raise their hackles. On the other side, AA in the past has often had an anti-intellectual and anti-research bias, exacerbated by ties between AA and the National Council on Alcoholism; e.g., attacks on studies that empirically question the assumption, "Once an alcoholic, always an alcoholic."

- There should be more research among potential clients of AA to determine how many never go or drop out early, and why.
- What patient variables (psychopathology, severity of dependence on alcohol, degree of alcohol-related consequences, etc.) relate to AA affiliation?
- What are the significant differences between AA old-timers and AAs who leave within 30 days?
- How can professional counseling most effectively facilitate AA involvement?
- What factors account for dropping out from AA at different points (e.g., 30 days vs. one year)? Are these factors different for people who stay sober versus those who relapse?
- Does drop-out from AA precede or follow relapse? What are the commonalities across AA meetings, in terms of language, procedure, and process?
- What gender and cultural differences are related to AA attendance, drop-out, outcome, etc.?
- How does the *structure* (as opposed to content) of AA help sustain sobriety?
- Focus on *process:* What constitutes the process of change? Questions need to be more global.
- Shift to a qualitative perspective in framing questions; include multi-level analysis; avoid reductionistic questions.
- There is much more need for a shift in research framework than for specific questions. Perhaps many of the most pressing questions of the past and future will have very different answers within a new framework.
- Longitudinal or cross-sectional studies spanning 20 years or more; do not stop with one year or three years as a measure of outcome or process. We also need to focus on the three to five years (or more) *before* entry into AA. What treatment experiences precede AA involvement? What is the chain of events prior to AA entry?
- It is important to look at processes that precede self-selection into AA, as much as treatment referral.
- Describe variation in ideology and practice in AA: (1) in the U.S., (2) cross-nationally, and (3) in other 12-step movements, through coordinated observational and questionnaire studies.
- Explore interaction between AA and treatment systems at multiple levels: (1) AA discourse vs. melding with therapeutic discourse; (2) "two-hatters": their role in treatment systems and their role in AA—what kind of boundary is there and how well do they maintain it [*ed. note:* "two hatters" are AA members who also work as professionals within the treatment system]; (3) treatment system interactions with AA as an organization—institutional groups, variations in what it means to be a "12-step based" treatment, effects of mandated AA attendance on the AA experience for mandated individuals and other AAs.
- Studies on natural history of AA membership (and treatment experience) in the context of drinking history and life experience history.
- Studies comparing samples of AA members with the general population (heavy drinkers and others) from which they come, following over time: difference in course of drinking history, in general life functioning, etc. If possible also study other treatment samples drawn from same catchment area.
- Study AA as a network and community, in the context of other networks and types of communities; effects on drinking and life history.
- What are the processes by which a person engages in AA? What are the processes whereby persons adopt the AA program of living that moves them toward sobriety?

- Is AA a fellowship, a program of living, or both? An AA program of living can be carried out independent of meetings. Can support networks and readings sustain an AA program of living?
- What is the role of higher power and spirituality in AA? How does spirituality operate with different populations? Is there a shift in spiritual definition over time?
- Issues about recruitment to AA and retention/dropouts over the long run (five years or more).
- What happens to AA dropouts? Do they return to AA, seek other help, or do nothing?
- What differences in AA effectiveness can be attributed to voluntary versus coerced AA participation?
- How does AA compare to other secular self-help groups, such as Rational Recovery, Secular Organization for Sobriety, Women for Sobriety?
- How does AA deal with members who have experienced relapse?
- What different definitions do AA members have concerning their own higher power? How prevalent is the doorknob really?
- Does AA have any harmful effects?
- The same questions that have plagued psychotherapy outcome research: how does it work, for whom, when, and why?
- We need to develop comprehensive means to measure change within AA. This *includes* methods or ways of understanding how individuals initiate and maintain sobriety; and secondarily, ways of tapping into the self-analysis or spiritual change that some individuals report.
- How can we begin a process of understanding affiliation and disaffiliation processes to the fellowship? Emrick's meta-analysis indicates some important differences (correlations) in terms of affiliation strength, yet on the whole we know little. Perhaps a stage model of AA attendance could help explain entry into AA.
- The dropout phenomenon needs to be explored further—does it lead to resumed drinking? How about alternative explanations to account for dropout? Why do longtime members between five to eight years of sobriety have a disproportionately high percentage of dropouts relative to other timeframes? What happens to these individuals?
- What accounts for a high percentage of U.S. individuals who cite AA as the primary factor in recovery, while European studies cite extremely low percentages naming AA as a factor in their sobriety?
- How effective is AA as a "treatment" resource compared with other forms of intervention?
- For what individual characteristics or types of problems is AA particularly suited?
- Why are some types of problem drinkers "put off" by their initial contact with AA? Why do some do less well?
- How does the cost-effectiveness of AA compare with other treatment modalities?
- What elements of AA are responsible for successful outcomes, and can these be used to improve the effectiveness of other non-AA programs?
- What is the impact of the popularity of AA, and its image of alcoholism, on the possibilities for early/brief intervention, and on attempts to broaden the base of treatment for alcohol problems?
- How does AA work relative to no treatment, minimal treatment, and alternative treatment? What processes distinguish AA from other approaches? What processes are most clearly related to outcome, and with what types of subjects?

- There is a real concern with whether one can find samples of alcoholics who are not polydrug abusers, and this may constrain the ecological validity of research.
- What are the effects of *mandating* AA?
- The questions asked are intimately associated with the model of AA adopted. If we view AA as a philosophy of life rather than as a treatment, the research methods of persuasion and attitude change become relevant. From the persuasion view: (1) Does adoption of 12-step beliefs promote change? (2) Are beliefs in different steps differentially associated with change? (3) Is initial similarity of causal beliefs predictive of adoption of 12-step beliefs? (4) How does attraction to group or fellowship facilitate receptivity to accepting the philosophy, and to change?
- For whom is AA an effective path of recovery? What client pretreatment characteristics are differentially associated with success in AA/12-step programs versus other approaches (e.g., brief interventions, behavioral approaches)?
- For whom is AA ineffective, or even harmful or detrimental to recovery?
- How can different AA groups be characterized? Potential domains might include levels of empathy, warmth, supportiveness, confrontiveness, hostility, aggression.
- Assuming that AA works for some people, what are the active ingredients: specific steps, social support, being sponsored, attendance, etc.? How important is capacity for spirituality (Steps 2–3, prayer, etc.)?
- Do different diagnostic groups affiliate at different rates?
- What are the behaviors of successful AA affiliates (those who do recover)? Are there clusters of variables that would differentiate different types of recovery programs "worked" by individuals?
- What concepts of God and spirituality are utilized by what type of individual (qualitative research)?
- What is the real (membership proportions) spread of AA among U.S. ethnic minority groups?
- How variable is the structure of AA meetings (speech content, etc.) across ethnic groups in the United States? What is the pattern of sponsorship in various groups? Does use of the 12 steps vary across ethnic groups?
- We need a random sample survey of AA members with data on drinking patterns, sociodemographics, problems, spirituality, etc.
- What constitutes affiliation?
- What is valuable in AA for people who do not work the program—who do not believe in a higher power—how do they stay sober? How do they use the groups?
- What is the extent of diversity in AA and how can this be measured (e.g., meeting styles, group structure)?
- How is informal power attained in meetings and in groups?
- What are the changes taking place in and out of AA that are affecting the fellowship? How is AA affected by the influx of mandated cases, treatment populations, etc.?
- How can we explore the complexity of AA and avoid reductionism?
- We need to understand more the process of affiliation into and withdrawal from AA. What are the barriers to affiliation? What are the types of withdrawal? Do people "graduate"?
- Which aspects of AA are active ingredients for whom? For example, which steps are active at what time for whom? Which aspects of the sponsorship relationship are active?

- What occurs with attitudes and beliefs as people contemplate joining AA as well as after people join and participate? How do beliefs affect outcome, particularly with an emphasis on change in beliefs as a correlate of AA involvement and behavior change?
- How can non-AA treatment be improved by identifying therapeutic ingredients in AA?
- How can professional treatment enhance or retard the benefits of AA?
- How can we best match clients to AA?
- Which change processes are occurring and crucial in AA? What is the role of humility, surrender, and powerlessness in effecting positive change?
- What is the role of the spiritual component of AA, as distinct from the psychological, behavioral, social?
- Given the plurality of AA groups, are there certain essential or common/necessary features that are definitive of AA?
- There is a need for more descriptive studies looking at and categorizing the variety of therapeutic activities that go on in AA—the variety of activities in meetings, what happens in informal networking, sponsorship relationships, anniversary celebrations, etc.
- There is a need to better understand AA affiliation and its relationship to different phases of recovery. For instance, AA encompasses (1) individuals in early recovery who enter and leave quickly, (2) those who celebrate one year anniversaries and then leave, (3) those who make AA a permanent feature of their lives. It would seem that AA may be giving these groups different things.
- What are the effects, possibly negative, of AA involvement on marriage and family?
- What is distinctive and yet complementary about AA when compared with professional help? How do the wisdom (knowledge base), practice (social skills), and social support offered differ from that available through professional help?
- What are the nature and consequences of the interaction AA has with professional help (rehab) and behavioral control (criminal justice) agencies?
- Methodological research is needed in this area; e.g., studies to improve strategies for obtaining high respondent rates and adequate representations of minority populations within AA.
- What distinctive outcome measures need to be developed to study AA and other self-help groups?
- Can the 12 steps be operationalized and tested?
- What strategies are currently used by counselors/therapists to facilitate client involvement in AA, and how effective are they? After client initial contact with AA, what follow-up strategies do therapists use, and how effective are these?
- What kinds of experiences do people have when they first attend AA? Are particular experiences predictive of successful affiliation?
- What theoretical models best explain variance in successful outcomes associated with AA—stress coping, developmental, etc.?
- If people return to moderate drinking, how does this impact their continued involvement with AA?
- There are important things that AA provides in a sense of values and meaning in life. To what degree is this an important factor in AA, and to what degree is AA unique (compared to therapist assisted or self-directed change) in this regard?
- Is there such a thing as a "good" AA group? Is it defined by size, stability of leadership, longevity of the group, length of sobriety of members, mix of members, percentage of new members who stick, etc.?
- How do 12-step processes compare in AA and in other 12-step groups?

- How are special-focus AA groups different from others?
- How important is Al-Anon involvement of family members in the recovery of AAs?
- How does AA's service structure influence groups?
- How do speech events differ among meetings, and how are groups changed or members affected by the prevalence of various speech events in meetings?
- How can we study the likely phenomenon that different people are helped by different aspects of AA?
- How do various kinds of coercion influence AA experience and outcomes?
- What constitutes sponsorship? How are sponsorship relationships formed, indicated, maintained? What do sponsors do? How much influence do they have on changes that occur?
- How common are spiritual changes, conversion experiences, etc.?
- What processes are necessary or sufficient for change within AA?
- More study of the organizational principles and rules of discourse in AA which may contribute to making it a more "feminine" institution in which, perhaps, women fare better than men, and in which men (as well as women) have the opportunity to explore or integrate more androgynous aspects of their being.
- Assessment of the qualities of meetings, both formal and informal components.
- Is it possible to construct a template of what "ideal" AA involvement or participation would be in order to measure the experience of individual members at a level of greater specificity than number of meetings attended or length of membership?
- How does AA involvement interact with individuals in different stages of change or recovery, and with people in relapse?
- Is there an optimal amount of exposure to AA for changes to occur in drinking, sobriety, or other life areas?
- What is sobriety? How can we measure processes like humility? These processes and mechanisms of change need to be identified in behavioral terms. It may be possible to define and frame behavioral anchors via the 12 steps.
- Search for client-AA matching by using not only drinking outcomes, but other nondrinking outcome measures.
- How does AA participation compare with spontaneous remission?
- Identify quantitatively testable hypotheses generated in AA literature. Be aware that the AA language system may be misinterpreted within the research community.
- It would be very helpful if researchers developing studies on AA could agree upon standardized measures for process and outcome. This would facilitate the development of a national or international database.
- Generally an important area of research is AA and early intervention; also relationship between level of alcohol problems/dependence and outcome in AA.

2. How Could Researchers Gain Access to and Cooperation of AA Groups?

- Approval must come from the local group.
- Principal investigators need to attend service board meetings. They must become known and reflect an attitude of respect.
- Researchers could start their own AA groups in the interest of research. It is unclear if such groups would really be AA.

- Researchers could work with "two-hatters" (those who are members of AA and working with the research team) to increase access to groups and understanding of AA.
- Compare treatment populations who do and do not attend AA.
- Researchers should go to open meetings and explain why they are there. They could also have AA members help with recruitment.
- Research teams should include some people in recovery.
- Researchers should recognize that getting research done is their concern, not AA's. Participation in research could be reframed as a way to help other alcoholics.
- Contact the Cooperation with the Professional Community (CPC) committee. Meet with the CPC, group secretaries, and state level service structure.
- Conduct focus groups with people who are AA members to develop strategies to recruit subjects, to brainstorm, to identify important questions.
- Use "interpreters" between AA and research. (An interpreter is a member of AA who speaks personally, but not as a spokesperson for AA.)
- Researchers should attend 90 meetings in 90 days.
- Researchers should tell the truth—the research may not be of any use to AA. However, if it might be of use, point that out.
- Assure the AA group of how you will protect confidentiality. Write down rules regarding confidentiality and show them to the AA group.
- Piggy-back onto state-funded evaluations of treatment programs.
- Give AA members the opportunity to participate in the design of measurement instruments.
- Closed groups present special problems. Make friends with members, collect data before and/or after meetings.
- Talk with the AA group at an early stage in developing the research protocol. Give AAs an opportunity to participate.
- Meeting schedules are not supposed to be used for research purposes, but they could be.
- Share the results of the research with the AA group.
- Develop research strategies respectful of AA's traditions.
- Perhaps present a research project as a way members of a group can contribute to the body of research knowledge on AA, which in turn could be useful in the future in helping other alcoholics become involved in the fellowship (i.e., as 12th-step work).
- Assure (and make sure you follow through) groups of feedback about results and interpretation of findings prior to publication.
- Restrict research to institution-based 12-step programs.
- Would it be possible to trade space to hold meetings for the privilege of observation and member contact? Researchers need to be able to offer something of value *to members*. Space or alternative supplemental help are the most obvious possibilities.
- There is little possibility of doing randomized clinical trial research—cannot manualize such a diverse treatment, cannot randomize interest, etc. Could do comparison research, naturalistic studies and $n = 1$ studies.
- Develop friendship with people in AA, outside of meetings.
- Respect the anonymity of AA members.
- Meet with key group members and explain the study.
- Go to a meeting early and leave a description of the study with the leader, and your name and phone number (leave several copies).
- Ask an AA friend to bring several copies of the study to an AA meeting to distribute (especially closed meetings).

- Identify yourself at open meetings and request that people who are interested stay and talk to you after the meeting.
- Be honest and if possible demonstrate some knowledge of the AA traditions and your desire not to violate these traditions. Be respectful.
- Attend meetings and learn about AA.
- Might work as a top-down, bottom-up approach simultaneously. A committee of researchers would be formed to deal with AA's central committee to identify problems and solutions to AA's cooperation with research. At the same time, interested individual investigators could contact local groups. This might be done through contacts with treatment professionals in disease model programs, etc. Some format would be set up for investigators to communicate with each other regarding progress, problems, and solutions. Eventually this might lead to a multisite network of AA meetings and contacts, which could be used for research purposes.
- Utilize AA "informants"—members willing to be trained and actually conduct the research (participant observers, etc.).
- Develop a really cooperative relationship, one where the object of research is respected and approached without preconceived ideas.
- See and conceptualize research as an enterprise whose objective is to develop knowledge about AA, knowledge which will help further treatment interventions for alcohol-related problems.
- Approach AA as a form of intervention that is probably very effective for some alcoholics, but which is not a panacea.
- Gain access by: (a) deep respect for AA and its practices, (b) pointing out— gently!—that it would help each AA group to be more effective if such information was available.
- More extensive use of recovering investigators and self-help consultants.
- Use AA's own principles to encourage participation (e.g., research knowledge could help the suffering alcoholic; AA has a policy about research).
- Use snowball or convenience samples.
- Advertise, on television, in newspapers or recovery-oriented publications, or place notices in strategic locations. Word such advertisements to share what their experiences have been like in their recovery efforts.
- Go to events heavily attended by recovering people, make announcements, give out questionnaires.
- Conduct a prospective study of treatment patients who are referred. As part of such a study, collect information from subjects' sponsors or other contacts within AA.
- Read descriptions by Rudy, Taylor, Johnson, Smith (cf. Kurtz, Chapter 2 of this volume, for complete references) on how they proceeded.
- Read Bill Wilson's series, "Let's be Friendly with our Friends."
- Have a working alliance with the State Agency on Alcoholism—they are often the gatekeepers to large samples of individuals with alcohol problems from a wide variety of ethnic and socioeconomic groups.
- Fully appreciate their framework of change, allowing own change schemas to accommodate to AA's (not applying our particular language/discipline to override their experience). Developing ways of understanding change for those with alcohol problems who attend AA versus those who don't; those who participate in multiple avenues of change (i.e., psychotherapy, church, other transformational groups that substantially impact personal change such as EST of the Forum), etc. Trying to partial out which is specifically associated with AA

involvement would seem to require a very comprehensive model of change that incorporates and integrates many different avenues influencing alcohol and personal change.

- The New York headquarters of AA should be shown the findings of surveys among social scientists and practitioners, and potential "clients" of AA, so that AA might improve their practices and their communications.
- AA should change their attitude that they must not change. The 12 steps are not as sacred as the Ten Commandments. Even our U.S. Constitution gets amended occasionally.
- Distribute previous papers by researcher to allay fears, show confidentiality, etc.
- Approach each group individually. No system permission is possible. Inform the local board, for their knowledge only.
- Understanding the culture of AA as fully as possible and approaching members with the *content* of questions reflecting an understanding of that culture.
- Link with indigenous leaders in the AA community who can influence others to participate (at the individual or group level).
- Building personal, trusting relationships between the PI and AA members. PIs must be willing to invest a lot of personal time in developing these relationships. Researchers must be willing to give back something to AA or at least be willing to have some sort of reciprocal or mutual relationship with AA.
- Offer information from the survey or research that would be beneficial to the AA fellowship.
- Develop relationships with state funding agencies that are involved in evaluating many treatment programs and are conducting surveys of state populations.
- Validate what AA has accomplished, express interest in understanding it better so that you can learn—it's not they that need to learn.
- Become familiar with AA, read literature, attend meetings, know the traditions, talk the language.
- Be meticulous in conforming to the traditions.
- Perhaps, after much discussion and interchange, AA would be willing to at least provide information to local groups on certain types of descriptive research that might help AA, such as information on the number and types of groups, group turnover over time, etc.
- Ask AA if it would like to know about its groups and members.
- Contact people who see alcoholics in nonalcoholism treatment contexts (physicians, courts, police, mental hospitals, etc.) and ask permission to interview/screen/work with their patients.
- The recovering alcoholic researcher is a double-edged sword—their own recovery produces bias, usually strongly for or against AA, but it increases access to groups, and credibility with AA.
- Assume an attitude of deference—a wish to understand AA and a willingness to recognize that research bias or narrow focus may lead to inaccurate conclusions about the data. Use "interpreters" as part of research teams.
- There is a difference between studying AA groups and individual members of AA. The latter is much easier. There is always the selection problem—differences between AA members who volunteer for research and those who do not. Studying AA groups will require cooperation with the New York General Service Office, but it should be pursued. No research should be proposed or undertaken without explicit cooperation with AA.
- Through cooperation with regional boards, research proposals can be drafted and perhaps circulated. Interested AA members or groups would then initiate

contact with the researcher. Proposals would best be brief and straightforward and include information not only on confidentiality, but on how the research could (or why it would not) interrupt the process of a meeting.
• Assign confidential code numbers to AA members to ensure anonymity.
• Pay subjects for participation in research? It is unclear if this can be done with AA members.
• Use conventional methodologies from treatment and longitudinal studies to preserve confidentiality.

3. What Special Issues Arise with Regard to Anonymity, and How Can These be Addressed?

• Researchers should read the long form of the *Twelve Traditions* to appreciate the concerns that AA has about lack of anonymity as a spiritual problem.
• AA members working on the research team need to be shielded from the identity of subjects—they may know them from AA groups.
• The anonymity tradition makes it harder to do longitudinal than cross-sectional studies in AA.
• Could a third party (say a group of AA members) be the entity that knows the identity of subjects?
• Should the unit of analysis be the group rather than the individual? This idea has been accepted well by some AA groups and is consistent with AA traditions.
• Newcomers present special problems; being approached violates their sense of safety and anonymity.
• Many issues around anonymity are not difficult to resolve. Subjects can be involved in studies of AA prior to being referred there, and this renders the anonymity issue moot. For other studies, done with those who are already members, anonymity is not essentially a problem. It principally becomes a problem in longitudinal studies, but here the use of codes would simplify matters.
• Common research procedures include the obtaining of collateral information. This is difficult because of anonymity, but not impossible.
• Difficulties may arise in the use of public databases (e.g., insurance records, DWI convictions, etc.) where no surrogate code like a social security number is available. However, some of the above strategies can be used there, such as prior consent.
• The bigger issue is how to track what people are doing and *assuring* them of anonymity—it is easier to maintain than to assure.
• Anonymity is an increasingly big problem with multiple drug use and complex treatments.
• Researchers need to seek a thorough understanding of the concept of anonymity and its meaning to the AA member and the AA meeting before embarking on research on AA.
• Survey studies would have to be careful not to sample the same person twice at different AA meetings.
• There is a need to be especially sensitive to issues of disturbing the natural context of AA by doing research on it. If investigators have too much of a presence in AA then it could distort the process.
• Closed meetings are a particular problem. Important processes occur during these meetings, but these cannot be observed directly.
• Some way needs to be devised to study sponsoring relationships. These are crucial to change and yet would be resistant to disclosure. Those sponsor/sponsoree

pairs that might agree would likely be a biased sample. This suggests the need for coordination at a general group level and larger AA organizational level.

- Use AA informants who don't identify who they use in research.
- Many of the issues regarding anonymity can be covered by usual human subjects procedures.
- Anonymity may be a special problem in the case of follow-up studies, especially when follow-up contact will be made outside group settings. A possible solution is to have data collection be performed by AA members or the GSO (unclear if this is possible). Other than that, only special guarantees provided by researchers and the trust of the respondent will solve the issue.
- We have used a person-generated code for collecting longitudinal data with anonymity. At second data collection, participants find their own prior form (i.e., the face sheet from the first testing).
- Within the Detroit metropolitan area, the University of Michigan Self-Help Research Center is tracking attendance for a 700-member self-help group by collecting the last seven digits of the social security number. Procedures were worked out with the self-help group to pass out and collect forms. They were also involved in the development of the forms.
- Anonymity is an issue when trying to study people in AA, but is not so much an issue when doing clinical trials in which subjects are randomized to AA.
- Anonymity is not so much an issue in research that involves observations at a single point in time.
- Researchers must be sure that potential subjects are aware that they are researchers immediately at entry.
- Ask the group ahead of time if you can attend and collect data.
- Researchers should make sure that AAs involved have a chance to give input on research design and items on measures.
- Collect consents with first names and last initials.
- Caution is needed in the use of stories in reports and presentations.
- Need to communicate to AAs that we understand and respect AA's traditions.
- Tap into very large samples of individuals who would agree to be followed over long periods of time. This would be a sample of convenience but it would allow us to follow both process and outcome events long term in the careers of persons with serious alcohol-related problems.
- Of course, the responses of AA members to survey questions are confidential. However, we cannot really draw good samples of AA members unless we can get access to unbiased lists of AA members in various categories, such as first-time attenders, attended for the first time a year ago (to study the differences between AA attenders and dropouts); the same for two years ago, five years ago, and perhaps then years or longer ago. Researchers can pledge confidentiality, and also anonymity in that lists of AA members are not to be used except in drawing samples. Researchers would attempt to meet with the General Service Office in New York to try to get a letter of endorsement for access to such lists, as well as data about the distribution of AA chapters for purpose of selecting chapters to be sampled (which is unlikely, given the traditions).
- Researchers would provide reassurances to the General Service Office and to all groups that might be included in samples. Much of the data collection could be carried out utilizing the self-administration technique worked out in *The American Soldier*, providing confidentiality and anonymity except for utilization of matching techniques to link each respondents' answers to the various forms.
- Distribute printed material detailing how anonymity will be protected.
- Emphasize that names will not be used.

- Issues are not substantially different from those of ordinary informed consent. The contract is with the individual subject.
- Educate AA groups and inform members of AA's policy on cooperation with research.
- Researchers who are AAs themselves face dual role problems. There are certain situations in which an AA researcher who is also an AA member may want to refrain from collecting data because of a too direct conflict of roles. This should be respected by other researchers.
- Theoretically, meeting schedules should not be used for research purposes.
- The biggest problem is the collection of longitudinal data, which is critical to a complete evaluation. Maybe we could attach a research number to an "AA name" and try to track more anonymously. However this would require special ways to contact these individuals.
- Use an anonymous or masked organization to contact these individuals that is under the control of AA intergroup or GSO that only sends the researchers the coded questionnaires.
- Use population-based samples that would include AA members indirectly rather than directly.
- Advertise and openly recruit samples of convenience that can be compared to the more official surveys conducted by AA in order to assess representativeness.
- If researchers are members of AA, they could have access to information of potential friends. Members of research teams should include both AA and non-AA members. All responses should be coded and AA members of the research team should not have access to even first names.
- Emphasize that they participate as individuals, not as AA members.
- Avoid collecting identifying information in studies without follow-up.
- Problems arise when researchers meet personal acquaintances or public figures whom they were unaware of as AA members and later meet them in normal social life.
- Another problem arises because AA members identify other members by full names; how do you speak of them within the project group or with members of AA?
- Anonymity will be a major problem in studying the AA group as a whole. Individuals have free choice in relinquishing their anonymity and often do, but it would probably be difficult and necessary to gain the cooperation of an entire group.
- Members may be unwilling to provide information that could be used to identify them.
- Solicitation of research subjects becomes complicated by anonymity and decentralization.
- Careful informed consent procedures and the use of recovering persons to review these procedures and to conduct research may help. Alternatively, the anthropologist's approach of showing respect and becoming a "participant-observer" may facilitate entry to the fellowship for purposes of research.
- Anonymity needs to be respected, but that is not unique—researchers gather data in a variety of investigations where the privacy of the respondents needs to be respected. The problem of anonymity from a research into AA framework is the initial identification of respondents. If we rely on volunteers we risk nonrepresentativeness. In a voluntary fellowship without clear membership it is difficult, if not impossible, to draw a sample. If we distribute questionnaires to participants at a particular meeting, we may get a unique finding based on the appeal of the group measured (step group, speaker group, time, location, etc.) and therefore draw false inferences.

- Treat AA groups as single entities with only aggregate data used.
- Will AA members agree to act as collateral information sources for subjects in studies? Ask!
- Anonymity refers to matters of public behavior, and that AA members are free to cooperate as individuals in research. Of course, assurances of confidentiality of data are essential, but perhaps may need more stressing than what is usual with human subjects. Of course, only volunteers can be evaluated and this necessarily limits the generalizability of any findings obtained. Nonetheless, anonymity should not present insurmountable barriers as long as we are interested in studying only convenience samples.

4. What Constitutes "True AA," and How Can Researchers Avoid Obtaining a Distorted Picture of AA?

- A clear description of the common ingredients of various AA groups is needed.
- Rely on self-definitions (i.e., a group is an AA group because it says it is), but carefully describe the nature of the group.
- Don't confuse AA with AA-oriented professional treatment.
- People randomly assigned to AA treatment should not be told how many meetings they need to attend. Participation must remain voluntary.
- Know the difference between "groups" and "meetings."
- AA has guidelines on how to join AA—use those criteria.
- Sampling AA groups in different parts of the country would be desirable due to regional variability in AA.
- An "environmental impact" statement for the research is needed. What is the likely impact of the research on the AA group? Can the impact be minimized? Reduce the chance that observing AA changes it.
- Strive to get a representative sample—self-selected samples of volunteers may be a biased subset of AA members.
- Most AA members do not stay with a particular group. They may belong to more than one group or switch groups. Don't sample the same subject twice.
- Sample a variety of types of AA groups.
- How about the nonattender who lives by the AA philosophy?
- Do more qualitative research to describe the kinds of AA groups.
- There are "dim light" groups that don't want to be known (e.g., airline pilots).
- Surely less "true" versions of AA should also be studied.
- More studies should attempt to focus on AA in the community (i.e., voluntary participation in AA).
- This is a research question that has to be answered. Studies will need to be done to characterize such things as the varieties of groups that are available to a given individual, the varying patterns and frequencies with which these groups are used, etc.
- The only common feature is the philosophy—there are no "true" or common methods.
- One way of thinking about the expansion and modification of Bill W.'s AA is that professionals and systems (institutions) adapted and changed the systems for their purposes. Another is that with a changing populace, Bill W.'s AA did not meet the need. Is there an AA (Bill W.'s) with spinoffs or is there a large AA with subdivisions?

- A dilemma—if AA exerts no central control, and its only rule is that people want to quit drinking, and the bonding principles are the 12 steps, how can *we* exclude the subdivisions or even hope to define the "true AA" beyond these points? Until the differences are demonstrated in *effects*, not simply philosophies, any part of the subset of 12-step, alcohol groups should be AA.
- There is no such thing as "true AA" beyond following the 12 steps and 12 traditions. Groups vary considerably.
- Avoid going to a couple of groups and making blanket statements about how all groups function.
- Avoid specificity and keep to generalities when describing groups and individual group functioning. We must keep in mind that groups and group functioning vary.
- Remain flexible and avoid "all or nothing" statements.
- It is important to study AA using qualitative approaches because quantitative approaches tend to fractionalize the program.
- Apparently there is no such thing as "true AA." The researcher has to carefully describe the nature and quantity of the AA experience of subjects in a particular study.
- A variety of descriptive and qualitative studies should be implemented to arrive at a clearer understanding of what AA is.
- It seems clear that while AA ideology is well known, what actually happens for AA members in various activities and in a variety of groups is less known.
- There probably isn't one "picture" that is "true" AA (as there isn't one alcoholism, chemical dependency, etc.). Also, AA is changing in response to social changes (i.e., polydrug abuse/addiction, treatment center involvement—even in-patient versus the move to outpatient treatment affects AA populations). So, by the time the research is completed, it is highly likely that the phenomenon will have changed!
- Avoiding treatment center influences, but "true" 1992 AA may reflect treatment center influences as a part of the picture!
- Perhaps a conditionally described group of "pictures" is the best we can do.
- Given the variation across groups, there may not be a "true AA." Perhaps self-definition is the best approach to identify AA versus non-AA groups.
- There can be distortion of group dynamics and structure because of observation. There are methodological ways to deal with that, but there will always be some change in group dynamics if an outside observer is present.
- This question assumes there is a "true" AA. Let's not assume so, but use the different approaches as naturally occurring quasi-experimental research designs.
- The importance of ecological validity must be stressed and the impact of the research operations should be monitored and controlled.
- To get a representative sample, studies should use acceptable sampling strategies to select AA groups for study and should consider collaborative or multisite studies to sample different nations or geographic regions.
- Studies should make a concerted effort to recruit community samples of people using AA, not just treatment samples—perhaps identifying subjects through such sources as the national household survey, the Epidemiological Catchment Area study, the NIDA survey of high school seniors, or the Rutgers longitudinal study.
- Need to standardize a cross-country or transworld set of characteristics that has validity with people who are in AA, and that universalizes what AA is: use literature, steps, traditions, use real rather than artificial groups, use community-based rather than treatment groups.

- Use the same criteria that the General Services Office uses for making up its directory.
- Use data from many different groups that are geographically distributed.
- Get feedback from knowledgeable insiders about data.
- Look for certain mixes: new in groups versus those with long-term sobriety (>10 years); those entering via treatment and those who do not.
- Look at AA away from the university, treatment centers, and other distorting settings.
- It is not for us to determine what is "true AA"—the need is to be open to and to seek out the diverse varieties.
- AA differs in different places—need to be sensitive to the sociological context.
- The heterogeneity of AA groups within the United States and the nature of the content of such meetings makes it difficult to quantify what "true AA" is and what it is not. A distorted picture arises out of researchers' views of the organization, namely that it is an organization committed to relapse prevention or that of others who report that its framework provides an opportunity for spiritual growth and change.
- What is missing are empirical, qualitative descriptions of what people take out of AA and use in their everyday lives, whether that be strategies for maintaining sobriety or whether it represents spiritual/communal or self-growth. To say that people who have successfully abstained from alcohol but who have not worked on their "egoistic, narcissistic" self are therefore "arrested" in their development misses some of the original impetus of AA—"to help alcoholics stay sober."
- We need a more balanced view of the change possibilities inherent in AA, and ways of adequately measuring them. To say that all alcoholics have an obsessional, narcissistic view of self is an overgeneralization, while focusing only on alcohol abstinence appears to be a sizeable underestimation of its potential effects.
- Content analysis of AA stories—what are aspects of the program that people relate as important to their sobriety?
- Use researchers who have experienced AA from the "inside" as "informants."
- "True AA" is both fellowship and program. The "program" part can be gleaned from literature. "Fellowship" occurs both in and outside of meetings.
- There is no monolithic "true" AA. Research should avoid stereotypic characterizations that imply homogeneity and seek to capture the diversity within AA.
- Avoid sampling sources that are not characteristic of AA as it was designed—as a voluntary affiliation. Coerced attendance, for example, is a different phenomenon. At least be cautious in interpreting treatment and judicial samples as "AA."
- Use caution in writing the discussion section of papers.
- Study many different groups and individuals in groups over time.
- Do more ethnographic studies and review the qualitative research literature. Talk to people about their AA experience. Find out what seems to make a difference.
- "True AA" consists of AA meetings attended by AA members whenever those meetings occur. AA-*based* treatment is not AA and should not be considered as the proper target of research into AA. Community-based AA needs to be researched more than it has been. Getting a representative sample with respect to gender, age, and ethnicity is essential.
- Qualitative participant observer studies are valuable, and building trusting relationships to gain access to normally closed meetings is important.
- With surveys, only those more enthusiastic and involved will tend to participate in research, or those not so "hung up" on the traditions. Those who are AA

conservatives are very wary of participating in research and may need more attention and explanation from researchers.

- True AA occurs in its naturalistic setting, unencumbered by research aims, protocols, etc. Community samples are the purest frame of reference, but suffer from self-selection.
- Development of a national database that integrates findings across studies.
- Develop a template of what "ideal AA" would look like and then assess individual experiences to see how near or distant they are from the ideal.
- Separate out practices and the 12-step principles so we can have distinctions that subjects can relate to.
- "True AA" includes: groups that adhere to the traditions, groups that are listed with central offices and GSO.
- Avoid groups based in hospitals that have treatment programs—they have mostly newcomers.
- Focus on groups that have not reworded the steps, such as SOS or Alcoholics Victorious.
- Study a randomized sample of AA groups (since we apparently cannot get a random sample of individuals).
- Be aware, in using informants, that eager informants may well be marginal to the culture they are describing.
- There is no "true AA"—it is polymorphous and changing. The crucial issue is to get enough data to describe central tendencies and the range of variation.
- "True AA" could be defined variously: (1) self-identification: everything that calls itself AA is AA, (2) legalistic: everything accepted by the GSO is AA, (3) exegetic: everything corresponding to the basic AA literature is AA, (4) prototypic of ideal: everything corresponding to some conceptually pure type constructed by a researcher is AA. The most important task would be to present a conceptually coherent and historically sensitive formulation of the main dimensions of variability within the set of family resemblances uniquely identified as "AA."
- One way to decrease bias is to use a range of frames of reference and probes. Another is to be aware of inevitable distortion.
- There is also a reverse effect: contact with AA has transformed the researchers. This meeting could not have taken place 15 years ago with any understanding across disciplines and points of view.
- Broaden geographic sampling.
- Consider how AA members differ from all alcoholics, and from people who visit and leave.
- Give up the idea that there is a "true AA," not because there isn't any such thing, but because such a goal will limit the exploratory process. If the research design is multileveled, cross-disciplined, and multitheoretical, a "true" picture should emerge over time. The quantitative approach will omit too much from the start and narrow the focus of what can be studied as a whole.
- It seems plausible and possible to combine quantitative and qualitative research. It makes for a more comprehensive, but more difficult, design, and reinforces the need for a multidisciplinary team.
- Researchers need to classify or specify the "type" of AA studied, as well as the "type" of members included in the research sample. Possible classifications of AA "types": inpatient based, community based, speciality (men's groups, women's groups, etc.). Possible classifications of AA members: gender, culture, treatment history, newcomer/neophyte/oldtimer, "voluntary" versus "involuntary" (court mandated, etc.).

- There is no one true AA; the nature of the decentralized fellowship encourages plurality. The research questions have to do with first identifying the diversity of AA and how the limits of diversity are maintained by the steps and traditions. AA appears to be variable both within a locale and in different geographic locations. There does seem to be a core or essence that includes the spiritual, insight, nonjudgment, openness, change focus coexisting with the somewhat dogmatic grounding of process by the 12 steps.
- Researchers need to attend AA meetings to "get a feel" for AA processes in action.
- Ask AA members what *they* consider true AA components or defining characteristics.
- Compare "old-timers" to new recruits to AA.

5. What Alternatives Are There for Identifying and Selecting AA Samples for Research?

- Use large general population samples.
- Advertise in newspapers, use posters.
- Advertise for specific subgroups (e.g., old-timers).
- Advertise in church/synagogue bulletins.
- Identify voluntary members of AA rather than those mandated to attend.
- Use grid of AA formats and do stratified sampling.
- Use the group as the unit of analysis. Ask for volunteer groups.
- Form a group of volunteers for research purposes. However, setting up a group for research would conflict with AA traditions.
- Recruit patients from clinical private practices.
- Go to closed meetings early and leave flyers with the secretary.
- Use opportunity samples, such as at conventions.
- Add a few questions regarding AA onto other, ongoing studies, such as catchment area studies, federally funded, longitudinal studies, or clinical studies.
- Use treatment programs that routinely refer all patients to AA.
- Avoid hospital-based groups.
- Enlist an AA member who is convinced of the need for research and use as a representative to groups.
- Sample AA groups for professionals. They may be more open to research.
- Go to 90 meetings in 90 days to develop personal contacts.
- Develop long-term personal relationships with AA members.
- Do not forget about people who are not AA attenders but who follow the AA program.
- If we violate AA traditions now, it will make it harder for future researchers to access AA groups.
- Perhaps there needs to be a guidebook on AA etiquette for researchers.
- Have AA members on research teams.
- Pool projects; draw one large sample to collect data for several investigators.
- Work with care providers to refer to certain types of AA groups.
- Obtain referrals from court and probation officers.
- Use of assessment and referral centers.
- Select broad samples of individuals, including those who attended AA only once or a few times. This might be done with newspaper advertisements or via other media.

- Prospective studies of individuals referred to AA from treatment systems, following all those referred, including those who only attend one or a few meetings.
- Accessing the network of well-established and well-respected AA members and approaching them with proposals for study.
- Use an external selection of individuals, some of whom would then be referred to AA. This mechanism was used by several others—the Ditman group, the Brandsma group, Diana Walsh's group—and has been very productive. It eliminates a lot of the problems that are due to anonymity and other issues. Of course, studies can be done in other ways. But this idea has much promise.
- Probability subsample surveys to catalogue experience.
- Select on a priori dimensions of group types for comparison: open/closed, coerced/noncoerced, special/general.
- Leave flyer at meetings. Announce at open meetings or go early and give to the secretary or chair at closed meetings.
- Friends who have shared their membership in AA with the researcher can be asked about meetings and asking other members about their willingness to participate in research.
- Using treatment populations to study later affiliation with AA has been criticized because it gives a biased sample of the entire AA population. That is true, but nonetheless treatment populations are not a trivial case, either in terms of numbers of people or significance. They represent the group we may be able to influence to go to AA, and we need to know whether or not we should do so.
- People might be identified through Minnesota Model treatment programs. Many of these programs have records of clients who might be contacted. This then could lead to selecting a sample of AA members by asking those in AA who have had treatment experience to nominate several other AA members to contact. Use of "two-hatters" in this process could be helpful.
- It would be worthwhile to look at longitudinal, prospective population studies of heavy drinkers, such as Bridget Grant's or Debbie Hasan's study. These people are a selected population of heavy drinkers who then might be followed to track AA involvement.
- Any group or intergroup office can furnish a list of groups and/or meetings available (often called "where and when").
- Go to meetings and let them know what you're doing. Many will be very cooperative.
- Take many samples in many different settings as AA groups differ in makeup, process, format, "climate," types of persons served, normative behaviors (expected and "not tolerated" behaviors), attitudes toward and use of spirituality.
- Possible samples: (1) members who are actually "using" AA, (2) AA dropouts, (3) AA members in the general population versus those who are in clinical populations.
- Identify subgroups: (1) draw "active members" from clinical populations, (2) follow-up those in the clinical population who drop out of AA, (3) identify such individuals in several population samples.
- Build a composite project for national data collection, with each investigator developing and analyzing part of the data and use of experts in selecting samples and collecting data.
- Interview "old-timers" and AA informants about varieties of AA and sample respondents from these groups.
- Use Beutler's grid to identify types of AA.
- Use "snowball" methodology using key contacts in AA.

- Representativeness is more attainable than random sample.
- Use group as unit of analysis and representatives (members) as spokespersons or key informants. Choose groups randomly from geographic distribution in a particular area using meeting lists. Informants from specific groups (chosen randomly) could be located through grapevine, informal channels.
- The treatment "window" is useful, but need to do substantial work with those with two or more years of sobriety.
- Gaining access to large, representative samples of AA attendees will require the very active involvement of those in the fellowship, to help in the development of trust and to measure as fairly and accurately as possible very poorly understood and distorted concepts of spirituality.
- Collect large samples of people in recovery who utilize different avenues of change for maintaining sobriety, including: the very large percentage of alcohol problem individuals who change without professional assistance or help from AA; those who have participated in AA in the past but who have dropped out; those successful affiliates who continue to participate. One way of collecting such information or groups is to specifically gear newspaper advertisements to recruit such populations. Although they are samples of convenience, they provide a wealth of quantitative and qualitative information about their change experiences. By accessing positively these samples, we are likely to greatly impact the negative biases that AA groups in general have with researchers.
- Delineate types of meetings, then randomly select some of each in a geographic area.
- Use any point source of referrals: screening service, DWI referral programs, employee assistance programs, hotlines.
- Go to meetings, or work with members to recruit at closed meetings.
- For open meetings, it is conceivable to conduct observational studies simply by attending and observing.
- Don't burden oneself with the requirement of having a *comprehensive* sample. One only needs to specify one's domain of study and not overgeneralize one's findings.
- Recruiting people who have ever been members of AA and have dropped out, or who consider themselves members but never go to meetings, might give us a sample somewhat different from that located by the usual means, and which also may yield new information.
- Ethical and professionally sensitive infiltration of AA culture, identification of key informal power holders in groups. Gain their interest and support of research project.
- Conduct multisite studies to obtain samples of sufficient size to conduct *sensitive* statistical tests.
- Find people in other health care settings who could be screened for AA involvement.
- Work with local AA CPC (Cooperation with the Professional Community) to gain access to all listed groups in a geographic area. Select a representative sample of groups.
- Form teams with AA members to work on research. Use AA members as key informants and raters to get measures of group process in various types of groups.
- Get clinicians/health care providers who refer clients to specific types of AA groups. Use to examine referral techniques and at least type of group in AA initially contacted.

- For treatment trials, if it is accepted that what is to be studied is therapeutic referral to AA, then sampling problems are simplified. Samples are defined by the frame in which such referral would occur.
- For descriptive studies of AA there is a need for characterizing AA in a quasi-representative way. Studies should use directories of groups/meetings (with appropriate ethical caution), and make efforts to perfect the list for primary sampling units, in order to derive a good sample of AA groups/meetings. This framework should be used for observational studies, group-level studies, observations.
- There are many useful exploratory studies that can be done with opportunity samples—attendees at an AA convention, sampling those coming in/out of a clubhouse or Al-Anon, etc.
- Work within AA's traditions.
- Use International Doctors in AA to help conduct research.
- Former AA members still sober should be compared to current AA members with similar duration of sobriety to ascertain which lifestyle changes are most important to sobriety.
- Subjects recruited for all AA research need to be identified as "attractees," meaning having positive expectations and motivation for affiliation, versus mandated" and "resistant" subjects.

6. What Outcome Measures Should Be Employed in AA Research?

- It would be useful—and challenging—to have an operational, measurable definition of humility. More generally, we need to develop a scale to assess the kind of spiritual change that AA intends to impact.
- Daily status measures (e.g., time-line follow-back, Form 90) would yield rich data for studying the temporal patterning of attendance, alcohol/drug use, etc. These also permit time-to-event analyses.
- Clear quantification of alcohol/drug use, problems, dependence.
- Abstinence.
- Number of relapses, amount of sober time.
- Changes in quality of life.
- Family assessment; interpersonal functioning.
- Reports of others regarding subjects' drinking.
- Objective verifications: breath tests, saliva stick, etc.
- Psychological adjustment measures—mental health inventory.
- Emotional growth, spiritual growth.
- Decreased negative consequences of drinking.
- Changed social adjustment—employment, marital.
- Subjective changes—quality of life, subjective well-being.
- Changes in apparent DSM diagnoses before and after.
- Insurance costs before and after, for AA members and families.
- Court costs, driving records, police visits, protective custody.
- Emergency room visits, inpatient hospital days.
- Mental health treatment.
- Measuring drinking outcomes is enough!
- Use continuous drinking measures.
- Spiritual well-being.
- Developmental level before and after; faith stages per Fowler.

- Ego-strength.
- Measures of health and longevity.
- Is the client helpful to others in their sobriety.
- The Hazelden/HEC data collection process needs substantial revision so that the quality of their outcome measures can be improved.
- Self-esteem.
- Social involvement versus isolation.
- Exposure to risky situations, and coping strategies used.
- Everything that Alan Marlatt said in his chapter.
- Other substance use, including cigarettes, coffee, licit and illicit drugs.
- Internal control and self-efficacy.
- Social network and social support; amount and quality.
- How well do groups adhere to AA principles; how well implemented are AA groups?
- I would favor relatively simple measures that are now used in other treatment outcome research: consumption levels and history, social consequences, and symptoms. Also look at criminal justice system involvement, interpersonal relations, family relations, psychopathology, CNS function, physical areas.
- Measures of AA involvement: attendance, amount of speaking done, number of phone calls per week to other AA members.
- Spiritual *activity*: frequency of prayer and meditation, etc.
- I would try to frame, "What happens to people in AA?" What is the effect of AA over many dimensions—behavioral, cognitive, affective, individual change, impact on couple relationships, family, etc.—in outcome terms. Qualitatively, what changes occur? Quantitatively, what variables contribute to these changes?
- Drinking behavior—patterning over time, variations in intensity.
- Subjective satisfaction, joy, fulfillment.
- Note the problems with regression to mean arising from measuring initial state in longitudinal studies—clients are always at a low point in life when they enter treatment.
- Importance of data collection, especially at intake, being separated from clinical process, preferably collected by separate staff.
- Types of AA groups attended, frequency, when and for what objective (e.g., Do you attend step group meetings when....).
- Steps worked at what points in recovery experience.
- Other activities within AA done for how long, and to what effect (12 steps, sponsorship, etc.).
- Use of alcohol or other mood-altering substances: how AA responded as a resource, what was useful.
- Spiritual formulation, how does higher power concept and relationship change over time?
- Al-Anon attendance by significant other, family adjustment issues.
- Models of addiction (e.g., Brickman).
- Attributions for relapse.
- Any outcome measures in studies of AA that will be conducted need to begin to standardize instrumentation; both process and outcome. Personality assessments need to have comparable criteria for matching the results of different clinical studies in meaningful ways.
- Certainly readiness to change alcohol behavior and perhaps a scale to assess readiness to engage with AA would be important measures to implement and develop. Readiness to change drinking practices is at best modestly related to AA participation. Standardizing alcohol use assessments and consequences of

drinking makes a lot of sense. Social measures, including quality of life, extent of spiritual and/or personal change will have to be included to help assess the extent to which involvement with AA produces deeper and more lasting (meaningful?) change. Beliefs about drinking, practices, and self-efficacy would also need to be assessed.

• As in all outcome research, there is a need to avoid dichotomous classifications of drinking/not driving and also to include more general aspects of adjustment. Thus, there should be detailed analysis of alcohol consumption, alcohol-related problems and dependence, using reliable, valid, and commonly used instruments. The usual strictures regarding biochemical and/or collateral confirmation apply.

• Estimation of cost-effectiveness, as well as simple effectiveness, is most important. Whether 12-step work should be regarded as an opportunity cost must be debated. Costs of treatment and health care utilization in general must be calculated before and after the AA participation under study.

• General psychological symptom measures—SCL-90, SCID I & II.

• Specific symptom measures, e.g., ADIS, HRSD, BDI, STAI, etc. for anxiety, depression.

• Systems measures of functioning—social support, Family Environment Scale, social functioning.

• Life Events scales.

• Values—Ways to Live Test, Rokeach Values Survey.

• Stages of change—SOCRATES or URICA.

• The seven areas addressed by the Addiction Severity Index (itself an excellent pre/post-treatment instrument): use, psychiatric status, relationships, legal, medical, employment, etc.

• Attitude change.

• Perceived and actual ability to moderate drinking without biopsychosocial consequences.

• Personality measures sensitive to important character change, since AA is focused clearly on character development. Measures that focus on self-absorption, such as narcissism scale of the new Minnesota Multiphasic Personality Inventory (MMPI).

• Document changes in support network; divorce, changes in friends, role of contacts made through AA, etc.

• Need clear measures of which part of the various AA practices the participants actually are engaged in—particularly those that may have shifted before the AA experience began.

• Measure of dependency on AA and family, to address criticism sometimes leveled against AA as fostering dependency.

• Measures of stigma, self-esteem, mastery, efficacy.

• Early experiences with AA.

• Purpose in life or meaning in life.

• Marital harmony, sexual adjustment, parent-child relationships.

• Liking People Scale, need for affiliation.

• Is it possible to operationalize the AA promises (from Big Book)?

• Acceptance of disease model, adoption of the beliefs of AA.

• How does AA membership affect neuropsychological functioning?

• I believe the social network aspect of AA to be very important, and this should be measured.

• Ideal versus real self discrepancies (shame).

• Personal Orientation Inventory or other measures of self-actualization.

7. What Would Be Promising Predictor Measures for AA Studies?

- Core variables: age, education, gender, race, prior AA exposure, prior treatment, severity of dependence, marital status.
- Conceptual level or field dependence.
- Spiritual/religious variables.
- Impaired (loss of) control.
- Motivation for change; commitment to abstinence.
- Client goals (abstinence, moderation, marital improvement, etc.).
- Conceptions of alcoholism (e.g., disease vs. habit).
- Value structure (e.g., self vs. community focus).
- Locus of control, including God control.
- Which steps correlate long term with sobriety.
- Ask "old-timers"—use their wisdom.
- Ethnicity, socioecomonic status, acculturation.
- Expectancies about alcohol's effects.
- Beliefs about God, higher power.
- Patterns of drinking.
- Perceived choice over method chosen.
- Court-mandated vs. voluntary.
- Meaning in life, occurrence of spiritual awakening, spiritual experience.
- Geographic proximity, transportation.
- Group process variables.
- Suggestibility.
- Previous exposure to AA and success or failure.
- Level of denial; type of denial.
- Ask what the client expects to happen in AA; will it be positive, will it help, etc.
- Level of AA use and commitment.
- Referral source, manner of referral.
- Use variables identified in Emrick's review.
- Quality of implementation within the group.
- Locus of control over drinking; general locus of control.
- California F scale—a measure of acceptance of authority. No one has even tried to replicate Cantor's finding, and it would be worth doing.
- Purpose in Life Test.
- Some cognitive measure of the type of thinking process that characterizes the individual; developmental level.
- Preferred defensive style.
- Coming from inpatient or not.
- Measures of coexisting psychopathology.
- Religious background.
- Need for affiliation.
- Severity of negative consequences associated with drinking.
- Perceived ability to control drinking.
- I would shift the frame again: How do so many different people—in gender, age, background, socioeconomic status—find a way to utilize AA? What mechanisms within AA, the steps etc., facilitate acceptance by so many, or what adaptations do people make to be able to use AA? This is virtually unstudied. I believe you cannot identify predictor variables without starting *inside* AA and examining the *process*.
- Employment status.

- Treatment experience.
- Involvement with drugs other than alcohol.
- Individual's skills and comfort in groups.
- Need for group support.
- Self-efficacy.
- Stages of change.
- Neuropsychological measures.
- Degree of internalization of AA beliefs.
- Qualitative descriptions of members that describe external events, important events, or thoughts that help promote sobriety.
- Try to standardize a set of predictors to be used across studies!
- Processes of change measures.
- Attributions about causes of drinking.
- Self-attributed social deviance (i.e., respectability vs. stigma).
- Distances between actual, ideal, and social selves, as measured for example by repertory grid technique.
- Impulsivity/sociopathy—MMPI internalization ratio.
- O'Dowd's resistance measure; MMPI dominance scale; repression-sensitization.
- Motivation or distress—SCL-90, GSI subscale, Inventory of Interpersonal Problems.
- Group Environment Scale or other group climate measures.
- Family history of alcoholism.
- Measures of health harm from drinking.
- Family environment supports.
- Having sponsor or not.
- See Brown & Peterson (1991) for variables identified as important by AAs themselves.
- Personality type: personality disorders, neuroticism.
- Level of depression.
- Ask for client's view of the best things in AA, and the worst things in AA.
- Satisfaction with AA.
- New friendships developed within AA.
- Definition of problem measure. Do individuals see drinking as the only problem or do they think there are other things that need to be changed in addition or instead? Those who are globally dissatisfied may be better match for AA.
- Nature of social supports. There is likely to be an interaction between processes used in AA and existing vs. absent network of social supports. Those with little social support are likely to benefit from social support of AA. Those with preexisting support systems may need this less.
- Predictors can only be properly selected once one knows what the groups researched normally do, and how groups vary.
- Extent of giving and receiving support in meetings.
- Contacts with AAs outside meetings.
- Reasons for wanting to change.
- Myers-Briggs Type Indicator.
- Previous attempts to quit.
- I have found that the ability to identify with other members is almost the most important factor in successful affiliation.
- Whether person is escorted to a meeting, has information on what to expect, has access to someone in AA immediately, gets a sponsor, is given a task in the meeting, etc.
- Support from family and friends to go to AA vs. to drink.
- Nature of experience in first few meetings.

- Whether spouse is in Al-Anon.
- Capacity for the spiritual—whatever that is.
- Sense that two-way communication with higher power is possible.
- Tolerance for differences, variety; inclination to give others the benefit of the doubt, see them as fallible and loving rather than as malicious or stupid.
- Ability to see, accept, and handle paradox.
- Past history of reaching out to others for help.
- Acceptance of label "alcoholic."
- Childhood emotional climate.
- It depends on what research questions you are asking, what the dependent variables are. Are we asking what predicts more AA *involvement,* longer membership, abstinence?
- Childhood abuse history.
- Look for linear combinations of predictor variables. Vital is empirical testing of whether linear combinations vary across different AA groups or dimensions identified by Moos's Group Environment Scale.
- Start from conventional lists used in psychosocial studies, but pay special attention to the blind spots in psychosocial research traditions: spirituality, mystical experience, community—rather than individual-oriented virtues, values, feelings, experiences; moment-to-moment aspects of mental functioning vs. traits or long-term orientations. Pay sustained attention to the context in which individuals are being measured—variables including aspects of coercion, life situation, etc.
- Self-concept and self-esteem.

8. What Alternatives Are Available for Conducting Follow-up in Longitudinal Studies of AA?

- Include AA measures in samples *already* being followed in other longitudinal research.
- Simply obtain identifying information at first assessment and track the sample as in other studies. There is no prohibition in AA against participating in research!
- I believe individual members from a community based survey sample would be willing to participate in follow-up assessments of spirituality.
- Identifying people by name is by far the best approach. By agreed code number is a second choice, but a much poorer one, because dropouts could not be followed.
- Obtain a secure agreement to follow-up *before* AA contact begins.
- Get commitment from a cohort of members.
- See Cahalan's chapter on longitudinal research.
- Identify a cohort of subjects with positive initial expectancies for help through AA, facilitate their entry into AA ("early recovery") and assess this group periodically to determine drinking behavior and changes in self-concept, social relations, and spirituality.
- Individual or small-N case studies.
- We designed (but then gave up as too complicated and unfundable) a repeated measures, cross-sectional design that covered five years. The same subjects were to be interviewed and retested three to four times over five years. Entry into the study was to vary from one week to 20 + years in AA.
- Cross-sectional designs covering a range of sobriety as long as 20, 30 or more years, and a range in age.

- Start from clinical-framed sample.
- Start from general population sample.
- Start by approaching people around AA meetings.
- Retrospective accounts from treatment and nontreatment participants.
- Surveys distributed to AA members.
- Surveys of non-AA attenders to find out about their working or non working of the AA program of living (use treatment outcome surveys to identify sample— this would provide a great deal of already-collected information about subjects).
- Use of existing treatment outcome databases for secondary analyses.
- Requesting specific AA items added to revised formats of existing treatment outcome systems.
- Use existing databases for exploratory and AA process description.
- Best would be a natural history study in which people are tracked through AA, but from a population in which some go to AA and some do not—all assessed prior to their choice to select AA or not and followed for five years.
- Put more detailed drinking questions in AA world surveys.
- Compare AA dropouts with newtimers (one year or less) and old-timers (five years or more) on variety of drinking and related biopsychosocial measures.
- Use of double-blind coding.
- N = 1 multiple baseline designs, or additive treatment and replications.
- Warner Schaie's sequential logged cohort designs.
- Regression-discontinuity designs.
- Naturalistic studies with model testing via structural equation modeling and survival analysis.
- Use of AA informants to track blindly identified subjects—have observer-members within AA track newcomers.
- Start in 12-step-oriented treatment centers.
- Some recovering AAs would likely volunteer to participate as a chance to carry the message.
- The usual good-sense research measures: good relationship with respondents, maintenance of contact between interview follow-up through phone or mail, having information on significant others who know where the respondent can be found, continuous presence in AA meetings, provision of incentives, etc.
- Perhaps if follow-up is done by AA members themselves (i.e., an individual known to the subject), the rate of contact will be higher. This may also help with anonymity concerns.
- Group follow-up rather than individual follow-up.
- Use follow-up phone calls and letters; provide postcards so that people who move can give a forwarding address.
- Best design is *not* pure longitudinal, except in rare cases. This is because of the effects of multiple testing occasions on the respondents. Better design: cross-sectional/longitudinal, in which carefully selected cohorts are followed for a year or two. One sample is receiving follow-up at the point another sample is just beginning. This gives samples of different points in history, and assesses effects of repeated measurement.
- Recruit individuals through randomized trials where one condition is assignment to AA, then use regular longitudinal research methods for tracking.
- Recruit individuals in AA who consent to follow-up study.
- Create unique identifiers with some sort of buffer between researchers and subjects that preserves privacy, but allows for individual tracking.
- One could observe a group over time, such as done in a study by Hazel C. Johnson (Ph.D. dissertation, University of California, Los Angeles, 1987).

- Follow individual subjects in single subject design with pre- and postmeasures at certain points in AA experience. Have these individuals keep logs on their meeting experiences, what happened, how they reacted, why they chose to go or not go, etc. This would be a good way to research when you have no funding or less time to devote.
- Follow through spouses or other collaterals.
- Study the life course of particular AA groups.

9. What Special Issues Are Likely to Arise in the Review Process of Proposals for Research on AA?

- There may be reluctance to consider funding research that does not match the usual clinical trial model.
- Peer review should be done by reviewers who understand AA.
- There is a need for a special seed grant RFP to help get ideas and methodology moving, in preparation for full application.
- How to create an openness to qualitative and exploratory studies?
- How to avoid using cheap but unrepresentative samples?
- The clinical trial format, appropriate for studying medications, does not apply well to such a variegated intervention as AA. We do not yet have the appropriate concepts and instrumentation to conduct clinical trials with AA, and there are more important things to study before the field is ready for formal trials.
- Reviewers may have unrealistic standards in rating studies of the type needed in this field.
- It may be important, in review of studies in this area, to constitute an IRG that is scientifically expert, familiar with the more qualitative side of studies likely to emerge, and relatively unbiased on issues of AA and spirituality (or at least balanced in biases).
- Researchers in the social sciences often have a low level of interest in spirituality. My own experience is that behavioral scientists are often hostile toward, rather than being indifferent to, spirituality. My concern is that a bias against spirituality may make it hard to get proposals to study spiritual behavior approved by review committees.
- Will IRG members have a bias against AA, affecting reviews?
- Should review committees include representation from philosophy, history, theology?
- An environmental impact statement should be considered in review of studies of AA. How will this research impact the normal operation of the group(s) to be studied?

10. What Other Ideas, Opportunities, or Alternatives Should Be Considered for AA Research That Are Not Covered by the Preceding Questions?

- What do treatment providers mean by the "disease concept"? How do AA members view that term? Do their views include a biopsychosocial aspect? Does it make patients or professionals responsible for recovery?

- Use AA philosophy to determine their tenets, and study how many AA members endorse the philosophy?
- Coercing people into AA is not a good idea. NIAAA might encourage principal investigators to make AA involvement voluntary. NIAAA, though, cannot become an advocacy group for any position.
- Matching studies imply someone other than the alcoholic selects the treatment. Alcoholics should choose whatever treatment they want.
- Try to understand AA within a community context (e.g., size of the community, number of groups available).
- Given the marketing of treatment programs, choice may not always be free choice.
- Recovery is a process, not a point.
- Informed consent when choosing treatments. Matching studies permit us to give people the best advice.
- Consensual agreement on what instruments we are going to use would facilitate comparisons across studies.
- Develop AA research clearinghouse for AA research instruments, bibliographies.
- The issue of the need to answer the question of the comparative effectiveness of AA must be distinguished from the narrower issue of the feasibility or desirability of randomized controlled trials. The latter may not be the best way of trying to answer the fundamental question.
- Support the idea of conducting randomized clinical trials, being careful to specify the characteristics of groups (e.g., using Moos' measures) and using sensitive measures of spirituality.
- Have another conference to set priorities on standardized instruments for assessment and follow-up. Perhaps NIAAA could set up a working group of researchers to pursue this over a limited time period.
- There is a real need to address qualitative as well as quantitative studies. Quantitative studies should proceed with existing or newly developing measures. However, there is much we need to know on a descriptive level about: (1) variability in AA groups and variability in structure, content and change processes; (2) the sponsorship relationship. Need for n = 1 studies of individual change in recovery.
- Conduct studies in a comparative framework (different regions of the country, different ethnic groups, different "special" groups).
- Studies using a variety of methodologies: historical research, ethnographic descriptions of meetings and members' history, descriptive surveys of membership with randomly selected members of groups, clinical trials of AA effectiveness.
- Research with ethnic minorities poses special methodological problems. Sampling design must take into account oversampling of these populations. Questionnaires need to be translated and retranslated. Interviewers need to have bilingual skills. Measures used must be cross-validated. Special data collection should cover acculturation, birthplace, and other variables of interest to certain minority groups.
- For prevention, analyze those institutions that successfully prevent alcohol use, then see if the processes there might be generalized to, for example, public schools.
- How do churches have such a massive antialcohol effect: Modeling, verbal norms, offering other options so alcohol is not needed, social support systems? What happens when they fail?
- Other studies might be proposed to evaluate different sampling strategies before the "big" study, a randomized clinical trial, is proposed.

- Review groups may be impatient with "process" studies and disinclined to fund them until AA has been found to be valuable for some people under certain conditions.
- Utilize correlational designs utilizing path analysis and other related techniques.
- Address the issues and difficulties in conducting randomized clinical trials of AA—especially community acceptance.
- Since AA is stories, some kind of content analysis of a variety of stories to determine what themes, if any, correlate with success or failure in sobriety.
- Develop some measure of "relationship" that will allow evaluation and analysis of what and how AA sponsorship works or fails to work.
- Need to question, verify (?) the validity of so much self-reporting.
- Have more open dialogues between AA proponents and behavioral scientists. Learn from some of the pitfalls and fruits of the psychotherapy outcome literature, which bears some striking similarities to the critical issues discussed at this conference. Specifically, adequately define what researchers mean by a process. To some it appears that this represents a belief while others treat it as an outcome.
- Develop key areas of research into AA, listing researchers who are interested in certain areas and allowing more expeditious networking.
- Review of the possibility that a heavy investment in AA research may undercut the development and success of alternative behavioral treatment modalities (self-help and group participation) that *might* work better than AA.
- AA may have accumulated too many unhelpful surplus effects.
- Spend more talent and money on research on the effectiveness of alternative behavioral treatment modalities in comparison to AA.
- Research on other 12-step groups.
- NIAAA should consider initiating an RFA to solicit studies that would focus on critical aspects of a thorough evaluation of the AA experience—process and outcome.
- Study 12-step users who are not attending AA.
- Clinical trials involving random assignment to AA or other interventions of subjects who see the interventions as equally attractive and whose profiles suggest that they are likely to do well in AA.
- Use of Moos scales and other "process" assessment tools to compare groups and monitor specific groups over time.
- Use of process measures in outcome studies.
- Derive our research from theory that has developed from extensive observation and qualitative research.
- Develop a national database that integrates findings across studies. Ideally, case variables could be developed and included in subsequent research. Thus, researchers have an intra-AA comparison group.
- Develop national AA library that includes: (1) AA-related instruments, (2) AA research to date, (3) updated directory of ongoing AA research scientists, (4) annual conference to disseminate information and encourage future research.
- Make sure not to compare AA to everything.
- Issue of court referrals and AA needs to be addressed.
- There is a process of recovery, and differential impact as different points in the process could be expected.
- Study of AA members and the concepts of powerlessness versus helplessness; individual responsibility.
- Study of the AA philosophy using its literature to determine what it teaches on such subjects as: who is appropriate for AA, what is "spiritual," individual

powerlessness, responsibility. Follow this with a survey study of AA members to see how many adhere to AA's written philosophy.

- There has been an undertone at the meeting of pulling away from the "pill-oriented" randomized clinical trial as the be-all of research in this area because (1) the design is not appropriate for a variegated intervention, (2) there are also other important things to be done, (3) we do not have the appropriate concepts and instrumentation to do it properly. These need to be developed.

- Treatment evaluation studies should always identify a professional or public intervention as the independent variable and be experimental or a randomized clinical trial. But, because AA is an interesting social phenomenon, it deserves to be studies on its own, qualitatively and historically. What should particularly be avoided is the combination of a treatment evaluation perspective and a nonrandomized, nonexperimental design.

- Are there ways to get the research findings we *do* have to have more direct effects on clinical practice, training, and government policy, including referrals to AA. Are there ways to get clinical expertise, though flawed and biased, into a form where it is of more research use?

- There are some clinicians who have *very* high rates of referral for AA engagement. What are they doing? Note Yalom's finding that group psychotherapy attrition fell dramatically when patients were educated about what to expect.

- Both fields—research and AA—have misconceptions about the other. Several conferences like this one, designed to understand the other's perspective, might help. I am concerned when I hear faulty assumptions about AA or vice versa. Use an integrated, multidisciplinary approach using "interpreters" across disciplines.

- How does "professionally facilitated early recovery," as in Project MATCH, compare to "self-selected" participation in AA for "first time" treatment for drinking problems?

- How do former AA members who are still sober believe that AA helped them, and in what ways did it lead to "permanent" changes in attitudes, social adjustment, etc.?

- Compare AA to other self-help groups that adopt a different theoretical framework, such as Rational Recovery.

- Can self-help groups be framed with alternative goals, such as moderation or balance in lifestyle habits (e.g., Weightwatchers format that would include other health habits such as smoking, exercise, drinking, eating, relaxation and mindfulness training)?

Contributors

John S. Baer, Ph.D., Addictive Behaviors Research Center, Department of Psychology, University of Washington, Seattle, Washington.

Margaret Bean-Bayog, M.D., private practice, Lexington, Massachusetts.

Linda J. Beckman, Ph.D., California School of Professional Psychology—Los Angeles, Alhambra, California.

Larry E. Beutler, Ph.D., Counseling/Clinical/School Psychology Program, Graduate School of Education, University of California, Santa Barbara, California.

Stephanie D. Brown, Ph.D., The Addictions Institute, Menlo Park, California.

Raul Caetano, M.D., Ph.D., Alcohol Research Group, Berkeley, California.

Don Cahalan, Ph.D. (deceased, October 1992), School of Public Health (emeritus), University of California, Berkeley, California.

Carlo C. DiClemente, Ph.D., Department of Psychology, University of Houston, Houston, Texas.

Chad D. Emrick, Ph.D., Veterans Affairs Medical Center, Denver, Colorado.

John Finney, Ph.D., Center for Health Care Evaluation & Program Evaluation and Resource Center, Department of Veterans Affairs & Stanford University Medical Center, Palo Alto, California.

James W. Fowler, Ph.D., Center for Research in Faith and Moral Development, Candler School of Theology, Emory University, Atlanta, Georgia.

Richard K. Fuller, M.D., National Institute on Alcohol Abuse and Alcoholism, Rockville, Maryland.

Frederick B. Glaser, M.D., F.R.C.P.(C), University of Michigan Substance Abuse Center, Ann Arbor, Michigan.

Richard L. Gorsuch, Ph.D., Graduate School of Psychology, Fuller Theological Seminary, Pasadena, California.

Jasna Jovanovic, Ph.D., Graduate School of Education, University of California, Santa Barbara, California.

Ernest Kurtz, Ph.D., Center for Self-Help Research, University of Michigan, Ann Arbor, Michigan.

J. Clark Laundergan, Ph.D., Center for Addiction Studies, University of Minnesota at Duluth, Duluth, Minnesota.

Laura Little, J. D., Department of Psychology, University of New Mexico, Albuquerque, New Mexico.

Klaus Mäkelä, Ph.D., Finnish Foundation for Alcohol Studies, Helsinki, Finland.

G. Alan Marlatt, Ph.D., Addictive Behaviors Research Center, Department of Psychology, University of Washington, Seattle, Washington.

Peg Maude-Griffin, Ph.D., Center for Health Care Evaluation & Program Evaluation and Resource Center, Department of Veterans Affairs, Palo Alto, California.

Barbara S. McCrady, Ph.D., Center of Alcohol Studies and Graduate School of Applied and Professional Psychology, Rutgers, The State University of New Jersey, Piscataway, New Jersey.

William R. Miller, Ph.D., Department of Psychology, University of New Mexico, Albuquerque, New Mexico.

Henry Montgomery, M.S., Department of Psychology, University of New Mexico, Albuquerque, New Mexico.

Rudolf H. Moos, Ph.D., Center for Health Care Evaluation & Program Evaluation and Resource Center, Department of Veterans Affairs & Stanford University Medical Center, Palo Alto, California.

Jon Morgenstern, Ph.D., Center of Alcohol Studies, Rutgers, The State University of New Jersey, Piscataway, New Jersey.

Joseph Nowinski, Ph.D., private practice, Mansfield Center, Connecticut.

Alan C. Ogborne, Ph.D., Addiction Research Foundation, London, Ontario, Canada.

Robin Room, Ph.D., Addiction Research Foundation, Toronto, Ontario, Canada.

J. Scott Tonigan, Ph.D., Department of Psychology, University of New Mexico, Albuquerque, New Mexico.

Rebecca E. Williams, M.A., Counseling/Clinical/School Psychology Program, University of California, Santa Barbara, California.

DATE DUE